Extensions of the Burkeian System

STUDIES IN RHETORIC AND COMMUNICATION
General Editors:
E. Culpepper Clark
Raymie E. McKerrow
David Zarefsky

"Hear O Israel":
The History of American Jewish Preaching, 1654–1970
Robert V. Friedenberg

A Theory of Argumentation
Charles Arthur Willard

Elite Oral History Discourse:
A Study of Cooperation and Coherence
Eva M. McMahan

Computer-Mediated Communication:
Human Relationships in a Computerized World
James W. Chesebro and Donald G. Bonsall

Popular Trials:
Rhetoric, Mass Media, and the Law
Edited by Robert Hariman

Presidents and Protesters:
Political Rhetoric in the 1960s
Theodore Otto Windt, Jr.

Argumentation Theory and the Rhetoric of Assent
Edited by David Cratis Williams and Michael David Hazen

Rhetorical Dimensions of Popular Culture
Barry Brummett

A Voice of Their Own:
The Woman Suffrage Press, 1840–1910
Edited by Martha M. Solomon

Reagan and Public Discourse in America
Edited by Michael Weiler and W. Barnett Pearce

Extensions of the Burkeian System
Edited by James W. Chesebro

Edited by James W. Chesebro

Extensions of the Burkeian System

The University of Alabama Press   Tuscaloosa and London

Copyright © 1993
The University of Alabama Press
Tuscaloosa, Alabama 35487–0380
All rights reserved
Manufactured in the United States of America

∞

The paper on which this book is printed meets the minimum
requirements of American National Standard for Information
Science-Permanence of Paper for Printed Library Materials,
ANSI Z39.48-1984.

Library of Congress Cataloging-in-Publication Data

Extensions of the Burkeian system / edited by James W. Chesebro.
    p. cm.—(Studies in rhetoric and communication)
    Includes bibliographical references and index.
    ISBN 0-8173-0674-9
    1. Burke, Kenneth 1897–   . 2. Communication—Philosophy.
I. Chesebro, James W. II. Series.
P92.5.B87E9 1993
302.2'01—dc20   92-31644

British Library Cataloguing-in-Publication Data available

Contents

Preface

James W. Chesebro

Officially formed on March 7, 1984, in Philadelphia, Pennsylvania, the Kenneth Burke Society held its first national convention six years later, May 4–7, 1990, in New Harmony, Indiana. A remarkable convention in many ways, the final session of this convention constituted a particularly critical moment in terms of this volume. In that session, entitled "An Interview with Kenneth Burke," Dale Bertelsen and I had been asked to lead a discussion with Burke, which would ultimately provide an opportunity for all members of the society to question and respond to him in person. My first question to Burke was intended to allow him to develop an idea he had been considering and exploring for some time: "What is 'operation benchmark'?" Burke responded:

The idea is this, the idea I have in mind: I am trying to decide just what the devil I am saying. I don't know quite the way to put it, this way or that. I learn something from you. You tell me how things are going. My point is that what I want to do is to create a scheme whereby you have to meet a test for being in the Burke Society, of which I am the founder but which was really made by all of the wonderful organizers who did such wonderful work. But as its founder, I just want to suggest that the way we do it, is that we call it "operation benchmark" in the sense that we start with what you say, but we only ask that you say, "Burke says it this way, I say this," with some such reasons. You may say more in the same direction, or you may change it in the reverse direction, or you may take it in another direction. . . .

We really are symbol-using animals, and we have to start from there. We have to have the notion of variance. Therefore I can't either prove or disprove that there's a God. The theory of language can't do anything with that or solve that problem. . . .

No one has to do anything. The only reason for having it [the Kenneth Burke Society] at all is that it names something and sets up a certain direction. I think that this idea of operation benchmark does that much. All you have to do, then, is to agree or disagree. . . .

I think that there has to be a lot of leeway in this business. I see no reason for being authoritarian. . . . The fundamental notion of choice in my scheme is difference.[1]

Extensions of the Burkeian System constitutes one of the first projects to meet the requirements Burke has established for his operation benchmark.

Extensions of the Burkeian System finds its origins in the scholarly contributions of Kenneth Burke. All of the authors of the chapters in this volume adopt stances that defer to Burke's initial contributions, ultimately casting their work as extensions of ideas and claims posited by Burke. Yet, all of the authors also make significant departures from positions Burke has articulated. The range of these reactions varies tremendously. Several of the authors cast their positions as augmentations. They offer supplements to Burke's claims that constitute logical additions to Burke's initial observations, but even these authors provide adjustments to the Burkeian system that make a difference in how the system is perceived and understood. Other essays are cast in a more challenging mode, arguing explicitly for alternative viewpoints. Displeased with Burke's analysis at a given point for one reason or another, they posit positions different than those advanced by Burke.

This preface is dedicated to three substantive goals. First, I want to establish a foundation from which the Burkeian system is viewed.[2] This foundation does not attempt to summarize Burke's major ideas regarding symbol using. Several such summaries are readily available.[3] Rather, I offer a sketch of Burke intentionally designed to humanize him and to suggest how the personal has affected the conceptions constituting the Burkeian system. Second, I identify some of the reasons why extensions of the Burkeian system are particularly crucial, if not essential, if the system is to continue. Third, I identify the ways in which the chapters in this volume constitute extensions of the Burkeian system.

Kenneth Burke: The Person and Source of Dramatism and Logology

A native of Pennsylvania, Kenneth Duva Burke in mid-1991 was ninety-four years old, a short, compactly built man, with pure white hair and goatee.[4] He was born in Pittsburgh on May 5, 1897. Since the early 1920s Burke has lived in a farmhouse on Amity Road in northwestern New Jersey in the rural area outside the town of Andover. By geographic location and immediate environment, Burke's life-style is intentionally rustic, seemingly charming, in some ways simple, if not isolated. Employing kerosene lamps for years, for example, Burke did not have electricity until the late 1950s and no running water until the 1960s. Certainly economics was a factor here. Rather than "increasing my income," Burke explains, "I've spent my life cutting down on expenses."

Burke is predominantly a professional writer, critic, and editor by occupation, not an academic. As a student, he did spend one semester at Ohio State University and several years at Columbia University. However, he failed to complete any formal university degree, "because," Burke recalls, "every course I wanted to take was for graduate students only."

Burke has taught at the University of Chicago, the New School for Social Research, and Bennington College (1943–61), and he has held any number of other short-term semester positions with a variety of other universities and colleges throughout the United States and Europe. Yet, he is not a traditional member of the university community of scholars. Not only is he not formally "credentialed" because he lacks a Ph.D., and a B.A. for that matter, but he also lacks the kind of academic concentration currently expected by most universities and colleges. At a time when universities and colleges expect a rather strict concentration in only one discipline such as literature, sociology, anthropology, or philosophy, Burke has ignored these divisions. His writings have drawn from all academic areas. Classifying himself as a "word man," "a student of strategies," and "logologist," he has not found the traditional academic divisions useful to any writer or critic whose focus is, in his view, "all language-addressed." Moreover, as Burke has put it, "I didn't want to go into academics, because in those days teachers only taught—I wanted to write." In characteristic informal speaking style, Burke now "just wants to go on with this goddamn stuff as long as I can."

Burke remembers that during childhood his first book was a dictionary. Presented to him without any real explanation as to its function, it was something Burke initially carried around with him, much as other children carry a teddy bear. Slowly, however, Burke recalls that he began to examine the dictionary as a book. The dictionary began to reveal the wonders of language to him. In this sense, Burke believes that his introduction to language usage was a self-discovery rather than a result of formal education.

By high school, the context for the study of language was even more clearly evident. Burke and Malcolm Cowley, a friend of his from age four,[5] belonged to a literary group that examined the French symbolists, Strindberg, Wilde, and domestically, H. L. Mencken. This literary exposure created a deep thirst in Burke, who now "lived for the idea of getting into Greenwich Village." The move to the Village became a reality, and Burke became part of America's first famous Bohemian subculture. A cluster of diverse but powerful literary figures came into contact with Burke such as Edna St. Vincent Millay, Allen Tate, Edmund Wilson, Stuart Davis, Hart Crane, Djuna Barnes, e. e. cummings, and Matthew Josephson.

Yet, Burke was shortly to make a life-style change. In 1922, he moved to his farm on Amity Road in Andover, New Jersey, where he has lived ever since. He ultimately made this life-style choice because he was, in his own words, "bored with the city" and "wanted to live in the country." In 1924, he published his first volume of fiction, *The White Oxen and Other Stories*.

As the 1930s approached, the Great Depression exerted a profound influence upon Burke. Although never becoming an official member of the Communist party, Burke flirted with the party as a true logologist would. Reacting to the depression as a national crisis in the evolution of democracy and capitalism, he proposed the use of the phrase "power to the people" instead of viewing the "masses" as "the workers."[6] During this same period, Burke's personal life was also "in crisis." Burke had married Lillian Batterham in 1919, with whom he had three daughters. He divorced her, however, to marry her sister Elizabeth ("Libby") Batterham in 1933, with whom he had two sons.

The 1930s were a period of tremendous productivity for Burke as a writer. In 1931, he published *Counter-Statement*, in which he argued that artists were pitted against the established social system. In 1932, in his first novel, interestingly entitled *Towards a Better Life: A Series of Declamations or Epistles*, Burke's central character, John Neal, writes: "Oh, I am very tired. I should like to fall into a deep sleep, and on awaking, find every single thing around me altogether different." By 1935, with the publication of *Permanence and Change*, Burke generalized his notion of crisis beyond his personal life and argued that crises and divergent perspectives were the central descriptors of all social interactions. In 1937, with the publication of *Attitudes toward History*, Burke maintained that all of history itself was a series of competing claims and counterclaims, which cluster into five major dramas that span and account for the entire human condition. The 1930s, then, were indeed a convoluted period of crises, but also productivity, for Burke.

The 1940s, however, began Burke's period of stability and constructive productivity. In 1941, in *The Philosophy of Literary Form*, Burke discovers, asserts, and defends a philosophy that appears capable of resolving the profound crises both Burke and humankind face. The word "dramatism" first appears in this book, and it is cast as a purifying and redeeming frame of reference capable of producing social unity. By 1945, in *A Grammar of Motives*, Burke offers a particular method—the *pentad*—for charting the nature of the drama of the human condition. In *A Rhetoric of Motives* in 1950, Burke cast social identification as the central dimension of all communicative experiences. In 1955, he published *Book of Moments, Poems, 1915–1954*. By 1961, the idea of identification permeated his new critical volume, *The Rhetoric of Religion*, which suggested that even "the subject of religion falls under the head of *rhetoric*" when rhetoric is viewed as a form of identification. In 1966, Burke published *Language as Symbolic Action: Essays on Life, Literature, and Method*, reprinting several of his earlier published essays, and *The Complete White Oxen: Collected Short Fiction*, which contained fifteen stories that had appeared in the 1924 edition. In 1968, he also published *Collected Poems, 1915–1967*.

Throughout the 1960s and 1970s, Burke constantly reasserted his theory of dramatism in reviews, essays, critiques, and poetry. Dramatism became an intrinsic feature of reality and was asserted to distinguish all purposeful human action from physiological and instinctive motions.[7] And from 1968 to the present, Burke has sought to "complete the task" by providing a comprehensive and philosophical conception of his views. Two key concepts came to define the system: *dramatism* and *logology*.[8] Philosophical in their orientation, "dramatism" was cast as Burke's label for his ontological system, while "logology" was identified as Burke's term for his theory of epistemology.

At the inception of the 1980s, Burke began to gain status as more than a minor literary critic. From the beginning of the 1980s, Burke has been increasingly cast as a recognized major social critic of the twentieth century. In 1981, Burke was awarded the National Medal for Literature. Likewise in 1981, the *New York Times* identified Burke as a leading American critic: "the strongest living representative of the American critical tradition, and perhaps the largest single source of that tradition since its founder, Ralph Waldo Emerson."[9]

More formally, in 1987, the *New Encyclopaedia Britannica* identified Burke as "one of the leading U.S. critics in the second half of the 20th century." The balance of the 1990s may well be a period in which Burke is celebrated as a profound social critic and thinker of our age. The tribute seems appropriate. Few critics have revealed the scope, imagination, insights, and dazzling concern for symbol using which Kenneth Burke possesses.

Overall, Kenneth Burke offers a unique view but one shaped by particular encounters and circumstances. For many, his system may be particularly powerful, but from other viewpoints, it is equally contestable. The issues are especially clear when Burke is compared with scholars who have offered alternative interpretative schemes. For example, in another essay, I have compared Kenneth Burke and Jacques Derrida. The comparison reveals some of the issues that can exist when examining Burke's system:

As a critic, Kenneth Burke is fascinated by the ways in which people socially construct different kinds of realities with and through the symbols they use. His critical tools are designed to reveal the potentialities of these symbolic systems. While also recognizing the limitations of these systems, Burke would preserve the right and need for people to use symbols as they do. In Burke's view, one perspective of reality does not deny another but merely reveals the incongruities which can exist whenever symbolic perspectives are employed. Accordingly, Burke would find little of value in the critic who would undermine or debunk symbol-using itself.

As a critic, Jacques Derrida holds that his task is to unmask false conceptions of truth, highlight concepts constructed through inconsistent premises, and reveal manipulative, misleading, covert, and subversive uses of language. Yet Derrida's agenda goes beyond "purifying" language use. His conceptions challenge traditional assumptions about language as a system for dealing with reality. As Art Berman has noted of Derrida's analysis of language: "language itself, having no origin in the immediacy of the perception of external reality, is by its very nature an ungrounded chain of signifiers."[10] Likewise, Derrida redefines the scope of human knowledge itself. Because human beings necessarily come to know through written and oral modes, they themselves know few *things*. They know only "traces" of what is real, for all conceptions of "what is" are symbolic, ultimately only "rhetorical fabrications."[11] Or, cast in equally useful terms, Derrida would dismantle all forms of linguistic determinism.

Burke and Derrida differ dramatically as social critics. Burke conveys a healthy optimism. In Burke's view, human beings can refashion, control and master society through symbolic manipulations. Derrida conveys a rigorous skepticism. In Derrida's view, human beings must regain control of their linguistically determined environment, challenge the symbolic systems which oppress and demoralize, and reaffirm the relationship between subjectivism and being. In any event, there is little doubt that Burke would view Derrida as a debunker, while Derrida would undoubtedly view Burke as a linguistic determinist. . . .

Ultimately, Kenneth Burke and Jacques Derrida posit two different views of language. For Burke, language is predominantly instrumental and secondarily expressive. Art is rhetoric, for Burke. For Derrida, language is predominantly expressive and secondarily instrumental. Rhetoric is art, for Derrida. (Chesebro in press)

Yet, this overview of Burke's life and intellectual contributions is intentionally "loaded." It seeks to underscore the ways in which the system Burke has proposed grew from the circumstances and the people he encountered. Others, experiencing and encountering other environments, may well have viewed symbol using in dramatically different ways.

Extending the Burkeian System: Motives for Growth and Development

No system of analysis is complete, for every scheme is shaped by the circumstances that brought the method into existence.[12] Circumstances change and alternative assessment methods become more appropriate. To use Burke's symbolic perspective, systems of analysis are linguistic schemes designed to affect human communication, thought, and action, but such rhetorics are subject to popular whim, growing, reaching a zenith, and later waning. To remain viable, a system of analysis must function as an "open system," responding to changing human conditions and adapting to shifting attitudes, beliefs, and actions. In this regard, even Burke's system of analysis must undergo transformations if it is to remain receptive to ever-changing human dynamics. Hence, it becomes appropriate, if not necessary, to consider extensions of the Burkeian system.

Furthermore, longevity itself has affected the Burkeian system, which requires that extensions of the Burkeian system be seriously considered. Burke has *not* had the luxury of reacting to a specific period of time and particular set of issues. His system has not been identified as a response to a unique decade or two or even as a counterresponse to identifiable events. His writings now span a seventy-year period, crossing a diverse set of intellectual "movements" and a vast range of circumstances, including various forms of massive global conflicts, which have each featured tremendously different economic, political, social, and ideological textures. His individual works have not been contextualized. Indeed, Burke himself has returned to his original works, often forty years later, and sought to adapt them, especially in new forewords and afterwords, to deal with emerging issues. Moreover, his books are frequently read from today's perspective. The "read" can be a difficult one. For example, *Attitudes toward History* was originally published in 1937. In its day, it constituted for many a meaningful and useful view of "the curve of history," which Burke cast as a progression from "Christian evangelism" to "medieval synthesis" to "Protestant transition" to "naive capitalism" and finally to "emergent collectivism." However, with virtually no changes in the original manuscript, the volume was also reissued in 1959 and 1984. Yet, a profound series of personal and societal changes had occurred throughout the world between 1937 and these reissuances. These transformations included two world wars, the emergence of non-Christian nation-states and cultures as global forces, the growing awareness and power of multiculturalism and feminism, the initial development of postmodern critical views in Western Europe and its spread to the United States, and the radical political and economic changes in Eastern Europe and the Soviet Union, to identify just a few of these many changes. They are not easily accounted for in the symbolic analysis of history provided by Burke in 1937. In these respects, Burke's longevity has functioned as a double-edged sword, allowing him to promote his system for a protracted period of time but also dating specific reference points that rationalized the system.

Moreover, an information explosion on a global level has also occurred, which requires that extensions of the Burkeian system be seriously considered. While Burke has focused upon the content of the print medium, information itself is no longer solely linked to print but has been enhanced by a host of visuospatial electronic media. Likewise, while Burke has responded primarily to the products of Western cultures, worldwide sources of information have rapidly escalated and increasingly dominate human understandings. Knowledge itself has become increasingly specialized, with a vast array of different disciplines generating massive volumes of technical knowledge. If the Burkeian system is to respond and adapt to these changes, it can no longer be the province of a single person. A concerted effort must be employed, which requires that the system be altered and changed as new information and new kinds of information are encountered.

Even on a methodological level, Burke's system must be reconsidered. Burke has provided explicit and convenient frameworks that invite their use without major modification. For example, Burke's pentad of terms—act, scene, purpose, agency, and agent—for analyzing motives appears almost universal, readily applied to any situation.[13] As I have argued elsewhere the system lends itself to being "viewed as a kind of 'tool box' from which any scheme of concepts can be extracted for any purpose. . . . Under such conditions, a 'stripped down' listing of Burkeian concepts might well be devised and employed as a pre-fabricated 'cookie cutter' for any and all criticism" (Chesebro 1988, 186). The outcome of using the Burkeian system in this fashion may ultimately be its own destruction:

"By analogy, the 'outline' of the neo-Aristotelian method proposed by Thonssen and Baird in 1948 [292–93] and then extended and expanded by Thonssen, Baird, and Braden in 1970 [308–11] did not promote the insightfulness of neo-Aristotelian analyses; in fact, for some [Black 1965], the outline began to constitute a 'mechanization' of the method, ultimately emphasizing the categorical nature of the system rather than its insightfulness" (Chesebro 1988, 186).

Finally, many of those applying Burke's system have sought to reflect as carefully as possible Burke's original intentions and meanings. Toward this end, Burke himself has frequently remained a central focal point when interpreting his scholarly contributions. Indeed, Burke has remained profoundly active during his later years, often modifying and revising his stated intentions for writing particular volumes and essays. For example, when the University of California Press released the third edition of *Permanence and Change: An Anatomy of Purpose,* Burke added a new afterword, *"Permanence and Change:* In Retrospective Prospect," in which he offered an alternative way of reading the volume that emphasized an ontological dimension (e.g., "Bodies That Learn Language") and four new "loci of motives" that had not appeared in the original publication ([1935a] 1984, 295–336). The revision is sufficiently explicit, for Burke concludes the forty-two-page afterword with this question: "How's that for a somewhat unwieldy revised version of the two sentences which the book, more than four decades ago, began by ending on?" (336). Particularly for scholars who have identified themselves as "Burkeian critics," these revisions may require a significant modification in assessing what Burke means and how his system is to be used. Moreover, Burke himself has functioned as a powerful motivational force, inspiring, encouraging, and helping many dramatistic scholars. The result has been that some view Burkeian scholarship as tied to Burke himself, and for some in an almost religious manner. Rosenfield (1989) has argued, for example, that Burkeian scholars constitute a cult in the discipline of communication. Insofar as the system is tied to Burke personally, as Burke nears retirement or when he dies, the system itself would be in jeopardy. An alternative is to view the Burkeian system as an ongoing product of a community of scholars, all of whom contribute to, extend, and develop the system, as new circumstances emerge.

The Contributions to This Volume

Each of the chapters in this volume constitutes an extension of the Burkeian system. The extensions represent the interest of each author rather than a systematic and concerted program for change. One writer has returned to Burke himself, focusing upon his life and offering new insights into the forces motivating Burke and the products Burke has generated. Others have reinvestigated and provided extensions of specific Burkeian methods, including his notion of media, the negative, and the representative anecdote. Others recast Burke's endeavors in a more political context, focusing upon technology as an antihumanistic and antiecological force. The volume concludes by reconsidering the philosophical system underpinning the Burkeian system.

While the chapters approach the Burkeian system from diverse perspectives, such diversity is particularly appropriate for a volume that explores how the Burkeian system should be extended. At this point in time, a definitive direction and program of research cannot be specified for extending the Burkeian system. Several probes, different in focus and emphasis, are currently required. Ultimately, the extensions may generate many, rather than one, system for analyzing symbol using. The chapters thus provide the kind of diversity now required, for they collectively emphasize the definitional, applied, methodological, theoretical, and philosophical levels which the Burkeian system affects.

At the same time, these essays may challenge readers, especially "Burkeian purists," who believe the central task is to implement the Burkeian system as Burke intended it. A brief sampling from these essays quickly demonstrates the point. In "A Field Guide to Kenneth Burke—1990," William H. Rueckert concludes that "Burke the published critic is one thing, but Burke the man or, rather, Burke the person and personality, is another and as such has had a powerful effect on many of us. He would not want to be, nor should we really want to see him become (though some have tried), a cult figure and thus lose him in the inevitable vagaries, vulgarities, and sentimentalities of personality adulation." In a similar vein but from a "media perspective," in his chapter "Instruments of His Own Making: Burke and Media," Robert S. Cathcart asks: "What is the future of Burkeian dramatism in a world where literature, specifically poetry, is being supplanted by video and cinematic images and where political rhetoric is conducted by telephone, fax, and TV spots?" And in the spirit of many of the chapters in this volume, Richard B. Gregg reports in "Kenneth Burke's Concept of Rhetorical Negativity" that he wishes "to 'employ' Burke's insights into the symbolic lure of negativity," but he adds, "I shall examine the rhetoric of negativity in my own way." In my view, Professors Henderson, Madsen, Blankenship, Thompson and Palmeri, Bertelsen, and Brock offer equally important, insightful, unique, and challenging analyses. Ultimately, this volume is grounded in Kenneth Burke's contributions, but it also offers major extensions of the Burkeian system. These extensions propose new ways for understanding and using Burke.

Organization of This Volume

This volume is divided into four major units. The units are unified by their common concern for the ways in which Burke's system can be insightfully and usefully extended, but they differ in the way in which this project is to be realized.

The first three chapters can be viewed as providing historical extensions of the Burkeian system, for each one reexamines earlier works by Burke. In "A Field Guide to Kenneth Burke—1990," William H. Rueckert focuses upon the intellectual origins of Kenneth Burke's corpus of writings, with special attention devoted to those who inspired Burke, influencing circumstances, the relationships among Burke's various contributions, and recent developments in Burke's thought. He offers an overview and evolutionary conception of Burke's major contributions. Implicitly arguing that a historical orientation adds new insight into the meaning of Burke's writings, Rueckert finds it beneficial to view Burke's writing within a developmental scheme. Kenneth Burke has also added to this historical perspective by contributing his previously unpublished essay from the early 1930s, "Auscultation, Creation, and Revision," which provides a new basis for reexamining the relationships between *Counter-Statement* and *Permanence and Change*. In "Aesthetic and Practical Frames of Reference: Burke, Marx, and the Rhetoric of Social Change," Greig E. Henderson focuses on two of Kenneth Burke's works—*Counter-Statement* and "Auscultation, Creation, and Revision"—written in the 1930s. He traces the dialectic of Burke's early works and examines the pivotal transition from literary criticism (the aesthetic frame of reference) to social and cultural criticism (the practical frame of reference). The argument suggests that the shift toward praxis in Burke's perspective is not as radical as it appears either to him or to others, and that even *Counter-Statement*—the most overtly aesthetic of his works—moves implicitly in the direction of an aesthetic-practical merger.

The second part of this volume, "Methodological Extensions," is composed of three chapters. Each suggests different ways in which specific Burkeian concepts should be recast as methodological tools for a critic. In "Kenneth Burke's Concept of Rhetorical Negativity," Richard Gregg returns to Burke's four essays on the origins of language published in the *Quarterly Journal of Speech* in 1952 and 1953, focuses on the notion of the negative, suggests how it can be cast as a meaningful concept for the critic, and offers applications designed to suggest how the concept "rhetorical negativity" can contribute to critical analyses. In much the same way, in "Burke's Representative Anecdote as a Critical Method," Arnie Madsen develops criteria for applying the concept of a representative anecdote to texts. Three speeches delivered by George Bush during the 1988 presidential campaign are analyzed through two distinct anecdotal approaches. First, the Bush Acceptance Address at the Republican National Convention is cast as an act representative of the entire set of texts. Second, "partnership" is an anecdotal form common to all of the texts, serving to represent the 1988 Bush presidential campaign. And in "Kenneth Burke's Conception of Reality: The Process of Transformation and Its Implications for Rhetorical Criticism," Dale A. Bertelsen posits that Kenneth Burke views reality as a transformational process rooted in a dialectical tension between biological and social dimensions. This view invites rhetorical criticism that analyzes the structural relations designed to maintain tension between ontological and epistemological modes. Such criticism is enacted through the identification of a principle of transformation that constitutes a theoretical statement about the strategies of symbolic action employed to maintain social cohesion and harmony.

In the third part of this volume, "Applied and Societal Extensions," the Burkeian system is cast as a program for activism. In "Kenneth Burke on Ecology: A Synthesis," Jane Blankenship provides a synthesis of Kenneth Burke's thinking on ecology by examining his "ecological attitude," providing a lexicon of pivotal terms used in his explication of that "attitude," and noting some connections between that "attitude" and the larger corpus of his work. In "Attitudes toward Counternature (with Notes on Nuturing a Poetic Psychosis)," Timothy N. Thompson and Anthony J. Palmeri focus on the nature of society's technological orientation, the "Counternature" it produces, and plans for a poetic corrective. After reviewing what Burke calls the "scientific rationalization" and the various psychoses that it has bred, the chapter outlines a comic frame of acceptance and suggests three paths to poetic action: education, agitation, and advocacy. It is a plan for those who wish to "take ecological action beyond recycling."

In the final part of this volume, "Philosophical Extensions," two chapters focus upon the philosophical foundations of the Burkeian system. In his chapter "Instruments of His Own Making: Burke and Media," Robert S. Cathcart extends Burke's traditional concerns for the written and oral modes of communication to the new technologies that increasingly influence human communication. Employing concepts central to Burke's writings, such as *agency* and Burke's extensive treatment of "technologies as instruments of the human being's own making," new types and kinds of communication dramas are described, interpreted, and assessed. Cathcart expresses concerns and hesitations with how Burke has previously examined media systems, and Cathcart proposes a dramatistic and logological reconception of media, a refashioning that would place media as the focal point for critiques "in a world dominated by the technological media of communication." But Cathcart's thesis is far more profound. It is ultimately philosophical, suggesting that the basic principles that have guided Burke should be thoroughly reviewed. Cathcart ultimately maintains that the Burkeian system must be significantly adjusted so that it is more compatible with the hyperreality of postmodernists. Finally, in his chapter "The Evolution of Kenneth Burke's Philosophy of Rhetoric: Dialectic between Epistemology and Ontology," Bernard L. Brock also focuses directly upon the philosophical assumptions guiding Burke's writings. He offers a reconception of Burke's major books in an effort to determine their central philosophical tendencies across three periods in Burke's writings. However, in contrast to Cathcart, Brock's purpose is not as clearly designed to offer an alternative framework for understanding Burke's writings. Brock seeks to make Burke's philosophical system explicit. He maintains that philosophically Burke's writings evolved and have reflected three different philosophical orientations that have ultimately created a philosophical system in which epistemology and ontology are dialectically related.

Editor's Notes and Acknowledgments

The conception for this volume began in 1988 as one component of the plans for the 1990 Kenneth Burke Society convention. Sheron

J. Dailey had agreed to serve as the chief planner for the convention, and in November 1988, at the first business meeting devoted to implementing these plans, I was asked and agreed to edit the volume of essays which the convention would generate. More personally, I undertook this task because Sherry Dailey was heading the convention effort. Sherry is a powerful source of inspiration and commitment whose influence goes far beyond what she suspects.

From this inception, it was agreed that the "call" for this volume would be as open as possible and ultimately designed to encourage original submissions from those new to the Burkeian system as well as the most experienced dramatists. In this regard, this volume has achieved its objective, for both established Burkeians and those new to the system are included.

A selection committee was formed to determine which essays would be included in this volume. The committee included Professors Dale Bertelsen, Bernard L. Brock, James F. Klumpp, and Timothy N. Thompson. This committee read the submissions in a blind review process in which the names of authors were excluded from essays before they were submitted to members of the selection committee. In all, forty-three essays were submitted and considered by the committee. Several of the essays, especially by those new to the Burkeian system, were resubmitted and reevaluated by the selection committee several times. In practice, the committee ultimately served as an editorial board, offering detailed and useful responses to authors on earlier drafts of their essays. Accordingly, the review process itself lasted over one year. Without the commitment, time, energy, detailed reviews, assistance, and patience of the members of the selection committee, this volume would not have reached completion.

At the same time, these extensions would be enhanced if forums were designed to engage the authors in direct face-to-face interactions and perhaps at points even in confrontations. The chapters present new concepts that warrant, not only extended dialogue, but the kinds of challenges that stimulate intellectual development. Moreover, the chapters contained in this volume raise related questions that indeed call for a subsequent volume, for critical issues yet need to be explored. The role, function, and utility of the Burkeian system in a multicultural rhetorical environment have yet to be addressed. Likewise, we need to determine if the Burkeian system can adequately explain and evaluate feminist discourses. Furthermore, feminist and multicultural theories need to be intentionally placed in opposition to the Burkeian system to determine the degree to which rather fundamental changes should be introduced into the system. We therefore still need to explore the degree to which the conceptions guiding the Burkeian system reflect and ultimately reinforce a rhetoric that serves an older, male, white, Anglo, heterosexual, Christian, and Western orientation. The Burkeian system needs additionally to be compared with systems of analysis proposed by scholars such as Michel Foucault, Jacques Derrida, and Jürgen Habermas. A single volume, however, cannot do it all.

Notes

1. This transcription, by James W. Chesebro, is derived from a videotape provided by John W. Kirk of the final session, "An Interview with Kenneth Burke," of the Kenneth Burke Society convention, May 7, 1990.

2. Authors disagree regarding how Burke's system should be linguistically characterized, as "Burkeian" or "Burkean," a discrepancy reflected in this volume. (Other authors have even preferred "Burkian.") The disagreement is at least twenty years old and was formally highlighted by Scott (1974).

3. See, e.g., Hyman 1955 (chap. 10, "Kenneth Burke and the Criticism of Symbolic Action," 327–85); Rueckert 1982; and Brock 1990b.

4. This analysis of Burke's personal life and related quotations by Burke regarding his personal life are taken from Kostelanetz 1981. An equally useful essay is Yagoda 1980.

5. For details regarding Burke's relationship with Cowley, see Jay 1988. Burke told me in a personal conversation that he believed Cowley 1985 had aptly captured the experience of extreme old age for a man.

6. Burke 1935b, esp. 89. Also, see "Thirty Years Later" (1966).

7. Burke explored these relationships in Burke 1968b. A more extended version of this essay appeared one year earlier; see Burke 1967.

8. Burke first published his discussion of these two terms in Burke 1983b. While editor of *Communication Quarterly*, I published an essay by Burke also entitled "Dramatism and Logology," which included Burke's essay from the *Times Literary Supplement* in its entirety as well as additional notes Burke added; see Burke 1985a.

9. The *New York Times* quotes Harold Bloom; see Kostelanetz 1981.

10. Berman 1988, 211.

11. Ibid., 208.

12. In Chesebro 1992 I explore in greater detail the motives for extending the Burkeian system.

13. For a convenient summary of Burke's pentad, see Burke (1945) 1969, xv–xxiii.

Part I

Historical Extensions

1

A Field Guide to
Kenneth Burke—1990

William H. Rueckert

Kenneth Burke was born on May 5, 1897, in Pittsburgh, Pennsylvania. He knew from an early age that he would be a writer, a man of letters, a word man, and he devoted himself with single-minded determination to achieving that end. Using his own terminology, we could say that he knew his own entelechy early, and prophesying after the fact, it is quite clear that he achieved it to perfection. Nothing was allowed to stand in his (or its) way, including formal education. By 1918, after brief stays at Ohio State University and Columbia University, Burke had decided that institutional education was too constraining for him, and he set out to educate himself, becoming proficient in whatever other languages he needed (mainly Latin, French, and German) and reading prodigiously in the literature of Western civilization—a process he was to repeat later, in a different way, when he transformed himself from a literary critic and would-be fiction writer into a social critic.[1] The early stages of Burke's career, which are very well documented in the Burke-Cowley letters, may be summarized as follows: like so many would-be writers, Burke was first a poet and then a short-story writer and involved himself in any way that he could in the literary life, first at Ohio State and then in New York City. He worked for and contributed to numerous little magazines and finally (in the early twenties) settled into a steady job as an editor with the *Dial*, which lasted until 1929, when the *Dial* ceased publication. Even as he was bringing his desire to be a fiction writer (he wanted to be a Flaubert, he said) to some kind of fruition with the publication in 1924 of his collection of short stories, *The White Oxen*, Burke was beginning to write literary criticism and so was discovering the true nature of his genius (and, I think we should add, coming to realize, just as Faulkner did during the same period, that he was a genius).

The early twenties were decisive for Burke: he married Lily Batterham in 1919 and in 1922 abandoned the city for the country, when he bought the first of his houses in rural Andover, New Jersey. He was to live in Andover the rest of his life, and he was to live there for many years in a countrified way, with an outhouse and no running water in the house (well into the sixties) and no electricity until midcentury.[2] Though he divorced Lily in the early thirties and married her sister, Libbie, in 1933, he never left his original place in Andover but simply moved down the road into another house. He was eventually to establish a kind of Burke compound there, which included his three daughters (by Lily) and two sons (by Libbie) and numerous grandchildren. The significance of Burke's commitment to the country and family should not be underestimated, for both played an important role in his life and the development of his thought.[3]

The early and mid-twenties were decisive in other ways. Though Burke was to publish another work of fiction in 1932—his important novel, *Towards a Better Life*—it became increasingly clear to Burke himself that criticism, not fiction, was his true calling and that theoretical criticism and the development of a resourceful methodology (as in the "Lexicon Rhetorica," in *Counter-Statement*), were his real strengths. *Counter-Statement*, Burke's first book of literary criticism, was published in 1931 and brings the first major stage of Burke's development to an end. Though it would seem that his novel should be treated as the terminal point in this first stage of development, it is so clearly both a terminal and a transitional work, symbolically enacting a major transformation in Burke himself, that it is best treated separately. The dismal failure of this novel with the public and critics marked the end of Burke's career as a fiction writer, though he was to publish one more "story" (more an autobiographical fragment than a story) in 1957, entitled "The Anaesthetic Revelation of Herone Liddell."

The end of the twenties and the early years of the thirties were crisis years for both Burke and the country. By the early thirties, Burke had committed himself to full-time writing as a career and was to make his living thereafter from his writing and various part-time teaching jobs. As was to be true throughout the rest of Burke's writing life, the troubles that afflicted the country and, later, the world were to have a profound effect on what Burke wrote and how he conceived of his purpose as a critic. The apparent collapse of capitalism as an economic and political system caused Burke to turn his mind to economic matters and to the relationship between economics, business, and the social good. Like many American writers and thinkers during this period, Burke began a serious study of Marx and other writers on social, political, and economic theory and history. As he turned from literary criticism to social criticism, he read widely in this new field in order to equip himself for his larger role as a social and cultural critic.

Even as he was doing this, his personal life was undergoing profound changes. Burke has written often about the psychological and emotional requirements of the breaking up of one significant relationship with a woman (or vice versa) and the beginning and development of another.[4] All of what he has said on this subject most certainly has a bearing upon the significance and importance of his divorce from Lily and his marriage to her sister, Libbie, in 1933. The importance of Libbie to Burke's life and work is made perfectly clear in the Burke-Cowley letters and was abundantly clear to anyone who knew Burke during the thirty-six years of his marriage to Libbie. All of his major books were written and published during this period (1933–69), and most of his major works—that is, the uncollected essays of the "Symbolic of Motives" and many other important essays—were also written and published during this period, as was most of his poetry. Burke has not published a new book since Libbie's death in 1969, so that it is quite legitimate to speak of the post-Libbie period in Burke's development—or, roughly, the period from 1970 to 1984, when the new editions of *Permanence and Change* and *Attitudes toward History* were finally published by the University of California Press.

Burke's shift from literary to social/cultural criticism—which was his way of responding to the stock market crash of 1929 and the depression—was signaled by the writing of *Permanence and Change,* a book which he says he had completed by 1933, though it was not published until 1935. As soon as he finished this book, Burke began work on *Attitudes toward History,* which was published in 1937 and is certainly the major work of the thirties. The tentative, exploratory nature of *Permanence and Change* is replaced by the certainties of *Attitudes toward History. Attitudes toward History* also reflected the development of the comic attitude, which was to stay with Burke from this point on, as well as the certainties of the "Dictionary of Pivotal Terms." The other work of the thirties, *The Philosophy of Literary Form,* which mostly collects Burke's essays on literature and brings his literary and social criticism into a conjunction in the theory of symbolic action and the critical methodology he was later to call indexing, brings the second major phase of Burke's development to a close. I think we can safely say that Burke discovered his life's work in the thirties, especially in the seminal *Attitudes toward History* and in the major essays of *The Philosophy of Literary Form*—such as the title essay, the essays on Freud, and the essays entitled "The Rhetoric of Hitler's Battle" and "Literature as Equipment for Living." Burke never deviated from the main tenets of the theory of symbolic action, and the four-part methodology developed in the title essay was the one he would use in all of his major textual analyses. Marx and Freud, Bentham and Nietzsche, so prominent in all the books of the thirties, would remain central to all of Burke's thought.

The next major phase of Burke's development—the central, mature phase, and the most productive in Burke's now very long and productive career—began in the early forties, when he started working on *A Grammar of Motives* and began teaching at Bennington, where many of the ideas developed in *A Grammar of Motives* and *A Rhetoric of Motives* were first tried out on his students. This phase lasted until 1966 and the publication of *Language as Symbolic Action*. The five major works of this period are really all of a piece, with one developing out of the other and the whole making up what we now know as dramatism and logology. With a few exceptions, all of Burke's major ideas are developed and ramified during this period, and the tetralogy of motives which he projected early—the grammar, rhetoric, poetics, and ethics (in imitation of Aristotle)—was really thought through and completed in one way or another. It was a massive undertaking and a truly remarkable achievement. Upon it Burke's real claim to fame rests.

However, it would be a mistake—and it is a very common one—to think that Burke's development and career end here in 1966 just because no new theoretical/critical book has been published since that date. There are three more phases to Burke's development, and I want to insist that we should acknowledge them seriously if we wish to have a comprehensive understanding of Burke's development and achievements. Burke's last published new book is his *Collected Poems* (1968), which is dedicated to Libbie Burke and published a year before her death. This book collects the relatively small number of poems Burke wrote up till 1954, which were originally published in his *Book of Moments* (1955), plus the large and varied number of poems he wrote from 1954 to 1968. With the exception of his long poem "Eye Crossing," written during the last sad year of Libbie's life and originally published in 1969, most of Burke's poems are collected in this volume. As Tim Crusius (1981) has so persuasively argued, we would be foolish to ignore Burke the poet, for it is in his poems that we can see almost more clearly than anywhere else the comic, ironic, and satiric spirit that is at work everywhere in Burke's work as a critic and that is so well known to anyone who has heard Burke speak and perform.[5] I would identify this poetic phase, one that is a product of the most creative and productive years of Burke's life, as the fourth major phase of his development.

The fifth phase of his development begins after the death of Libbie with the work that Burke began publishing in 1970. I will call it the Helhaven phase because his Helhaven satire is one of the major works to come out of it. In that satire and in other essays published during this period, Burke arrives at the conclusion that, because humans are symbol-using animals, and because technology is made possible by symbol using, humans' entelechy is technology, and high technology (or post–atom/hydrogen bomb technology) is essentially and potentially both ultimately homicidal and suicidal. In other words, after many years of thinking and writing about technology (a theme that appears as early as *Counter-Statement*), Burke arrives, during this late phase of his development, at a kind of ultimate, ironic, satiric vision of the ultimate, essential nature of the human species. This final tragic vision of humankind is the counterpart of Burke's earlier comic vision, but it is not really separate from it, for Burke has argued all along that criticism is essentially comic; only by critically scrutinizing the human condition does one arrive at this ironic tragic vision wherein our genius may be our undoing.

The final phase of Burke's development—though perhaps it is presumptuous of me to speak of a final phase until Kenneth Burke lets go and leaves us and we have access to the work he has been doing over the past five years (since 1985 and the "In Haste" essay that appeared in *Pre/Text*)—lasts from the late seventies to the publication of the new editions of *Permanence and Change* and *Attitudes toward History* in 1983–84 with their new afterwords— their "Retrospective Prospects." The works of this period consist of summarizing essays Burke wrote—such as "Variations on 'Providence'" (1981b)—in which he tried to reduce his major ideas to a few essential theses or propositions. Another example of such a summarizing essay is "(Non symbolic) Motion/(Symbolic) Action" (1978a), which, like the end of "Variations on 'Providence,'" is also written as a series of paragraph-long propositions.

Burke has been writing and publishing now for seventy years. That is a tribute not only to his longevity but also to his persistent creative energy. Only a couple of years ago, into his nineties, he was getting ready to embark on yet another project, to have one more go at arriving at the ultimate answers he began seeking in the thirties when he first understood not only that he was a genius but what the nature of his genius was, and what the burden of it would be. Burke certainly knew when he was writing *Attitudes toward History* that his genius was to be a critic—not just a literary critic, which, in a sense, he has been all of his life, but a critic in the larger sense, a critic-at-large, as Simons and Melia like to put it. He probably knew even then that the burden of the critic is knowledge and that, in the resonating line from De Gourmont which he quotes in his "Eye Crossing" poem, "Intelligence is an accident, genius is a catastrophe."[6] Why? Because in the case of Burke the critic, genius is intelligence pushed to the limit; it is the compulsion to use this intelligence, no matter what burden of fulfillment and knowledge is placed upon one as one goes on fulfilling one's genius to the end of the line, to the end of one's time, even if it means that one arrives, near the end, at catastrophic knowledge. Though he must have wanted to stop his efforts, and must have been tempted to do so at some point after Libbie's death, Burke has never relented in his quest for knowledge that would serve (if not save) humankind and has never given up the most fundamental of all the critic's beliefs— which is that knowledge can and, it is to be hoped, will save us. The negative of this, of course, is knowing that knowledge will not and cannot save us from ourselves, which is an irony close to the essence of Greek tragedy and to Burke's tragicomic vision of the symbol-using animal that is, thanks to its genius, "rotten with perfection."

1924–1931

The White Oxen (1924) is Burke's first published book. The fifteen stories that make up the book were written between 1919 and 1924, as were the three shorter stories he added to *The Complete White Oxen* (1968c). The final story in the latter, "The Anaesthetic Revelation of Herone Liddell," was written and published in 1957. These stories, plus Burke's novel, *Towards a Better Life* (1932), make up his total output as a fiction writer. Read in the context of Burke's overall development and career, *The White Oxen* tells us some interesting and valuable things about Burke's beginnings. His earliest serious aspiration as a writer was to become an American Flaubert, or a writer whose whole life was dedicated to his craft, and whose craft was the carefully written, well-made story or novel. To borrow the title of the first essay in *Counter-Statement*, he wanted to become an "Adept of Pure Literature," or literature that was written solely for its own sake, as a kind of formal and rhetorical exercise. In a sense, that is what he achieves in *The White Oxen*. Without exception, the stories are immaculately written and well made; the stories as a group are exercises in different styles and different fictional modes. The progression from "The White Oxen," the first story, to "Prince Lan," the final story, is a progression from the completely realistic and ironic to the completely fantastic and symbolic. In between, there are other stories in the realistic mode and in the symbolic mode, stories in which realism and fantasy are alternated, stories with recognizable characters and consecutive plots, and stories with disjunctive plots or three completely separate plots and unrecognizable characters like Treep and Arjk. Some of the stories are comic; many are ironic or have an ironic twist to them; some are broadly satiric; many are extremely witty. Overall, inventiveness, experimentation, and variety are clearly operative principles as Burke works his way through a range of short fictional styles and modes. When one finishes this book of stories, one has a sense of having read a book with almost no content by a writer with a very witty, cerebral, and playful mind. The Burke one meets in these stories is the Burke one meets many years later in the poems, the Burke who loved to tinker with the medium, to create humorous, often ironic effects; who could never resist a satiric jab here and there, whose mind both saw and played around corners.[7]

I do not mean to suggest here that the stories or, later, the poems are frivolous, because they clearly are not. The stories are serious writing of a particular kind, writing that is more interested in itself—what it is doing—than it is in saying something. It affirms what it is by what it does, which is, as Burke says in *Counter-Statement*, to create certain effects. When Burke began to abandon his aspirations to become an adept of pure literature and turned to literary criticism (to writing about literature rather than writing it), he shifted the whole focus of his aspirations and energy. When he returned to fiction writing in 1928 and began his semiautobiographical and highly symbolic novel, *Towards a Better Life*, he was far beyond the formal exercises he put himself through in writing the stories that make up *The White Oxen*, even though one can recognize some of this same motive in the early, elegantly written "declamations" that make up the first part of the novel. In between these two fictional works Burke conceived and wrote the essays that make up *Counter-Statement*, the book that signals the fact that he has found his true vocation—criticism.

Counter-Statement is really Burke's defense of the seriousness and serious *social* function of art, the artist, and the critic. Literature (which is usually what Burke means by art) is equipment for living, as he shows in his essay on Mann and Gide (Burke [1931] 1968, 92–103) and in the theoretical essay "Program" (107–32). As

Burke tries to show everywhere in the book, writers are counter-agents, and their works are "counter-statements"—or should be—in the sense that they tend to respond to the excesses of their own time and place and work against them either to promote change or to restore a healthy norm. It is this countermanding role of the artist and of art that Burke the critic—first the literary critic and later the social/cultural critic—will adopt and perfect. Reading *Counter-Statement* again after reading and rereading all the rest of Burke, I notice not so much the theory of form or the critical machinery of "Lexicon Rhetorica" (though both served Burke very well in the years ahead) but Burke's defense of Mann, Gide, and De Gourmont, and his defense of the revolutionary humanistic function of art in the "Program" essay. Burke's lifelong battle against overindustrialization, against technology, against scientism, against the oversimplifications of fundamentalism, fanaticism, and bureaucratization begins in this book and forms the basis of his defense of the writer and of literature and, roundabout, of the critic. "Certainties," Burke says in "Program," "will always arise, impelling men to new intolerances. (Certainty is always cheap, it is the easiest thing of which man is capable. Deprive him of a meal, or bind his arms, or jockey him out of job—and convictions spring up like Jacks-in-the-box.) Thus, we can defend the aesthetic as anti-practical, anti-industrial, anti-machine because the practical, the industrial, the mechanical is so firmly entrenched" (113). Burke is not just being perverse here, nor is he playing the devil's advocate. He here states—as he does in the title of his first book of criticism—one of the themes of all of his later work and describes, with great accuracy, what the function of critics is to be in relationship to their own society and time.

It seems unlikely that one could have predicted Burke's future development from *Counter-Statement*. After the fact, we see certain obvious connections; before the fact, it is quite another matter. Though it was not published until 1931, *Counter-Statement* is basically a work of the twenties, a kind of precrash, predepression work that belongs to Burke's life as a man of letters—a would-be fiction writer, a sometime poet, an editor of a literary magazine, a music critic, and a literary critic. Though *Counter-Statement* addresses the question of the relationship between literature and society, it never does so with the seriousness and intensity that was to characterize all of Burke's work in the thirties and after; it remains, after the fact, a work by a literary critic who has not yet developed a real sense of the larger social context which we find at work in *Permanence and Change*, *Attitudes toward History*, and *The Philosophy of Literary Form*.

1935

The change from *Counter-Statement* to *Permanence and Change* is a huge one, as is the later change from *The Philosophy of Literary Form* to *A Grammar of Motives*. It is easy to say that Burke changed from being a literary critic to being a social/cultural critic: that is, from the smaller to the larger domain of the critic, whereby literature and the function of the critic are absorbed into a much larger and more inclusive context. But this hardly indicates what happened to Burke. For one thing, all of his references change, indicating that he again underwent a massive program of self-education in preparing himself for his new role as a social critic. In a transitional study written in the early thirties called "Auscultation, Creation, and Revision,"[8] Burke uses a metaphor that is much to our purpose here. The metaphor in the first word of the title suggests a comparison between the critic and a doctor who is listening to the patient's internal symptoms with a stethoscope. The patient is society, and the doctor-critic is Burke, who was in the process of changing from a literary to a social critic. The patient/society is sick, and the doctor/critic is going to determine the nature of the illness and prescribe a cure—a process that is clearly suggested by the second and third words of the title. That is exactly what Burke sets out to do in *Permanence and Change*. Rather than specify the requirements of the good life, he writes about ultimate matters, such as human purpose, the permanent human needs throughout history, and how they have been and may now be adequately satisfied in the flux and change that is history. But we should never think that Burke is going to abandon his first love—literature, poetry—and he never really does until much later.[9] Instead of analyzing individual works, as he does in *Counter-Statement*, or discussing literary form, he here turns poetry and the poetic motive into metaphors for the good life. They become the corrective "rationalization" needed to counter the dangerous, combative misemphasis of the current capitalistic and "scientific" rationalization and the inadequacies of the old religious one. The church, Burke says, is "like a big deserted building, with broken windows and littered doorways" ([1935a] 1984, 65). The "corrective philosophy" that Burke proposes in this book is one in which "the center of authority . . . [is] situated in a philosophy, or psychology of poetry rather than in a body of poetry"; it will be a "rationale of art" whose purpose is to promote an "art of living" (66).

Burke makes these statements at the end of part 1 of *Permanence and Change* and ramifies them throughout the other two parts of the book. Burke not only has an extraordinarily retentive memory but demonstrates an amazing ability to bring apparently completely unrelated writers and ideas together to make his points. This is why he calls the middle section of the book "Perspective by Incongruity"—a phrase that well describes an analytic technique Burke was to use in all the rest of his books and talks and which tended to make many of his more conservative readers and listeners angry, resentful, and distrustful. By the end of this book, Burke has worked out the cooperative creative moral/ethical "philosophy of Being"—a conception of the "good life," of the "poetry of action," which he will adhere to in all the rest of his books and essays. This position and its commitments are well summarized in the conclusion to *Permanence and Change*, where Burke explains what he means by the poetic or dramatic metaphor as "key," and why it is that the poetic cooperative metaphor must be a corrective to the competitive metaphors (the us vs. them metaphors) that have "plagued the Western-world with increasing violence" so long. I think we need to remember, when reading and thinking about Burke, that the Western world and, in a sense, much of the rest of the world have been at war or engaged in devastating revolutions during all of Burke's adult life (from 1914 on).

Interlude—1932

This is perhaps an ideal place to discuss Burke's important, highly symbolic semiautobiographical novel. Burke has said many times that the novel names his number; that one cannot understand him without understanding this novel; that it is about the breakup of his first marriage to Lily and his developing relationship to Libbie, his second wife; that he killed off some highly individualistic and destructive part of himself in the novel in the scapegoat character of John Neal and the profound changes that occur in him in the course of the novel. Burke has written repeatedly about this novel in his letters, in various footnotes and afterwords and forewords; in fact he has written a whole essay about it ("On Stress, Its Seeking")[10] and has argued with most interpretations of the novel.

This elegantly written novel tells the story of one John Neal (or, punwise, kneel), who begins the novel as a cynical, mean-minded, manipulative character given to Nietzschean aphorisms of the most cynical, negative kind. Very basically, it is the story of John Neal's relationship to four women: Florence, Genevieve, his wife, and the girl in white. The kindest way to describe Neal's relationships to all of these women is to say that he is despicable. This is especially true of his relationship to Genevieve, who, though she is married, loves him and comes to him whenever he needs her. Neal repeatedly treats her most cruelly, especially near the end of the novel, when he falsely accuses her of betraying him, puts her to obscene tests of fidelity, drives her out to solicit for him, and finally drives her away. It is this final act that precipitates the great change that occurs in John Neal in the last part of the novel. The change is classic, in the sense that as a result of his own actions in his relationship to Genevieve, John Neal slowly comes to knowledge of what he was like up to that point in the novel. He was, to put it nicely, a despicable human being, a user of everybody, especially his women. As he comes to knowledge, he is driven more and more into himself and begins to break down—an event which many critics take as a sign that he goes mad, but there is very little that is mad about John Neal at the end. In fact, he is all wisdom at the end, when he writes a series of unsent letters to Genevieve in which he acknowledges the cruelty of his behavior toward her; or in the recapitulation chapter, in which he again admits his faults and guilt; and especially in the final somewhat disjointed chapter, "Testamentum Meum," where it is even clearer what he has learned, what he has purged out of himself (or symbolically, out of Burke), what he now stands for, and, most important, where he asserts that he will rise again, profoundly changed.

Following Burke's own leads in his theory of symbolic action, could we not say that in this novel, by writing this novel (which we know was a very painful experience for Burke, especially at the end), Burke symbolically purged himself of the negative traits that made him unfit for Libbie (the woman Burke says he adored and for whom, he said, he wrote all of his books just to keep proving to her [and himself] that he was worthy of her)? Could we not say that the symbolic function of this novel for Burke was to purge himself and make himself worthy of Libbie and a better life? The novel preceded his marriage to Libbie in 1933, but it did not precede his relationship to her. In depicting a character who finally does learn to kneel at the end of the novel, Burke depicts a character who goes from a kind of Nietzschean, highly self-centered and individualistic view of the self which makes him incapable of love, to a kind of completely opposite view of the self—the view that is depicted in the last three chapters of the novel as John Neal comes to knowledge and undergoes his changes. This change, by the way, is also similar to the one that Burke went through when he changed from an artist to a literary critic and then to a social critic; from the artist who wrote and the critic who addressed himself to individual works and authors, to the critic who addressed himself to society with its cooperative needs and behavior.

Towards a Better Life consists of unsent letters—that is, of a series of reflexive acts by John Neal—to his "friend" and rival Anthony. Two of the last three chapters of the novel break this form because one chapter is unsent letters by John Neal to Genevieve; the last chapter is Neal's testament and is simply called "Jottings." In both of these, as well as the recapitulation chapter, John Neal admits that his character was his destiny; he was no victim of fate or bad luck but the originator of his actions. Hence, it is his character that must change, and does. It is quite clear that Burke, in the fictional person of John Neal, is addressing his symbolic self throughout this novel and that the novel does function as his symbolic action, allowing him in the mysterious ways of symbolic action to purge himself of his burden (his negative traits) and the guilt that goes with them, allowing him to cleanse himself and make himself ready and worthy for both the new relationship to Libbie and his new role as a social/cultural critic. Whatever Burke says about how to interpret the title of the novel, I think we should take it at face symbolic value and realize that, by writing the novel, Burke was able to move toward a better life. Unlike *Permanence and Change*, which he says he put together in order to keep from falling apart, in this book he took himself apart in order to put himself together in a new way, to prepare himself for the new roles he was to enter into with Libbie and as a social/cultural critic.[11]

1937–1941

As Burke was finishing *Towards a Better Life*, he was casting about for the most appropriate way to begin the second phase of his career. After writing and rejecting various projects, he settled into the writing of *Permanence and Change*, which he says he finished in 1933—the year he married Libbie. *Permanence and Change* is a book of beginnings, an exploratory work in which Burke tries to get his bearings as a social critic and to define his own orientation. Having rejected Communism (but not Marx, whom Burke was to draw upon in profound ways right up through *A Rhetoric of Motives*), Burke commits himself to the poetry of action he describes so eloquently at the end of *Permanence and Change*.

However, it is not until *Attitudes toward History*, which was published in 1937, that Burke moves from exploration to self-assurance and certainty and writes what is his major work of the thirties. Even after fifty-three years, *Attitudes toward History* is still an exciting and thought-provoking book to read (and reread), especially parts 1 and 3, where we do not have to contend with

Burke's somewhat tedious, problematic, and very partial account of Western history. I do not mean to dismiss part 2 of the book, with its economic and political analysis of Western history as a five-act drama culminating in "Emergent Collectivism"; after all, it is at the end of part 2 (Burke [1937] 1984, 166–75) that Burke develops the *comic frame*, which is one of the main achievements of this book and one of Burke's major contributions to our intellectual equipment for living. The same can be said for the "Dictionary of Pivotal Terms" with which Burke ends the book. Like the "Lexicon Rhetorica" of *Counter-Statement*, the "Dictionary" indicates clearly that Burke has now developed a terminology (a set of concepts, a calculus) that equips him to analyze and interpret social dynamics in a way that suits him—that is, in a way that is consistent with his view of the role of the social critic and the obligation of the critic to provide society with the "corrective" knowledge and perspectives that it needs to stay sane or regain its sanity. As Burke says at the end of part 2: "The comic frame should enable people to *be observers of themselves, while acting*. Its ultimate goal would not be *passiveness*, but *maximum consciousness*. One would 'transcend' himself by noting his own foibles. [It] would provide a rationale for locating the irrational and the nonrational" (171).

Another achievement of this book is the way in which Burke again—as he had done in *Permanence and Change* with the poetic metaphor as key in the analysis of social behavior—brings poetry and social criticism together in the section entitled "Poetic Categories." Here he uses poetic categories to define and characterize recurrent attitudes toward history ("strategies for living"). He also uses this chapter as the occasion, early in the book, to define comedy and isolate it as the sanest and most civilized of frames of acceptance. The best of Marx, Freud, and Veblen, he says, is comic. Whatever poetry may be, Burke says, criticism had best be comic ([1937] 1984, 107). Burke himself is often wonderfully comic in the way he writes, as in the comic interpretation of T. S. Eliot's deadly serious *Murder in the Cathedral* (83–86).

The resourcefulness of this book is hard to pin down. The theory of symbolic action is here in germinal form throughout part 3 of the book. Marx, with his emphasis on class structure and the economic basis of social action (property relationships), is everywhere in the book. Burke's deepening awareness of the significance of Freud is present in all of his many references to literary works and symbolism, and to the irrational and nonrational motives that operate in social behavior. The "Dictionary" is a storehouse of useful concepts. The book is full of techniques for the analysis of symbolism wherever it is found and everywhere suggests ways of bringing literary and social criticism together, a task Burke was to deal with at length in *The Philosophy of Literary Form*. And finally, emerging out of the whole book, in bits and pieces as one goes along, and in the very way that Burke does things, are Burke's well thought-out conceptions of comedy, a comic vocabulary, the comic critic, the comic attitude toward history as the most persuasive frame of acceptance, as the most "peaceful" and peace-promoting attitude and approach to the drama of human relations. Burke was always a yea-sayer, however dark and ironic some of his perceptions are; he has always been in the great American tradition of James, Whitman, and Emerson, just as his contemporary and fellow critic Lewis Mumford was.

It is hard to let go of this book, just as it is hard to put down *A Grammar of Motives:* one always wants to dwell in it and on it for a long time, unpacking its many treasures.[12] Much of what he was to do later is anticipated in this book, as one realizes reading it again with the rest of Burke in one's head. Burke's other work of the thirties—aside from a great many reviews—is *The Philosophy of Literary Form*, which collects essays that he wrote during the thirties and, in the title essay, shows us the profound effect that teaching, which Burke began to do in the later thirties, will have on his work. In this book Burke goes back to his first love—literature and literary criticism—and works out both the basic theory of literature and the critical methodology that will later be the basis of his poetics as he developed it in his *Symbolic of Motives*.

In the title essay Burke works out and applies his theory of literature as symbolic action, mostly in an analysis of the works of Coleridge. In this same essay, he elaborates on the four-part methodology he first used in *Attitudes toward History* and anticipated in the theory of form (the "Lexicon Rhetorica") in *Counter-Statement*. Like most of Burke's methodologies, the one developed here is very simple and extraordinarily resourceful when applied to *any* verbal or symbolic structure. Later, in "Fact, Inference, and Proof in the Analysis of Literary Symbolism" (Burke 1954), Burke was to call this methodology "indexing." The way to find out what is going on in a verbal structure, Burke says, is to find out first what goes with what, or what equals what, or what is identified with what. This obviously would include metaphors. Burke and others have called this *cluster analysis*. Second, one also has to find out what versus what, or what is opposed to what. Burke has called this *agon analysis*. Third, one must also pay attention to what follows what, or to the progressions in a given work. Burke called this *progressive form* in *Counter-Statement*, but it is perhaps easiest to think of it in rather conventional terms as structural analysis, which studies the progress or development from beginning to middle to the end of a given text. Finally, Burke says, one must study the *transformations* in a given work, or determine what, if anything, changes or is transformed into something or someone else—as in the case of John Neal. This methodology is used by Burke throughout his career, in the many extended analyses he did for the *Symbolic*, the *Rhetoric*, and *Language as Symbolic Action*, and most extensively in "Verbal Action in the *Confessions* of St. Augustine," in *The Rhetoric of Religion* (Burke [1961] 1970, 43–171).

The theory of literature as symbolic action, with "symbolic" meaning both verbal and the usual something that is both itself and stands for something else, is Burke's functional poetics and his protest against purely aesthetic theories of literature and the New Criticism's tendency to deny both a personal and a social function to literary works. In other words, it is Burke's way of insisting that literature is equipment for living, both for the person who wrote the work and for those who read it. Its function is primarily social for writer and reader. According to Burke, literature has a purgative-redemptive function; catharsis is central to the theory of symbolic action, just as it is to the theory of tragedy Burke later worked out in his essays on *The Oresteia* and *Othello*, which are part of his *Symbolic of Motives*. We need to remember here, as we do everywhere in Burke from the thirties on, his deep, humanistic commitment to the proposition that, as in the comic frame of *Attitudes toward History* and later in the motto of *A Grammar of Motives*, resolving conflicts by means of words (i.e., symbolically) is usually better than resolving them by actual physical means. To put it as simply as Burke sometimes does, it is better to write a poem about killing somebody or to settle one's scores verbally than it is to go out and actually kill someone. Diplomacy is always better than war.[13] Burke has spent most of his mature years as a critic trying to warn us (one of his favorite words is "admonish") against the causes of war and killing. The *Grammar* and the *Rhetoric* are catalogs of these causes. As every reader of Burke knows, the motto of *A Grammar of Motives* is toward the purification of war; one of Burke's most frequent reminders to us is that books should be written to promote tolerance and speculation. Burke must have been shocked by the death sentence laid on Salman Rushdie by fundamentalist Muslims for writing a novel, just as he has always been disturbed by the ideological rigidity, the fanaticism, and the lack of imagination displayed by the fundamentalists in any religion, and by the ethnic and racial hatreds that have led to so many killings in our time. Few critics have ever taken literature and the powers of the word quite so seriously as Burke nor argued quite so persuasively for its therapeutic personal and social functions in the many text-centered analyses and interpretations that he has done in his role as literary critic.

Before leaving the thirties and this text, I want to point out that *The Philosophy of Literary Form* is a lot more than the title essay and Burke's attempt (or second attempt, really) to formulate the first principles—the philosophy—of literary form. Also included in this book is the admonitory essay entitled "The Rhetoric of Hitler's *Battle*," which is really a kind of paradigm of all of Burke's later work on the seductive, destructive inducements of ideological and political rhetoric which comes to a head in part 3 of *A Rhetoric of Motives*. There is also the essay entitled "Freud and the Analysis of Poetry," in which Burke not only acknowledges the importance of Freud in his work but indicates, by way of Freud, why he too is so interested in what he calls the "demonic trinity," or, as he so wittily puts it, in showing that sewers are what churches are for (Burke [1941] 1973, 259). Burke's obsessive concern with the hidden, the disguised motive behind the expressed one, with the secret, often guilt-ridden and destructive motives behind apparently straightforward, often altruistic, and seemingly innocent actions began in the thirties, especially in *Attitudes toward History*, and figures prominently in all the work of the next period.[14] Finally, we should not forget such basic Burke texts in *The Philosophy of Literary Form* as "Semantic and Poetic Meaning" (138–67), where Burke again pits poetic against scientific, and the apparently very simple but extremely important "Literature as Equipment for Living" (293–304), which states the most basic of all propositions for Burke's thinking about literature.

1941–1966

Burke's central period began in the early forties (when he also first began teaching at Bennington College) and lasted through 1966. There is no way in which the five works of this period can be dealt with adequately in a short, omnibus chapter such as this one. The five works are *A Grammar of Motives* (1945), *A Rhetoric of Motives* (1950a), his "Symbolic of Motives" (done, really, by the late fifties and published as separate essays but never assembled by Burke into a book), *The Rhetoric of Religion* (1961), and *Language as Symbolic Action* (1966b). Out of this period, and as the culmination of the work he began in the thirties, come dramatism and logology, the twin towers of the inclusive language-centered system and methodology Burke worked out between 1940 and 1966. Dramatism had as its overall object the working out of a language-centered grammar (a logic; a dialectics), a rhetoric, a poetics, and an ethics. The first three were completed and, though no "Ethics of Motives" exists as such, Burke certainly worked out the moral/ethical basis of dramatism in such essays as "A Dramatistic View of the Origins of Language" (Burke 1952a, 1952b, 1953a, 1953b), which locates the genius of language, and hence of humans, in the moral negative, and in the tour de force which concludes *The Rhetoric of Religion:* "Epilogue: Prologue in Heaven" ([1961] 1970, 273–316), where Burke lays out the essential features of the drama of human relations according to dramatism and logology. Logology has as its ostensible object a working out of the relationship between the Word (Christian theology) and words, on the assumption that, since theology is the perfection of the use of words, it can be used as a paradigm for the study of all uses of words. Logology in its ordinary meaning is simply the study of words (words about words), but as Burke develops and uses it, throughout *The Rhetoric of Religion* and everywhere after 1961, as the main resource of his criticism, logology takes on a whole array of special meanings peculiar to Burke's way of looking at and talking about the world (the natural, the human, the sociopolitical, the supernatural, and, of course, the verbal).

In 1963 (or thereabouts) Burke wrote his extended definition of humans as the symbol-using animals (1966b, 4–24), and this action, more than anything else, tells us what the real purpose of dramatism and logology is.[15] It is not so much that Burke spun his system out of this definition as it is that, at the end (or near the end) of working out his system in *A Grammar of Motives, A Rhetoric of Motives,* "A Symbolic of Motives," and *The Rhetoric of Religion* Burke is able to make what he considers to be a definitive statement about the nature of humans, the human condition, and the drama of human relations. This definition is both the culmination of all his previous work and a point of departure for all the work that will follow in the next twenty-five years. In other words, Burke is not just a critic who enters and leaves history periodically with an essay here and a book there, as the occasion demands or will and energy make possible. He is a critic who enters history and plans to make his mark and become a significant permanent part of history by making an original contribution to our knowledge and understanding of ourselves and the drama of human relations. Burke's motives were to follow and use his genius to creative and constructive ends, however eccentric these ends might at first seem. For years, many people regarded Burke as a maverick, someone who was very difficult to place, hard to read, and nearly impossible to understand. He was thought of as a literary critic long after that had ceased to be his primary concern; it was many years before people in many disciplines began to understand the profound corrective social purpose behind his work and its wide range of applications. Burke did not live the way other critics did; he refused to be institutionalized; he was self-taught and often distrusted by the bureaucratized intellects of other formally educated critics; he was, in many ways, so far ahead of his time that other critics had a hard time figuring out what he was doing, and why, or what they could do with it. It was not really until the seventies that the establishment in many different disciplines finally began to understand what Burke was about and to recognize and honor him and his achievement.

In 1961 Burke ended his twenty years of teaching at Bennington and took his one-man show on the road, crisscrossing the country many times with his wife, Libbie. He has been on the road ever since, preaching the dramatistic/logological word. Many of the essays in *Language as Symbolic Action* were first given as talks; almost everything that Burke has published since 1966 was first given as a talk and in one way or another is either an explanation of, or a defense of, dramatism/logology as a system and methodology against all comers—against N. O. Brown in an MLA confrontation; against Marshall McLuhan, Buckminster Fuller, B. F. Skinner and behaviorism; against scientism and reductionism of any kind; against more technology as a solution to the problems caused by technology; against purely formalist literary criticism; against Northrup Frye; against archetypal criticism and myth criticism; against any explanation of the human condition and the drama of human relations which Burke considers an oversimplification. One oversimplification is any scheme which denies the dualism (mind-body, motion-action, verbal—not verbal, nature-language, symbol using—animal, humans-nature) Burke has insisted upon from the very beginning as necessary to an adequate account of the human condition and the drama of human relations. Others are any account that shifts the stress off moral action and drama as the key to the human drama, or any account which fails to acknowledge the primacy of words, of language as the essential characteristic of the human animal; or, odd as the converse of this may seem, any account that fails to acknowledge the fact that we are *bodies* that must learn language.

Why stress this adversarial part of Burke's development and career? Because it is such an essential part of all that Burke has done since 1945, and it is a function of Burke's quite dogmatic assertion, part of a somewhat paranoiac conviction that he must fight his way out of the corner he is always being backed into. After 1945, he felt more and more strongly that he had in fact, in dramatism/logology, discovered and formulated truths about the human condition, the drama of human relations (especially in the sociopolitical scene), and humans' relationships to nature, supernature, and counternature that are so essential, so basic, so important that they can and should be pitted against—seen in relationship to—other prominent views on the same topics put forth by his contemporaries.

Briefly, synoptically, here are some of the high points of the five works from this period.

A Grammar of Motives *(1945)*

The contributions this book has made to our intellectual equipment for living and to our own conception of ourselves as critics include the following: the pentad and the ratios and the other terminological resources of Burkean dialectics worked out for us here as analytic tools; the carefully worked-out philosophy of action that forms the conceptual center of this book (in chapters 3 and 4 of part 2); the theory of substance; the theory of language and the assertion that the study of language is the key to knowledge of the human species; the carefully worked-out and often restated conception of the nature and role of the critic (the whole book embodies—or, as Burke would prefer, enacts—the critical intelligence at work); the conception of criticism as comic, as hypochondriasis—that is, the study of our own human foibles, of our diseases that we may better understand and live with them; and the conception of criticism as cure (it works, always, toward the purification of war). And, finally, in these contributions we encounter some of the early permanent tenets and methodologies of dramatism (*before* logology).

A Rhetoric of Motives *(1950)*

In moving from the *Grammar* to the *Rhetoric,* or from logic, dialectics, and substance to rhetoric, to identification and persuasion to action or attitude, Burke moves from philosophy to the sociopolitical scene. Burke's interest in rhetoric dates back to the twenties and *Counter-Statement* and persists all through the work of the thirties. The theory of literature as symbolic action is essentially a rhetorical theory in which literature functions as self-persuasion and as a persuader of the reader. The theory of identification as the chief persuasive device in rhetoric goes back to *Attitudes toward History* and the work Burke did there on cluster analysis and symbols of authority; it is also one of the essential parts of the four-part methodology Burke develops in the title essay of *The Philosophy of Literary Form*, there going under the name of equations, or what equals or goes with what. Burke argues in *A Rhetoric of Motives* that it is through the manipulation of identifications (sometimes overt and sometimes covert) that one persuades others to the attitude or action that one desires. And he says that it is in the sociopolitical realm that we should really study this because not only is politics impossible without rhetoric but all kinds of hidden, secret, and often dangerous identifications act as hidden persuaders in most of our sociopolitical life. Much of this is certainly not new with Burke, as he acknowledges in the first third of the book.

It is when Burke comes to the sociopolitical hierarchy, by way of Marx, Bentham, and Carlyle, that he adds a whole new dimension to dramatism and the role of the dramatistic critic. By its very nature as a hierarchy (a graded social order of higher and lower classes), the sociopolitical order is charged with highly symbolic identifications and is intrinsically persuasive, with those in the lower classes always being powerfully attracted to and persuaded by what is identified with the classes above them to mount or move up the hierarchy. Burke says that this causes a pervasive, widespread hierarchical psychosis and results in members of one class wooing members of another class, usually higher up, but not always, for members of higher classes often woo those in a lower class, as with gods and humans (the extreme case of reversal), or aristocrats and peasants, or higher classes and rural types.

Burke's conception of hierarchy and the hierarchical psychosis, joined up to rhetoric (identification and persuasion, whether active or passive), is so fertile a concept that once Burke has finished exploring or ramifying it in his typical fashion (in parts 2 and 3) by working his way through what he often calls the "range" of meanings intrinsic to the concept, he convinces us that hierarchy and the hierarchical psychosis are everywhere in both benign and malign forms and that we must arm ourselves against the malign identifications and persuaders inherent in any hierarchy, and especially in the hierarchically infused rhetoric which we use and which assaults us in our daily lives by way of the media. Burke develops a methodology which he calls socioanagogic criticism for analyzing the social mystery that is present in hidden symbolic form in all hierarchic schemes, whether they are ethnic, religious, political, ideological, or sexual. He does this in part 3 of *A Rhetoric of Motives*, the densest, most difficult, often most obscure part of this book—even for a veteran Burkean. Much of the obscurity comes from the fact that Burke—always afraid of and always the enemy of war and victimization in any form—is convinced that in every hierarchy, at every level of it, there are secret identifications which are in reality inducements to violence and victimization, to what he calls the "kill."

The book begins with examples of how poets symbolically kill off parts of themselves in their poems, thus adopting the resources of poetry and symbolic action to nonviolent solutions to their problems, much as Burke did in his novel *Towards a Better Life*. The book ends with a section entitled "The Rhetorical Radiance of the 'Divine'" and is filled with examples, mostly from literature, of how this powerful persuader from the very top of the hierarchy (doing things in the name of God) is used for good and ill. *A Rhetoric of Motives* ends with this eloquent passage, which probably renders better than almost any other passage in Burke his conception of the role of the dramatistic critic and the passion of his commitment to this task:

> But since, for better or worse, the mystery of the hierarchic is forever with us, let us, as students of rhetoric, scrutinize its range of entrancements, both with dismay and in delight. And finally let us observe, all about us, forever goading us, though it be in fragments, the motive that attains its ultimate identification in the thought, not of the universal holocaust, but of the universal order—as with the rhetorical and dialectic symmetry of the Aristotelian metaphysics, whereby all classes of beings are hierarchally arranged in a chain or ladder or pyramid of mounting worth, each kind striving towards the *perfection* of its kind, and so towards the kind next above it, while the strivings of the entire series head in God as the beloved cynosure and sinecure, the end of all desire. ([1950a] 1969, 333)

"A Symbolic of Motives" (late 1950s)

What I have called Burke's "Symbolic of Motives" was really mostly finished by the mid-fifties, though parts of it were not published until later. For example, "On Catharsis, or Resolution" was published in 1959; "Catharsis—Second View" was published in 1961; and "The Thinking of the Body (Comments on the Imagery of Catharsis in Literature)" was published in 1963. However, these three essays were written long before their publication and are part of the manuscript entitled "Poetics, Dramatistically Considered," a 391-page typed text, which Burke was circulating to his students of the Indiana School of Letters in the early and mid-fifties.[16] As Burke says in a letter to Cowley, he was distracted from assembling and completing his "Symbolic" in book form (a most uncharacteristic action by Burke) by his discovery of and working out of logology, which resulted from a series of talks he gave at Drew University in

1956 and 1957 on theology and language. It was these talks, which he expanded into the three main essays, that make up *The Rhetoric of Religion*, mostly during his stay at the Center for the Advanced Study in the Behavioral Sciences at Stanford University in 1957–58. The "Epilogue: Prologue in Heaven," in which Burke lays out all the coordinates of human history, according to dramatism, was not finished until 1960.

We will never know what else Burke might have written as part of the "Symbolic," had he done the usual careful introducing, revising, and shaping that was always part of his final preparations of a manuscript. Nor will we ever know, alas, exactly how he would have arranged the existing material into his usual tripartite division. What we do know is, as with the first two motives books, most of the material for the "Symbolic" was conceived and written during a five-year period from 1950 to 1955, just as the material for *The Rhetoric of Religion* was conceived and written during the next five years, and *Language as Symbolic Action* was both written and put together during the next five (1961–66). One is tempted to say that Burke had a series of five-year plans, all but one of which came to fruition in published books. The "Symbolic" did not come to fruition as a book, for reasons known only to Burke, but Burke's dramatistic poetics is certainly complete in the sense that all the essential elements of it are present in the existing published essays—some of which were included in *Language as Symbolic Action*, some in the Hyman and Karmiller (1964a, 1964b) double volume, *Perspective by Incongruity and Terms for Order*, and some of which remain where they were originally published.[17] In other words, anyone who wishes to study the "Symbolic"—certainly Burke's major statement on the nature of literature, its function and significance as an act of language, and his most comprehensive presentation and demonstration of the methodology developed for the dramatistic analysis and interpretation of literature—can readily do so. No account of Burke's development and significance as a critic could be complete without making the achievement of his poetics a part of that accounting. Because it does not exist as a book—just as Burke's work since 1966 is not yet available to us as a book—does not mean, as some of Burke's critics seem to assume, that he has no dramatistic poetics or that he has done no significant new work since 1966 and the publication of *Language as Symbolic Action*.

The central concept in Burke's poetics is catharsis, just as it was in his theory of literature as symbolic action, and its representative anecdote is tragedy, because tragedy, better than any other kind of text, best illustrates Burke's dramatistic theory (as developed in the third part of *A Rhetoric of Motives*) that the hierarchical psychosis is everywhere with us and everywhere a threat, and that in *imitating* various forms of this hierarchical or social "tension," tragedy activates and releases this tension in us and vicariously purges off, as imitations (not realities) do, the more dangerous parts or aspects of it. Literature thus has an essential social function as equipment for living. The classic texts for the study of Burke's dramatistic poetics are *"Othello:* An Essay to Illustrate a Method"; "Form and Persecution in the *Oresteia"*; "The Language of Poetry Dramatistically Considered" (which includes the essay on *Faust,* part 1); and "Fact, Inference, and Proof in the Analysis of Literary Symbolism" (which lays out the methodology called indexing).[18]

Reading these essays, and the others which make up the "Symbolic," one can readily see why, when he wrote this material, Burke thought of poetry and of his poetics as the culmination of dramatism. In the first place, the scourge of the drama of human relations—the hierarchical psychosis first introduced and developed in *A Rhetoric of Motives*—is confronted and purged off in literature; it happens in poetry, because with the freedom that goes with the exercising of the imagination, human beings are able to perfect the use of language, to go to the end of the line with any set of possibilities, verbal or otherwise, and in this way follow out the genius of the entelechial principle (which is what makes us rotten with perfection). Finally, the critic, in analyzing and interpreting great literary texts, can practice and preach the corrective comic perspective of criticism (first introduced in *Attitudes toward History,* refined in *The Philosophy of Literary Form,* perfected in *A Grammar of Motives),* which always involves a movement toward knowledge and the fundamental secular assumption of all Burkean criticism, which is, that if it cannot save us (which is what religions promise to do), at least it can help us.

So why did Burke abandon his "Symbolic" and develop logology? In a sense, he did not really do that at all: he completed his "Symbolic" and moved on, in the next five-year plan, first to logology (1961) and then to the completion of the whole dramatistic enterprise by 1966, when he finished the final five-year plan of this productive period of his life. He was sixty-nine when this period came to an end, seventy-two when Libbie Burke died in 1969, and still as feisty and vigorous as ever.

The Rhetoric of Religion *(1961)*

Logology, which Burke first develops in *The Rhetoric of Religion* and then uses in almost all that he writes after 1961, sometimes as if it existed by itself, and sometimes in conjunction with dramatism and its coordinates, is ostensibly the study of words and is based in the most fundamental of all dramatistic assertions: that humans are symbol-using animals and that the best way to study humans is through an intensive study of their distinctive trait—language, with the stress on symbol using as an action. However, by the time Burke is finished working out logology, he has decided that it is in theology, not poetry, that we find the perfection (the entelechy) of symbol using, and by working out a series of analogies between Christian theology (symbol using that comes to a head in the Word—the Logos) and symbol using that comes to a head in god-terms, or in something like Plato's forms, Burke establishes the main coordinates of logology as a methodology and perspective. The rest of *The Rhetoric of Religion* consists of Burke's applications of logology to two Christian texts—St. Augustine's *Confessions* and the first three chapters of Genesis—and his comic "Epilogue: Prologue in Heaven" (imitating the beginning of part 1 of Goethe's *Faust*), which consists of a dialogue between TL (The Lord) and S (Satan) before the creation and fall, and translates or transmogrifies the whole history of humankind from the beginning to the end of time, from Genesis to Revelation, into dramatistic and logological terms. In some way, *The Rhetoric of Religion* is one of Burke's most definitive texts, as well as one of his densest and most complex.

It is definitive because so much of it seems so final: logology is Burke's final methodology for the study of words. Using Christian theology as a paradigm for the study of words allows Burke to discuss first and last things over and over again in his own terms as he works his way, chapter by chapter, through the *Confessions* and, in almost tortuous detail, through the Christian or biblical narrative account of the creation, fall, covenants, redemption by way of the sacrificial Christ, and apocalypse, and the timeless cycle of terms implicit in the idea of order which he says is intrinsic in this narrative or rectilinear account.[19] In the "Epilogue: Prologue in Heaven," the Lord explains to his cooperative interlocutor, Satan, the whole mighty moral drama of human relations as it develops inexorably from the dramatistic fact that humans are the symbol-using animals. No purer Burke in his maturity can be found anywhere else, and Burke in his maturity is almost always dense and complex, often pursuing a hidden agenda one must figure out, as he analyzes texts with exhausting thoroughness and intellectual ingenuity and writes, when it suits him (as it does in the "Epilogue: Prologue in Heaven"), with great wit, humor, irony, cleverness, and inventiveness on the most serious of topics, reminding us, as he does himself, that we better take things seriously, but not too seriously, lest we puff up and burst in our self-satisfied pride.

Language as Symbolic Action *(1966)*

The Rhetoric of Religion is a great text, a great moment in Burke's development. What follows is something of an anticlimax, but only in relative terms, for *Language as Symbolic Action* is really the most complete single-volume presentation of mature Burke that we have, or are ever liable to have until someone does a reader. It is probably Burke's most carefully arranged, most thoroughly annotated, and most diverse and representative book. After the fact, it seems like the most perfectly planned and timed book that Burke could have done at this date. It is a book that sums him up, or, more accurately, sums up the achievements of the four previous books and moves forward from them, in some of its essays, by applying logology and especially by applying the dramatistic poetics to a variety of new texts. It is good to remember, when thinking about *Language as Symbolic Action* and what is and is not included in it, that in 1964 Hyman and Karmiller edited and published *Perspectives by Incongruity* and *Terms for Order*, which consist of essential Burkean selections from *The White Oxen* through *The Rhetoric of Religion* (1961) *and* include some of the most basic essays from the "Symbolic" but omit any selections from either *A Grammar of Motives* or *A Rhetoric of Motives*.

What Burke does in selecting the material for *Language as Symbolic Action* is include all the major essays he wrote and published between 1961 and 1966, most of which are developed from either dramatism or logology or a combination of both, and many of which were written as attempts to finish off the "Symbolic"—which Burke kept announcing as forthcoming during the early sixties. In addition to this material, Burke includes essays from the early fifties that were written for the "Symbolic," such as "Form and Persecution in the *Oresteia*" (1952c), "Goethe's *Faust*, Part I" (written 1954–55), "Vegetal Radicalism of Theodore Roethke" (1950b) and "The Thinking of the Body" (1963), which was written in the early fifties but published later. And finally, because it is so essential to dramatism and the whole moral/ethical drama that is central to it, he includes the four-part "A Dramatistic View of the Origins of Language" (1952a, 1952b, 1953a, 1953b).[20]

Collected Poems (1968)

With *Language as Symbolic Action* we come to the end of this long productive and creative period in Burke's development. After 1966, Burke was never to return to literary criticism or literature in any significant way, though he was to continue to write poetry into the seventies and in the early seventies conceived and partially wrote his satiric piece "Helhaven." Many people seem to think that Burke's career and development end after 1966—in part because they do not take his poetry seriously, and in part because there are no further books to deal with and *Language as Symbolic Action* seems (falsely, I think) so inclusive. Burke's *Collected Poems* was published in 1968. If we added his "Eye Crossing" poem, which was originally published in 1969, the year Libbie Burke died, and later, in 1973, in a longer version, with an elaborate commentary on the poem by Burke, and the few poems he published after her death, we would have, if not all the poems Burke wrote, at least all that he has been willing to publish. Anyone who really wants to understand Burke should read his poems. There is the critical self and the poetic self, both of which have comedy and the comedic in common. Wit, humor, irony, satire, self-irony, mind play, verbal play, puns, a love of formal tinkering and of aphorisms, a sense of the absurd, including the absurd in his morbid, sickly "selph," therapeutic laughter, comedy, including the comedy of the human barnyard—all of these are part of Burke's poetry. They are also part of Burke's performing self and, in different ways, of his "comic" self—as in "Epilogue: Prologue in Heaven," in *The Rhetoric of Religion*. Though it is not as obvious as it might be from the letters that Paul Jay selected for inclusion in the Burke-Cowley letters, these are also traits of Burke's letter-writing self, including, no doubt, the many letters he wrote when angry or somewhat tanked or "alkylined" and put in his unsent letter file.

The *Collected Poems* is a joyful, high-spirited book, appropriately enough dedicated "To Libbie," who brought so much joy into Burke's life.[21] It was Libbie Burke who arranged the puzzlelike Flowerishes that appear in this book (1968a, 88–92 and 297–300), which, taken as a whole, represent the essential ironic nature of Burke's mind, critical perspective, and final vision, as well as his belief that there is no unearned wisdom. Irony gone sour becomes cynicism and debunking, neither of which Burke ever allowed himself to lapse into—though he must have been tempted at times, especially after the death of Libbie. But Burke had his final say against the destructive debunking in *The Philosophy of Literary*

Form, and he was always saved from cynicism by the laughter which was a part of his irony.

Burke's lasting fame will certainly not depend upon his poetry, nor, for that matter, upon his novel, both minor works in relation to his criticism, but works nonetheless, which name his number for us because they are also his symbolic acts. Some part of the complex personality of this native American genius and some of the burdens which go with being a genius get expressed and purged when the fictional and poetic voices speak and Burke uses himself as a text. This is probably nowhere more obvious and illuminating than in Burke's last story, "The Anaesthetic Revelation of Herone Liddell," an obviously autobiographical "fiction" which he wrote after a traumatic, but minor, hernia operation when he was sixty, and which he describes as a kind of symbolic "recovery" sequel to his novel, *Towards a Better Life*, another fiction about other traumatic events written twenty-five years earlier.[22] Returning to the poetry, this personal element is certainly obvious in another symbolic work where Burke also uses himself as text, the "Eye Crossing" poem Burke wrote while he and Libbie were living in Brooklyn during the last painful year of her life, when Burke, in a reversal of roles he must certainly have understood and appreciated, literally became Libbie's keeper. As Burke has said so often about the writers he has studied, we would be foolish to ignore and not make use of the evidence provided us about Burke, and his motives, by these fictional and poetic works. As he said long ago in *The Philosophy of Literary Form:* the critic should use all that is there to use in trying to understand what the great creative minds are doing in their works and how any or all of it impinges upon our own lives.

Burke's most productive period began in 1933 with his marriage to Libbie and the writing of *Permanence and Change*, his first symbolic act as a social critic. This transformation is certainly symbolically enacted in his novel *Towards a Better Life*. It is therefore most appropriate and significant that his last published book, after thirty-six productive years, should be a book of poems dedicated to Libbie and that his last major poem, "Eye Crossing," should come out of a "context of situation" in which Burke has become the keeper of the woman who changed his life, at a time when she is clearly dying from an irreversible, untreatable, fatal disease—and one which must have driven both of these wonderful, always active and creative people to the edge of madness. Fortunately, Libbie died before she became completely helpless. Burke, of course, went on, and as I write in January of 1990, he is still going on.

1970–

By way of closure, I want to consider what Burke has and has not done since 1970. What he has not done is as important as what he has done because it is responsible for the fact that we will not be able to assess the final stages of his development and career adequately until he is dead and we have access to all the work of this period. To use his own phrase, Burke has chosen to exist in his scatterhood ever since the death of Libbie because he has refused to assemble and publish any new books. Instead, he has traveled around a lot, even going to Europe for the first time, shortly after the death of Libbie. He has spoken, performed, and been in residence at a great many different places. He has been the subject of numerous conferences devoted to him and his work and has become the subject (or object) of numerous new books, dissertations, and essays on him and his work by people in many different disciplines, including European scholars, who finally discovered him. Special issues of journals have been devoted to him, as have special sessions at regional and national conferences. And finally, during this same period, as Burke has almost literally scattered the seeds of dramatism and logology all over America, he has been rewarded by receiving many honorary degrees—this critic who never even bothered to get a B.A. degree—and many awards in acknowledgment of his achievements. In sum, and somewhat ironically, it is during this period after the death of Libbie that he finally became what he set out to be in the twenties: a famous person, an acknowledged authentic American genius, like Faulkner, with every bit of his fame *earned* by the labors of his mind and the power of his written words.

But let me return briefly to Burke in his scatterhood: Burke (1) has simply declined to put his "Symbolic" together as a book, which the University of California Press (or many others) would gladly publish,[23] and (2) has refused to, and refused anyone else permission to, put together a collection of the important major essays he has written since 1970, a collection which, like *Language as Symbolic Action* or *The Philosophy of Literary Form*, would have summed up the work of the last twenty years and would have put an end to the common delusion that his development came to an end in 1966, with his last published book. Basically what Burke has done since 1970 is turn himself into his own best advertisement for himself and his ideas. This is all well and good, but in a sense Burke has scattered himself instead of gathering himself, as he had done in the past, into a book, or books, which could be read and reread, studied and absorbed in relationship to his other books. I have discussed the lost "Symbolic"; let me here discuss the essays Burke has published since 1970, up to and including the "In Haste" piece in *Pre/Text* (1985b).

The work since 1970 can be divided into two groups and discussed rather briefly. During this period, Burke apparently is goaded by two objectives. He sums himself up as concisely as possible, or he attempts to employ the dramatism/logology construct as a way of thinking about the world to the end of the line.

The first group consists of what I will call the Helhaven (or language/technology) material, after the title of the satire Burke published first in the early 1970s. When Burke conceived this anti-technology satire is not clear, but it figures prominently in the two lectures that make up *Dramatism and Development* (1972a) and in the 1974 "Why Satire" essay, which is his most complete version of the satire and one of his major statements on the relation between language, rationality, and technology and on what we need to do about the threat posed by high technology.[24] In this material, Burke moves his thought forward and arrives at what is surely an essential part of his final ironic vision of humankind and the drama of human relations.

If language and hierarchy were the major themes and concern of Burke's work in the forties and fifties, and if language and theology were the major concern of his work in the late fifties and sixties, then we can say that language and technology were the major concern of his work in the seventies. Burke's interest in and concern with technology—especially the high technology that developed during and after World War II—goes way back to the thirties. It is a central concern in *A Grammar of Motives* and becomes a specter haunting Burke's mind beginning with the development of the atomic bomb. However, not really until the late sixties and early seventies does Burke begin to explain technology, and especially the high technology of Western culture and America in particular, in dramatistic and logological terms. That is, he links it to symbol using and gradually works toward his ironic formula that human beings' entelechy is technology. Human beings' specific genius is for symbol using; the final genius of symbol using is no longer the godhead, but high technology is; in and by means of high technology, humans have arrived at the ultimate, at secrets of life and matter, and so have the capability of creating and manipulating new life and of destroying life itself, or at least all human life, and perhaps the planet earth as well. Humans, in other words, thanks to symbol using and technology, have become the godhead because, as a result of their genius—their desire to know and understand and control everything—they have arrived at the knowledge which gives them the powers once attributed to God.

This final vision of Burke's is most clearly worked out and presented in the second Helhaven essay, "Why Satire, with a Plan for Writing One" (1974), and in his bicentennial lecture, "Towards Looking Back" (1976). In both of these essays, Burke makes extensive ironic use of Whitman and the romance of technology so prominent in his poems and essays and in nineteenth-century America's general view of itself. Whitman's dream has become our nightmare, Burke says, and the only real question any more is whether we will be able to use all the knowledge and power we now have for good or ill. More technology will not solve the problems already created by technology; only a neohumanistic (poetic, comic, and antitechnological) corrective vision or perspective can bring an end to our slow pollution and destruction of the earth and its atmosphere, and us along with it. And Burke, ironist that he is, and good ecologist that he has always been, must doubt whether such a corrective vision would have any persuasive power in the seats of real power: science, economics, and politics.

Burke's thought has evolved beyond the hierarchical psychosis that so dominated his thinking in the fifties and early sixties. Burke has moved from smaller (literary criticism) to larger (social criticism) and later to global orientations. Burke has consistently tried to take on larger and larger questions and move his thought toward the all-inclusive, ultimate questions. In his Helhaven works, or those essays concerned with language and technology, Burke has certainly arrived, by his own dramatistic/logological route, at the final, ultimate question about humans, the symbol-using animals: Will the creative genius of humans, a function of their innate, inherited genetic endowment, their ability to create symbol systems (primarily language), and their ability to learn and use symbol systems (we are bodies that learn language, Burke says) take us to the holocaust, the apocalypse? Or, can we use our knowledge and power to save ourselves from ourselves, somehow controlling both the suicidal and the homicidal motives that seem intrinsic to the drama of human relations?

These are among the last questions Burke asks. They may seem like questions of the seventies, but they seem less and less historically limited as we enter the nineties, plagued and harassed, even as we are served and helped, by technology and its products, especially by the products of electronic technology. I do not wish to present Burke here, toward the end of his career, as a doomsday thinker. He is not, nor has he ever been. Even as he contemplates our possible self-caused doomsday, he satirizes it and proposes, as usual, his comic corrective neohumanistic perspective. In doing both, he is fulfilling the admonitory role of the critic, a role he adopted in

Permanence and Change and to which he has been faithful ever since. Burke's Helhaven satire is basically very simple and well worth contemplating if we wish to understand some of the end thoughts of this remarkable man. In the satire, Burke has the lords of high technology—the small elite group that has benefited the most from high technology and its products—build a space bubble on the moon (Burke calls it counternature) that exactly reproduces what they are used to on earth. But of course it is all artificial. At the point where the lords of high technology have polluted or destroyed most of planet earth and made it uninhabitable, they get in their spaceships (themselves products of high technology) and set forth for Helhaven, the ironic punning name of the space bubble on the moon, also a product of high technology. There they will live happily ever after in their counternatural setting.

Whither after this, one might ask? Well, in a sense, Burke returned to himself and his own development after Helhaven, summing himself up, exploring the implications of his refinement of his dramatistic definition of humans (from humans the symbol-using animals, to we are bodies that learn language), defending dramatism/logology as a system or position against his traditional adversaries (scientism, the simplifiers, the behaviorists, the warmongers and polarizers, the politicians, the technocrats, and any others who did not appreciate the merits of the dramatistic/logological perspective). His defense of himself can best be seen in an essay such as "(Nonsymbolic) Motion/(Symbolic) Action" (1978a), and his summing up of himself can best be seen in an essay such as "Variations on Providence" (1981b), which ends with a section entitled "Counter-Nature: Fulfillment *via* Technology" and consists of thirteen summarizing logological propositions. Finally, as he has been doing here and there ever since "Curriculum Criticum" (Burke [1931] 1968, 213–25) was added to the second edition of *Counter-Statement*, Burke recapitulates his own development, most notably in the extensive interview which appears in *All Area* No. 2 (Burke 1983a), in the two long afterwords he adds to the new editions of *Permanence and Change* and *Attitudes toward History* in 1984, and the long "In Haste" piece written for the special issue of *Pre/Text* (1985b) devoted to him.

Epilogue

Many others have been commenting on Burke and summing him up since the great revival of interest in his work began in the mid and late seventies, a revival which has thus far resulted in four important new books on Burke (with more forthcoming),[25] the formation of the Kenneth Burke Society, numerous conferences devoted to him and his work, especially by those in communications, and a flood of essays.

One would have to say now, in the 1990s, that Burke has finally gotten his just rewards (recognition and appreciation, understanding) for a long creative and productive life. However, the returns are not all in yet, nor will they be for some time to come—certainly not until the archives at Penn State and elsewhere are more complete. There must still be a treasure trove of material in Burke's house at Andover, as well in the thousands of still-uncollected, unpublished letters. The Burke-Cowley letters, valuable as Paul Jay's selection of them is, represent but a partial selection from that long and important correspondence. A forty-five-year span of Burke's life (1943–88) is inadequately represented in Jay's collection (which stops at 1981), and many crucial events in Burke's life and in the history of his time never figure at all in the published letters. No one really knows (except the poet himself) how many unpublished poems Burke still has in his files, or how much other material he wrote but never published. And there are his so-called papers—the voluminous notes he is always referring to, and the drafts of his essays and books. No one has yet written a Burke biography, and Burke, for reasons of his own, has always refused to write anything but bits and pieces of his autobiography. No one has ever really written about Burke as a reviewer—he has written more than 150 reviews in his life—and only a few of these many reviews have been collected and published (in *The Philosophy of Literary Form*). I do not mean to suggest that Burke should be picked apart and worked over the way Faulkner has been, only that large quantities of essential material (including tapes, videotapes, interviews, remembrances, notes on and accounts of his many lectures, performance and prolonged stays at various institutions—to name a few) remain to be collected, assembled, sorted out, and, where feasible, published in book form if we are ever to arrive at a comprehensive view and assessment of this remarkable man's achievements.

Burke the published critic is one thing, but Burke the man, or, rather, Burke the person and personality, is another and as such has had a powerful effect on many of us. He would not want to be, nor should we really want to see him become (though some have tried), a cult figure and thus lose him in the inevitable vagaries, vulgarities, and sentimentalities of personality adulation—a tendency we can see quite clearly in the 1985 *Pre/Text* special issue devoted to him. He is a great man as well as a great thinker. He is a person of extraordinary generosity toward all those who were genuinely interested in his work. He is a person of great integrity who has lived what he believes in, affirming in his life-style at Andover with Libbie and his family what he argued for and against in his writing. He is a person of great honesty, often telling us the truths about ourselves, our country, and our times that we did not really want to hear, but which we knew to be true. And he was a great teacher for those willing to pay attention to what he said and did in and out of his writing, with the doing (the actions of the mind, the way he went about things) as important as the saying (the truths, the ironies, the aphorisms, the pronouncements scattered through his works and conversations).

Finally, no one (since my own efforts in *Critical Responses* twenty years ago) has undertaken the extensive and difficult task of reviewing and evaluating the now rather considerable amount of scholarship that has been done on Burke, going back to the pioneering works and coming forward to the huge amount of work done in the seventies and eighties by scholars in many different fields, here and abroad.

Notes

1. I want to note here that I have made no serious attempt to acknowledge or in any way to interact with the considerable amount of work now in print about Burke, either in the chapter itself or in the endnotes that follow. This "Field Guide" is based on my reading and rereading of primary works by Burke, including his letters to me, and on many years of thinking and writing about Burke. It is now possible, I think, to meditate on Burke as a whole, and that is what I have tried to do here, taking no specific doctrinal or "discipline" approach and trying to acknowledge and account for all of his significant works.

I have drawn here upon Jay's invaluable collection of letters (1988). My only regret about this selection is that so much of it is devoted to the early years and not enough to the amazingly productive (for Burke) years from 1943 to 1981. I hope that someone will do a second volume of selections from this rich exchange of letters between these important but quite different American men of letters.

2. I first visited Burke in Andover in the early sixties after *The Rhetoric of Religion* was published and last visited him there in 1968, during the last year of Libbie Burke's life. By then, Libbie was in a wheelchair, and Burke had modernized because of her condition. He put in a regular bathroom, ran water into the house, and had a well dug and a septic system put in. During all of my other visits during the sixties, he was still using his outhouse and carried all of his water into the house in galvanized pails from the well next to his house. Libbie Burke was a truly remarkable and wonderful person who understood her husband and his genius perfectly and knew exactly how

to deal with and get along with this volatile and difficult man. They were an amazing couple. We used to visit them with our pack of kids and dog, whose name was Burke. Dealing with my dog at Burke's house was, to say the least, highly comical.

3. Burke gradually bought up all the land between the original two houses, as well as land across the road, where his pond and tennis court are located. He also bought and restored a pig barn across the road where his daughters and guests stayed. His grandchildren built a house down the road. Libbie, who was an excellent painter, had a studio in the woods up behind the house. The original house was down the road from where Burke and Libbie lived. My memory of my visits there is one filled with people, especially family. Burke's daughters lived in New York City and would come out on weekends, as would some of the grandchildren. Burke's sons were still around when we first visited. I remember long evenings of eating, drinking, and talking. Then, as now, Burke was a fabulous talker and arguer, as well as a truly remarkable drinker. He also loved to walk, especially at night, after hours of drinking and talking, and would take you out for long walks on the dark country roads, talking all the time, as vigorous as ever, even as you were about to drop from exhaustion and alcohol.

4. See especially *Attitudes toward History* (1937), the title essay of *The Philosophy of Literary Form* (1941), and "Freud and the Analysis of Poetry" in *The Philosophy of Literary Form.*

5. Crusius has also written brilliantly on *The White Oxen* and *Towards a Better Life* but has apparently not published either of these essays. Again, I read them both in manuscript and am somewhat puzzled by the fact that they are not in print.

6. See Rueckert 1988, in which I discuss this poem and the Helhaven satires at length.

7. Frank (1969) has written an illuminating account of these stories. For some reason, we tend to overlook Frank's excellent book on Burke, with its many fine insights into Burke and his work. He writes about Burke with considerable wit and wisdom and brings a welcome European perspective to bear upon this unique American critic.

8. See "Curriculum Criticum," *Counter-Statement* ([1931] 1968, 213–25). Crusius is apparently one of the few critics of Burke who has read and thought about this previously unpublished manuscript. Crusius 1988 is a fine analysis of the manuscript and its implications for the study of Burke.

9. Burke's last significant essays in literary criticism are all in *Language as Symbolic Action*, even though he did occasionally return to the subject of literary criticism in some of his later essays and reviews.

10. This essay has since been published; see Burke 1970. Burke sent me a manuscript copy of it (thirty-eight typescript pages) shortly after he wrote it in 1966 on the occasion of the republication of his novel by the University of California Press. See also his prefaces to the first and second editions of the novel, his preface to *The Complete White Oxen*, his afterword to *Attitudes toward History* (389), *Language as Symbolic Action* (338), and the many references to the novel in the Burke-Cowley letters, as well as Jay's (1988) comments on it in his introduction to part 2.

11. An adequate account of this novel as symbolic action would require a long, carefully documented analysis of the text, using Burke's own methodology, especially of all those scenes and passages involving John Neal and his women, particularly Genevieve; and of part 3, where the transformation of John Neal occurs, along with the strange episodes involving Alter Ego, which are vaguely homosexual, and the episode with the mad girl in white, in which John Neal seduces an essentially helpless female.

12. Burke has made it even harder to let go of this book with all of the additions he has made to it since the first edition. Not only do the many long footnotes take one off in many different directions, but the "Dictionary of Pivotal Terms" is deliberately designed as a nonsequential stimulator and recapitulator at the end of the original edition of the book. To the first edition, Burke added an introduction, an afterword, and "Appendix: The Seven Offices" when the second edition was published by Hermes in 1959; and to all of this he added the long (fifty-five-page) "Afterword: *Attitudes toward History:* In Retrospective Prospect," to the third edition, published by the University of California press in 1984. Much could be made of the difference between the original (1937) and the final (1984) structure of this book. See my keynote address "Criticism as a Way of Life: Criticism as Equipment for Living," *Kenneth Burke Society Newsletter* 6, no. 2 (October 1990).

13. Burke never denies that some wars and revolutions have to be fought; he only argues that many large- and small-scale wars are senseless and need never be fought. Many of these senseless wars and killings take place because of ideological differences which have hardened into implacable fanatical commitments, often supported by literal-minded interpretations of "holy" texts, whether political or religious. Lebanon would epitomize what Burke means by senseless wars. There, Muslims fight Muslims, Muslims fight Christians, Christians fight Christians, both fight Jews; but all of this is also happening in other parts of the world: Muslims fought Muslims in the Iran/Iraq war and killed each other by the millions. Muslims fight Hindus in India; Catholics fight Protestants in Ireland. Ethnic, racial, religious, and political strife occur all over the world these days, and much of it is due to the way in which words are used and interpreted and the apparently incurable human desire to group together with one's own kind *and* exclude or destroy those who are different—whether of a different color, a different race, a different religion, or a different ideology. When Burke dedicates a book to the purification of war and writes at length about dialectics and the basic principles of discussion and debate so central to democracy as a political system and criticism as a way of life, he is pleading for one of the most profound aspirations of all thoughtful people in the twentieth century, a century in which hundreds of millions of humans (and who knows how many other living creatures) have been killed in wars, in the name of the state, in the name of God, in the name of democracy, in the name of Communism, in the name of right, in the name of racial purity; he is writing out of desire for peace, out of a deep desire that a way can be found to minimize the polarizations and, in many cases, the goals of empire that have caused all these wars and killings. The developments in South Africa

in early 1990 are a splendid example of Burke's assertion that we can purify war by means of talk—discussion, debate, and negotiations.

14. Burke's interest in these matters is certainly compulsive and obsessive and comes to a head in his relentless pursuit of evidence of the presence of the demonic trinity (the fecal, the sexual, and the urinal), where one might least expect it. Burke's search for evidence of the demonic trinity is often a hidden agenda in many of his analyses of texts and is based on his assumption that there is always some form of sin and guilt hidden in every text (and life) which must be purged. This explains his frequent search for puns and his development of the technique he calls joycing—which he uses to coerce words phonetically until they become images of the demonic trinity. His most notorious example of this, and one that outraged many critics, is his assertion that the famous lines from the end of Keats's ode "On a Grecian Urn"—"Beauty is truth, truth beauty"—really mean "body is turd, turd body." His most extended discussion of this matter can be found in "The Thinking of the Body" and "Somni ad Urinandum" in *Language as Symbolic Action*. He also says that *towards* in the title of his novel contains (punwise) tords, or turds.

15. Parts of this definition were written much earlier, and Burke was to tamper with and modify his definition somewhat in later years by saying that we are bodies that learn language, rather than symbol-using animals, and that we are unique because, of all other species, only humans have a foreknowledge of death. Still, my point is essentially correct and is corroborated by Burke, who says that one does not ever really start with a definition like this one but arrives at it, bit by bit, phrase by phrase, until it suddenly comes to one whole and sums up all the essential parts of one's thinking. Only after arriving at such a definition can one then start from it in the work that follows—which is exactly what Burke has done since 1963.

16. Interesting as this manuscript is, it is clearly only a *draft* of Burke's poetics. See my discussion of Burke's "Symbolic" in *Kenneth Burke and the Drama of Human Relations* (Rueckert 1982, 230–37, 288–92). Burke was a great reviser, and it seems perfectly clear that any final version of his "Poetics" would have been much different from this draft.

17. It seems likely that Burke would have included "Symbolic Action in a Poem by Keats" in the "Symbolic." This essay was also included in *A Grammar of Motives*. In Hyman and Karmiller (1964a), the following selections are part of the "Symbolic": "From Three Definitions" and "Othello: An Essay to Illustrate a Method"; and in Hyman and Karmiller 1964b, the following selection is part of the "Symbolic": "Fact, Inference, and Proof in the Analysis of Literary Symbolism."

18. Calling these essays the classic texts is somewhat misleading. I call them classic because two of the essays develop the theory of tragedy and the theories of imitation and cartharsis that are so central to Burke's *Poetics*; one essay lays out the basic methodology (indexing) in great detail through an analysis of Joyce's *Portrait*; and the fourth essay lays out Burke's whole theory of poetic language and the freedom he associates with it, develops his theory of the text, and finally, applies both in a brilliant, detailed analysis of

Goethe's *Faust*, part 1. However, there is considerably more to Burke's "Symbolic" than what one finds in these four classic essays.

19. No one-sentence account of this essay on the first three chapters of Genesis can possibly reveal the complexity and ingenuity of Burke's dialectical spinning out of the tautological cycle of terms he says is implicit in the idea of order. The beautifully symmetrical chart in *The Rhetoric of Religion* ([1961] 1970, 184) gives some idea of the complexity of this endeavor and the ways in which Burke tries to relate the dramatistic account of the creation and the drama of human relations to the biblical account. This whole essay pursues at much greater length a distinction Burke first made in *A Grammar of Motives* between logical and temporal, or between the ways in which a narrative or rectilinear account of things simply lays out in terms of scene-agents and actions what was logically prior to the temporal account. To show how this is true, Burke generates the whole biblical account of Christian history from creation to apocalypse from an analysis of the cycle of terms implicit in the idea of order.

20. This essay is certainly the culmination of Burke's dramatistic thinking about the nature of language—a way of thinking that he began in *A Grammar of Motives*. Had he written his projected "Ethics of Motives," this essay would have been central to it. In asserting that there are no negatives in nature and that it is language that adds the negative, especially the moral negative but also the kind of negative we get in irony and abstractions, Burke makes crucial distinctions between nature and language: the preverbal (nature before man), the verbal (nature with language and man added), the postverbal (language and language created infused back into nature by man), and the metaverbal (the realm beyond language, arrived at by means of language).

21. Burke's dedication in *A Grammar of Motives* is also "To Elizabeth, Without Whom Not," which, symbolically at least, is the perfect pairing for the motto of that book. Burke's other dedications are interesting: three books—*The Philosophy of Literary Form, A Rhetoric of Motives*, and *Language as Symbolic Action*—are dedicated to his patron and friend, James Sibley Watson, who, with Schofield Thayer, provided the chief financial support for the *Dial*. In saying Watson was Burke's patron, I mean that he provided Burke with a fixed amount of money for many years, beginning, I believe, in the thirties; Watson probably helped make it possible for Burke to devote himself full-time to writing. Burke dedicated *The White Oxen* to his first wife, Lily, and *Permanence and Change* to his mother and father. His first short book of poems, *Book of Moments*, he dedicated to his "Sparring Partners." All the rest of his books are without dedications, which has always seemed a little strange to me. And only *A Grammar of Motives* has a motto; but then, it might well be the motto for all of Burke's critical works. The wording of the dedication in *A Grammar of Motives* proved to be somewhat prophetic in the sense that no further *new* books by Burke have been published since Libbie's death in 1969.

22. Except for some of his long poems, such as "Eye Crossing," "On Flood Times of Sinkership," and "Introduction to What," the Herone Lid-

dell story is probably the most obvious and the best example of Burke using himself as text—something he also does in some of his essays. In this story, Burke starts out with his hysterical and certainly paranoiac reaction to the minor hernia operation, with all of its bodily indignities, that he is about to undergo. All the first part of the story is body obsessed and somatically concerned. The second part of the story deals with the revelation and Burke's (Herone's) dreams, and is psyche centered. Who but Burke would analyze his own dreams for us, or tell us how important it is to listen to one's unconscious. In the third section of the story, entitled "Haunted by Ecology," Burke (Herone) explains that being so obsessed with his body and its mortality naturally got him to thinking about symbol using and the specific human genius. In this section, we have a brief summary of dramatism, which Burke then uses to explain himself to himself, especially the relationship between psyche and soma and humankind's duality. From this, in good Burke fashion, he finally gets to ecology and the ways in which humans, because of their symbol-using genius and especially because of the technology that symbol using makes possible, are destroying nature. So from his initial concern with his own body, Herone (Burke) finally moves to the much larger concern with the relationship of human beings to nature. This movement from the concrete, highly particular and personal to the global is most characteristic of Burke, especially from *A Grammar of Motives* on, as is the analogy he works from between the mind and body, the psyche and soma, and human (the mind) and the world's body. The last part of the story has Herone (Burke and Libbie) in Florida recuperating by the sea. Most of this section of the story is about Herone reading and meditating on the dying Keats's letters. If we remember that Keats, like Burke, is a word man, a symbol user, this reading of Keats's last letters will make more sense to us. Many of these letters are concerned with poetry, with symbol using at a high and refined level. Herone recovers at the end of the story, in part by having young Keats die for him from his bodily affliction, which was consumption. A lot can be learned about Burke from studying this story, just as it can from the study of any of his other fictions and poems where he deliberately confesses to us by using his private self as his text—whether in disguised form, as in the story, or in frankly open, undisguised form, as in the long poems. Burke's commentary on his "Eye Crossing" poem, which he wrote in response to student analyses of the poem solicited by his friend Henry Sams at Penn State, is revealing, especially since it is written so soon after Libbie's death.

23. In fact, Burke probably lost sight of the original conception of the "Symbolic" he was working with in the fifties. See the list of what Burke thought might be included in the "Symbolic" in 1978 in Rueckert 1982, 291–92. The logic of this list is hard to figure out, except that most of the items have something to do with literature, and anything published in *Language as Symbolic Action* is omitted. Basically, it would be another omnibus collection of Burke's uncollected essays and would resemble *The Philosophy of Literary Form* in the sense that it focuses on literature and literary criticism.

24. I have written at length on much of this material, in Rueckert 1988 and Rueckert 1982, 128–62.

25. These four books are White and Brose 1982; Lentricchia 1983; Simons and Melia 1989; and Henderson 1988. The second edition of my 1963 book on Burke, *Kenneth Burke and the Drama of Human Relations*, with a long new chapter covering Burke's work from 1963 to 1981, was also published during this period (1982). These books have certainly altered the way we think about Burke. Lentricchia's book, an aggressive defense of the social function of criticism which uses Burke as a basic text, is especially suggestive, and Henderson's book finally makes an attempt to see Burke in relation to other language theorists of his time. The other two books are collections of essays which provide ways of reading Burke by people in a variety of disciplines. In addition to these books, a number of highly sophisticated critical minds have made extensive and interesting use of Burke, including Hayden White, Clifford Geertz, Sherman Paul, Harold Bloom, Bernard Duffey, and Wayne Booth. Thames's "Selected Bibliography of Critical Responses to Kenneth Burke, 1968–1986" (Simons and Melia 1989, 305–15) gives some indication of the range of work done on Burke as well as the range of his influence. However, his bibliography is far from complete, and much good work has been done since he completed it. Much interesting work is now in progress by a new generation of Burke scholars.

2

Auscultation, Creation, and Revision
The Rout of the Esthetes
Literature, Marxism, and Beyond

Kenneth Burke

Contents

Spring during Crisis
(Foreword)

In the course of preparing some Last Words ("In Retrospective Prospect") for two of my early books (*Permanence and Change* and *Attitudes toward History*) which are being reissued by the University of California Press, I became quite entangled among recollections of that pesky period in which those books were written and first published (1935 and 1937 respectively). I kept tending to get back into all that, while also I kept undoing much of such redoing. But the item to which these paragraphs refer (it was written several years earlier), was never published.

And for a good reason. The first editor to whom it was submitted rejected it; and I was so disheartened, I submitted it to no other. I was almost demoralized. The editor who rejected it (his own magazine, *Hound and Horn*, would be discontinued not long after, itself too a victim of the troubled times) had been quite hospitable to my work. He had published three chapters of my novel *Towards a Better Life*, then "in progress." And since it's about a man cracking up, the author (who didn't feel so safe himself) promptly withered away when the editor wrote that he was turning it down because it seemed "unreal" to him. Under the circumstances, the editor couldn't have picked an adjective that might disturb me more.

But now, ironically, I think of offering the piece for publication precisely because the editor was right. The thing *is* "unreal." But its very "unreality" is what might recommend it now to a reader's attention as a kind of "document" that "reconstructed" some of the moody tentatives (erroneous trials) let loose during those days. Some variants of the article's attitudes are now here among us. But even the similarities turn out so differently that my "unreal" text "faithfully" depicts conditions of *those* times, unless, damn it, the pages will be judged to reflect only my own personal conditions, as though the responsiveness, however "real" in itself, was "really" responding to a world that was not "really" there at all, outside mine own respondings, as when, having at one point got saturated with Milton's prose, I let some of it rub off ("unreally" indeed!) onto or into the tonalities of some sentences.

Precisely like now, our naggingly recurrent momentary moods were in effect saying "Where turn?" So we turned all sorts of ways. That at least should come through as *wholly real*. What gridlock times they were!

Against my principles, I am grateful to the journalists for grinding that term into us after their fashion, during a strike of transit workers. They did a good job in making people so familiar with its literal meaning, since thereby it was prepared to do service as an exceptionally accurate metaphor for suggesting the state of mind that one gets into not only when there is a traffic jam, but even when things are going, as they usually do, every which way, like being unable to make up their mind.

One sets up the term thus: Begin with "grid," the better to fare forward *(pour mieux sauter)* into "gridlock." There, despite the jam, one thinks of "grid/lockstep." At first glance, that looks even worse. But look again, and lo! even in "lockstep" there are the makings of a going forward somehow, whereat in the very midst of the vexations there arises promise enough; namely: "gridlock/steppingout"—and once again one is on the way towards somehow picking up momentum.

Out of those gridlock times, I remember a dream (it turned up a bit later than this "Crisis" piece) in which President Wilson was consulting me. I let him have it straight, no pussy-footing. I forget exactly what I said and he said. But even at the risk of seeming boastful, in the cause of sheer historical factual accuracy, I should testify that our president was visibly impressed.

[probably written between 1930 and 1934]

Spring during Crisis
(Preface for a Work Left to Languish)

If there is a state of affairs which one considers regrettable, one may speak with bitterness against those people and those institutions to which, by his way of thinking, the responsibility is most directly attached. Or he may not do so at all. Thinking the repulsive conditions changeable by peaceful methods, he may avoid defiance, not as alien to his mood, but as unsuited to his purpose, which is rather to cajole and wheedle—the noblest of such pleas being perhaps Milton's *Areopagitica*, in which, though Milton on many other occasions had proved himself a master of filthy invective, he chose to address the Parliament with a strategy of ingratiation that a man could invent, I believe, only by being first a violent man and then putting a check upon his violence. I know of no more astounding maneuver in all literature than this campaign of Milton's against a government censorship of books—and I can even believe that we today still enjoy some measure of freedom for our press because the arguments against official licensing were made so dignified at the source. Crude editorials will now and then appear, and seem to bolster up the cause—but they are, deep down, supported by this one magnificent pamphlet of Milton's—as a cause does not recommend itself by its own merits; it becomes a worthy cause by being recommended worthily; it is a radiant cause when some poet has made it radiant.

In the *Areopagitica*, however, the problem of exhortation was relatively simple. There was a definite body, the British Parliament, to be addressed; this body was contemplating a definite measure of suppression, the official censoring of books in the name of civic welfare. The prime matter of tactics to be considered was as follows: How ask persons who favor one course of conduct to adopt another instead; and how affect them without wounding the important prejudices that lie behind their choice? I should call the resultant pamphlet a kind of sublime tail-wagging—as when the weaker avoids trouble with the stronger by an aggressive friendliness, disarming the big idiot by subtly suggesting that strife is simply not on the day's program.

Strife? Beneath all Milton's unction there is such a sharp distribution of forces, such yielding here and concentration of heavy artillery there, such pursuing of advantages, as to suggest nothing quite so much as the movements across a battlefield. In the *Areopagitica*, of all his pamphlets, Milton is most at war, since the most wit is here required of him. Particularly in works where he is lambasting the enemy for the delectation of those who agree with him in advance, he is not warring—he is swimming with a current. Authentic war calls more of oneself into play. The most military moment (by our inverted concept of the military, the veerings and deployments of appeal), the most military moment came with the exalted use of a particularly questionable aspect of the modern world, the patriotic mechanisms which enable humble men to become boastful, and peaceful men to become pugnacious, by simply thinking of themselves as groups. If our English people are as remarkable, he says in effect, as all good Englishmen know them to be, why could we not trust them to make wise choices in the matter of books without government supervision of their reading; in so wholesome a nation even a thoroughly vile and subversive literature could be distributed with safety, our own moral and intellectual soundness being guaranty enough that we would reject it. And with his well-timed pictures of England as the great eagle, staring unblinded at the sun, he has finished off his work of making an adequate refutation impossible—he has lifted the national coxcombry to the plane of nobleness, and then used its overwhelming nobleness against another coxcombry which he had left in its originally unexalted state. He has taken the politicians' praise of Englishmen, made it into a more gorgeous thing over a long stretch than they could even have imagined in glimpses, then put it in such a context that they could not advocate their censorship without turning against a love of country which, after their tepid ways of stating it, must have startled and scorched even them, leading them to respect in Milton's words what they had rightly despised in their own. A person who has choked at the sight of soldiers advancing in unison might conceivably choke also when he first came upon this neat spectacle in Milton, the use of a menacing prejudice to destroy another menacing prejudice, his way of easing the differences between himself and his audience on one matter by stressing their agreement on other matters, and the scoring of a point without the slightest suggestion of a triumph—the gracefulness, the unction, the tail-wagging, the mock-naive failure to make it clear that the author had just extricated himself from a considerably tangled knot.

When faced with a regrettable state of affairs, one might think of this pamphlet by Milton, asking himself whether improvement by methods of cajolery is possible. If, on the other hand, he chooses the methods of wrath, insofar as his work is effective it will be effective in contributing to the strengthening of differences, in bringing about such an array of opposites as makes further gains by cajolery almost impossible. A whole literature of this second sort would serve to draw a line; it would influence no one in the sense of changing his attitudes, but it would certainly add to the sharpening of the attitudes already latent. Where there was a preference, there would now be an intense desire; a misgiving would be heightened into a dread; a dissatisfaction would become a deep resentment; an inchoate jangling group would divide into two groups, each given a character as the result of literature precisely as figures in books are given character, by the intensification of some traits and the neglect of others. Wheedling having given place to defiance, we should get factions that would rather break than bend. If we distinguished them roughly as oppressed and oppressors, and found them some obvious mark whereby they could tell themselves apart, we may say that, instead of calling upon the oppressors to cease oppressing, we should now call upon the oppressed to cease permitting themselves to be oppressed.

Let us start with the fable of the wind and the sun, how they saw a man walking along a road, how they laid a wager as to which could get his coat from him the sooner, how the wind tore at him ferociously but only made the man wrap the coat more tightly about him, and how the sun, by a few minutes of benign and peaceful shining, very effectively induced the man to doff his coat of himself. However, there are two major errors in this fable. The first is the implication that the sun did not attain his end by violence, whereas the increase of molecular activity caused by his bombardment must have been enormous (our inverted concept of the military). The second error arises from the fact that the author of this fable was unfair to his wind, palming off on us a relatively feeble wind and not the sort that rips houses from their cellars or hurls trees into other counties. A really capable wind could have got that coat off, by genuine wind-methods, though it may have left little of the wearer, or even of the surrounding real estate, in the process.

Of course, a literature may equip people so well for relentless advance that it equips them for nothing else. To be made into a good bullet is to be made into a good thing for others to fire as they see fit. So those trained by slogans must, to be fortunate, have pure luck in their choice of leaders. They must possess that most difficult form of all initiative, initiative in the selection of the person that shall guide them out of their inertia. If, then, they choose a man who really does understand the issues, and is incorruptible, and is not murdered, a mere trumpet-call will be enough to set them in the right direction. Even if we assume the best, however, I see no permanent security in such a solution, since what is gained with the help of a correct choice of the first leader can be retained only by the correct choice of subsequent leaders—as the slogan, in its stimulating inaccuracy, fails to tell us exactly what we are after, and thus fails to give us ways of knowing which procedures (social, legal, administrative, etc.) are really the ones to assist our purposes and which, however they may seem on the surface, are intrinsically a menace. Such a slogan as "liberty, equality, fraternity" seems to have been perfect for leading a mob to get things but did not give it adequate insight into the ways of holding what it had got. So we must go on picking people by their faces, and always picking rightly—yet complex as the problems of society are at present, they are very simple as compared with the complexity we should encounter if we tried to lay down the principles of a wise choice of leaders.

For my own part, I have read my Bible well enough to make no single choice between the sun and wind, knowing that there must be a time for each. I have wondered just how much could be done by pleading, if people really did remember how to plead, if they came fancifully to a rich man's door in thousands, all on their knees, and weeping. Then again, I have wanted to be nothing more than a bullet, or a tiger's claw, sent suddenly against the pink flesh of some damned liar, some damned liar who fattens while his damned lies contribute to the wretchedness of millions. And there have been other attitudes. At times, for instance, anything less drastic than a complete rebeginning has seemed to me like a mere expedient, a kind of symptomatic remedy, open to the objection against all symptomatic remedies, the gruesome and hilarious objection that the dose for the stomach ailment finally affects the liver badly, the dose for the liver in turn affects the heart, the dose for the heart affects the kidneys, and so on, circularly, as we bolster each complaint by providing a cause for some new complaint. Society would, by this outlook, be the House That Jerry Built—as money makes thieves, thieves make policemen, policemen make graft, graft makes investigations, investigations make elections, elections make money—one can start at random, anywhere, and draw these useless circles. So we may come to feel that the mere transference of a railroad, say, from one group's hands to another's is practically no change at all, however much the social order might be languishing, at a given time, for precisely this transference. In sum, one feels that new instruments of control, when set up, need in turn further instruments of control.

From this antinomian position several different moods can arise—

all on the same day. One can think of turning evangelical, and trying to advocate directer ways of living, a return to conditions wherein the nature of desires and their appeasements would be clearer, so that we should require only rudimentary kinds of good judgment to make the proper choices, should not have to be exceptionally wise to do the wise thing, as a dog, when you toss him a bone, need not be a skilled economist to snatch at it. Surrounded by a world of controversies, a world crying for enlightened decisions when even a philosopher could not be sure of deciding which enlightenment, I thought vaguely of a rebuilding more in accordance with the fundamental dogmatisms of the body. For a man so skeptical that he would not make one statement without adding "maybe," "possibly," or "perhaps" is nonetheless a citadel of unquestioning faith—viz. the myriad of correct decisions that go to make up his body, the unwavering cellular discriminations of metabolism, the acceptances and rejections of his organs. The human hulk is but the concretization of sound principles, or it is so at least until it likewise has made things too difficult for itself (by growing old)—and I felt that if our ways of living were simple enough for us to be making the correct social choices by simply making the correct physical choices (as projected into their closest mental equivalents), we might then honestly consider ourselves in the way of a real revolution, while anything less thoroughgoing than this would be a mere palliative, all the conflicting schemes falling together into one design, if viewed from this great distance, as the French and Germans confronting each other in the last war must have made simply one battlefield to a good eye on Mars, and by this notion schools as different as Communism, Fascism, and Social Planning would all look alike, all being minor sectarian quibbles of the same orthodoxy, a respect for the complexities of industrialism and "efficiency."

Allied with this, but more temperate, was a kind of non-cooperative relaxation, a welcoming of corruption. If the world, that is, has developed many powerful institutions which need still more powerful institutions to control them, why not avoid the whole issue by a mere collapse, corresponding to a sudden insensibility from too much tax upon our sensitiveness, or corresponding to a healthy child's balking at subjects in the curriculum which are not linked with his concepts of the future? If a force is to be controlled, why not make it controllable by weakening the force? This, I thought, might be accomplished, for a while at least, by a simple refusal—sometimes lethargic, sometimes insolent, sometimes viciously satirical—to accept the current criteria of distinction and ambition which best uphold the worthless aspects of our culture. I made vague allowance for some "minimum" society, preponderantly a group of small agrarian landowners, untaxed by either the state or mortgage, and so restored to a barter economy which might enable them to avoid their sociological confusions by enabling them to avoid the confusions of finance. Yet I am talking only of a mood, not of a project—for I am wholly aware that this negative policy, if actually carried out, would be little other than the rock upon which a set of unsleeping affirmations should be based. Follow the implications of this mood, try simply to plot your life in accordance with it, and you would end—like any industrialist—by having a lobby in Washington.

Impatience, despair, and their simple reversal in the humor of trench morale: impatience at the thought of how ghastly much the voice-of-God must learn, as compared with what it knows, about the ailments of our institutions. Despair at the thought that, difficult as it is, even under the best conditions, to get these matters clear, there is the further obstacle of highly organized misinformation, the bewildering interaction of stupidity and greed, aloof collaboration of perjurors and slinkers with outstanding educators and editors in high repute even among themselves—an entire national network now so well established, so thoroughly written into the texture of our customs and institutions, that it would really need no further briberies to perpetuate it—yet briberies perpetuate it too, briberies by the overt exchange of money, and covert briberies by threatened loss of privilege, so that we have, all working together, helped by the vocabulary of a nation, by our distribution of possessions, by the channeling of opportunity, we have (in deadly alliance without the disgrace of collusion) the mutual assistance of honest convictions, and of bought convictions, and of convictions both honest and bought. And since all this is implicated in the very mechanisms by which our millions of people provide for the existence of one another, we cannot get at the rotten portion without seeming to endanger all. The situation would be dismal enough if it were under the guidance of the keenest and most conscientious men, investigators least liable to pervert their findings in the interests of some prejudice or prerogative. Even if they were given a free hand, full access to all the documents, the goodwill and assistance of the entire nation, which simply waited, obedient and imploring, for their conclusions. Add then the fact that the elements making for obscureness happen to be in as orderly a shape as anything in the nation, and you have reason enough to let your impatience become despair. There is a vast amount of our culture well worth the saving—you think desolately at precisely this moment when there seems the least likelihood of its rescue—in the archives alone, there is a depth, and a refining melancholy, and a machinery for contemplation, which we should greatly cherish. Whereupon we might shift quickly into humor, the laughter of trench morale, contenting ourselves with the thought that, in a moment of respite before calamity, everything is still here, and we can get a little human warmth by playing diverse factors one against another, making an administrator's statement look foolish in the light of a religious belief, making the religious belief look foolish in the light of some new custom, making the new custom look foolish in the light of some law on the statute books or some canon of taste, in this way using all that has been handed down to us, really relishing our traditions for one last time by our very trifling with them, since humor comes richly out of the past.

Thence to the attitude which has many times come to the assistance of things as they are, making people who are not unjust acquiesce to injustice, the attitude to which we might most properly erect a national monument, the attitude which befits one if one is a man, and on a boat, and the boat is sinking, and there are no women and children on the boat, nor are there means of salvation enough for all, the attitude of *sauve qui peut*, of devil-take-the-hindmost, an attitude adopted, not because we are a brutal people, but because we have not seen our way clear to establishing the organization for not being brutal. It takes tremendous genius, in a bungling way, to develop a national system of doing things, with each one of one hundred and twenty million people contributing somewhat to the process (even though his contribution consists modestly in kissing the flag that gave him a medal in exchange for an arm, or in saying a sentence which someone else said to him and which happens to interfere with some greatly needed alteration)—so, when we have done this once, it is expecting awfully much of us, as a nation, to ask that we do it again. If we have organized, and the organization has its brutal aspects (an organization, mind you, is not merely in the laws, but also in the ways of seeing and doing that lie behind those laws)— if we thus have a system, and the system is all that we have, so that it has in its favor the one indubitable fact that it is already there, whereas there are at least a dozen hotly advocated schemes for replacing or repairing it, and if the system happens to give off some portion of brutality as a by-product, and we do not know how to avoid the giving-off of this by-product without changing the system itself, and we can most effectively change a system by just having the change occur, so that we are someday told by a thinker, to our surprise, that it actually has occurred—there we are, each waiting to join a new crowd, though we must all have made the crowd before each of us can join it; arriving at which point our typical country-man, if he has anything left to give, gives twenty-five dollars to organized charity, puts it down on his tax statement as one hundred twenty-five, and earnestly hopes that the unfairness which is too much for him to remedy will not include him and his family among its victims. Though he might wince at so stating it, the suffering of millions becomes a margin of safety to him: when he "retrenches," they "pull in their belts"; when he pulls in his belt, they starve; and should the pinch tighten to the point where he must starve, by then they should have attained the initiative of anguish.

That spring, with a vague sense of impending calamity, I went back to my unkempt Jersey farm, even having decided that as a kind of "terror insurance" one might, as well as not, put in a few extra rows of potatoes. For if a disorder in the transport aspect of distribution should arise to match the disorder already present in the purchasing aspect, so that it became as impossible to bring supplies to people's doors as it now is to get the supplies beyond their doors, we should have potatoes in the cellar—and occasionally, besides the cooked ones, we could eat a portion raw, as a preventive of scurvy. Terror-insurance was cheap—for in any case one should profit by the exercise and if the potatoes were not needed sinisterly, they could be used the following year as seed. I liked the idea (trench morale; in New York the financial stringency has given rise to a whole group of such rebellers, who are honestly in favor of some violence, yet have a little haven somewhere along the commuting fringe, which they recall, not proudly but comfortably, when they think of Paris mobs pattering down the streets like big rain-drops). After a sour winter in the city, several months given over to a study of really nasty documents which did many of my outstanding compatriots no great honor, I was prepared for "escape"—and so inverted has the world become, that there is actually an "evasion," an "avoidance of realities," in a program for spending a solid spring, summer, and fall among the fundamentals of sensation. By looking at the expertly modulated contours of hills, I would be closing my eyes. In a daily firming of muscles there would be a relaxation, even a flabbiness. Turning my face heliotropically upward toward the blazing Father God the Sun, I would be obscuring the issue.

I admitted as much—and gathering up the family, including the pup, who was small enough to be transported in a cardboard box with square holes cut here and there for ventilation, I started off on a slow train which—it being early spring—was heated both by steam from the engine and by slanting sunlight. The pup, Ping (so called because Pong was his brother), in his eagerness to see, would stick his nose into one of the holes, thus blocking his vision and leading me to realize that had he been less eager he would, by not pressing so tensely forward, have avoided plugging the hole with his nose, and so would have seen much better. I thought of calling the attention of all my daughters to this parabolic fact, but I was not quite sure of what it was parabolic, and insofar as dogs recognize by scent rather than vision, his nose was exactly where it should have been.

Through the windows of the train, the sun fell upon us out of a stark naked sky. And under the simple exhilaration of the season, superimposed upon my memories of so sour a winter, I whispered "Spring during Crisis," and felt very much as I might have felt had some plague or earthquake or revolutionary madness fallen upon the city, as though the city were lying across the river even now in the grip of tetanic spasms, with the people churning about like the sufferers in some crude illustrator's version of Hell, while we had somehow managed to reach this train, which would carry refugees into a vague hinterland of safety. Our luggage, a fairly orderly assortment, I pictured as a jumble of our few transportable possessions, shoes, books, silverware, bread, vegetables, canned milk, the whole hurriedly wrapped in bedding. And as the train still lay champing at the station, I imagined that it was not merely waiting for the exact split second of its scheduled departure—but that, on the contrary, there was every reason for a hasty get-away, and even now fireman and engineer and train hands were working nervously to repair some damage done the machinery by the cataclysm (the social or geologic cataclysm, on this point I was not clear)—that even now a boat was landing a few hundred yards away, bearing a stricken swarm which, if the train could not immediately be started, would overwhelm us.

Just then the train did start—and one would hardly have realized, as it moved easily out of the station, that we were leaving such a mangle and torment behind us, the gently accelerating motion seemed so alien to their frenzy, their outcries as they trampled one another, the tearing apart of families. The danger now over, I moved a few seats forward to leave my wife with all the travel annoyances of restless daughters and a yelping pup (he was not grateful for our remembering him at our moment of flight; he merely felt that, confined in a box, he was no longer loved; he probably thought that he was being punished for having sneezed or scratched his ear, as pups consider all our rules for pups thus arbitrary), I sat at this safe distance and opened a book. It was Barron's, Clarence W. Barron's, and it repeated what various enterprising financiers had told him. I found it, on the whole, a very dull book—but this year, as penance, we have all had to read the most abominable stuff (I think I read all winter without coming upon a single sentence that had resonance in it, a literature of books by bookkeepers, dismal accounts of accountants, telling you how one corporation did something, and then supposedly telling you something else by telling you how another corporation did the same). One reads such matter as though he held his ear to a crack, expecting no splendor, but hoping for usable information.

Splendor versus significant gossip. There has been talk of renouncing poetry—and one striking fellow, who got a prize in Paris for a poem, forthwith came forward to make it clear that he would now turn his mind to more serious things. (Was I beginning to doze, as the train stretched its busy length across the Jersey Meadows?) I have been made uneasy by such treacheries to the Guild—for if one had spent a whole lifetime studying the values of literature, and had finally come to the conclusion that poetry was a secondary matter which threatens to divert us from a concern with really fundamental forces, the least he could do would be to carry his secret to the grave. Instead, what we actually find is a striking fellow who wrote a poem crowned in Paris, and who now thinks of some plausible flourish, rushing forward with tinny doctrines to add his vaudeville weight to the confirming of an illiterate public in its illiteracy, and getting somehow the notion that one has somehow made himself remarkable. Biblically, I have granted that there is a time for everything; but it never occurred to a person until a few years ago that each time he goes to eat, or to shave, he must formally renounce all poetry. When an invader came upon a peaceful people, and the call went forth to lay down hoes and take up muskets, this was not construed as a renunciation of hoes. They took up muskets that they might return to hoes. And if one wishes to convince me that a concern with pure literature is inapposite to the season, I should at least point out to him that there are two deductions possible from this premise, since one may either say, "So much the worse for pure literature" or "So much the worse for the season." Besides, what is the difference between pure and applied literature, poetry and propaganda? Literature must always have its "gravitational pull," by which I mean that it must always be directed towards some worldly situation. Literature is the manipulation of vocabulary in such a way that it provides us with the images, the motions and emotions, relevant to a situation. If there is to be a storm, poetry (pure literature) and propaganda (applied literature) will both deal with it, insofar as they have relevance, insofar as the writer is aware of the storm in its incipiency. The poet will prepare us for this storm by saying, "Beware, a storm approacheth," while the pamphleteer will handle the same matter by saying, "Go thou, and buy rubbers."

To make it clear that there is no categorical breach between the poem and the pamphlet, could we speak of pure literature (poetry) as "incentive" literature, and of the pamphlet (propaganda, applied literature) as "kitchen sink" literature—and could we not value "incentive" literature in that it serves above all to remind us why we should wish to abolish all that we, in our "kitchen sink" approach, complain of? "No one walks unpunished beneath palms," says Goethe—and that is what we must feel entitled to expect: the sort of punishment that comes of walking beneath palms. The poet should refuse to let his countrymen be content with less—and he should let no writer of quick articles persuade him that there is not, in these remote imaginings, a direct bearing upon the contemporary unimaginings. How in the devil's name did they work this: how did they contrive it that the conditions which have constantly threatened to deprive us of our poetry, by compelling us to expend nearly all our energies upon theories of credit, are now backed by a sanction, so that poets turn from their poems with zest, for it now seems as natural to denounce poetry in the name of "conditions" as it once did to denounce "conditions" in the name of poetry. And though I have seen photographs of Soviet leaders playing chess, I find that the deep cunning and immersion which, if properly devoted to art, might involve one in the fundamental maneuverings of the king and queen and bishops and knights and rooks of the mind is considered sometimes a mere self-indulgence leaning towards the psychopathic, and sometimes even a direct crime against the state.

They have forgot that things come out of a well, that in poetry there is a prodding, that in a mere recital of calamities, in exposures, recommendations, and affidavits you have, in the end, but grounds for growing sick of recommendations and affidavits. The facts are not enough. Or rather, they may be enough up to the eighth or ninth time—but what if we must rehearse them daily? Even revelations of the godhead had to be ritualized before the people could be induced to concern itself with these revelations regularly. But if the pamphleteers had their way, they would think it enough to reveal again and again, without dance-steps. And when the public had finally sneaked off to dream in the feeblest dream-literature, they would complain that the public was evading by closing its eyes to the important realities of the times—but I will tell you that the public would be evading something more fundamentally ghastly than ill-adjustments of finance: it would be evading, not a depression in industry, but a depression in prose. For if you are to maintain its attention upon things which are at bottom disagreeable, and which people wish were different, you can do so only by making these things different—which is to say, by embedding them in literary happenings, making the story of corruption a graceful or fanciful or witty thing.

After a sour winter in which, being too far removed from the enemy, I fought with friends, it was comfortable and sweet to be moving towards spring—even towards a Spring during Crisis. I thought of a kind of inventory-song in which all these factors would be intermingled: pre-Marxian trees and birds, an even positively anti-Marxian pond aflutter like little aspen leaves beneath a privileged-class sun, injustice lying somewhere behind the hills (the margin of safety inexorably narrowing upon greater and greater numbers of people); these factors being intermingled with questions—what is admirable about our institutions, what despicable; how much should we have to tolerate, whether we considered it despicable or not; should palliatives or complete reversals be aimed at; is there a quackery of the virtuous (in uplift and revolution); what is the alignment of forces, and can there be but one; what things arise by planning and what arise of themselves; can a people, without understanding historic processes, act correctly; what sentences, lodged in the public mind, are pivotal, in that they make for the maintenance of the present order, or for a change of order; which of our two theories of material well-being do we really act upon, or act upon more often—the theory of oppositionist prosperity (that some prosper at the expense of others), or the theory of integral prosperity (that for some to be greatly prosperous, all must be fairly prosperous)? I thought of bringing business and metaphysics within the same frame of reference, as Veblen first taught us, making no distinction between a question as to what is included under the head of "depreciation" on the books of a utility corporation, and the question of those delicate sounds heard at times in the mythical country of Hudson's "Crystal Age" or on that island where Prospero had employed his spare time to such advantage.

Above all, I thought of discussing, at some length, the matter of Edgar and Margaret—of whom, up to this point, I have heartlessly said nothing. For though I have loved them, I confess also that I have watched them, finding their troubles "symptomatic." Their minds, it is true, have often been very much upon themselves and each other—yet I believe that they have been as distinctly moved by the contemporary disorders as though they had considered nothing else. Their disturbance also, it seemed to me, might be woven into the indeterminate text—partcularly if one may still subscribe to the "spotlight" or "case history" school of narratives, the Leibnizian, Goethean, monadic, microcosm-macrocosm theory, the notion that in certain individuals there can be concentrated an experience typical of the group, or that in such individuals the workings of factors most deeply affecting the group can be observed most clearly. Edgar and Margaret, if they are moving as they seem to be, would belong here.

Meanwhile, we had climbed out of one train into another, out of the second into a car—and now, after five miles of furrowed roads, we had arrived. The house, though unoccupied for months, had been untouched (another winter might be different). A farmer from the next valley stopped as he was passing—and when I had asked him about conditions here, and he had told me of several men who had, in a kind of tiny unlabeled local revolution, appeared in a body and thrown themselves upon the township, to be given work forthwith, he surprised me by suddenly becoming filled with something which he very much wanted to say. And then he told me, not very neatly, that if things did not improve before many months, there would be "blood let in these here hills." I did not take him very seriously— except to note the fact that he would not have been interested in such remarks a few years back. This meant that the arrows had veered, the coordinates of his thinking had been changed; but I felt confident that, for all the outrageousness of his words, the underlying change was very slight. Unfortunately, even if he had stood, this once peaceful man, with a murderous hog knife at someone's neck, the underlying change in the coordinates of his thinking would have been slight. The slogan of the new is but a fresh way of touching off the old.

Spring? There I had been, toasted in a train, looking out upon an unimpeded sun that raced me across a sky of uniform blue, except for the grading of paler blue that went along the ridges. By the time we reached the house, the sun was lost behind a uniform dirty greyness. A damp wind had risen, with an occasional sprinkling of snow. Gradually the burden of the air increased—and then came an enormous wastage, millions and millions of little snow units, each with its own special quality of skill in its construction, being simply squandered across the countryside, unused, undesired, even despised by the natives, clinging heavily to the stocks of last year's goldenrod, and gradually covering with sound snow the slush of the storm's beginning. I huddled against the stove, still reading Barron, while the wind was strong enough, and the snow was wet enough, for spasmodic swishings to attack the windows. The lamp globe was dull, but I was too unenterprising to clean it. Instead, I stood the lamp on a chair, close against the stove, and sat following the yellow page while beyond the white precipitation in the edges of the windows there was a tangled white descent, and beyond this was blackness. A dismal page, being read at a dismal time. In the dirty yellow light, shivering because I had too soon opened myself to spring, I read these unlovely notes of a man who had got very fat, and died.

"All property is potentially debt, or nothing but the representation of indebtedness. The land owes the farmer its annual crop, and the building owes its proprietor the rent. All the world is in debt and lives by debt," he wrote—he too thus commingling metaphysics and business, as here he seems to have shown us theories on the "productiveness" of credit built into the very nature of the universe. And since even McKinley was once a bimetallist, before Mark Hanna raised a sixteen million dollar campaign fund to elect him in the interests of "sound money," what more natural and more human than that Barron, even Barron, should have shared in that strange ennoblement over silver, when men got famous for falling into the posture of Calvary during currency disputes, so that an actual demon stirred him, for one paragraph, in the rigors of '93, and he cried out Byronically, "Conservatism is hide, skin, skull, bark, protection; but the blood of youth, radicalism, growth or expansion bursts the bark, grows a new shell, expands the skin, and finds its own protection. The two forces of youth and age make life and limit it." He goes further: "Enterprise is sap, expansion, growth, advance circulation; it needs the money of circulation, it must have silver or a substitute for silver." Then turning viciously upon gold, he summarizes his accusations: "Conservatism wants to be paid in a dearer metal, it wants the money of reserve, it wants sluggish money of most universal market." And he asks himself, "Which will win, conservatism or enterprise?" unmindful that the two might be the same. Following this dangerous period (the youthful fury of his page suggests that he must have been courting the future Mrs. Barron at the time), he settled down to a very steady and commendable existence, the curve of his own concerns following somewhat the curve of the entire nation's concerns so far as political and economic matters go—for with him, as with the nation, the keenest critical acumen between the election of 1896 and the present was expended upon the discerning evaluation of individual financial ventures while the structure underlying such ventures went completely unexamined. So, in his lack of partisanship, his placid, adulatory noting of "what they said," his work becomes more damning than many an intended philippic, as the reader inevitably supplies in his own mind the interpretations which Barron sweetly omitted.

Well, perhaps it was right to call an advocate of silver radical, since the whole question of money was made terrifying by such a quarrel. For if the time should come when great capitalists had finally cornered all the silver too, what more natural than that the farmers should next propose a sub-silver currency—clay dollars maybe. To have two metals sanctified is, for such a monotheistic people as we, to risk losing faith in any metal. And faith obviously is at the bottom even of something so apparently "realistic" as business. Barron had discussed this too:

It is really faith acquired or inherited that does the big things in the world. John D. acquired faith from his Bible-reading mother, and borrowed all the money he could to store oil when it was going to waste and considered of no value. He had faith in the value of the author of that oil. Harriman was the son of a clergyman who never earned more than $600 a year, but he was brought up in a religious atmosphere of faith and in faith he never faltered, whether rebuilding the Union Pacific when the men who appreciated him said that it could never be worth it, or filling in across the apparently bottomless Salt Lake to make a shorter railroad route. People who have no faith may be terror-stricken and swept off their feet before unknown and unmeasured adversaries.

Then it is no accident that our word for "credit" comes from the Latin "to believe." And it is not insignificant that the greatest monopolist of credit, the deceased Morgan, should, when pressed for definitions by a lexicographically minded congressional committee, have introduced the strangely unbusinesslike term "character" as the basis of credit, when the entire nation (himself included) was attempting to found credit upon the collateral of fluctuant stocks and bonds, with their forever bobbing "base line." Belief, of all things, is needed—belief not only in the borrower, but in the very structure of borrowing. For if one single dollar, when owed long enough, would owe its creditor the entire world in interest charges, and there are billions of invested dollars each competing for this astounding prerogative, what less than *faith*, simple *faith*, a secularized adaptation of Tertullian's *credo quia absurdum*, will enable us to have *confidence*?

The note which affected me most complexly, as I sat forlornly by the stove, the family asleep now, the sleetlike snow sprayed in gusts against the windows, was a brief reference to Barron in Damascus: "W.B.T. said, as we walked in Damascus last evening, that he lost $3,000,000 in Sinclair." Oh, we were in the streets of Dimeshk esh-Sham—perhaps near the banks of the Abana, a deep and rapid river that cuts the city, converting aridness into exceptional luxuriance. There were minarets, domes, golden crescents emerging above the foliage of the gardens. In this center of piety and trade, piety and trade under other schemes than ours, how easy it was for us to penetrate their errors, not by reason of superior insight, but simply through having different errors of our own. There had been momentous massacres here. There was much splendor behind dreary walls. Perhaps we had passed the house of Naaman the leper, or had visited the spot where the apostle, with not exactly apostolic dignity, had been let down from the wall in a basket. Or we had stood by the east gate, which Paul had entered after his personal revolution—or perhaps gone through the street which is called Straight, where the chosen vessel unto the Lord had languished until the disciple Ananias came to him, so that the scales fell from his eyes, and he took food and was strengthened, and he was certain days with the disciples which were at Dȧ-măs'cus. And straightway in the synagogues he proclaimed Jē'ṣus, that he is of the Son of God. And all that heard him were amazed, and said, Is not this he that in Jĕ-rü'sȧ-lĕm made havoc of them which called in his name. We had been walking through a history-laden city, bewildering mosaic-work of our history and history wholly alien, and W.B.T., turning to me, said, "Yes sir, I lost three million at one clip in Sinclair Oil."

I went outside. The snow had stopped, and I ventured a prophecy. I prophesied that a dry, roaring wind would burst in from the West, and that after several hours of bluster, every last shred of cloud would be torn out of this sky, and all above us would be a sterile, frigid calm, our house jutting right out against the sharp stars. The next morning there would be a few blinding hours until this unnecessary snow had melted down, and been sent speeding through the valleys towards the Delaware. And the sap would resume flowing.

This was wish-thinking—but even wish-thinking can be correct.

Introductory Note

This book considers, among other things, the factors behind that somewhat remarkable phenomenon, the "rout of the esthetes." Here was the case where an entire literary generation, as soon as the word "esthete" was leveled at them, promptly "cleared out." It was generally felt that the exigencies of the times made such a move advisable. Before "clearing out" myself, I thought I would take one last look around, to see if anybody had left anything of value in the hastiness of departure—and sure enough, I discovered lying about unclaimed, a Philosophy of History, a Psychology, an Apologia for Art, a Methodology of Art, a Theory of Criticism, some valuable Archives on the trends of Modern Literature, and a number of devices for relating the whole to the contemporary scene. The present short book aims to give an inventory of these things.

However, I would not want to confine a reader's attention to so limited a field as one year's critical movement. I am concerned with the specific issues insofar as general principles may be projected beyond them. The book, in this sense, should be as valid if the particular writers and careers I have in mind were purely imaginary. I am interested in these local literary processes as they may be related to broader biologic or historic processes. And I hope that the reader, accordingly, will consider them as hardly more than a "case history." Similarly, my discussion of "Marxian method" in literary criticism is framed ever with an eye toward "what is next."

Roughly, the stages of my exposition might be outlined as follows:

I begin by granting the all-importance of the present economic difficulties, and by considering some efforts of literary criticism to take these into account. I try to show the disorders and uncertainties which have been brought into criticism by the economic crisis. Especially I seek to indicate confusions in the way of those critics who, aghast at contemporary disorders, would meet them by a "conversion" mechanism, by the adoption of new standards in direct opposition to those they had formerly held, thus hoping as it were to prepare for the social "Revolution" by a revolution in their own minds.

In particular I re-examine the nature of the "romantic, individualist protest," "obscurantism," the "Ivory Tower," and "leisure class" thinking, since such are considered essentially candidates for the discard—and I try to show that the present "collectivistic," "conformist" tendencies do not differ in psychological fundamentals from the earlier tendencies which they are supposed to replace.

In sum, by what I call the "Saul-Paul reversal" I seek to show that the reborn "collectivist" is simply the old "individualist" over again, that there is no fundamental difference in the basic patterns of his thinking. This I call a "genetic" account, as it discusses the attempted critical reversal from the standpoint of psychological origins.

I then turn to what I call the "logical" account, considering this same matter from the standpoint of the Marxian doctrine of "antithesis." Karl Marx, that is, lays much emphasis upon an antithesis between an exploiting, bourgeois class and an exploited, proletarian class. Each of these classes, by Marxian doctrine, has its special cultural standards. Accordingly, the Marx-inspired critics seek to advocate a "proletarian" literature which will be "antithetical" to the "bourgeois" literature of the past. I try to show some of the difficulties of this attempt—and in the course of doing so I find myself compelled to consider the reasons whereby Marx arrived at the doctrine of "antithesis" in the first place. I thus seek to restate briefly his underlying theory as it has been applied to esthetic values.

In this discussion I attempt to show that the Marxian thesis can be manipulated in non-Marxian ways, and can provide a "sanction" for some of the very trends in art which the "converted" Marx-inspired critics would attempt to condemn. I also attempt to show that Marx's so-called scientific theory of history is not scientific at all but involves judgments about the nature of the universe which science cannot make, and ambiguities of definition which make the rigorous Marxian prophecies impossible.

Along with this discussion of Marxian thinking as it applies to questions of esthetic values, I seek to develop methods of interpretation beyond Marx. In particular I use behavioristic doctrines as to the nature of our thinking to show that Marx's "bourgeois-proletarian" dichotomy gives a faulty explanation of human psychology, as it overstresses the changing social or historic aspects of thought and neglects the "constants" of human physiology. That is, insofar as the human body remains a "constant," we may expect to find corresponding "constants" in the human mind—a consideration which, as I attempt to show, has an important bearing upon the doctrines of Marx. (In brief: if we consider the human body as the "initial economic plant," we find the notion of antithesis greatly restricted in its usefulness, since "proletarian" overlaps upon "bourgeois" in proportion as the *environmental* and *organic* relationships of both classes are identical.) I also introduce the newer Gestalt or Configuration psychology, as it bears upon the general question of "meanings," to show how the discoveries and formulations of this school take us beyond the simplicities of Marxian determinism.

On the basis of these points "beyond Marxism," I consider the probable trend of literature in the future, and reconsider—in the light of what has gone before—the literary trends of the last hundred years, culminating in the conversion of the "esthetes" to Communism. In connection with this last point, I deal with a peculiar paradox: How, for well over a century, the "esthetic" attitude had been distinguished by its attack upon "profit-economy" ways of thinking—and now, just as this attitude begins to claim general acceptance beyond the field of literature, the esthetes' *victory* is pictured, amusingly enough, as a *defeat*, and was even so considered by the esthetes themselves.

In concluding, I question the fitness of the "Saul-Paul reversal" as a way of dealing with the altered scene. I point out how thoroughly imbued it is with peculiarly nineteenth-century ways of thinking, and I offer reasons for suspecting that these ways of thinking must be "translated" somewhat, if we would adapt them to the conditions of our century.

On the Chimeric Nature of "Realities"

They shut themselves up in their own private world—a contemporary critic has warned us, when speaking of certain poets—they cultivate their own private fantasies, encouraging their private manias, ultimately preferring their "absurdest chimeras" to the "most astonishing contemporary realities," and even ultimately "mistaking these chimeras for realities." The critic did not say exactly how we may distinguish between a chimera and a contemporary reality. There might be grounds for considering many a headline in the daily press more chimerical than the elaborate cosmogony of a Plotinus, particularly as a reader of the *New York Herald-Tribune* finds that an entirely different world occurred on a given date than if he had read the *Daily Worker*—which suggests that there might as reasonably have been a dozen other "real" worlds for that same day, if we but happened to have the business organization for putting them together. Or some application of the Taylor System might seem peripheral to the "realities" touching upon the psychological machinery of man, whereas the metaphorical vision of a Blake could seem quite central, handling as it does the basic proportions between ourselves and our imaginings. If one chooses to turn the matter round, taking as "realities" the various contingencies of business and politics which have come to have prior liens upon us (mortgaging us while we slept), one will of course turn from an awesome night to get his understanding by a glance at the bought stars on the ceiling of the Grand Central—and I will grant that one should rather not have a toothache than know the very secret of the universe (unless the second advantage automatically procured the first). I will further grant that there is, today, a pronounced social toothache which makes any universal concern somewhat remote until this nag of economic pain is quieted. I would only ask that we find some way of making the distinction between "chimeras" and "contemporary realities" more serviceable—so we shall know exactly what we mean when we warn against a poet who, after reinforcing his initial brilliance by years of study, succeeds merely in shutting himself away in a world of "chimeras," whereas the silliest typist, hurrying home at rush hour, can pick up the first newspaper she happens to lay her hands upon, and find the "most astonishing contemporary realities" there, all over its pages.

We might tentatively speak of primary, secondary, and tertiary worlds, with a different order of "realities" for each of them. If some acquiescence to universal patterns is primary (as with the periodicity of growth and decay; or as learning of the mind is analogous to learning of the body, by habits under repetition, and by the development of callosity from rubbing); and if some primitive or natural society, in which tools are hand-shaped and appeasements are doglike, is secondary; then our own coordinates (wherein we must steadily observe graphs of foreign trade, credit expansion, gold supply, purchasing power, and the like) must throw us into a tertiary world. And poets who concern themselves somewhat with the first two orders might seem "chimerical" as viewed from the third; for it is "real" now to watch each week the index of last week's carloadings; and it is chimerical, it is a living among queer castles, when the world all falls together at the touch of resonance, as in some opening of a psalm, some lament, say, how "by the rivers of Babylon, there we sat down, yea, we wept."

There is good reason for such a turning away. The man who says, "Why plot the curve of hog production when there is no graph of groans?" is overlooking precisely the fact that human miseries and elations lie behind the proper reading of these bare economic charts. The disorders of the tertiary world are real enough—for they are doing damage, and anything that does damage is real. The question simply is whether we may adapt ourselves to these contingencies, recognize the menaces of the tertiary world as menaces, without being forced to conclude that concerns with anything else are proved, once and for all, chimerical.

There have been various situations in human history, distinct enough from one another to have called forth distinct kinds of thinking and imagery as the way of dealing with them. A still further situation arises (today's)—and it naturally leads us to ask what works of the past, or what methods carried into the present out of the past, are relevant to it. A poet might conceivably have written to bring his fellows through a time of flood, and written very well, yet might seem "inapposite" to us, and even unsympathetic, if we were suffering now under drought. Again: some situations have lasted over longer periods than others, so that the poet who dealt with them remained "apposite" over a period correspondingly long. Other situations, enjoying only brief periods of hegemony, have enjoyed these intensely, though the situation they displaced rated higher in general importance both before and after the temporary eclipse. Thus, a man who said a sentence in San Francisco shortly after the earthquake was more likely to be talking "on the subject" if he referred to the phenomena of "earthquake love" (the stressing of brotherhood and mutual assistance in disaster) than if his sentence were wholly upon the matter of monogamistic love, which has been a fairly live issue through several centuries. There is no fundamental difference between one person angered for a minute, and a whole civilization engrossed with some one cultural problem for hundreds of years: in either case there is a situation out of which apposite statements will arise. The one angered man may shout oaths, afterward tempering them by quick revision into lesser oaths; and similarly, the "leading minds" of the civilization will put forward many enterprising statements about the cultural problem, revising themselves and one another—the processes of the man momentarily engrossed with anger will simply be drawn out, by slow motion, through the successive generations of engrossment with the one cultural problem. Nor do situations come only one at a time: some poets have been involved in the imagery of surfeit even while others have been involved in the imagery of deprivation. It is a mere convenience of history to picture the world as all being romantic at once, or naturalistic, and so on. We may, however, decide what we shall call the "key" situation of a given era; and having laid down a few salient rules of thumb for telling this "key" situation when you see it, we may examine art from the standpoint of its relevance to this "key" situation.

"Realities" Are "Key" Issues; the Present "Key" Issue Is Economic; Therefore, "Realities" Are Now Economic

The matter is not so simple as it could be. One might say that a book which sells hundreds of thousands of copies has automatically proved its greater "relevance" to the day than a book which sells only a few, thus allowing the whole question to be settled by an accountant. Critics do at times coquette with this notion (though naturally they refrain from testing the relevance of criticism by the same measure)—but just as often they are found struggling to prove the relevance of some writer in whom the public takes no interest at all. Perhaps a book can be relevant in many ways, as both finger-exercises and disappearance at lesson-hour are relevant to the study of the piano. And the critic who would pronounce a popular work less relevant than some comparatively neglected work by a member of his lodge would simply have to say that the popular work was relevant to *a* situation but not to the *key* situation.

If we assign the maladjustments of our commercial structure to the "tertiary" world, and if we at the same time admit that these maladjustments are the directest known cause of misery to millions of people throughout the world today, we may conclude that a writer who now neglects this "tertiary" structure and its ills is neglecting the "key" issue of his age. He grows "chimerical" in direct proportion as he moves away from the "key" issue. He may happen to deal with one of the coexistent situations. A man who has the district agency for the distribution of some automobile, for instance, and is straining like a fiend to dispose of his quota, may at the same time be thinking of marriage. This thinking-of-marriage is also a situation, so the poet might be as relevant to this particular man's concerns by talking of marriage as by talking of agent's quotas. So if the poet puts forth an innocuous love idyll, and the sales agent takes a fancy to it, the critic who would call the idyll irrelevant under such circumstances must mean that the question of love itself is not now "pivotal," does not rate high enough in the hierarchy of burning issues. Or the critic has another way of condemning this work. He can say that the love idyll is relevant to the agent's troubles about his quota, but relevant in a most deceptive way, being relevant in the sense that it enables him to take his mind off his quota-troubles (thus, relevant in the sense that disappearance at lesson-hours is relevant to the study of the piano). In giving us the concept of "escape" or "evasion," psychoanalysts left it vague enough for practically anything to be defined as the evasion of something else. A man who goes inside a house can properly be said to evade the outside; a man who goes up the road is obviously evading going down the road. Thanks to this pliable concept, whatever the critic finds a reader taking an interest in (be it love, metaphysics, tennis, chess, pictures of mountains, fishing, stories of geographical explorations, or investigations in child psychology) can be described by the critic as an evasion of what the critic has decided the reader *ought* to take an interest in (as, let us say, a comprehensive economic explanation of his quota-troubles and of the political moves by which he might remedy them).

Were we to have in mind some general idea of the present "key" situation—as the critic did who accused certain poets of neglecting the "realities"—we might, when objecting to a poet's work as irrelevant, have more or less clearly in mind four rough categories under which the erring work would fall. The work might be simply neutral, with no appreciable bearing upon the contemporary scene at all—as let us say, the catalog of ships in Homer. It might be relevant, but not relevant enough—as I have seen books praised for picturing the miseries of the proletariat, the critic at the same time complaining that these miseries were not linked clearly enough with the doctrines of Karl Marx. Or the work may be relevant but "evasive," the classic example being the great Christian *dèbâcle* pictured by the prelates, who are said to have prevented revolution on earth by promising longsufferers a successful revolution in heaven, where the last should be first. Finally the work may be very relevant—too relevant in fact—since it may bear totally upon the key situation, but offer a solution which the critic considers dangerously wrong (thus could Fascist appeals in the cause of national aggrandizement be condemned by Communists). The categories are not clearly demarcated—when denouncing a book, the critic often seems to be tossing it indiscriminately among the four, but in a general way they seem to cover the ground: books simply irrelevant to the key situation; books relevant but inadequate; books relevant but "evasive"; books whose kind of relevance is positively dangerous.

Category of the Irrelevant

Under the head of the simply Irrelevant we might have two concepts. The work may be neutral in the sense that it does not apply to the key situation at all, or in the sense that it applies equally well to other situations. Offhand, one would say that there was no relevancy at all in a story about an evil worker of magic who, when a rival had stolen his knives, cut off little children's heads with sharp shadows (though even a story apparently as neutral as that might conceivably be given a symbolic relevance to the present if contemporary meanings were "read into it," as with the satire underlying *Gulliver's Travels*). The broader and more significant aspect of the Irrelevant is in the property of general application. The poet's material, that is, may lie across many historical situations—as either a Communist agitator or a bourgeois lawyer on a canoe trip might conceivably observe a fat, lazy moon if they were resting, or a very brisk moon if they were in brisk movement; or as Pavlov conditioned his dogs to salivate at the sound of a bell under the czar, and can make them salivate similarly under Stalin. This is the region of observations and fancies which are not "weighted" as regards the particular issue now pivotal, since they apply to broader situations. Incidentally, in this region lie many discoveries which can be "weighted" if one chooses to weight them. Thus, whereas the investigations of the Symbolists were as far removed from political warfare as one can imagine, their disclosures can be easily adapted to political purposes by the manipulation of associative groupings (as the enemies of Trotsky exemplified when, in exiling him, they included in the edict of excommunication the names of several unsavory reactionaries, thus subtly dishonoring him by his contiguity with images of dishonor). And the conditioning of Pavlov's dogs is an even clearer case in point—as the motion pictures of Hollywood and the Kremlin now work to make their publics salivate under totally different stimuli—the mouths of the Russians being made to water at the sight of a bourgeois, and the mouths of Americans to water at the sight of a Red.

Category of the Relevant but Inadequate

Perhaps highest in the category of the Relevant but Inadequate comes the literature of romantic, *individualistic* protest. It seems generally felt that what we require today is armies: armies of nationalists, armies of revolutionaries, armies of voters, armies of readers, armies of buyers. And if there is such a strong practical necessity of our all doing the same, and opposing ourselves to others who are all doing the same, it is quite natural that this practical demand should find its parallel in an esthetic canon. There have, of course, been armies of individualists too, as possibly the revolutionary armies of France, and as Trotsky says was true of the Russian army when it first turned against the czar:

For millions of soldiers the revolution meant the right to a personal life, and first of all the right to life in general, the right to protect their lives from bullets and shells, and by the same token their faces from the officers' fists. In this sense it was said above, that the fundamental psychological process taking place in the army was the awakening of personality. In this volcanic eruption of individualism, which often took anarchistic forms, the educated classes saw only treachery to the nation. But as a matter of fact in the stormy speeches of the soldiers, in their intemperate protests, even in their bloody excesses, a nation was merely beginning to form itself out of impersonal raw material. This flood of mass individualism, so hateful to the bourgeoisie, was due to the very character of the February revolution, to the fact that it was a *bourgeois* revolution.

The underlying schema here seems to imply a process of emergence out of the impersonal into the personal, and thence to the super-personal (out of the undifferentiated into proud and ambitious singleness, and out of singleness into the collective). So the Protestant trends of individualism are found relevant in the sense that they make for protest against the circumambient ills, but inadequate in the sense that they resist the full neo-Catholicizing trends of Fascism or Communism as a unified way of coping with these ills. The people, it is felt, must be taught how they can take things without stealing, or how they can slay without murder—and to contrive this they must act in groups; otherwise, as individual protesters, they are mere thieves or terrorists, and not very effective ones at that. The philosophic doctrines behind individualism, it is true, generally assume fundamental collective linkages: linkages with God, the universe, historic processes, essential biologic needs, a masonic band of similar-minded individuals who have moved various distances along the uncharted thirty-three degrees of initiation from which one is excluded only by blackballing himself. And even anarchism is but a theory of *brotherhood* to which the soundest objections are not that it is reprehensible but that it is too difficult a way of life for ordinary people to build a world upon. But in general we may say that individualism has been more fruitful in emphasizing the negative, the refusal to acquiesce; and the objection of the "neo-Catholicizing" collectivist would seem to be that, in fostering the spirit of non-cooperation as regards the enemy, the individualist has fostered as a by-product a spirit of non-cooperation as regards his allies. Thus individualism has been at once a splendid way of keeping men aroused, and a poor way of helping men to remove the factors that aroused them.

"Relevancies" and "Inadequacies" of the Romantic, Individualistic Protest

I know of a bank clerk (literally a bank clerk), forced by the exigencies of living, to live a life little in keeping with the seasons, to fulfill other men's certainties, while certainties of his own went necessarily frustrate. He knew, as he stood counting coupons in a cage, that at that moment the sun was being squandered across thousands of square miles, and that he would see none of it, except as much as he ate out of a can, or as had not yet been put away by the time the bank had struck its balance that evening. At night this young man, who firmly believed that he would live but once out of all eternity, yet gave the sharpest hours of his life to counting coupons in a cage, sneaked off to his room and read French novels— not particularly good ones, but intelligent, and at least non-bank, while on occasions he even found such a writer as Baudelaire, who tautened again the slackening cords of his resentment. Here was literature serving to foster romantic, individualistic protest, keeping something alive in him which would otherwise have dwindled under the constant corrosion of its inappositeness, under the discouragement of its unfitness for bank-needs. It reinforced the coordinates of thinking and imagining by which he could resist the serving of a blind employer's purposes. In giving him the signs to steer by, in prodding him to recall that there were other possible orders, it prevented his internal surrender to a gnarled and unnatural way of living—not in the sense that he did not appear as promptly each morning as the others (he did), but in the sense that he refused to accept his life as "dignified" by its place, or any place, in such an inefficient scheme. He reacquired from his reading the encouragements by which he could reject a doctrine of service entailing treason to his own mind and body and affections; thus fortified by texts of varying sturdiness, he could warn himself that a mere languishing in drugs, or a fantastic attachment to a pig, would mark a more justifiable way of life than this, since it would demand less clogging of the pores of his humanity. He naturally tended to formulate an individual integrity in the face of what he considered social collapse, and to value self-imposed obligations above the obligations imposed by a society deemed despicable. In the evening he met cronies, in the catacombs of some greasy bar, where they came together like plotters, that each by his company with the others might bolster himself against his own correspondingly purposeless situation.

Here is the "case history" which might sum up both the genesis and the content of romantic, individualistic protest. Were the disgruntled man also a writer, he would give us something ranging from the Byronic-Baudelairean down to "the efforts of sensitive Richard Robinson to maintain his ideals against the blundering malice of society." If he were a literary sophisticate, he might also permit himself certain investigations in method, even though such experiments bewildered people who were not investigators in method. And to justify himself he might reason, more or less clearly, that insofar as the public has accommodated itself to bank-needs, any writing that does not surrender to their surrender will have the effect of being written in code anyhow; for one can be an obscurantist in even the simplest of sentences, if he happens to say things which other people do not need to hear or which they perhaps even need to leave unheard. So, although a poet wrote straightforward, his work could become the equivalent of mirror writing simply because the rest of the world was turned backwards—and on beholding so great a breach between "commercial" and "poetic" purposes, he would not mind making it still greater by waywardness of style.

There is a basic discrepancy between what our bank clerk would prefer, or thinks he would prefer, and what the imperatives of his society require him to accept. Hence we might place him: "One man's attempts to maintain personal integrity despite the disintegrating forces of society." Or the same pattern might be stated with a greater show of objectivity: "An organism feeding upon its environment, and maintaining its integrity as an organism by assimilating some elements and rejecting others in accordance with the 'logic' of its own existence." In either case, we have the fact of an *individual* at war—this is his pattern of experience as a citizen; as a reader he will want it symbolized, and as a writer he will symbolize it. And whether reader or writer, he will most likely have a devout desire to see both the individual and the struggle idealized, as though he could not consider his difficulties worth taking into account esthetically unless both he and they were magnified. As part of this magnification he may even take pleasure in a tragic outcome—since there is no better way of dignifying a cause than to suggest that it is worth dying for, and there is no better way to suggest that it is worth dying for than to picture someone as dying for it. Also, in tragedy there will be a vicarious expiation—for one is never quite comfortable in being at odds with one's fellows; so if one is writ large, and one's sins are writ large, then one can atone in the large by dying—yet this tricky state of affairs will serve at intervals to cancel off his transgression against the group, and so leave him "absolved," and thus prepared to begin his transgression anew, for the "katharsis" of tragedy is famed as a way of helping one to accept one's fate, in the case of the Greeks helping them to accept their fates as well-to-do slave-owners, and in the case of our rebellious bank clerk helping him to accept his fate as a rebel; so it is no accident that so "final" a thing as tragedy usually marks a beginning, as the slaying of the god in the Greek goat-song long preceded the flowering of Periclean Athens, the Crucifixion was the symbol for ushering in Christianity, the great individualist tragedies of Shakespeare came nearly two centuries before the full social unfolding of individualism, and labor agitation began with plays of labor agitators dying (not until the Cause has triumphed may we expect the comedies and the satires, showing the champions of the downtrodden grown fat and prosperous while their hearts bleed).

Another mechanism behind the idealization of the issue will be a "compensatory" one. As Ouspensky has pointed out, if one stares at red, then stares at white, one "compensatorily" sees green—which suggests that "compensation" may be a property of staring. So our "subject," if he is sufficiently engrossed in this opposition between himself and his group, will stare at it until "compensations" arise. He may, for instance, stare at the disproportion between himself and the enemy forces so steadily that these forces take on gigantic proportions—and then, by staring at these magnified forms, he will necessarily see in his speculations a magnified self as the only self equipped to cope with them. Thus, by the sheer strength of his preoccupation with this matter, he will have increased its scale, thereby incidentally laying himself open to the burlesques of any who, detecting the man in germ in the book he writes, accuse the poor devil of mere self-adulation. There may be some justice in this accusation too—but why should one not adulate oneself at least in proportion as he has adulated his opponent? If he has turned his wearisome bank-cage into a dungeon, why should he not see the man imprisoned there as a monster? The relative strengths of the two factions are still untampered with: and "compensation," we might say, becomes a register of the degree of his preoccupation with his subject.

Category of the Relevant but "Evasive"

At the mention of "compensation," however, we find ourselves on the outward limits of the Relevant but Inadequate category—and many a critic would say that we have already entered the category of the Relevant but "Evasive." Far from seeing the heroics on the pages of our romantic individualist as a "compensation" arising out of firmness, the critic might insist that there is nothing here beyond a mere feeble wish-fulfillment, a day-dreaming, a gratification of the man's thwarted desire for importance by imagining a "keyed up" state of affairs wherein he becomes important. The only objection I can see to this objection is my presumption that everyone would like to be important; so we could not attack a man on this ground unless we were writing a Swiftian attack, an attack upon the human race in general, whereas if we wish to discredit some members of the human race while exempting others, we cannot complain about the "desire for importance" per se, but must merely question the particular ways by which the people under suspicion hope or try to make themselves important. And if the critic feels that there is a key situation which must be appropriately dealt with, even if he thought the poet a self-adulating ass, he could not logically complain on this score unless he had demonstrated that self-adulation makes one categorically unfit for handling the key issue. Arriving at this point, we note that many of our most active participators in great popular emancipatory movements have been endowed with a degree of self-concern which less volcanic people have even found funny, while the example of Rousseau suggests that a great engrossment in one's own frustrated preferences can be a strong basis upon which to erect a scheme in behalf of other people's preferences, if the experiences of the individual and his group happen to be sufficiently analogous. If our objections, as here hemmed in, are confined to a particular kind of self-adulation, the critic's complaint might then be that the poet was being "evasive." The critic might say that the poet, by converting his problem into a "mythology," had in effect closed his mind to the "real" nature of the problems (as would also be the case with a reader reading such a work). The poet had "evaded" reality in the very act of accepting it, since in making it bigger, he had made it something else.

There is something to be said for this, though the objection does not apply only to the literature of individual protest. "Mythological magnification" seems to be the poet's way of singling anything out for attention, since it is hardly different from mere *clarification*, and may correspond in the field of imagery to the process of abstraction in the field of concepts. Any pointing is a "lie" in that it destroys the "natural proportions" of the object pointed at, by making it "bulge above its fellows" with meaning. Thus, "mythological magnification" may be the same as "indication," the kind of significant distortion we get when a jumble of facts is given an order, seen to be a constellational grouping with reference to ourselves, as when we "interpret" a figure in the distribution of certain stars, though this figure depends for its validity upon the particular position of the earth with relation to these stars. If "mythological magnification" is anything else than the mere stylistic equivalent of pointing one's finger, if it is also "evasion," there is a possibility that the American poet least often accused of "evasion" is the one most open to attack. I refer to Whitman: how, by "Whitmanizing" that vast century-long real estate boom which has been America, he was able to make himself an "Answerer." Through converting a very hard-headed movement into its ennobled equivalent, through "looking at a traveling salesman and seeing an angel," through translating a business deal into the terminology of mystic migrations and cosmic elations, through taking a man who went to a certain spot for profit and discussing this man as though the divine fellow had responded to some peculiar call, some deep and gentle prodding, Whitman so prettified the policies eventually making for our expansion in the Caribbean that the most sincere anti-imperialists of Europe could find in his work an acceptable guidance and illumination. Thus, whereas Poe, who never once closed his eyes to the discordant relationship between the things he admired and the things his countrymen sought, was welcomed in Europe by the quizzical Baudelaire or Valéry type of mind, Whitman's self-deceptive mythology for "answering" to the needs of American commerce was heralded by the practical agitators, the "activists," as a wholesome and inspiring facing of the issues. Not Whitman's surrender, but Poe's fight, was called "evasive." Whitman seems to have been received as a prophet for a very remarkable reason: At a time when the tertiary world was coming to make tremendous demands upon us, so that even poets felt the need of adapting their Babylonian and Mediterranean archives to these immediate compulsions, Whitman found a perfect way of making the tertiary world seem primary. People tend to become twice buried—first resigning themselves to something which they dislike, and next changing their desires so that they can cease to dislike it. When indirect schemes of existence no longer disturb us, they have quit disturbing us only insofar as the imagery of a directer existence has died from the mind—we blunt ourselves to the glimpses of primary and secondary worlds in order that we be not hurt by the requirements of the tertiary one. Hence, critics felt the growing authority of the tertiary world even as they were prevented from fully welcoming it by their criteria surviving from a more "earthy" culture. It was a dilemma for which Whitman offered the perfect solution, by simply looking at a stock-jobbing proposition for the promotion of a new railroad and seeing it as a reaching out of hands. Our Rotary Clubs are the poorer poems of Whitman, the ones which he, being dead, could not revise. In Whitman there is latent a mechanism of "evasion" as thoroughgoing as the prelates' promise of the revolution in heaven, since it is a device for silencing criticism as to the fundamental movements of our country. Whitman will, it is true, protest against "injustice" (one must go far to find an unjust despot who has not done as much), but the basis of his method, as an adjustment to the happenings about us, is a profound acceptance by euphemistic translation (as with the old Greeks who, believing the left side unlucky, induced warriors to fight on the left flank of the army by calling it the "well-named").

Further Paradoxes of the "Evasive"

There is still another unexpected paradox about the matter of the Relevant but "Evasive." Though utopian literature is frequently chosen as a supreme example of the evasive, since it enables people to close their eyes to the sufferings about them by enabling them to dream of some ideal world existent in the mind, one has history itself to bear witness that in sweet and placid Utopias the most ferocious revolutions may lie concealed. Could a man, by reading, keep his mind closed all day and every day to the disturbances about him, the evasiveness of books which picture lovely existences, as contrasted with the harshness of our actual environment, would be fairly well established. I, for my part, admit that I would concern myself with nothing else, and would go dreamily on, devouring one picture of loveliness after another, while the whole damned world toppled all about me. But if the critic thinks that there is any serviceable evasion in such books, let him choose a particularly good one, let him live in a set of fancies slavishly suited to his mentality and his desires, and then, when he has laid down his book, let him go into a stenchy subway and look at the putty-faced guard operating the doors of the subway train, a man who has lived in solitary confinement under the earth for several years, and whose most recurrent thought is a terror lest someone wrest this privilege from him. Or let the critic read on, until there is a knock at his study door—and his family enters wailing, to announce the sheriff. All that I mean is this: If literature could keep us closed, then we should be fools not to stay closed with the aid of literature—but literature which closes us for a few hours, only to expose us all the more brutally a few hours later as the imperatives of non-literature and anti-literature again crowd upon us, is like that early day of spring I recall, when I opened myself to spring too soon, and so, when the snow came at evening, I shivered as I had never shivered in January.

Turning now to dingier Utopias, those crude pictures of worldly success which have formed so large a portion of our verbal and cinematic imagery in America, we find that these too could easily be interpreted as making people dissatisfied with the situation in which they find themselves. The "society drama" was a good vehicle for selling new styles of clothing and automobiles, when these could be bought. It built up a corpus of imagery, very serviceable to manufacturers as to what the "good life" was, suggesting exactly what one should get to attain the good life—and so long as these things could be got, it certainly acted to foster an evasion of any other interests. But if these things could not be got, what then? Would not this same literature merely serve to aggravate unrest? And is that not why, though a few years ago we heard of nothing but our "higher standard of living" (our accumulations of bought products), we now read featured articles in the news telling how some leading commercialist has praised "things of the mind" as a sounder road to the good life than was the constant purchase of commodities? By granting our critic that the "success" literature was the perfect machinery for "evasion" under the set of conditions formerly applying, we bring up the possibility that its relevance may be of a different sort if these conditions have materially changed. The fact that it was evasively relevant to one situation may make it irritatingly relevant to another. And if this literature was evasively relevant to a situation of prosperity, in that it enabled people to glorify their prosperity, what of its relevance when so important a factor in the situation as prosperity itself has been eliminated? The scheme had made people feel that they *ought* to buy, if they hoped to have rating in their own and other people's eyes. So when people no longer could buy, the scheme could very easily become a direct cause of pain, and hence of resentment and unrest. In substance they had been given a picture of the good life, they had been convinced that the good life is to be sought here and now, and then after economic upheavals they found that further progression towards this good life was interfered with.

There is a tendency to draw too thorough an analogy between the flattering materialistic dreams sponsored in the vulgus by our "success" literature, and those once sponsored by the priests—yet there is an important difference between them. The promise of success in heaven very effectively lifts the issue beyond the reach of pragmatic testing; in fact, once such a cosmic order is accepted, each added deprivation becomes one more harbinger of ultimate reward. But the promise of prosperity at one's present address and forthwith can very soon leave one bitter if prosperity comes not (particularly if, within this promise, there is implicit the awful suggestion that only by financial advancement can a human being respect himself). The great cause of so much turbulence in the history of American labor has not been labor agitation—for there is a deep dislike of protest in the American mind; the American would much rather "conform" if conformity is possible, not out of cowardice, but because conformity was one of the qualities most called into play in the quick upbuilding of his nation (a nation, like a house, is most quickly put together if the parts are standardized). So although the American laborer has been almost wholly without an ideology of protest (as compared with the strong socialist leanings in Europe for over half a century, whereas in America the region of protest was left to the "evasive" poets), he has yet protested often and violently. These protests have probably arisen because he was indirectly equipped for protests after all, since his belief in the materialistic aspects of the good life brought him so quickly to degradation and despair whenever his possibilities of material advancement were hampered. Teach people that the essence of a culture is in purchases, and if their purchasing power becomes impaired you may blow up a continent.

The "Push Away From" as prior to the "Pull Toward"

Though I offer these considerations to suggest that it is not always easy to assign one brand of literature definitely to one category, I should also admit that critics are fully justified in attempting to establish the "evasive" kind of relevancy if they can do so. We know what it means to have incipient cancer, and to take opiates instead of going under the knife. And if the tertiary world now suffers an economic cancer, so that we cannot safely think of anything else until it is removed, a critic is rightly jealous lest systematized evasions turn our efforts to matters which, however valid they may be as subjects for human contemplation, either lack the importance of a menace or are in themselves menacing in that they disguise a menace. There are two opposing tendencies in the human mind: the tendency to shirk to avoid the unpleasant; and the tendency to grapple with a knotted problem, even in our sleep, until it is solved. And the two conflicting tendencies, working together, can have a very sinister effect, leading us to find a *solution* for the problem, but to make this solution of a pleasant nature which permits us relaxation—hence "evasion" by a leaning toward symbolic cures in place of realistic ones. The symbolic cure may enable us to put a grappling and a shirking together (as with our bank clerk who atoned for his breach with society by picturing himself dying of it—he thus letting the *lex talionis* work symbolically, canceling his debt through retribution by proxy). So if we feel that there is an economic problem, to be met on economic terms, we may see any deflection of emotions as a risk; we may even be worried to note greater promiscuity than usual, or greater withholding—for once strange exaltations enter to obscure the issue, we can expect in the end some general alighting upon a wholly deceptive enthusiasm, ranging anywhere from love-feasts to a slaughtering of niggers in the name of God.

To say that human beings are primarily involved with matters of adjustment is to say that they are forever solving problems. Incentives, in other words, are fundamentally negative. Food is not initially an invitation to eating—hunger is the incentive, and food is found by experience to be the thing which one must "move toward" in order to "move away from" hunger. Thus, it is no accident that the nihilistic has often preceded the revolutionary. For besides the mere analogy between social growth and bodily metabolism, which suggests that some of the social waste is to be carried off if the anabolistic process is to provide the cells with fresh sustenance, there is also the fact that the negative is real and indubitable, whereas the positive that matches it is a kind of discovery by trial and error. The infant soon learns that food is the proper expedient for the stilling of hunger; but the infant has a very limited range of experimentation at the time this "problem" first arises. When hungry, it can try shouting, it can try squirming, it can try sucking, not much else. It tries all three, and eventually discovers that the third expedient is the most effective (though it will still try the others at times; and if the issue is complicated a little, as when the child has a colic caused by hunger, it may in its distress become so confused as to the nature of its problem that it will even push aside the breast frantically). If it had a greater opportunity for experiment on this important subject, it might need years to learn the exact expedient for stilling hunger, and in the scope of its trial-and-error process we might even find it doing such exceptionally inappropriate things as praying, reading "escape" literature, and voting for Mr. Hoover.

This doctrine, I know, is abhorrent to common sense, which holds that an incentive is a definitely imagined thing, drawing us toward it like a siren or a divine beacon—and I should hesitate to offer it did I not have the authority of so keen a man as Mr. Bertrand Russell to fall back upon, particularly the chapter on this subject in his book *The Analysis of Mind.* According to the view of common sense, he says, "What comes first in desire is something imagined, with a specific feeling related to it, namely, that specific feeling which we call 'desiring' it. The discomfort associated with unsatisfied desire, and the actions which aim at satisfying desire, are, in this view, both of them effects of the desire." His contrary view, which I have been trying to state in my own words, is that "the primitive non-cognitive element in desire seems to be a push, not a pull, an impulsion away from the actual, rather than an attraction towards the ideal." He cites the example of food (and incidentally, this example might be carried into adult life as well; for we have some-times heard a man, after some illness or an unbalanced diet, com-plaining that he is hungry "for something"; he himself is unable to decide what this "something" is, so he goes to the cupboard, looks over all sorts of things, even cinnamon, until his eye alights on the "right" thing, the vinegar cruet perhaps, and vinegar promptly be-comes the "incentive"; yet he had gone to the cupboard, earnestly requiring vinegar, with no notion at all that it was vinegar he required). Mr. Russell also cites the vagaries of sex in which, despite the imperiousness of the unrest, the sexual "negative" arises compa-ratively late in human development, so that the range of experimen-tation is now considerable, with the result that people can spend a whole lifetime trying to still their sexual hunger in extravagantly inappropriate ways. This explanation, it will be observed, can omit entirely the picturesque psychoanalytic concept of "repression" and a "censor," a legalistic borrowing which has generally given rise to the plethora of "escape" and "evasion" charges. Mr. Russell could simply say that, instead of "escape," one failed to find the "ideal" that would best fit the actualities of his particular discomfiture, being largely misguided by reason of the various false leads in his training and vocabulary.

The fundamental negativeness of our impulses is a distinction not without grave practical import. Mr. Russell's explanation, for in-stance, would account perfectly for a symptom of drug addiction once considered primary by doctors, much to the misfortune of addicts. It was noted that opium-eaters developed, besides their need for the drug, a distinct opium hunger, a craving for the *taste* of opium. Accordingly, when the hypodermic needle was invented, earnest practitioners who had no need of metaphysics in their daily rounds decided that the craving of the palate could be eliminated were they to administer opiates by injection, since the patients would thus never learn the *taste* of opium. Great was their exalta-tion on finding this subterfuge for removing an important lure to relapse—and they were some time in discovering that the mor-phinist, instead of a craving for the taste of opium on his tongue, now suffered a greedy fascination at the thought of a hypodermic needle puncturing his veins. The dreaded negative (the "withdrawal symptoms" under morphine hunger) remained the same in either case; but the nature of the positive, the attracting image, the "ideal," changed in accordance with the prior tactics of administration.

Increasing Definiteness of the "Pull Toward"; Greater Precision of the "Ideal"

This priority of the negative also has an important bearing upon the problem of literary criticism. For one thing, it should throw light upon the literature of romantic, individualistic protest, a literature in which the "negativistic" aspect was very pronounced. Here the documentation as to the "away from" has been vast, and of a generally uniform tenor. In some way or other, all the romanticists were proclaiming their indubitable dissatisfaction with the environment in which they were placed. Their attitude is perfectly epitomized in Melville's words, "not so much bound to any haven ahead as rushing from all havens astern," or Baudelaire's "Anywhere out of the world." They were all suffering from an illness, or from some radically unbalanced diet, the result of an inadequate existence, of some sort or another, forced upon them by the social machinery among which they moved (whether it was forced upon them as it is forced upon a subway guard, or forced upon them by more devious compulsions as it is forced upon a pampered young heir, does not here matter to our purposes). So they were hungry "for something," and they went to the cupboard, and the variety of things they wanted there is indeed fantastic. One shouted in elation when his eyes fell upon the vinegar cruet—another, turning green at the very thought of vinegar, plunged into the honey pot. And whatever food each wanted, he wanted it so intensely, its discovery was such a revelation to him, that he could not imagine how anything else than this could be the generic need of all mankind. In a civilization so warped that everyone was living an unbalanced life, no one could rest until he had proved himelf balanced: hence a *mania for the normative* raged alongside an infinitude of personal norms. It also looks silly when we apply the matter to foods, where we are easily cynics and know that tomorrow we will turn against the things we enjoy today—but when the needs become "spiritual" needs, our ready admissions about the relativity of tastes drop away; and when we cannot prove to ourselves that all people *do* want the same thing, we compromise by saying that they *should.*

Today, out of myriad protests (a century of vivid social criticism which, it is safe to say, has left not a single act or interest or fleeting thought of mankind without its well-documented detractors), we now find that a sifting-down has taken place. And as large fortunes have been sifting into fewer and fewer hands, so the multiplicity of trials and errors seems correspondingly narrowed in the search for the positive that will match our negative. The movement to Tahitis became practically impossible as Western methods were "evangelized" throughout the world, and primitive peoples grew merely "corrupt," losing the finer aspects of their own social orders and coming in contact only with the harsher aspects of ours. A kind of "sub-Whitmanizing" took place, as romantic authors tried to accommodate themselves to the unescapable world by a deliberate glorification of its vices: toughs, drinking orgies, sexual promiscuity, bull-fighting, etc. They tried to persuade themselves that they were getting from the tertiary into the primary by way of the brutal. But a strictly economic factor came more and more into prominence. Whereas the old romantics had said, "The system is despicable; do not surrender to it," authors began to look about them, to see literally millions of people begging for the chance to work; and they concluded, "Why, you couldn't surrender to this system if you wanted to. You can't even 'knuckle down' and behave. If your spirit of old imaginings is broken, and you are willing to do nothing but push some button or turn some screw to the end of your days, and for a pittance, even on these groveling terms you can't continue." Or otherwise stated: Our existence has been made more and more dependent upon purchases, and we have become less and less able to purchase. The romantics were dealing with broader ills—and if ever this immediate issue is solved, we may find that we still have a strong negative at work in us, a "pushing away" for which the corresponding "pull toward" has not yet been formulated. Meanwhile, there is a crucial dilemma of a strictly economic nature, which might be removed by appropriate action of a strictly political nature—and the *Cause*, for all its ennoblement in some quarters, is at bottom a very realistic project for taking full account of the fact that we now live by purchases, and that our economic institutions must be so altered that the possibilities of purchase are properly extended to all who would live. Thus, those jealous of "evasions" feel that they have found the particular "food" for our "key" hunger of today, and they do not want us, by the vagaries of trial and error, to experiment with inappropriate "ideals." By facing "realities" in this sense, they would mean dealing with an important economic ill on economic terms; and they would call any other way of dealing with this ill an "evasion" or a "chimera"—and I do not see why any one should care to say them nay. If there are further and deeper changes still to be undergone, may this immediate revolution of expedients soon be accomplished, that the fundamental revolution can begin.

Mr. John Maynard Keynes has written,

At present the world is being held back by something which would have surprised our fathers—by a failure of economic technique to exploit the possibilities of engineering and distributive technique; or, rather, engineering technique has reached a degree of perfection which is making obvious, defects in the economic technique which have always existed, though unnoticed, and have doubtless impoverished mankind since the days of Abraham. I mean by economic technique the means of solving the problem of the *general* organization of resources as distinct from the *particular* problems of production and distribution which are the province of the individual business technician and engineer. For the next twenty-five years, in my belief, economists, at present the most incompetent, will be nevertheless the most important, group of scientists in the world. And it is to be hoped—if they are successful—that after that they will never be important again. But during this horrid interval, when these creatures matter, it is of vast importance, that they should be free to pursue their problem in an environment—for they, with their mixed subject matter, are of all men the least independent, as the history of their theory shows, of the surrounding atmosphere—uninfluenced, as far as possible, by the bias of the other motifs.

It is no insult to a burning issue to hope that it will someday cease to be burning. Mr. Keynes says that the "defects in the economic technique which have always existed, though unnoticed, and have doubtless impoverished mankind since the days of Abraham," have now been "brought to a head, or at least brought to notice, by the radical changes in modern technique." The issue, always a burning issue to some unfortunate members of the community, whether they knew it or not, has become a burning issue for almost everyone, since we live on purchases, and thus must live on purchasing power. The one important consideration (for our purposes) which Mr. Keynes has omitted from this statement (though not from the implications of the article from which the statement is taken) is the fact that not only economists, but literary agitators and political allies, must take an important part in this work. The problem is not purely a problem of economics—for were the economic expedients completely formulated, there would still be the business of getting them adopted. Here enters the whole field of persuasion—hence, at this point we move into the field of literary criticism. Hence the admonitions of critics who are jealous lest literature obscure, rather than assist, our meeting of this problem. Hence, no wonder that the jealous should become at times too jealous, suspecting the most harmless doctrines as "rival" doctrines. For if a man so much as plays a game of tennis he is, for the duration of the game, "evading" the burning economic issue. While the game is on, he is lost hopelessly among the "chimeras."

Category of the Relevant but Wrong

Add now a further consideration. Suppose we have stopped to note that tennis is a game particularly characteristic of the "enemy." We are now about to move beyond our category of the Relevant but "Evasive" into the category of the Relevant but Wrong. It is not tennis, however, but the privilege making tennis possible—leisure—that has usually been brought into question. Having called the key situation economic, and having decided that this key situation cannot be remedied until economic privileges restricted to the few are distributed among the group, the critics note that high among these privileges is leisure—and strangely enough, instead of advocating leisure as one of the good things to be seized by those they would emancipate, they ferret out and condemn all "leisure class" thinking as a prime characteristic of the enemy. If the logic is not completely cogent, however, they do arrive at their position by emotional agglutinations which are quite understandable. If a pillow has been sat upon by the beloved, it becomes an appealing pillow; if sat upon by the "enemy," we may think of it with loathing—and leisure is the pillow upon which the enemy sat. Or again, recall the old pope who, concerned for the welfare of his flock, and noting that many immoral ballads were written in the Ionic mode (the mode with intervals corresponding to those in the key of C), banned this mode from the church as being itself immoral. And conversely, we have actually heard a man in the new mood scorn all logic on the grounds that logic was once an "enslaving device" of the Roman Catholic schoolmen.

Similarly such words as "conservative" and "revolutionary," though they are properly but technical terms for designating an attitude toward a situation, are allowed to take on an emotional tinge, a note of approval or suspicion, under the implication that a writer should be categorically one or the other—so the critics now in favor of change will impugn a past writer as conservative without stopping to consider that the situation in which this man lived might best have been improved by the mildest forms of criticism, as one might better budge a strong monarch by pleading "Come now, your Majesty" than by shouting "Down with the King." Can even an arch-rebeller deny that there must have been times in the world's history when it was extremely appropriate to have the merely "ameliorative" attitude of the conservative—as it might be in America even now, had not our industrialists already been too revolutionary, had they shown more of the quietude of certain enwrapped poets now under suspicion for expressing them, and less enterprise in their financial imaginings (for we learn in their own words that they have made "revolutionary" contributions to the icebox, the shoestring, et cetera). Had we but been conservative enough in half our thinking, and not surrounded ourselves with a clutter of cheap newness, we might without disaster permit ourselves to be conservative in the remainder of our thinking. But a new tool is only a half-invention—the invention not being complete as a social contribution until we have also invented the way of controlling it. If some men suddenly took to poisoning city reservoirs on a grand scale, we should have to develop new practices for taking this strange appetite properly into account; as regards our past ways of storing water, our new means of protection might even seem "revolutionary"—and there is some evidence that the reservoirs of decent living have thus gradually been poisoned. So, as we claim that a revolutionary in Paradise would be an ass, we must by the same token admit that a non-revolutionary would be very inappropriate in our present anti-Paradise—but that is no grounds for attempting to place a categorical stigma upon conservatives, and then, having established it, to broaden it out until it touches everyone who is not exactly as revolutionary as oneself, and in exactly the same way.

"Smugness" is another word that dissolves under scrutiny. I ceased speaking of "bourgeois-smugness" when, at the John Reed Club, I heard Marx cited with John-Reed-Club-smugness. Smugness is not the property of one person—it is a name for the relationship between two persons, one of whom has let his mind go dead on a certain issue while the other is very much in agitation on this same issue. "Smugness" is the word which the agitated mind applies to the quiescent mind as an indication that this discrepancy between the two minds has been observed. We are all smug on some matters—we are all smug now in the once very unsmug belief that the earth goes round the sun, so smug that a man who held the opposite belief would probably go quite mad in arguing with us. And there are dreadful proletarian smugnesses: as with slum-dwellers who know so firmly that they should be good Catholics, should burden themselves with a whole kitchenful of children, and should keep Tammany in office.

Leisure and the "Error of Limitations"

Similarly with the attempts to dispose categorically of the "leisure class mind." True, there is the woman kept in a rich man's stable. There is the one-piece harem. She winters, let us say, in the South and summers in Europe. She daily tends and nourishes those parts of herself that frame her feminine core, and she may even perfect her accent that her flesh be somehow made more delightful to the man that claims her, or to an occasional pilferer. She is "leisure class," to be sure—but I see no fundamental error in her ways. We may hold it against her that she receives the vital issues of the day too glancingly; we may point to an "error of limitations," since she is closed to many important factors, as in some ways the parson's wife is similarly closed (however little each may relish the juxtaposition of the other). Both she and the parson's wife are specialists, like the insects—penetrative as regards a certain limited range of motions, but completely unaware of all else. Yet it is no error per se to sun oneself as graciously as one can. And this same "leisure class" opportunity may be utilized broadly by a person of broad intellect—as I can imagine nothing more "bourgeois" or "leisure class" than the origins out of which Mr. C. K. Ogden's remarkable *International Library of Psychology, Philosophy, and Scientific Method* arises, yet these books bristle with fecund speculations which, though there is a continual willingness to check them against observation, to restrict hypothesis by the test of empirical data, often lead to inferences more fanciful than the uncritical reaches of an ecstatic. Indeed, as we follow the rigors of these books, we understand why the economic theories now serving to glorify the proletariat were formulated by a man posessing precisely those advantages of leisure which at that time were open to the bourgeois class alone.

If the mere use of a special privilege is in itself a derogatory sign, even though the man who used it was personally powerless to change the institutions by which such privilege arose, then we are all reprehensible as regards good beef. It (good beef) is certainly entitled, in the eyes of heaven, to revolt against us if it can find a way of doing so, but in the interim we will not permit it to call us sadists for enjoying it with mushrooms. Were any single individual in the leisure class personally responsible for the maintenance of special privilege, I should say that he required a special type of mind, of an especially unpleasant sort, to maintain these privileges for himself while denying them to the collectivity. We might even see the makings of such an individual in our pudgy and hard-working president. But as a matter of fact, the personal responsibility of the average person enjoying the privileges of the "system" (be he a Guggenheim or a young "revolutionary" author touring Europe on a Guggenheim fellowship) is no greater than that of any worker suffering under the lack of them—it may be less in fact, since the worker should obviously take the initiative in bringing about a change, as he is the aggrieved party, and the aggrieved party is the one properly to bring suit in the courts of history. ("Bring suit in the courts of history"—that is, organize in protest; and he will be surprised how many of the maligned bourgeois he will find on his side.)

One cannot logically condemn leisure for arising out of inequality unless one shows that leisure cannot rise out of equality as well. And it is even doubtful that a person of the leisure class would be unfit to deal, profoundly and sympathetically, with the fundamental miseries of the proletariat. Though not goaded by the incentives of material necessity, he might bedevil himself with the problems of workers. In order to feel the issues with the same force as downtrodden or unsupported colleagues, he would, it is true, have to make up the difference by being much more imaginative than they (as many a "leisure class" poet of the past was, conversely, a proletarian of the pen who outstripped his leisure-class colleagues by being more imaginative, in leisure-class imaginings, than they; and I even knew a poet who worked fourteen hours a day in a packing house, but devoted the remainder of his time to leisure). One can easily imagine a privileged young heir who had seen the inside of a factory or the outside of an employment office only when slumming, yet had precisely such an imaginative curse upon him as filled him with a deep, unreasoning fear of poverty. The mere enjoying of a privilege, even if enjoyed at the incidental expense of other men, does not "brand" a person. A sweet old lady remains a sweet old lady, though you prove that her sweetness is really a luxury product, financed by warped child-bodies working at the looms of her deceased husband's cotton mills—a sweetness that may remain sweet precisely because, through hiring others to bear the strain of annoyances, she may be enabled to keep her sweetness from being put to any acid test. The sweetness of another old lady, who had remained sweet despite a life of hardships and disappointments, might be a more remarkable thing; and it would, since rarer and more difficult, rightly be considered more of a triumph, but not more of a sweetness unless it was, in itself, regardless of origins, sweeter. This is one of the reasons, in fact, why the problems of protest are today so complex. People need not be "vicious" in proportion to the damage that underlies their privileges. A Neronic tyranny arises out of the character of our institutions.

Wherein Leisure Is Demagogically Defended

When I realize how many desirable human qualities and privileges have lately been brought into question by the theorists of emancipation, I can imagine a demagogue among critics, haranguing laborers, and inveighing against these other critics, thus:

"It begins to seem that the petty bourgeois critics, who have come to the support of labor, would in spite of themselves try to cheat the workers all over again. For even while conceding the workers their right to participate in the ownership of the means and sources of production, these critics would warn the proletariat that certain amenities of thinking, certain elegancies of past poetry, certain charming kinds of ironic tolerance and melancholy, must be shunned as a special prerogative and property of the favored classes. Presumably they would confine the workers to a kind of rough and illiterate writing—and to substantiate their position they would call up the very course of history. By pointing out that 'thou wert' is feudal, or aristocratic, and that 'you were' is bourgeois, they would insist that 'you was' is all that is left for the proletariat. They warn you against gentle poets, while weeping over a coalminer—yet what can they hold out to this coalminer but an eventual opportunity to surround himself with the materials of poetry? Unless the future is to justify itself by being a pretty future, let us remember that the future has adequate protection in merely not being born. And instead of turning against poets because these poets cannot corral voters, let them consider the plight of poets and the plight of coalminers as identical, thus framing their agitative pamphlets to remedy both. Let us even dare say that the world might become so bearable a place, so like a garden in the morning (as those with eyes turned back upon the past restore this past to the future) that people will be smug, conservative, leisure-class, loving elegance, delighting in keen scholastic ergotisms, startling one another with accounts of the most ingenious personally pursued chimeras, given to conceits, to badinage, to the plumbing of abstruse methodologies, entertaining guests with outrageous caricatures of their friends' peculiar habits, and like the old East, relegating to the class of professional soldiers and thieves the ambitious merchants who scheme in behalf of individual aggrandizement. One dare expect all this, except that it will be obtained at the expense of no man—it will be there for all, and people will vie with one another in difficult relaxations, some, it is true, merely causing themselves to rot with sexual or alimentary gluttony (it will not matter if their illnesses die with them), while others will think of both physical and mental things in terms of athletic firmness, denying themselves no excess through absurd reasons of restraint, but being moderate nonetheless because the over-indulging of one preference would involve the slighting of another. I have seen photographs of Soviet leaders playing chess, as empowered proletarians, in a leisured moment, manipulating chimeric symbols brought down from a feudal order—and similarly, why may not workers consider as their own all the subtle maneuverings of the king, and queen, and bishops, and knights, and rooks of the mind? The critics are moved by a strange sense of sacrifice. They feel that every man should give up something for the Revolution; and as they would not like to give up their apartments, they have compromised by sacrificing a few gentle, conscientious, but not wholly apposite poets. Or since some literature, written for rich men, has been elegant, we may find fragile fellows heralding works as strong and fit because couched in a loose and not very difficult vernacular which they would lecture their children for using in the presence of a rival. Indeed, by some strange lacuna between their thesis and their behavior, they see no discrepancy in praising crude sentences and using their pay to buy themselves fine furniture. These men's houses are as neat as they can make them— and so you are entitled to consider all the aspects of mental neatness open to your efforts. In this way also you will further avoid the charges of 'defection' that are laid against you when, in seizing opportunities for personal advancement, you turn against your fellows. I would not for a moment build a set of exhortations upon any hope that you would remain loyal to a principle when you could advance yourself by denying this principle. I say simply, 'Be treacherous whenever treachery will profit you; but there will be so damned few of you that have a chance at profitable treachery, that you will remain allies after all.'"

Fallacy of the Swindled Poles

If a man considers some proposition inconsistent, generally it is enough for him to present his proofs. In the presence of these new proposed impoverishments, however, when critics are eager to bring into question all sorts of elegancies in past art, advocating cultural sparsity in the name of proletarian advance, a discussion confined strictly to logic would leave our orientation too incomplete. One of the most significant traits here is the *excessiveness* of their step, requiring so many choices and exclusions *beyond the logical necessity*—thus we may suspect an emotional factor, to be explained by theories of genesis involving the emotions. In other words, we must turn from the logical to the psychological. So I herewith offer a hypothesis, which interests me primarily by reason of a little paradox contained in it: That the broad esthetic reversals proposed in the name of the collectivity really stem from the critic's individualistic origins. By this account, there is the old romantic rebel speaking in them, deep down, and not so much disguised as one might think.

We have already mentioned the pillow which takes on different *meanings* according to the views of the sitter upon it, and the strange way whereby the mode in which "Home Sweet Home" and "Old Black Joe" are sung became immoral. If a stepmother is cruel and has a wart, warts mean to the stepchild cruelty—so the symbolism of a wart will vary as our past has put warts on cruel stepmothers or kindly, ineffectual old clergymen. And it is told that in a mill town, where there was a large colony of Polish mill hands, they had been so regularly cheated by people who gained their confidence speaking fluent Polish, that the best swindling thereafter was done in English. One can conceive the process: how their Polish syllables, being spoken during the protected years of childhood, had cohered with their deepest images of comfort; how this welding had been made all the stronger by their exposure in an alien country where their bosses spoke only a few Polish words of command, and these disdainfully, with an almost purposely wrong accent; how sweet it must have been when a man came to them, offering bad stocks that would supposedly make them rich and comfortable, saying it in soft Polish, not in harsh, wrongly pronounced command-Polish, and so linking the pathos of the future with the pathos of the past; one can imagine the wrenching when the investments were proved worthless, and in the breaking of past and future asunder they also underwent the breaking of a more fundamental logic, a snapping of the connectives between their hope of well-being and the very speech in which they thought. Consider the patience of such people, that they did not promptly run amok (in their need of simplicity, that they might decide quickly who the enemy was, as in random lynchings), making anything outside themselves the enemy, dividing the world into the rough compartments of Self and Non-Self, and finding relief by letting Self strike any portion of Non-Self that happened in the way. Such madness, or metaphysics, would have seemed quite just to me—yet these people did in actuality merely turn to English-speaking crooks, testing the equally blind cohesion between their hopes of prosperity in America and their respect for English as the language of authority ("authority" in turn, perhaps, being made to look like "good authority" through the unsuspected collaboration of their religious cohesions, since God was both "authoritative" and "good").

Our acts are latent in these associative alignments of our thinking—as a banker, since "bank" is welded to "safety," gets his money for gambling from people who deposit their funds with him because they abhor gambling (an awkward welding which often results in his keeping his profits for himself and sharing his losses with his depositors)—and those who would budge their countrymen are really faced with little more than the strategy of welding new associations and unwelding old ones, so that the formerly feared looks desirable and the formerly tolerated looks fearsome (a change obtained, in the devious ways of poetry, by putting a burglar's mask on a president and giving the outcast a cross). Accordingly it is not at all exorbitant that, in the midst of great national heavings, when several millions of people were in acute distress, an acrid cry should arise among some New York literary men to turn against certain conscientious but not wholly apposite schools which had generally been the admirations of their youth. It was as though one could not properly start the Revolution without first killing off a few poets. The critics, having decided that a reversal was needed, were prepared at least to make a pattern of reversal in their own minds by turning against their one-time literary mentors. In the belief that the external world needed a reshuffling, they modestly prepared for it by a reshuffling within—and whereas, but a few years ago they had hoped to develop their understanding by the gradual inclusion of new areas (the "chambered nautilus" or "coral island" method of upbuilding by small accretions), they now prepared to be struck blind and then suddenly see, getting their new affirmations by negating what they had been, undoing past cohesions with one brutal rip (the method of Saul become Paul). So we find one critic warning us that his old Symbolist masters were no longer serviceable as "guides"; we find another, who had written a lovely book of verse picturing the Poet against the World, now suavely burlesquing this whole way of seeing; we find another even risking ribald comment by warning against leisure-class traditions while himself teaching at a university (school, σχολή, leisure); and though Goethe's entire outlook is based upon the awareness of change, we find another condemning him for having accepted change in the chambered-nautilus way rather than in the terms of a Saul-Paul reversal.

Genetic Account of the Saul-Paul Reversal: At-one-ment for the Sin-against-Society

This call for simple reversal arises, I submit, from the fact that no man of the present generations devoted himself to letters in America without a thorough grounding in the pattern of our bank clerk's wretchedness. Illness, grotesque appearance, disordered family life, hypochondriac imaginings, inability to conform, through awkwardness, timidity, or sullenness—such were the experiences he lived among, and for such there was a wealth of archives amassed by brilliant men. I do not for a moment take these traits at their face value. In each of these so-called weaknesses there is a power (and the poet who remains a poet does so because he is on their power-side). Why in God's name should a trait which is to serve a man at forty or fifty—after much reworking—show in a good light at eighteen? The best promise should be in the worst gawk. In any case, I take it as a general rule that one's first significant explorings in literature are made at a time when a great curse is upon him—and if you will follow me no further, you will at least follow me in this: That one reads avidly in his "formative" years, that formative years are distinguished most of all by their formlessness, and that this formlessness, in an eager adolescent reader, is made most painfully apparent precisely by his daily contemplation of much that is well-formed—since even a work of fiction so overwhelming to its maker that it was merely slung together will generally have a pronounced consistency about its characters, and each of these characters will be a portion of the young reader, an incipient trend of his own, here expanded into a dominant principle of conduct, so he lives among all sorts of inducements to make himself think of his own fluctuant nature as a set of wasted potentialities, his discomfiture being aggravated, in this test-period of adolescence at least, by the thought that a non-literary brother could establish himself by starting anywhere, that he could become a shoemaker simply by learning to mend shoes, that he was on the road to being an engineer as soon as he entered a school of engineering, whereas the discipline of art was a vaguer matter, which some acquired by being doctors, others by studying old texts, and others by hopping freights, or making love, or getting shot at, so one had no label by which he could know for a certainty that he even had hold of the right thing.

He rotted—before he had really come to life, he rotted. If a man does not always have the same newspaper heroes as the rest (and for exactly the same length of time), if one does not shout always for the home team, if one has (in a work of art) met with mockery for something which his fellows accept without question, there is deep within him a gnarling. He is subtly pitted against others—yet he is in no shape to be pitted against others, for though he may not admire the quality of their attainments, he is unsettled by the undeniable concreteness of them (concreteness, the formed—as against his formlessness). He cannot hold his position soundly enough to silence his own internal murmurings. He does not so much as know how to surrender. Perhaps, under a slow distress, he makes slowly the division between Self and Non-Self which we had expected to see made suddenly by the swindled Poles under their sudden distress. Picture him, then, as unpresentably as you like, restive, with documents enough to start him on countless lines of thought and too scant to finish him on any, blunderingly at odds with his fellows, and uneasy at being so, despite all boastfulness—and note how, out of this repugnant chaos, he gradually constructs himself a tiny kernel of cosmos, and builds it more firmly, as one by one he comes upon those authors who, without his even knowing that they existed, seem to have shaped their speech especially for him, giving him exactly the terms (in images, in the particular things singled out for approval, disapproval, and mere neutral notice, in personae and the quality of their acts) that best handle his particular complexities and enable him to set his momentary glimpses of life into a larger structure of meanings. Henceforth he has a rock—or rather, the beginnings of a rock, for there is still much fundamental shiftiness, uncertainty in matters of affection, the niggardliness of proofs that he is at last moving forward (when all about him there is such a general insistence that one should move forward, and there are so many generally accepted criteria as to just what moving forward is). In any case, he now has two dominant moods: one of misgiving, as he thinks of those about him whose interests are not sufficiently his interests; and one of strength, as he finds in certain poets the specific for his difficulties. But what is more natural than that these years, for all their fullness, should become profoundly distasteful to him, so that he would, in open or hidden ways, cringe at the thought of living through such an amorphous period again, dislike it so basically, so in the very marrow, that he will dislike anything associated with it: a particular house, a particular city, if he lived there at that time, and thus even the particular poets and philosophers who had then been his mainstay? And much later, when some public issue arises to which he can attach himself, when there is some cause of general betterment or emancipation to which he can subscribe, we may find him doing so in a most surprising fashion. We may find him, under the aegis of "contemporary realities," settling the old scores of his childhood—sallying forth, aglow with intensity, to wipe out his earlier crimes against society. Happy at last that he can think of himself as one of an army, he proclaims his restoration to the collectivity by damning the poets who had once upheld him during the painful years of his division. He slays the earnest dead men who had been the fulcrum of his development, and who had really become his masters in so subtle a sense that he is obeying them even as he makes this show of renouncing them. And would not this atonement be particularly pleasant if, under the guise of joining the collectivity, one were really inviting the collectivity to join him, as one presents a stimulating plan for reconciling old differences between the Self and the Group by having the Group change its ways in accordance with one's private ideas of the desirable? One plucks up precisely because he thinks he sees a way of making a world after his own heart—whereupon there may be a flowing back and forth in blissful collective faith—plus the final purging of the critic's lingering adolescent sin, as he replaces the associative weldings of those years by their simple opposites. The individual may slough his individualism, now that there is a promise of the collectivity's being made over; he may cease to think of his separateness, now that he hopes to induce society to abandon those malpractises which had led him to proclaim his separateness in the first place—and one recalls Lenin, how by his stubborn individualistic will, his personal integrity upheld through years of social ignominy, he maintained a code so particularistic that it advised thieving for the cause of honesty, lying in the cause of truth (he thus remaining personally firm in a moral order so naturally making for personal decay that it even admitted hypocrisy as a basic stratagem—a Gide could not have gone further). And we find the Collectivist state founded upon an exceptional concentration-point of individualism, who forced his private convictions upon the minority for the good of the minority, in order that this minority in turn might force its ways upon the majority for the good of that majority. Such bewilderments suggest that sectarian differences are but the varied stressing of a common orthodoxy, just as, looking back upon the dogmatic distinctions of the early church, we find it hard from our alien point of view to demarcate the opinions for which people burned from the opinions solemnly endorsed as Tridentine creed. In fact, the very struggle over "personality" recalls an old church quarrel, a dispute over the divisions of the Godhead, arising in great measure from the fact that in Latin the word *persona* meant an actor's mask, thence secondarily an actor's role, and thence by further derivation the role of a player playing a part in actual life. Thus, to match the distinctions between the individual and the collectivity, we find the Book of Common Prayer speaking of "three persons and one God," while the old Gnostics had argued whether the man Jesus was a distinct person from Christ. As an outcome, though the Latin word *personatio* means only "resonance," people emerged from the churchly dispute with something so priceless as a "personality," and the path was presumably cleared for a peasant in the French army to become more of an "individual" than Socrates had been.

It is not hard to see how one's thinking inevitably follows in the thought-patterns of his group. When a man, because his language has nouns and adjectives, finds a simple projection of this grammatical arrangement in the very nature of the universe, with "substances" for nouns and "attributes" for adjectives, or when, because his language can turn the word "green" into "greenness," the man discovers "greenness" as a thing in heaven, and finds that each individual green thing is green in that it shares this archetypical greenness, therein he makes his bow to the collectivity, pays his tribute to the genius of his people, though they consider it advisable to put him to death for an impious divergence from their ways. There are, on the surface, two kinds of artist, the gangster and the lone wolf—but we must remember that the lone wolf of art is calling always to some band that may come to be, and calling in the medium transmitted to him by some band that very definitely is or has been. In any case, the individual and the group are so hopelessly merged that any fundamental distinction here seems impossible— and rather than a breach, we disclose two modes for stressing the same awareness: a strong sense of relationship between the individual and his group. It is for this reason that we can trace the "individualist" emphasis and the "collectivist" emphasis back to precisely the same origins.

Adaptation by "Thought in General," as against Adaptation by "One Particular Brand of Thought"

Our entire section, up to this point, has been directed to showing the difficulties in the way of laying down "passwords" that will clearly distinguish friend from enemy, once the purely economic issue is broadened to include the whole range of imaginative literature. There seems a fair reason for holding that literature generally strengthens the imaginative and critical abilities of man—but as soon as we attempt to fix, once and for all, the effects of some particular school of literature, we run into a situation which remains clear exactly in proportion to our skirting of it, and suggests somewhat St. Augustine's paradox: "What is time? If you ask me, I do not know—but if you do not ask me, I do know." Critics who would make rigorous categorical distinctions, selecting certain thoughts as per se sterile and certain others as blanket indications of a "fruitful psychology," must assume that the effects of a given work or school are uniform upon all readers, otherwise their inclusions and exclusions on the grounds of social efficacy become pointless.

One may, it is true, having decided to discredit some school, be cunning enough to catch it "off its guard," at one of its weakest moments, but such a procedure is better suited to debating than to critical inquiry. On noting what dangerous end a certain way of thought *can* serve, people may define this end as the revelation of its *true* function. Once having shown that religion *can be* an opiate or *has been* an opiate, they feel entitled to call it an opiate always, despite the many known times in history when religion has made men act more as a stiff injection of cocaine or strychnine might do; they prowled, they jerked, they leaped at shadows. Opponents of a doctrine interpret some weak or faulty manifestation, perhaps even some perversion, as affording a glimpse into its "true inwardness"— which might be like damning chairs by proving that all the chairs made by a certain manufacturer collapsed. As the sitter was photographed sprawling upon the floor, the "real purpose" of chairs would be made evident. So, many who would pick some literary school, or some way of thought, for categorical attack, first select its obvious vices and then "interpret" its virtues as being merely these vices in disguise. Yet strangely enough, though Marxian doctrine is at present the prime stimulus in the attempt to discredit wide areas of literary excellence by such a method, there are exponents of the Marxian principles who deny that Marx's theories apply to the particular work of art at all. The theories, by this interpretation, would account for the arising of science and art in general out of man's productive equipment, but would grant the possibility that, once having arisen, the arts and sciences could obey demands of their own. Thus I quote from a book, *The Basic Principles of Scientific Socialism*, by an author whose admiration for the doctrines of Karl Marx is unqualified:

Certain learned critics, who ridicule the entire conception of historical materialism, believe that they can embarrass or completely overthrow it by one seemingly puzzling question that they are so fond of putting. "Do you mean to say," ask these savants, "that when a scholar makes a discovery or an artist creates a masterpiece, his accomplishment is merely the result of the promptings of necessity, of the economic requirements? What is the relation between the productive forces and those great intellects of scholars and scientists which must certainly have an influence upon historical evolution?" This question, enigmatic as it may seem, betrays a lamentable ignorance on the part of its formulators: We are primarily concerned, not with the single inventions and discoveries of science and art, but with *science and art in general*. According to historical materialism, science and art are not divine gifts, but the results of the perpetual struggle which man wages against the forces of nature. It is only through this struggle that man forms the desire and the will to reveal nature's secrets. Since this desire, the striving for scientific knowledge, has been developed through a separate instinct, it is no longer necessary, according to historical materialism, that every discovery be accounted for by a special economic cause.

Did Marxians generally base their critical exhortations upon this scheme of artistic genesis, rather than upon their "once a bourgeois, always a bourgeois" scheme of highly sensitized detectors for revealing the dangerous bourgeois virus lurking behind the most innocuous of exteriors, one could find little to complain of. Expanding the interpretation of the paragraph just quoted, we should see *literature in general* serving the practical purpose of equipping us in the "struggle for life" by *keeping the mind open*; and out of this statement we should draw the obvious critical exhortation that the best way of keeping the mind open would be by admitting the fullest possible range of literary responsiveness, on the grounds that each specialization, no matter what its limits, derives from its specializing some insight. We might seek to rate schools by our "error of limitations" concept, showing that some works took more factors into account than others—but we should eliminate entirely the notion of the "error per se" contained in the Saul-Paul reversal. We are happy to find some grounds for this schema in the statements of an exponent and admirer of Marxism—since it would further serve to explain why speculations and imaginings can continually be taking one beyond the strict requirements of his "class," and it gives us a basis in historical materialism itself for understanding how a coalminer might, for a few minutes, be able to follow a train of thought regardless of where it led, though it led to something so "subversive" to his needs of the moment as a forgiving of the checkers employed by the company to underweigh his load. Or again, it might help to explain that "lure of the esthetic" which made the philosophers of the "enlightenment" in France fashionable reading among the aristocracy, suggesting precisely a *transcendance* of class interests as an explanation why the presence of these men was sought to grace the aristocratic salons. That is, out of the requirements of struggle in general arise the implements of intelligence and imagination; but these, once having risen, *may* operate regardless of strict particularistic necessities. One can, living on a mountaintop, "see this condition through" even to the point where he comes down into the valley, as Faust arrived by study at the discovery that he had studied at the wrong times. And while it does seem reasonable to suppose that, were all the factors in a man's environment known, we could (by knowing the precise "combination" of his temperament) predict the nature of his output, there are too many environmental and personal factors of a non-economic nature for us to account for him by the coordinates of economic causality alone. Economic factors should certainly show their influence, since a man lives among them, and thus must adopt an attitude toward them just as he is likely, if he lives in the Australian brush, to adopt a pronounced attitude toward the Australian brush. But there is a big difference between saying that a certain attitude *takes a certain factor into account,* and saying that the attitude is *determined* by the factor.

However, this whole question as to the nature of esthetic "adaptability" has moved us out of the strictly psychological sphere in which we sought to account for the critics' exhortations as arising (by the Fallacy of the Swindled Poles) out of an attempt to reverse themselves in the cause of "atonement." We may now abandon our "genetic" approach, to discuss the same matter from the standpoint of logic.

Logical Account of the Saul-Paul Reversal: The Search for Antithesis

The logical basis of the Saul-Paul reversal seems to stem from the thesis-antithesis-synthesis schema as borrowed from Hegel and re-vamped by Marx. Since, by this schema, the thinking of the bour-geois oppressor will call forth "antithetical" thinking on the part of the proletarian oppressed, critics are now busy trying to help the inevitable course of history by discovering which of the thoughts thought by a bourgeois are bourgeois thoughts, so that they may advise the proletariat to think antithetical thoughts. The task is not an easy one. It is not a bourgeois thought, for instance, to observe on a sunny day that the sun is shining (yet if you observed too many sunny days in succession, the observation might become bourgeois since it tends to make for your "acceptance" of things as they are). Many thoughts can be simply anybody's thoughts. A thought does not become a typical bourgeois thought just because a bourgeois thought it, any more than the thought that water runs downhill becomes a typical French thought if thought by a Frenchman. So the decision as to what the proletarian Antithesis shall be, depends pretty much upon the things in which one happens to have been interested. The reborn bourgeois critic will try to become prole-tarian by negating his own individual past.

It is a kind of "open season" for criticism. Antithesis, coupled with the pliancy of the "escape" or "evasion" concept, enables one to shoot arrows at random into the air with perfect confidence that, wherever he turns, he will find them sticking in the hearts of his friends. There are, of course, some limits. Few critics, feeling that the bourgeois philosophers often talked good sense, would counsel the conscientious proletarian to adopt nonsense as the wholesome Antithesis—a kind of tentative Saul-Paul reversal which the French

Dadaist group entertained for a season (though I will admit, the man who damned logic as an enslaving device of the Roman Catholics came dangerously close to such a simplified kind of "insight"). The issue is nearer to a borderline when critics, noting several examples of "style" in bourgeois masterpieces, damn style as bourgeois in the interests of proletarian rescue.

As a kind of *tu quoque* refutation, we should note that although critics have invited poets to encourage all kinds of Antithetical discoveries, they usually confine their admonishments as closely within the frame of classic-bourgeois argumentation and exposition as they can manage (differing in this respect greatly from the spirited Dadaists, who carried their Antithesis consistently through their critical methods as well, dutifully replacing bourgeois order with anti-bourgeois disorder in everything they wrote). But it is doubtful whether the Marxian advocates of Antithesis, though condemning poets for their failure to abandon traditional "bourgeois" presentation, have written one single paragraph which does not have its ample prototypes in bourgeois criticism, stemming from such classic methods of inductive argument and such traditionally "environmental," "evolutionary" thinking as most strikingly distinguish the contributions of the nineteenth-century bourgeoisie. Surely if the breach between bourgeois and proletarian were thorough enough to justify a proletarian Antithesis, this breach should cut as deeply into our critical methods as into our "creative" ones (particularly as the Marxians are generally agreed that the old Platonic dualism between "form" and "content" is a myth, so that a new fruitfulness of content should automatically manifest itself as a new fruitfulness of form).

Of course, we may take observations and change their "weighting." A *Franzosenfresser* play written in German by a Hitlerite might be "reweighted" by our simply renaming the symbols in translation, making the French villain a German villain, and the German hero a French hero. We note a primitive Antithesis of this sort in the different "weighting" of Russian and American films. But such a mechanical shift is surely not the thing which advocates of Antithesis have in mind. It barely scratches the surface of our thought-patterns. Show me a Britisher thrilling to the Union Jack, and then show me an American thrilling to Old Glory, and as I turn from one to the other, I shall not expect the "new and fruitful." And I shall not be surprised to find that the "critical exhortations" behind the Union Jack bear a very close resemblance to the "critical exhortations" behind Old Glory. And conversely, where I do find a similarity in critical exhortation, I shall be led to anticipate a corresponding similarity in the sphere of the "poetic" or "imaginative."

The Extravagance of Antithesis: Wherein We Offer a Philosophy of History Which Makes a Distinction between an Antithesis and a Difference

The dilemma of the Antithetical has the further drawback that it is not a concept necessary to account for the facts. Despite Marx's great dislike of metaphysics and his desire to offer us a purely "scientific" explanation of history, he has built upon a term too metaphysical in its very nature for him to get quite clear of its "genius." Hegel's dialectic was a vast and novel scheme for giving us a metaphysic of history. Marx attempted to use his basic concept upon which to found a "science" of history. Yet, although the scientific method is based upon the "law of parsimony," the concept of a progression from thesis to antithesis, and thence to synthesis, is unnecessary. The processes of historic adjustment can be discussed without it.

We may say, for instance, that there are periods of comparative integration, periods when the customs and institutions, the attitudes and the economic practises of a people are sufficiently in tune with one another for the whole to present a general picture of consistency. I do not mean that there are not "ills." There may be a large slave class, for instance. But if this slave class, by reason of some doctrine, is induced to remain a slave class, the presence of this slave class does not constitute an "ill" in our purely technical sense of the word. *A society is integrated in this technical sense when its institutions enable one to do what they require of him, and its standards enable him to want to do what he is doing.* Were the slave class to develop a pronounced doctrine which made it resent its position as a slave class, and were this doctrine to stimulate slave disorders of one sort or another, we should say that to this extent the integrity of the cultural unit was impaired. If some of the priesthood began to read strange texts, thereby coming to the conclusion that the creed to which they subscribed was faulty, the integrity of the culture would be still further impaired. Or a new invention that changed the value of slave labor would even more clearly serve as a disintegrating factor. In other words, there has come a time when the culture must include "new matter." This new matter may be in the nature of an idea which changes the nature of people's desires and acquiescences. Or it may be some new device, which requires people to alter their ways of living, and hence secondarily their ways of thinking. As such divergencies mount, the cultural integer finds itself less and less able to assimilate the new matter within the terms of its traditional thoughts and institutions.

At this stage, desires are greatly out of line with requirements, so that we find people acting purely on the basis of "necessity," while feeling that if they did the things they "really wanted" to do, they would risk extinction or pauperization. Others, in their attempt to strike a balance between desires and requirements, teach them-selves to *want to do* desperate things, things which make for new turmoil in themselves, like men who hire out as mercenaries, or as high-pressure bond salesmen. Clearly, some of the culture's terms and methods are out of tune with other of its terms and methods. If it is to become an integer again, it must alter its frame of reference, taking care of the new matter by the discovery of a new order.

The society now suffers a disintegration, or reintegration, or both (depending upon the stretch of time one selects for his interpreta-tion, and the extent of the area one selects for his definition of a cultural unit, and somewhat upon the historian's personal notions as to what the "good life" is). In any case, we are faced with the spectacle of a society including new matter, or failing to include it, or first failing and then succeeding. And if it does enlarge and reshape the cultural frame appropriately, it may then become a new *integer*, possessing a new *order*, and a new set of *meanings*.

Technical Grounds for Being Mystical

This schema, which lays the emphasis upon a Difference rather than upon an Antithesis, has the further advantage of orientating, without the use of Freud's ambiguous and legalistic "escape" con-cept, the vigorous nihilistic, negativistic, mystic movements which arise during the period of pronounced disintegration. Far too much power and enterprise and intellectual brilliancy go into these move-ments for them to be dismissed as a kind of feeble-minded slinking-away. One cannot decide categorically that "nihilism" is one of the enemy's passwords, and thereupon assign a dynamo of human thought like Dostoyevsky to some category of weakness, when by the same token the most trivial party-member on a Communistic committee becomes valiant for his bold facing of "realities." Surely "insight" is too difficult to be obtained by merely joining a club. In any case, there is evidence that the mystic movements, arising at such times, display a deep sensitiveness to historic issues.

As the old cultural integer progressively reveals its breakdown, the "potential" mystic feels the corresponding breakdown in the whole trend of thought by which the cultural integer had been established. As the old trend of thought shows its inability to en-compass the new matter (to naturalize it so that the new matter becomes a thoroughly assimilated element, as a language, in its most spontaneous stage, borrows foreign words by completely distorting them to make them conform with its own "genius"), several other trends of thought tentatively arise. The authority of the old trend is "spiritually" broken before the authority of a new trend is established. At this point the contemplative realizes that, by following any one of the various rival trends of thought, we should get a different world, with different insights, than we should get by following any of the others. At this point, of all points in a cultural history, it is possible to see or to sense that when we have adopted a vocabulary, the conclusions we shall eventually arrive at are already contained in our terms, that in triumphantly coming upon our conclusions, we are simply thinking things through to the point at which we began, merely making the implicit explicit. For by each vocabulary things are classified in a different way. The man who offers a new terminology will generally bring forward three kinds of suggestions: he will show how, by his vocabulary, a concept formerly considered unified can be divided into two concepts or several; how concepts formerly considered independent of each other can be brought into one; and how the new concepts are sometimes simply on a different plane of discourse than the former ones, "cutting across" them on the bias. By making new patterns, new sortings, new identifications, he is—to all practical purposes—making new things. So the Marquis of Queensbury rules for loving and hating, wanting and shunning, singling out and neglecting, et cetera, are subtly altered—in accordance with the new groupings, we may have to love some components formerly of the hate class, some formerly of the love class, and some toward which we had not had attitudes of either love or hate. It is by such machinery that a shift in vocabulary may eventually lead to a whole new world, since our attitudes toward the various groupings we think of as "things" determines our conduct toward them. As new thinkers come on, to take up the vocabulary where their predecessors left off, they may carry the line of inferences far beyond the anticipations of the first formulators—just as one man, making up a new set of terms on Monday and juggling them, will have all sorts of "discoveries" by Saturday which had never before crossed his mind.

Here is a kind of disguised mandarinism, as the "mystic" sees it (a situation somewhat analogous to writing a new poem, not with direct bearing upon the world, but also with reference to a famous poem already written), as one would touch upon associations from life and literature both were he, like Laforgue, to write a contemporary work called *Hamlet*, since the work would have "meaning" to us not only in the light of our actual Hamletic experiences, but also in the light of our acquaintance with the character in Shakespeare. The writer, and his corresponding reader, would not be stepping directly from life into Hamlet, but from life-and-Hamlet into a second stratification-of-Hamlet, the new vision being lighted in part by flashes from the older one. Yet Shakespeare himself could not have written the second Hamlet—Laforgue's—nor could Laforgue have seen his Hamlet as he did without the first Hamlet to make a groove for his imaginings. It is probably an awareness of this process which explains the great predilection for parallels in certain modern poets, the tendency to retell old legends, out of an alien setting, by finding for them their contemporary "equivalents," the poets thus giving us some further insight of a quasi-mystical nature by permitting us to consider the same things in two vocabularies at once.

To the mystic, then, history becomes the following-out of one line of thought, where other lines of thought might just as "reasonably" have been followed. And when a new thinker is born, to carry on some one historic line of thought, it is as though a man had come into a room, found people there discussing some matter, and after he had listened long enough to get the drift of their conversation, had begun putting in remarks of his own, accepting *their* remarks as the basis of *his* remarks, "proving" his points on the strength of the points which the other speakers had taken for granted. The "innovator" is a man who, after a certain trend of conversation has been going on for some time, goes back a few sentences to some point that was made and partially neglected—and from this partially neglected point he develops a line of thought somewhat different from that which the subsequent course of discussion had taken. The "coordinates of thinking" may thus seem to be all in the air at once, supporting one another but unsupported—as I once heard of a boorish fellow who contrived, despite his boorishness, to cultivate the acquaintance of many outstanding people. He had very little to offer beyond his sycophancy, so his contacts with the great were always on the point of collapse. Yet he kept himself at the very top of the world by getting the distinguished Mr. P's introduction to the well-known Mr. Q just before Mr. P had reached the limits of endurance, and then getting Mr. Q to hand him along to the famous Mr. R just as Q was ready to cry at the sight of him. Vocabulary, seen in this way, might seem to provide the most "illumination" at moments when it gives us glimpses of possible realms beyond it.

If a man has gone this far in distrusting speech, he can readily go still further. Even the instruments of precision by which science "discloses the secrets" of the universe may then be called the projections, not merely of our senses, but also of our vocabulary, as they reveal things in accordance with the set of meanings which guided their construction. The entire universe can thus become a crowd of beckoning symbols; for once speech is considered merely "symbolic," it is only one more step to considering action itself as symbolic, so that every specific act, colored by the contingencies of the tertiary world, becomes a mere mode or manifestation of some deep-lying universal process (as Whitman could convert the sales drive into a reaching out of hands). This suggests a way of carrying symbolization far beyond the mere sexual symbolization of the Freudians, as the mystic would say that the sexual yearnings are but the conventionalization of a still profounder yearning, and instead of considering the sexuality in dream symbols as indicative of a fundamental sexuality, they would say that the "real" underlying universal patterns merely adopt sexual modes in dreams as they sometimes do in waking experience. As evidence of this, they would adduce the very observations that Freud has adduced, but reinterpreted. They would point out the important respects in which the symbols of dreams are not sexual at all—and instead of considering this non-sexual aspect as the sexual in disguise, they would say that the sexual aspect tends in our society to disguise the other aspect, which is a mere revealing of fundamental experiential patterns. That is: a man desiring "communion-in-the-absolute" might symbolize this by imaginings of junction, sexual junction naturally being among them—and the psychologist, in disclosing this one feature, would take it as indicating the nature of the image in its entirety. But the image, the mystic would say, is really an image of *communion*. And as evidence that it was an image of communion, and not merely an image of sexuality (one mode of communion), he would point to the fact that it was not more obviously a sexual image—but had to do with the workings of an engine, or with a boat coming into port, or a breaking into tears when someone had called.

All such antinomian concerns are much less likely to occur, as a general movement at least, when one trend of terminology enjoys authority. If a vocabulary is in full vigor, backed by the comparatively smooth workings of the social institutions and customs to which it is fitted, people are naturally more set upon plumbing the depths of this given vocabulary than upon deciding which vocabulary they shall plumb.

The Dilemma of Proletarian Denudation

The proposal that we supplant the notion of Antithesis with the notion of a mere *difference* (as the cultural integer undergoes disintegration in its attempt to encompass new matter) would also fall in well with the readily observable data of the "cultural lag." By the "cultural lag" is meant simply the fact that some significant changes in our social ways are not paralleled by the simultaneous changing of *all* our social ways, as our attitudes toward a given situation, and our devices for controlling it, will naturally be preserved in our speech and our institutions after the situation has changed. The historic process, as here defined, would also be in accord with Mr. Russell's remarks on the priority of the negative, which we discussed when considering the psychology of romanticism. The change of some social characteristics while their "companion characteristics" lagged unchanged would give rise to a discrepancy which would be felt first as a mere lacuna, a "push away from," and only later might there arise some general agreement as to a definite image or "pull toward" for producing again an integration among the jangling factors.

But above all, an explanation of history which can merely say that thinking becomes *different* from what it was, rather than *antithetical* to what it was, would have the signal virtue that, while taking care of the facts, it would also avoid the "dilemma of proletarian denudation" which leads our Marxian critics into such desperate straits. The concept of antithesis was fruitful enough in Hegel, as when, by combining *being* with its antithesis *non-being*, we get a synthesis, *becoming*—hence *becoming* is the "reality," composed of the unreals, *being* and *non-being*. Taken over into Marx's historic progression, it nearly draws his disciples into speculations as to what should be the proletarian opposite of a sonnet, or the antithesis of a tone-poem by Debussy—and whether there is some simple workers' reversal of a cathedral other than a cathedral stood on its head. It completely misguides the functions of critical enquiry and exhortation growing out of the economic issue. It leads to a kind of sentimentalizing or infatuation which makes critics only ask how literature may be made "fit" for workers, while they neglect the other possible adjustment: how workers might be made "fit" for literature.

No wonder that, in the fields of both critical and imaginative literature, the proletarian Antithesis should be a toy confined primarily to the reborn bourgeoisie. "Proletarian" writing, as defined by the Marxian critics, is consumed generally among the intellectual classes, and peripherally in the Oranges. Who, working in a factory, wants to read about working in a factory? The factory is an image for students and clerks. White collars is the image for the proletariat. In other words, *if you are seeking for a genuine proletarian antithesis, you will find it in the bourgeois things which the proletariat lacks.*

A Sample Society

It is not enough, however, to complain against Antithesis merely on the grounds that the concept proves troublesome to critical theory. Perhaps we should also consider the concept as it is employed in the theories of Marx himself. And we might begin our inquiry by constructing one of those mythical "first-man" societies, so loved by economists, to illustrate the development of social institutions.

There was once a very pious society which held that fire was sacred, and they had a definite ritualistic prescription for showing their reverence. This society held that, since man and woman unite with each other, any symbolic likeness to this process should be taboo as regards the sacredness of fire—and accordingly, fires should never be made with sticks that had been bundled together. This society did not know how to make fire; but it owned some—and it had many provisions for making certain that a nest-egg of fire was kept continually on hand. Now, there was a villainous fellow, a genius or a recidivist, who had decided that this magic taboo was false. He was an outcast of the worst sort, generally disliked by his tribesmen, a kind of blasphemer who found nothing so delightful as sneaking off into the forest and secretly outraging his tribal standards by the rubbing of sticks, which he later would add to the sacred pyre. As a result of this malpractise he found the secret of fire-making. The discovery was too momentous for him to keep quiet about. After brooding in a kind of agitated silence, rushing about nervously, finding sleep impossible, he decided that he could contain himself no longer. And on a particular holiday, when the priests assembled to bewilder the populace with their cheap magic, our recidivist arose, called upon all the people to observe him, and taking up two dry sticks, proceeded to kindle a fire before their astonished and horrified eyes. Naturally, the man was promptly cooked alive on the very fire he had kindled.

Weeks passed. Or rather, moons. Then one day, as the result of disaster or oversight, the vestal fires went out. The attempt to steal fire from a rival tribe ended only in a terrific slaughter. The priests consulted. The transgression of the Recidivist was in the minds of all. Suddenly one old patriarch remembered an injunction handed down to him, by successive ordinations, from the sacred Fire-Hyena that had been the God and Founder of the tribe itself. This injunction was that, should the sacred fires go out, one could make everything all right again by pronouncing, very slowly, the syllables "Aboozle." The priests broke into glad outcries. The populace, awaiting anxiously outside the tabernacle, took heart and danced in frenzy. For naturally, by a slight "exegesis," it could be proved that the Sacred Hyena meant precisely this: "It is all right to rub sticks together to make fire, if you say 'Aboozle,'" thereby establishing a line of prophecy-after-the-event which culminates in our contemporary neo-Thomists. Hence, we have "new material," and we see the institutions altered to fit the needs of the new material.

Things now dropped back into their old unexciting ways again. The priests proved to the populace that the sacred lore had always contained the secrets of fire-making (in a subtler sense, of course), and they cited the clear and indubitable evidence of the syllables "Aboozle." The making of fire became a common pastime. People began making fires all over the place, naturally being careful to say "Aboozle." A man with nothing else to do would amuse himself and the children by making a fire. Of course, there was still the "sacred fire," carefully tended at considerable expense to the community, a "cultural lag" which in this case did not do much damage directly, although it did require the tribe to support an unconscionable number of rather otiose and heavy-eating priests. But profane fires were there for all, until even children began making fires. As a result, a child burned himself—and the comic little fellow was thereafter so wary of fires that people began to say, "A burned child dreads the fire," and parents very seriously warned their children against fires. Here we have a standard somewhat "antithetical" to the Aboozle device, even though the bourgeois-proletarian dichotomy was not yet established. Aboozle was suited to the new device for fire-making in that it furthered the use of this device; but the injunction to be careful of fire was "antithetical"—it was a standard for *regulating* the powers of the device rather than for *furthering* these powers. The benefits and dangers arose out of pretty much the same situation, applying pretty much to the same people. And perhaps this thesis and antithesis find their ennobling synthesis in the family hearth, which established both a way for fires to warm us, and a way to keep fires from burning down our house, a *furthering* and a *regulatory* process in one.

But let us turn now from this crudely interpreted society to the social process as interpreted by the doctrines of Karl Marx.

The Marxian Philosophy of History: Relationship between "Culture" and the "Productive Forces"

Marx's philosophy of history is a comprehensive scheme for tracing the relationship between social institutions and the physical background in which they arose. If we refer to all the characteristic mental phenomena of a given society as its "ideology," meaning by this term the laws, sentiments, customs, standards of the desirable and undesirable, religious convictions, and the like, we may say that Marx offers an evolutionary account of the processes by which environmental factors determine cultural factors. His ways of dealing with social evolution are analogous to Darwin's doctrines of organic evolution. That is: The organism is seen as developing organs that served the particular end of assisting it in its struggle against the rigors of environmental factors; its own implements, therefore, like the eye or the thumb, might be called "weapons" attached to the body; but when it had developed the most effective weapon of all, the human mind, evolution in the human species became generally confined to mental evolution. New weapons, from now on, were no longer integral to the body: they were implements or tools ("inventions") entirely disconnected from the body.

Social evolution is concerned with the cultural changes, the shifts in ideology, that accompany the use of new implements. The implements are called by Marx the "productive forces." By his schema, since a society adopts an ideology suited to the environment in which it arose, and since the most significant change in environmental factors is the change caused by a change in the "productive forces," it follows that the nature of the "productive forces" determines the nature of the ideology. Thus, the sentiment of "brotherly love" would be explained as arising out of the social advantages of cooperation, since brotherly love would be the sentiment that best encouraged cooperation. Or in our little fable, we saw an institution involving fire-worship altered to fit a change in the nature of fire as a "productive force," when a new device (the process of fire-making) had been discovered. A change to vestal fires from no fire at all would of course have been much broader, and would have required much broader shifts in ideology. Thus, tribal communism, with collective ownership of the society's wealth, was natural to the conditions of the hunt, since the best results could be obtained by foraging in groups; but the shift to agriculture and cattle-raising led to the institution of private property, since people could now obtain the best results by working tracts or tending herds individually or in small groups. The quarry obtained by foraging had been obtained by the functioning of the group as a whole, so that uniform sharing was natural—but now, the working of individual tracts made for a situation wherein the individual amassed goods in proportion to the amounts he had raised, with a resultant differentiation in sharing.

A given society is not a completely homogeneous organism, however, for the productive forces do not affect the society uniformly. One group in the society will have a different relationship to the productive forces than another group may have. One may enjoy the advantages of the productive forces; another may receive mostly the disadvantages. Thus whereas, in our sample society, we had found that the same people might meet both the advantages and the disadvantages of fire, Marx says that a stratification arises, with one group basking in the warmth, and another forever getting burned. He sees such an environmental and ideological division in society at the present time in the division between capitalists and workers. Thus, we should not expect to find one homogenous ideology for the whole society. Instead, we shall find antithetical "class moralities," two opposed ethical and esthetic systems, their differences widening as the environmental differences widen. This opposition must become more and more acute until it leads to conflict. The conflict is inevitable because the group now profiting by the nature of the productive forces (the bourgeoisie) is unwilling to permit any radical change in our social institutions, whereas the nature of the productive forces themselves requires such a change. Today, instead of the small form or herd, or the individual craftsman, our typical method of production is by vast collective effort. The institution of private property (so well adjusted to a time when we had the small, individual unit of production) must now give way to collectivistic institutions matching the collectivistic nature of our modern productive methods. Under conditions of mechanical specialization, few workers turn out a product that does not require the cooperation of the group. Only in a few of the arts, in fact, and in the rapidly vanishing small farm, does individualism survive as a method of production.

To substantiate his contention that the institution of private property (with all its attendant ideology) is unsuited to the collective nature of our productive forces, Marx offers an objective test. The maladjustment, he says, should manifest itself as economic crises, which arise from the fact that mass production requires mass consumption, whereas individual appropriation of profits for the use of a few interferes with mass consumption. Because of this institutional misfit (which proclaims itself a misfit by the fact that it interferes with the operating of the productive forces), not only must the economic crises increase in intensity, but a gradual pauperization of the masses must take place, until the situation becomes acute enough, and the suffering group (the proletariat) is large enough and powerful enough, to accommodate the social institutions to the new environmental needs. An understanding and propagation of these principles will help in the work of making the proletariat "class-conscious"; and a formulating and strengthening of the ideology fitted to collectivism will thus be an integral part of the proletarian "class morality." This class morality must be developed antithetically to the individualistic ideology (the bourgeois ideology of private property), which enables a small class to enjoy great privileges, but does so in a way that grievously interferes with the working of the economic unit. In summary, the institution of private property is condemned, not merely on the score of *injustice*, but on the grounds of *unfitness*. It *must* give way to collectivism because the environmental factors *demand* collectivism.

Roughly in Agreement with the Marxian Theory of Profits, We Herein Confine Ourselves to Marxian Doctrine As It Affects Critical Exhortation

We have omitted from this summary all of Marx's specific economic analysis radiating from his theory of the "surplus value of labor." Our purpose here is not to examine economic expedients—particularly as we recognize, on the face of it, how far superior a collectivist economy of some sort would be to our present intolerable lameness under orthodox capitalism. Even the capitalists themselves are coming to perceive the growing impossibility of "exploitation" for private profit under the capitalist ideal. The Ford doctrine of high wages, if capitalists could but muster courage enough to admit its full implications, should suffice in itself to reveal the capitalist dilemma cruelly: That employers-as-a-group can only take as profits from employees-as-a-group the money which they give to these employees in wages or to the state in taxes. It is a bitter thought—that society is playing a kind of "poverty poker" wherein, after you have taken so much from a man, you must carry him in the game at your own expense. They will naturally close their eyes to this desolate thought as long as they can, trying at least to put off the evil day by the subterfuges of "credit," preferring an uncollectible IOU to an outright giving, but thereby making the end all the more inevitable through the dynamics of compound interest. So we find bankers, who would only too gladly dote on thoughts of "exploitation," now forced to worry for the prosperity of workers, in order that the workers may in turn make the manufacturers prosperous, and the bankers may then take their handsome toll of prosperity through the machinery of investment and savings. Or again, when employers-as-a-group have lowered wages among employees-as-a-group, they have done worse than merely lowering the collective buying power; for by lowering buying power they also lower prices, which is to say that they increase the value of the dollar, and thus increase the "real cost" of all fixed charges against their plants. Every dollar paid in interest on loans becomes a bigger dollar, becomes harder to get because it buys more—and as the basis of modern business is credit, when wages have been lowered throughout the country the industrialists increase the relative burden of their interest charges in proportion to the drop in prices.

So we are only too willing to recognize the acuteness of Marx in foreseeing some of these economic dilemmas nearly a century ago—and we do not see how the present machinery of production can be kept at work unless "profits" are more evenly distributed.

Fortunately, the two pivotal points of Marxism on the political and economic side do not require for their acceptance the acceptance of Marx's entire doctrine as to the origins of culture. One of these principal tenets (that the wealth of the people must be increased, not merely on the grounds of *justice*, but as a sheer economic *necessity*) is now common to doctrines other than Marxism; and the second (that people best get results by banding together) never was peculiar to Marxism. Accordingly, we dare hope that, by and large, a Marxian type of solution will prevail in the economic field, whether it prevails specifically as Communism or not. And we may confine ourselves here to the Marxian theories as they affect the formulation of criteria for the evaluating of purely cultural activities.

Is There a "Marxian Sanction" for Romanticism?

Marx's theories as they apply to matters of literary criticism hinge particularly on the critic's search for the ideological equivalents of economic collectivization. If our ways of thought accommodate themselves to the environment, and economic factors shape the environment, and the distinguishing characteristic of the productive forces today is the *collective* methods involved in their operation, it would follow that the older, romantic, individualist pattern of thought should give way to a greater "catholicity" of response. Our modern methods of production, in which no worker is engaged in the production of an entire commodity, but each joins with countless others in a vast cooperative effort, would bear some analogy to the old communistic conditions of the tribal hunt, conditions under which no man could properly call the quarry his own, and which were accordingly marked by an absence of private ownership and a corresponding presence of extreme homogeneity in the thinking of the tribe.

There is, however, one important difference between the modern collectivity of effort and the tribal collectivity of effort. Namely, the tribal hunt was in itself a homogeneous affair: all the men engaged in the hunt performed an identical function—and this procedure, by Marxian theory, should certainly manifest itself in a collectivist ideology. Would not this very doctrine of Marxism, then, provide the "dialectic" sanction for romanticism, since our modern "hunt" requires the most thorough "departmentalization" that the world has ever known—and romanticism (individualism, subjectivism) can clearly be the mental counterpart of specialization? The thought suggests the possibility that society is now composed of an enormous "heterogeneity" of environments, giving rise to a similar heterogeneity of ideologies in obedience to Marxian doctrine—for if it is our relationship to the "productive forces" that distinguishes our environment, then the sand-hog is clearly in a different environment from the railway engineer, and the environment of a hard-working chemist is widely divergent from them both, perhaps even overlapping considerably upon the "environment" of a "leisure class" student who is using his income to support himself while he follows the science of chemistry. Even in "proletarian" Russia, we see the unmistakable signs of an agrarian-industrial dichotomy, and of a breach between "laborers" and "experts," presumably because of the fact that each of these groups has a different "productive" environment. How much more reason would we have to expect a multiplicity of attitudes in American life, where the processes of departmentalization have been so much more fully developed? Did we know nothing about the literature of America, did we only know the nature of American commercial and industrial procedure, we should—from Marxist theory—be led to expect that we should find in American literature strong romantic, subjective, and individualist elements to parallel the quality of extreme specialization that marks our productive forces. And since this specialization will presumably remain an important aspect of modern collective production, we may expect it to remain an important aspect of our ideology. Unless the chemist is also to be the doctor, the sand-hog, the carpenter, the manicurist, the actor, and so on ad nauseam, we may expect to find many different relationships to the productive forces, each relationship having its ideological individuality. For heterogeneity is as much the mark of the modern collective hunt as homogeneity was the mark of the old tribal hunt.

Indeterminate Position of the Poet

If the group as a whole cannot be defined as engaged simply in "collective" effort in the old tribal sense, the position of the writer is even more indeterminate. In some ways he still remains, even in collectivized Russia, the typical "one-man" enterprise. Even inventing has left the ways of literary production behind, as organized effort in the research laboratory takes the place of "inspiration." In the production of the motion picture scenario we do see some instances of "collective" effort, with one man furnishing the story, another the scenario, another the jokes, another the "sob-stuff," another the verses for the song numbers, et cetera. But in general the artist is in the stage of private initiative, still "cultivating his own garden" (which may explain his frequent sympathies with the vanishing individualist farmer, despite their many disputes over questions of virtue, and may also explain why, in Russia, he enjoys the privileges of private copyright for his books). But if even the Russian writer is a private trader in a productive environment generally collective, in another sense we may say that even the most arrant individualistic American writer is involved in cooperative enterprises—for if we were accurate, we should certainly designate as collaborators all the other poets and critics by whom a writer, no matter how subjective his concerns, was induced to write as he does—and particularly among his collaborators are the masters whose "line of thought" he carries on. Or by pursuing this same analysis, we can recognize that even the most thoroughly romantic poet was always deeply involved with "collective" productive forces, since he was using the most collective implement of all, the corpus of linguistic symbols amassed by the group. For this reason, though he went to a desert island and wrote there, he would not be conducting a strictly "private enterprise," his every concept taking him back to the social unit out of which it arose.

Because he always works with this most collective implement of all—human speech—he will naturally show the vicissitudes of its history in his work. So where specialization has become so total as to develop distinct ideologies and even untransferable terms (a specific word in one science or discipline being totally omitted from another, though it may be a fulcrum of explanation in its own branch), we may expect the writer to manifest his sensitiveness to this ideological heterogeneity by abandoning in large measure the practices best suited to ideological homogeneity. If one has an audience, for instance, so thoroughly uniform in ideology that they all titter when you mention the name of Hoover, or groan when you mention the name of Trotsky, insofar as one's work is to elicit groans and titters his task is considerably lightened. A thoroughly grounded ideology is like a set of flags: pull out the appropriate flag, and people's bosoms swell. A society, or class of society, marked by strong ideological homogeneity is a vast, complex assortment of

Pavlov's dogs. It is usually an age of great objective drama, as the artist gets his effects in a subtle way by arranging our Hoover-titters and Trotsky-groans in keenly mounting sequences—and that is certainly much more fun than talking about oneself, as the artist tends to do more and more under the breakdown of such homogeneous responses.

Even under conditions of complete ideological homogeneity, however, the artist may have a "disruptive" influence. For once he finds that the responses of a society are completely codified, so that the particular kind of salivation is established for each particular kind of bell, he will start ringing these bells at all hours of the day and night, until we simply will not respond to their stimulus any longer. He will cry "Wolf" until the cry of "Wolf" fails to arouse us. Or he may do something much subtler to corrode the ideology. He will confuse the simplicity of our response by ringing at the same time one bell which should turn us to the right and another which should turn us to the left, so that we become all atremble, caught in the cunning "pity and terror" combination which Aristotle discovered in the tragedians of Greece. When an ideology is intact, an artist can get powerful effects by this device until the ideology is not so intact, whereupon he must turn to the ringing of "remoter" bells, as he begins exploring the outer and less worn edges of the ideology. He may even find, just on the borderline of subjective specialization, one last opportunity to use the "pity and terror" catharsis—as we see in Wagner's romantic symbol of the *Liebestod*. Here, by merging under the one symbol of a "love-death" both *capital punishment* and *forbidden sexual union*, our last ambitious writer of Greek opera was able to synthesize gratification with renunciation, thus getting a kind of sublime club-offer (as the sexual "fall" and the "fall" into death were combined, sin-and-expiation in one, transgression sanctioned by its symbolic melting into retribution)—and I am told that after the premiere of *Tristan und Isolde*, the bells were ringing all over Berlin. But of course, in proportion as an ideology crumbles, the range of such possibilities is lessened. And we may ask ourselves whether the modern hunt will ever become homogeneous enough again—while specialization of the productive forces goes on apace—to make for this kind of "impersonal," "objective" art on a grand scale.

The Ambiguousness of "Suitability"

If this re-examination of Marx leads to a quasi-Marxian sanction for a state of literature which critics condemn in the name of Marx, an examination of Marx's schema for the description of historic processes leads us to another difficulty. In the first place, the matter of the "causal" relationship between environment and ideology is not quite so clear as it seems on the surface. In saying that an environment gives rise to an ideology which is "suited to" the environment, we may find that our concept of "suitability" is ambiguous. In our sample society, for instance, we found two ways in which a mental adjustment might be "suited to" the operation of the productive forces. The syllable "Aboozle" was suited to their operation in that it better enabled people to kindle fires—but the injunction to beware of getting burned was equally suited to this productive force. In one case the suitability consisted in the furthering of the use of the new discovery—in the other the suitability was regulatory. Thus, both new highways and traffic laws are suited to the automobile. The ambiguity suggests that we should analyze the situation in another way if possible, in order that we may not erect a causal principle upon so uncertain a base. "Suitability" might easily be made to accommodate both of these antithetical aspects if we meant by "suitability" simply "taking a factor into account." If there is a flood, for instance, an ideology is suited to the flood insofar as it stresses flood-thoughts. And if the flood is an outstanding environmental factor, we may expect many people to have flood-thoughts (to do with the power of floods, the danger of floods, the value of floods in bringing silt for the soil, the annoyance of floods, et cetera). If there is a drought, we may expect an "ideology" of drought-thoughts. If, during the drought, a man has a secret supply of food while people about him are starving, he will presumably think such drought-thoughts as apply to his cachet of food: the possibility of its being discovered, the question as to whether he should share some, and so on. Those in an antithetical position, the starving, will presumably think such drought-thoughts as refer to their desire for food, and perhaps to their suspicion, on observing him still somewhat plump, that he might have a hidden food supply and that they might find it. Their antithesis, however, leaves all in complete agreement as to the desirability of food.

To speak of an ideology as "determined" in this sense is simply to mean that people will think more or less "on the subject." But the ways of thinking on the subject may vary considerably, and all the thoughts are "suitable" in our definition insofar as they arise out of exposure to the "subject" in some form. (That is, even in drought, a child shut up in a courtyard and fed regularly might think, not drought-thoughts, but play-thoughts. This child's thoughts would not be suitable at all. A man who was dying from the effects of deprivation under drought, however, would be thinking very suitably, very much on the subject, if he in ravings saw vast banquets of food and drink.)

Wherein Determinism, Once Thought the "Gloomiest" of Doctrines, Serves to Smuggle in an Appealing Contraband Consignment of Optimism

Such considerations greatly complicate our ideas of economic causation. For instance, we see that so far as suitability in this sense goes, any number of ideologies are suited to the present situation: Fascism is very much "on the subject"; international rivalries for the right to exclusive exploitation of foreign markets are on the subject; a praying Luddite who came forward with a vision and swayed the people with a fervid desire to smash their machines would be talking on the subject—and any one of these solutions would be "economically determined" in that it arose out of the current economic difficulties. Mere race suicide by drastic birth control would also be "suited to" our dilemmas.

The fact is that Marx, by the ambiguousness of the "suitability" concept, can smuggle in some contraband optimism under the misleading label of scientific rigor. He suggests that there is *one right solution*, and that economic determinism forces us eventually to accept this one right solution—yet he proves his thesis by adducing nothing more than proof that *people tend to think on the subject of their advantages and misfortunes*. The concept of strict causation could be omitted entirely; in fact, it *should* be, for Marx's "scientific" theory of history arose at a time when science was much more dogmatic as to the nature of the universe than it is now, and as a result the theory is vitiated by purely metaphysical pronouncements which modern science could not permit itself at all. Since the religious outlook was generally "spiritual," tending to make for equivalent metaphysical systems of "idealism," the sciences of the early nineteenth century, as positivistic and anti-religious, considered themselves quite "scientific" in holding to materialism. Since then, science has been subjected to as strict an examination of its own methodology as it once inflicted upon the methodologies of religion and metaphysics, with the result that it has learned to forgo metaphysical judgments except on the grounds of "personal guesses," confining itself *as science* to the study of relationships, which is its proper sphere. It is content to say, "Tell me a certain set of relationships, and I can tell you a certain other set likely to follow" (tell me where Jupiter "measures" as being today, its orbits and speed as interpreted by our measuring instruments, and I will tell you where to look for it next year within this same scheme of measurements). Even in the strict physical sphere pronouncements as to the ultimate nature of "matter" are admitted to be impossible, and "prediction by the concept of causality" has given place to "prediction by the statistical method." How much more obviously, then, are we forced to "leave an unfilled gap" between the mental and physical spheres of investigation—at least until that time when we shall have a definite principle, capable of empirical demonstration, for converting the manifestations of one sphere into the manifestations of the other. At present, as Mr. Russell has pointed out (though he himself inclines to the hypothesis that the universe is monistic, composed of one homogeneous "neutral stuff" which is manifested sometimes as "mind" and sometimes as "matter"), there is no "scientific" justification for postulating such monistic identity until we have a common term for shuttling between physical and mental phenomena. At present we do not have such—the kind of "attraction" which we observe in the "gravitational" phenomena of physics being of a totally different order from the kind of attraction we observe in the "associational" phenomena of psychology. There must be a common formula for the "attraction" of images and the "attraction" of bodies before it becomes strictly "scientific" for us to synthesize the two realms of discourse. Hence, a strictly "scientific" theory of history must make only such kinds of predictions as it can make without a doctrine of monistic/materialistic causation.

If we do omit this, we are left with an abundance of evidence, supplied by Marx himself with great acumen, to indicate that people tend to think on the subject of their environment, as affected by their productive forces. But to say as much is to realize that we have no reason for supposing that there is only one way of thinking on the subject, or that people must inevitably come to think this one way. Even the analogies of organic adaptation suggest that there is, at least, a hierarchy of solutions, some better than others, as we find in the development of the eye, which was certainly an excellent weapon in our environmental struggle since it enabled us to see, but would have been a still better one had it enabled us to see like both an eagle and an owl, and would have been still better had it enabled us to see around the corner. Indeed, examples from organic evolution would even suggest that, despite the environmental demands, the adaptation needed for survival may not be developed at all. And if Marx attempts to give us a purely technical, non-personal test for disclosing by the "dialectic" method an inadequate adjustment, suggesting that a faulty adjustment is betrayed by periodic crises, he thereby suggests that society never did develop a completely "suitable" ideology, since history has always been marked by some "unrest."

The great emotional appeal behind Marx's purely intellectual formula arises, of course, out of the optimistic promise implicit in his determinism. By combining an ambiguous concept of the suitable with an unproved causal theory as to how the physical determines the mental, he gives us heart to face the discouraging contemporary complexity. He suggests that the "right" ideology must inevitably arise out of the new environment. As might be expected, the ambiguity can be traced to the very end of the system: it explains why Marxians can continually refuse to admit an inconsistency between their doctrines of economic determinism and their great emphasis upon the value of propaganda. While they are eager to show how a bourgeois, as the result of economic determinism, *simply cannot help* thinking bourgeois thoughts, they exhort the antithetically placed proletariat to *please think* antithetical proletarian thoughts. This discrepancy always bewilders the non-Marxian, who can never understand why the bourgeois learned his lesson so easily under the promptings of historical necessity, whereas the proletarian, who was exposed to antithetical promptings, still requires considerable coaching. The matter is cleared up, I believe, if we recognize the ambiguousness of the "suitability" concept. That is, the bourgeois does think thoughts suited to his bourgeois setting (thoughts, let us say, of having hidden some food in times of drought), and the proletarian does think thoughts suited to his proletarian setting (thoughts of resentment, of deprivation, of unhappiness, of despair, of suicide, of stealing, of sabotage). But the Marxian objects that these thoughts are not *suitable enough* to bring about the proposed Marxian solution. In other words, the Marxians offer in collectivization a plan which they think suitable to the situation arising out of modern productive methods. They think this much more suitable than, say, a vast wave of slaughter and birth-control, or a wholesale scrapping of machinery as advocated by our praying Luddite. And they say that people *ought* to think this way (moral imperatives) because people *must inevitably* think this way ("technical" imperative—historical necessity).

Confusions Avoided by the "Integration-Disintegration" Concept of Historic Movement

We may avoid these confusions by eliminating the metaphysical assumptions with which Marx vitiates his "science" (though I admit we may lose our appealing contraband of optimism in the process). We may say that as a society reaches a point of cultural disintegration under its attempt to encompass "new matter," this state of disintegration is felt very pronouncedly as the "negative," the "push away from." In time people come to propose various kinds of "pull toward." Each "pull toward," each "attraction toward the ideal" which is proposed as a counterpart to the "propulsion away from the actual," is really a different set of "meanings," as it attempts to orientate us by putting our discomfitures into an interpretive "frame." And implicit in such a framework of meanings there are conclusions as to the kind of action required to remove the discomfitures. High among these rival frames of meaning is the Marxian frame. Therefore its advocates may offer it *on its merits*. And since they consider it the *highest* solution in a hierarchy of possible solutions, they must plead for it. And they plead for it *precisely because they have no causal guaranty that it will prevail.*

There are indications that something very much like it will prevail. Collectivism, that is, may prevail because it is the *least revolutionary* kind of solution, the kind of solution that can be obtained with the minimum of basic change in our patterns of thought. The solution of the praying Luddite, for instance, is obviously too radical for any of us to entertain it seriously. "Machinery is here to stay." Whether we are in the bourgeois or the proletarian environment as regards modern productive methods, we have all—bourgeois and proletarian alike—accommodated ourselves to the authority of the productive force in the sense that we do not propose to scrap it, whatever social disorders its technical advantages have caused us. That is, we already have a "mechanized" ideology so ingrained in us that Ghandi's "hand-loom" solution is almost unthinkable. So we may advocate the Marxian solution over against the Luddite or the Fascist or the race-suicide "ideals" on the grounds that it is the most "conservative." This is a good argument, since revolutions are generally the most conservative things imaginable, shaping their whole course in strict accordance with the given society's past—but it justifies us merely in foreseeing some generally Marxian solution as the kind likely to recommend itself to the people, and is far too shaky for us to erect a theory of historical necessity upon it.

My purpose in raising these questions, however, has not been to bring discouragement where we formerly had that optimism so beloved of all Americans from our president up. It is to attack the notion of Antithesis, the "dilemma of proletarian denudation," which our Marxian critics would bring upon us if we do not question the deterministic aspects of Marx's theory. By replacing "thesis-antithesis-synthesis" with "integration—new matter—disintegration or reintegration," we omit the grounds for the Saul-Paul reversal which is causing so much confusion in critical admonishment. If we consider that one environment is "different from" another rather than "antithetical to" it, we are not led to seek a proletarian art as something antithetical to a bourgeois art—we merely realize that the two arts may have varying degrees of overlapping and distinctness, in rough correspondence with the varying degrees of overlapping and distinctness of the two environments. Our recognition of the fact that people "think more or less on the subject" will justify us in expecting that the "typical" bourgeois will betray in some way the influence of his hidden food supply, and that the "typical" proletarian will worry about losing the job which he detests—it will not justify us in supposing that all the thoughts of each group must be made antithetical by reason of this antithesis.

Indeed, it is hard to understand how strictly antithetical judgments could lead to protest at all. If you enjoy privilege A, and keep it for yourself, and I am denied privilege A, but by reason of an antithetical ideology I do not consider it a privilege, on what basis should we quarrel? If you covet leisure and I glorify toil, then we might live amicably in an exploitive relationship, whereby you enjoyed your leisure at my expense and I admired myself for toiling. There seems to have been some such placid adjustment of antithetical ideologies between the rulers and the ruled in the heyday of Catholic feudalism. We quarrel insofar as our ideologies are identical, insofar as you want to keep for yourself what I want to take from you. Practical agitators instinctively allow for this fact by picturing to the proletariat, not a special proletarian heaven, but the possibilities of their extending to themselves prerogatives now retained by the bourgeoisie. They take into account the fact that revolt must arise out of a synthesis of ideology, not an antithesis.

Wherein We Play the Permanent "Organic Productive Forces" against the Contemporary "Social Productive Forces," Thus Restoring in Part the "Human Substrate"

We might even point to a doctrine in Marxism itself which should guard us against the simplicities of Antithesis. If Marx holds that our thinking is affected by our productive forces, he inevitably brings up the possibility that a past ideology would be retained as long as the past condition of the productive forces was retained. Marx's entire dialectic was framed as an attack upon the "human nature" school, the older absolutist economists who tried to explain our social institutions on the basis of a human "constant," a generic "human nature" which remained the same under all conditions and thus showed up again and again as the "old Adam" in us. Marx refuted this school by showing the adaptability of man to differing environmental conditions, revealing the fact that man's ideology was altered as his environment was altered, and using this fact as evidence that man's thinking is determined by the productive forces which shape his environment.

However, there are important respects in which man's "environment" has not been greatly altered since the beginning of history. For the organic productive forces, the weapons integral to the body, have remained unchanged, so we might expect some vestiges of an ideological "constant" in keeping with this constancy on the part of the organic productive forces themselves. Such a thought would suggest that we could not simplify our esthetic canons by envisaging the literary problem in terms of a strictly bourgeois-proletarian dichotomy, as there should be some ideological overlap of the groups corresponding to this identity in the organic productive forces of both groups.

A Mind Helping the Body Think

Had we, in gaining levers, lost hands, such considerations would not arise. But insofar as we retain hands, and insofar as levers themselves are merely stronger hands, we may expect us all to have "hand-thoughts." That is, through all of us there will run patterns of thinking to duplicate the hand's function of "grasping." Other human "constants" overriding the bourgeois-proletarian dichotomy can suggest themselves ad libitum: "pugnacity" as the brain's equivalent of the fist; "love of clarity" as the ideological projection of the eye; bodily muscularity "made mental" as logical firmness or as aggressiveness of style; the function of the palate finally leading to canons of "taste," since criticism would be integrally grounded in the assimilative and rejective processes of digestion. Our interests, sentiments, impulses, desires, "values" should manifest some "constant undertone" in proportion as the nature of the organic implements involved in their "determination" remained constant.

If a fish were to "think," his thought-processes might bear a close analogy to glidings and quick flips of the tail (in which sense it is not at all hard for us to imagine him as "thinking"). It is only when we try to liken his thinking to verbal thinking that the notion of his thinking seems incongruous, suggesting the atrocious puns of the rude, extremely linguistic animals in Alice's Wonderland. At least, we know that the fish has a set of "meanings" just as we do—for we can see him learn new meanings ("widening his ideology") under a change in the nature of his productive forces (as when he is put into captivity and learns that food is something sprinkled on the surface of the water each morning subsequent to certain agitated appearances above the water which he would formerly have considered menacing). The primary qualitative difference between the fish and the philosopher in these matters seems to be that, whereas the fish can swim better, the philosopher can deny it. But there is evidence that his thinking follows man-patterns, just as the fishes should follow fish-patterns, paralleling his behavior as his behavior is shaped by the organic "productive forces." Thus, when the child is paddled:

"We are fundamentally offended," exclaim certain nerves. "Be pugnacious!" shouts the fist. "Let us criticize the enemy," the alimentary tract proposes; "I mean, let's digest him." "With my proverbial love of clarity," the eye observes, the eye which, as Schopenhauer has told us, made the sculptured Apollo hold high his head that he might gaze all about him, for the sheer Grecianness of gazing (so says Schopenhauer when growing eloquent about the eye and its symbolism, though naturally, to be eloquent about the eye in sculpture you must be eloquent about something else—in this instance, the head-case for the eye, not the sculptural eye itself, for the stony eye in sculpture should be covered with fig-leaves); "With my proverbial love of clarity I have investigated this situation, and I fully recognize the forms and colors that go to make up the offending agent." And Justitia, that fine sense of heavenly fairness, of transcendental weighing, that comes of balancing oneself on two legs, solemnly pronounces, "Touch not a hair on yon gray head; in youth it sheltered me, and I'll put up with it now."

It is true, I am not content with this as an explanation of the whole process. The entire account might just as well be stated otherwise—and instead of accounting for our thought-processes as an outgrowth of the organs, we might (in a neo-Spinozistic way) see the thought-processes and the organic processes as dual manifestations of some prior, unifying design (just as we could not say whether a man swims well because of an unctuous quality in his thinking, or writes unctuously because he can swim well, and so we might compromise by considering the thought-behavior and the water-behavior as the same pattern in two different orders). In any case, though the complexities of the modern tertiary world would suggest that complexities can arise without design, and that accordingly even so complex an organ as the eye may well have been developed more out of stupidity than as the result of wise central planning, we should be as justified logically in reversing our scheme of the relationship between the physical and the mental by adopting something like Bergson's notion of the *élan vital,* which is based primarily on the converse scheme, making the aim prior to the organ, rather than the organ prior to the pattern (hence, *pugnacity* would lead to the invention of the *fist*). The matter is all the more bewildering in that the *uses* of a device do not always indicate its *purpose.* Airplanes, for instance, can serve to carry serum across snow barriers to plague-stricken cities, or as a convenient means of dropping bombs upon them, but it is most likely that neither use was an instigation to aeronautical invention. To assume with Marx that a productive force dictates the nature of its future activity (that it contains one kind of use, and that society will adapt its ideology to this use) is to overlook the fact that gunpowder was discovered in the Orient independent of its discovery in the West, and that it was used there for pretty sky displays alone, and not until the West brought its ideology to those far shores did Orientals learn the "real" use of gunpowder. A device is almost as ambiguous in its use as an exponent in mathematics: put the exponent 12 above a, and you get a^{12}; put it above $-a$ and you get $-a^{12}$. So the productive device, like the exponent, may simply raise the power of any ideology, as airplanes raise the power of mercy in carrying serums and the power of vengeance in carrying bombs. A device, that is, gets its "nature" as an environmental factor partly from the nature of the ideological scheme into which it is introduced. To consider it "pure environment," of an unchanging essence or character which it possessed regardless of the particular pre-existing ideological combination into which it was introduced, would be to admit another absolute into a dialectic scheme.

Mr. Robert Briffault has dealt with this "subjective" aspect of the environment when he says that the adjustments of a society to environmental conditions "are products of antecedent as well as of actual social conditions." In other words, one adjusts himself to the productive forces not purely in accordance with the "nature" of the productive forces themselves, but also in accordance with his society's *earlier* adjustments to *other* productive forces, since these earlier adjustments are preserved in his ideology. Thus: "The pastoral people who lose their cattle and turn hunters will differ considerably from the hunters who turn pastoralists. The effects of their pastoral tradition will not be obliterated. Adjustments to similar conditions differ according to the cultural history of a people, that is, according to the traditional contents of their minds." This amounts to saying that the new environmental factors themselves vary their character in accordance with the previous mental character of the society into which they are introduced.

Thus, we need not be surprised to find different orders of thought co-existent. If the method of hunting in groups made for "collective" thinking, there is evidence that, whatever the nature of cooperation, the individual who lives or dies as a *unit*, did not let the collectivist aspects of his ideology destroy the individualistic pattern that parallels this unitary aspect of his existence. Thus we find that in many collective-minded groups of savages there is a sense of personal identity so pronounced, so much stronger than the personal sense of the most arrant modern individualist, that the people who hold a similar personal view in modern society are generally confined in asylums for the insane. I refer to what M. Lévy-Bruhl has called "mystic participation," and what modern psychiatrists would call either "ideas of reference" or "acute paranoia," according to the intensity of the symptoms. That is, the savage had so strong a sense of personal involvement in natural processes that accidents were inconceivable to him. If a tree fell in his path and injured him, the event was "purposeful," designed to *injure him personally*, and he promptly set about to discover what malign god or man was implicated in this vicious business. And out of this sense of personal involvement in processes which to us seem "impersonal," he spun a whole magic ideology which naturally was coordinated with his "collectivist" imaginings as well (so that the transgression for which he was being punished was conceived as possibly having been committed by some other member of his tribe, "retribution" as well as quarry being shared in common).

All such considerations should suggest the nature of the critic's dilemma in trying to base his exhortations upon the simplism of a bourgeois-proletarian dichotomy. The art of the bourgeoisie, that is, does not arise purely out of a strictly bourgeois ideology: in part its ideology is the ideology of the "human substrate," the patterns of thought common to all men insofar as the "organic productive forces" are common to all men. Since bourgeois art is thus *both* bourgeois *and* human, a proletarian art developed by strict antithesis would be meaningless, as it obviously could not be inhuman or non-human. Even if we omit the point raised in our quotation from Mr. Briffault (who suggests that the "nature" of a social productive force is not absolute, but varies with the mentality of peoples), we still have grounds to question the Marxian theory within its own terms, by adducing a Marxian principle to indicate the presence of a "human substrate." Antithesis, therefore, must become very modest in its application; and the critic, instead of throwing out wide areas of literature in the name of Antithesis, must confine his bourgeois-proletarian divergencies to strictly party differences, particularities of the vote, questions of legal method, etc., recognizing that when he moves into the broad sphere of imaginative art, insofar as both sides of the dichotomy are "human," their art must overlap.

The Present State of Language and Ideology (the Chief Productive Force of Writers) As It Affects the Problems Peculiar to Writers

Incidentally, in the course of this discussion, we have smuggled across another concept of the "suitable," but this one also is in Marx. That is, we say that the ideology is "suited to" the productive forces when the pattern of thinking is similar to the environmental pattern. We find this concept of suitability the very fulcrum of Marxian optimism, for by showing that the nature of modern production is collectivistic, he leads us to expect a similar collectivist pattern in the ideology.

Pursuing this Marxian principle, we come across considerations that should complicate the forming of collectivist standards in the field of art. Language is now undergoing a kind of conscious evolution entirely different from the collective aspect of its growth. To a large extent, language now develops out of "terminology," a very obvious process of conceptual naming. This kind of growth would seem to be in direct contrast with the natural collectivistic principles of linguistic growth. According to the mimetic theory of Sir Richard Paget (a theory which he offers in place of the old "bow wow" school, which held that speech arose out of onomatopoetic naming), language arose as "gesture speech," not a way of naming, but a way of expressing attitudes. At first these attitudes were probably expressed by the set of the entire body, as a terrier's back bristles when he expresses the attitude of rage, or his tail wags and his body relaxes to express an attitude which we, without tails, convey by saying "I like you." No, even now we do not wholly convey our meanings in this way. If a man said "I like you" in thunderous accents, frowning and clenching his fists, we should have the most uneasy doubts as to his real attitude. A good actor still expresses his attitudes by the set of the entire body; a fairly expressive person uses facial gestures to a large extent; and those who would draw one card when they have four aces can conceal their glee only by the rigid donning of a mask, the "poker face," that says nothing because it changes not. Sir Paget suggests that by greater and greater economy, this gesture speech which generally began with the whole body was localized in the facial muscles, and thence even many of the facial gestures could be dropped as the conveying of attitudes became generally confined to the throat and the sounds issuing from it (the "tone of voice" probably conveying different meanings, before this in turn was made more precise by sounds being schematized into words).

The origins of speech, by such a doctrine, might be seen in a word like "ouch," which even now is not a naming, nor is it the onomatopoetic equivalent of anything, but clearly expresses an attitude, a sense of displeasure at being hurt. It will be noted that the utterance of the word distinctly necessitates a baring of the teeth—and the gesture of baring the teeth is certainly the proper gesture to go with being hurt, since it is clearly a threat of vengeance against the instrument that does the hurting. If one objects that the word is not generally used as a threat, but is uttered when the hurt has been accidental, thus expressing our personal grief rather than our resentment, we may explain this fact as arising out of the later discrimination between the intended and the accidental, a distinction which, if we are to believe M. Lévy-Bruhl's account of *participation mystique*, the savage lacked completely when a tree fell across his path and hurt him. The tree was considered a spiteful agent, and thus well merited a threat. Further, there are not occasions lacking when kindly old ladies, bumping against chairs in the twilight, have not only cried "ouch" but have struck at the chair vindictively.

Again, we have already noted the thinker's unconscious tribute to the collective genius of his language when he offers us universal groupings and identifications in keeping with grammatical groupings. We may choose to account for this by the concept of pattern (as a *Zeitgeist* thinker might do, saying that the groupings in the thinker's cosmogony would naturally reveal the same pattern as the grammatical groupings in his speech, since they both arose out of the same cultural pattern). In any case, we must recognize the pronounced tendency of language to "freeze" traditional patterns of thought, thus readily tempting the thinker to follow these same patterns spontaneously in whatever corners of his thinking happen to escape his critical caution.

Marxian Simplism Inadequate as a Way of Analyzing the Poet's Productive Force

Today a definite attempt is being made to circumvent both these aspects of speech, and one need accept neither the theory of gesture-speech nor the notion of grammatical thinking to recognize that, under departmentalization, logicians are attempting to develop a kind of logic which will remove thinking as far as possible from the uncritical pitfalls contained in the "collective" speech, while concepts are continually being introduced in special departments of research which will avoid as much as possible the emotionality and metaphorical or "picture thinking" aspect of the collective speech, attempting to designate a mere awareness of processes that shall be as devoid of "attitude" as possible. Roughly, we may say that here, as the result of departmentalization of the productive forces, we face a host of problems which, though applying to the collectivity, cannot be appropriately treated by the thought-processes of the collectivity. Hence, the most collective of all enterprises, human speech, is not merely strongly affected by "individualist" thinking (or "group-individual" thinking, if we attribute the rise of a terminology to a specialist and his colleagues); in addition, it definitely requires for its development a pronouncedly "un-collectivist" state of mind if the appropriate ideology for the new productive matter is to be developed.

Such considerations would throw an entirely different light upon certain contemporary work which Marxian simplism leads the critic to condemn as unsuited to the present nature of the productive forces. Let us consider the experiments of the "verbalists." We need not concern ourselves here with an evaluation of what has been attained by people like James Joyce, Gertrude Stein, or the general group studying "the word" in the publications of Mr. Eugene Jolas. We wish merely to indicate why the concept of Antithesis, leading to an exhortation for "class-consciousness," and thence to an automatic denigration of those who by their punnings plumb the "unconscious," is an inadequate way of handling the issue. If the state of the productive forces distinguishes an environmental problem, it follows that the "verbalists" are deeply alive to the "contemporary" in their technical concern with speech.

We may take Joyce's later writings as a case in point. There is little doubt that words contain their verbal overtones (that when we say the word "man" in a certain context, we may also "glance at" such words as "Manhattan—manahatta—perhaps thence even Whitman and broad-axes, and the reconciliation of tertiary and primary worlds," while in another context the same word may have fluttering about it such outlaw punning images as "mandrake—mandragore—man-dragon," yet we should not say "outlaw," as they cannot arise and be outlaw, though the context "logically" would seem to furnish no grounds for these loose-ends of association). In his *Principles of Literary Criticism* Mr. I. A. Richards discusses this fluctuant matter as "free imagery," and in his *Seven Types of Ambiguity* Mr. W.

Empson handles linkages of somewhat the same sort, though in the second case they often seem to be discussed too much in terms of purely literary associations, as might apply to a literary scholar whose memory for quotations was exceptional. Joyce would appear to be dealing with a kindred problem—yet it does seem regrettable that Joyce has not found some clearer way of incorporating in the text his processes of revision. Roughly we might say that, instead of giving the dictionary background of a word (its "family history" as regards Latin, or Anglo-Saxon, etc.), he gives it an experiential background—but when we see three versions of the same passage (as printed in the appendix of Mr. Edmund Wilson's *Axel's Castle*), we realize that his telescoped words mean more if we have the history of their construction. Perhaps we should see them transformed before our very eyes, under successive accretions, instead of having to "guess back" when we have nothing but the final manifestation to guide our "guesses." It is too much like seeking a new Darwinian descent for each separate word, whereas the Darwinian descent should be laid before us as the really interesting part of the show. If I understand Miss Gertrude Stein's injunction correctly, the "opus" in works of this sort is not in the finished product but in the "operations" by which one gets to the finished product. *Madame Bovary* is a classic—a disclosure of the steps by which Flaubert got to *Madame Bovary* might be a classic of a different order, the perfect esthetic culmination of an "evolution-minded" century.

Such literature may at present have its highly unsatisfactory side. For one thing, as a way of *revealing* processes it is much less efficient than the examination of rudimentary hysterics and madmen has been so far. Its final contribution may be, if science ever makes us wholly at home in such matters, that the work is here done much more *suavely*, by a fuller and more vigorous mind, than in the case of the unbalanced. However, the point to be emphasized here is not the matter of results, but simply the fact that Marxians could not, by strictly following their own theories, object to the *nature* of such investigations. The productive force determining the literary conduct of a writer would not merely be found in the circumambient devices for non-literary production (such as factory conditions, transportation methods, disorders of marketing and financing). A very important formative environmental factor affecting him as a writer should be the state of the implement used in his particular department. In other words, the quality of a writer's efforts may respond to the quality of the available linguistic devices—and in these at present we must note a pronounced heterogeneous aspect, *with collective contributions arising out of individualistic methods, in many cases the procedures of the entire departmental group being radically altered within a few years by the formulations which an individual, working in total or comparative isolation, eagerly contributed to the very collectivity that had scorned him or had ignored him.* Nor can we test the *use* of a discovery too promptly. Pasteur first made his reputation among brewers, because his experiments with germs had made more precise the nature of yeast. One can imagine a good Marxian at that point, pushing him off the earth in the name of Antithesis, for an investigation so "evasive" to the matter of the bourgeois-proletarian dichotomy.

Wherein We Attempt to Re-apply
Some Marxian Principles in Ways of Our Own

If the sentiment of mercy or brotherly love is explained by Marxian tactics as arising out of the fact that such a sentiment furthered the powers of the productive forces through promoting the state of mind under which cooperative effort is best promoted, what sentiment might we expect to be called into prominence through the present nature of the productive forces, *departmentalized cooperation?* The sentiment best adapted to such conditions would seem to be the sentiment of *tolerance*—hence the Marxian logic might lead us to claim it as no accident that, for all the battling of the modern world, there is a tremendous degree of tolerance observable throughout the entire field of human thought. Where our vital interests seem at stake, we are recalcitrant—but we have come to learn that there are very many matters of disagreement on which our vital interests are not at stake. There is, of course, some guild boastfulness, as when you hear a student of medicine and a student of mathematics arguing about the relative importance of their disciplines, and you realize that one shares the prestige of Pasteur, while the other is a kind of Galileo-Newton-Einstein *in parvo*. But there is a general tendency to be meek in our judgment of fields not our own, to refrain from any but the most tentative opinions until we have equipped ourselves in the fundamental data of this field. It is not the "specialist," the "subjectivist," who knows once and for all the divisions of good and bad in every scheme of human activity. It is the "classicist," the "catholic," who knows this, the man orientated in a firm ideological homogeneity such as existed par excellence in the old tribal collectivity and as the Marxian critic would like to see rigidified for the proletariat. Even naive people are tolerant today, as compared with the "great minds" of eras marked by firm ideological structures. Nearly everyone can take a "tentative interest" in schemes of thought other than his own, and precisely because they are other than his own. Everyone is a kind of miniature anthropologist, strongly affected with a sense of moral and esthetic relativity, interested observationally in the comparisons and contrasts between his culture and other cultures, and finding divergencies noteworthy. One will listen entranced to any sub–Marco Polo describing the logic of a strange people, and though his risibility is touched now and then by the clashes between his ideology and theirs, such laughter is not merely "superior" laughter, for laughter is generally aroused by ideological discrepancies, as images incongruous to one another are juxtaposed. The "classic" attitude has vanished—that ideological fixity whereby the alien, in simply being alien, became "barbaric."

The wise Marxian, at this point, will have cocked his ears. Tolerance! Have we gone all this distance to get to Tolerance? Tolerance would be a superb sentiment for the contemporary scene. One could raise a goodly chest of several millions of dollars, if he could but convince the donors that the money would be effectively spent on Tolerance. The wise Marxian sees the whole joyous picture, the Gentle Reign of Tolerance—the poor tolerating their poverty, and the rich tolerating their wealth.

Muddle of Anomalies, Antinomies, and Dichotomies

Well, we have said that there are organic productive forces as well as those evolved by society. And if the contemporary state of the productive forces evolved by society makes for tolerance, *the organic productive forces would not think of tolerating the intolerable*. Tolerance must cease when our vital interests are at stake—thus does the human substrate speak as opposed to the social accretions. The dictates of our organic forces require that primary *intolerance* which a grass-root must have in resisting a daisy-root. The same tribe that engrosses us with its strange customs will infuriate us if it tries to destroy us. By the Goethean principle, we have considerably widened the range of the "tolerable." But when the "intolerable" encroaches upon even the most rudimentary demands of the body, when the intolerable tells a man that he cannot, under present conditions, get the things which the general ideology calls necessary to his self-respect, and if this intolerable state can be shown to arise out of man-made arrangements, we must consider ways of removing it and substituting other man-made arrangements in their place.

Tolerance, intolerance; specialized effort for the good of the collectivity; individualistic protest serving as the nucleus of a group;

subjectivism assisting in the objective formulation of processes; one man's private enterprise furnishing terms and images to the most collective of all human enterprises, language; the general muddle of anomalies, antinomies, and dichotomies—what would all this suggest if not the possibility that our key word for today would be "complexity"? And at least, if we ask that the distinctive trait of modern thinking be complexity, we find a quasi-Marxian sanction on looking about us and noting the exceptionally complex pattern of the modern productive forces. What simple antithesis is possible here—when we see "leisure" giving rise to some of the world's most valuable "works," and observe an "exploiting" class bent stupidly but earnestly (because necessarily) over the problem of improving the welfare of the "exploited." And far from a simple conflict between capital and labor, we find a long history of how capital and labor "hunted together" in the empirialistic exploitation of non-Occidental or generally "backward" peoples (quarreling among themselves only as to the relative division of the spoils). And we find this same capital-labor dichotomy confused by the interlocking of interests in the two groups as opposed to the agrarian group, as industry preyed upon the farmer for over a century and the laborer, however niggardly his share of the quarry, got it by joining in a common expedition with the capitalist-industrialist which is now culminating, to the great disaster of capital and labor alike, in the complete pauperization of the agrarian group. I quote from a newspaper article a paragraph which made me gasp as I realized the ruthless kinds of confiscation lying concealed beneath that cooperative and orderly warfare which is economic warfare. What invading army, I thought, ever carried off as much, ever took such mighty toll in tribute and plunder, as industry took from the farmer while the "invasion" aspect of the process went unnoticed:

At the time of George Washington, 95 percent of our population was engaged in agricultural production. From that time until the era of Woodrow Wilson the abundant agricultural surplus paid for the imports of capital which went to build up our railroads and to develop our industries and cities; it paid for the interest on that capital; it paid for the importation of raw and manufactured products that were needed to build up the great industrial plants which were being erected in all parts of the country. Truly agriculture stood supreme as the source of national wealth. It was the foundation of American industrial society.

And these agrarians, who built up industry by their "abundant agricultural surplus," own not one fragment of this industrial wealth. Indeed, about 50 percent of them have become tenants on the very lands they once owned, and of those who have remained owners, most are staggering beneath a colossal burden of debt. Any wonder that the laborer does not find himself in simple opposition to the capitalist? Any wonder that he distrusts an oversimplified picture of himself as in direct conflict with his employers' interests? Any wonder that the laborers of one section will join with the capitalists of the same section, to obtain legislation (such as tariff measures) which will benefit both at the expense of some other section? As Mr. George Soule has written, when discussing the failure of the Marxian, Communistic philosophy to attract the proletariat despite its misfortunes: "The intra-labor conflict is real enough, even when the class conflict languishes. This fact in itself presents a challenge to the Communist point of view. What is the chance, in any highly developed capitalist country, of a united labor front strong enough to carry through a revolution of any sort? Those who, according to the Communists, are misleaders and traitors, are so prevalent in every non-socialist nation that they assume the aspect of a natural phenomenon, not to be exorcised with moral indignation."

Such a situation is far too complex to be adequately handled by the simplism of bourgeois-proletarian antithesis. The worker instinctively appreciates the "integrity of interests" which now affects all members of the nation. And rather than thinking of the problem in terms of a strict division in class interests, he might compare our society to a large business corporation riddled with nepotism, and requiring some such "revolution" as might be instigated by an "efficiency expert." The stockholders and coupon clippers who take most of the profits might be compared to the holders of "soft jobs" in such a limping organization. The officers and directors fall into the picture as "overpaid proletarians" (like the American technical experts in Russia). There are conflicting interests, but not "class" conflicts.

Cannot one say that we must, in a society living by purchase, have a general availability of buying power; cannot one say that such a readjustment is tremendously necessary; cannot one say how we should vote or act to bring about the requisite change, without attempting as a literary critic to found literary judgments upon a simple Saul-Paul reversal? There is a simplicity of action, when the aroused genius of our organic productive forces speaks. There is the ideology, born of the body, that will not forever tolerate the intolerable. But such simplicity, though it attained its end tomorrow, would leave us just as squarely facing all the complexity of our socially evolved productive forces. A revolution which attained its ends by "oversimplification" would most likely leave a simplist heritage which made for its own undoing. At least, events in Russia suggest that "dichotomies" do not vanish in a "classless" state, as the struggle between the Stalin faction and the oppressed Trotsky Opposition reveals a "class" division of the strongest sort one can imagine, namely, between those *in office* and those *out of office*, a division which in Russia can also entail a worker's dismissal from a factory for the expression of Opposition views as is the case in capitalistic America. And as an evidence of how the discredited Trotsky "complexity" of open discussion and constant criticism may serve as a better adjustment to modern conditions than Stalin simplism, Trotsky has written: "In the heaviest years of the past— in the period of the underground struggle under tsarism, in 1917 when the country passed through two revolutions, during the following three years when twenty armies were fighting on a front 7,000 miles long—the party lived a seething inner life. All questions were freely discussed from the top of the party to the bottom; the freedom of judgment within the party was unqualified." Yet a few years later, when all difference of opinion is silenced, when Stalin's policies are obeyed like the dictates of an absolute monarch, when conformity within the party is of the strictest and when foreign obstacles are diminished, we find that tremendous errors in the development of the productive program have been allowed to grow without warning, as the excessive upbuilding of heavy industries leaves the workers without consumers' goods for themselves or for delivery to the peasants in exchange for food. We find, in the gagging and exiling of an obviously sincere faction, an instance where the entire Russian state has suffered from the simplism of intolerance whereas the complexity of tolerance would have brought a benefit. We also find arising a condition of office-holding which, though the beneficiaries are now unquestionably actuated by the best of motives, could readily metamorphose into mere bureaucracy which might develop a powerful self-perpetuating function in that politics and industry tend there to become identical.

Such considerations do not, in themselves, discredit a simplist solution. But they do suggest that the simplist solution is not adequate to the maintaining of the contemporary productive order, which requires the complexity of critical inquiry rather than the simplism of enthusiasm and faith. A simplist solution might make best for a return to a simpler productive order—as were our hypothetical praying Luddites to arise and were their Ghandi-like doctrines to be generally followed. And perhaps it is no accident that the nearest approach to Marxian Communism has prevailed in a nation in which something like 93 percent of the people were agrarian, non-industrial at the time of the revolution. One must not confuse the simplicity of the principles underlying our modern dilemmas with a simplicity in our ways of coping with these principles. A social tangle might arise out of the simplest maladjustment imaginable, and yet society may have carried this pattern so thoroughly through the manifold aspects of its thinking, customs, institutions, and needs, that the process of unknotting it can be tremendously complex. To avoid the unbeautiful plight of the "muddle-headed liberals," it is not enough to adopt an oversimplified clarity. Marxian lines of reasoning themselves might suggest that, to retain the present highly complex system of production, we require, not the Saul-Paul reversal, but the Goethean "chambered nautilus–coral island" complexity.

Man's Inborn Right to Consider the "Unweighted"

Insofar as environmental conditions may be intolerable, the "convictions" of the organism itself will demand resistance. But as the oppressive forces are not the kinds of forces to which the organs in themselves are best equipped for resistance, this organic resistance must require, for its orientation, a set of purely intellectual "meanings." We are pretty close to observing the simple dictates of the organs, for instance, when we see miners, farmers, or unemployed veterans blindly congregating to protest and perhaps to do violence or to peacefully bring up the *image* of violence in the minds of those from whom they ask help. This purely organic resistance is made more effective as broader meanings are presented, illuminating the local difficulties, for instance, by an interpretation involving social institutions in general (as the Marxian theories of profit do). Meanings are simple, close to the organic, when we hate the "Cossacks" that club us on the head. But such meanings are almost worthless in the present issue; in this issue we are required to regulate our organic responses in accordance with a set of meanings which explains why the Cossacks are there to club us on the head at all, and why we, who are normally peaceful people preferring sloth to activity, should find our heads in such a startling position. Hence, we must redefine the opponent, seeing him not merely in terms of people, but in terms of a "system," a system so much possessing a genius of its own that were all the "oppressors" to up and slay themselves, while leaving the "system" intact, we should in a few years have the same oppression all over again, new oppressors arising from among the formerly oppressed, since the "system" categorically makes for such a state of affairs. So the organic intolerance must be directed, not specifically against a few policemen, but against something so remote from a particular scene of violence as *laws and institutions in general.*

To be able to see as much, one must be able to see much more. The mind, to grasp meanings of this sort, must have a kind of "expansiveness" or "stretchableness" which enables it to grasp meanings of very many sorts. It must be such an agent as continually plays over the human scene (and I am referring not to the mental activities of some exceptional person, but to the processes of inquiry and notation which distinguish *any* human mind, the general qualities of observation, curiosity, criticism that we find operating, now in an abstruse metaphysician, now in the crowd at a ballgame). It is because the mind has this free play, because it concerns itself with all sorts of things, like a puppy out walking with his master, that we can lay before it some *new* meaning, some new way of grouping the events about us whereby they are fitted into larger schemes than is observable through the mere sensory phenomena themselves (some way of interpreting a club on the head, for instance, by a broader scheme of interpretation than is presented in the simple facts of the clubbing).

In sum, *it is because the mind is capable of functioning on all sorts of issues, that we can lay before it a set of meanings as to the nature of the key issue.*

Hence our resistance to the Marxian criteria of relevancy. Hence our resistance to their admonishments when they see a mind deeply concerned with issues other than the key issue, or when they observe this mind framing its critical standards in accordance with a different frame of reference than bears wholly and exclusively upon the key issue. The equipment which enables a mind to see things in accordance with their interpretation can only arise out of an *equipment for interpretation in general.* Thus, in one sense, we may say that as regards the play of the mind there is no key issue. The key issue for this "productive force" is merely the need of fullness and pliancy in the matter of thought itself. The mind must be capable of a general tolerance, even if only that it may settle accurately upon the kind of intolerance requisite for one specific situation. It must be capable of great complexity, if only as the soundest way of selecting one set of meanings as the interpretation of one specific scene. Through its general ability to range across "neutral" areas of thought, the mind becomes best suited for dropping with authority upon some "weighted" area.

"Souvenirs for All"

So we shall not feel called upon to admit the Marxian criteria too strictly into the field of ethical and esthetic judgment. Nor need we completely exclude them. We might say that, like the antithetical leisure-class lady sunning herself, they are marked by an "error of limitations" rather than by "error per se." Their fundamental doctrine, if kept within its proper limits, seems unimpeachable. It might be stated thus: "A certain attitude, involving a collectivized protest against the present political and economic order, would be immediately serviceable at this point in our history. Books can reinforce this attitude. Critics can discuss in what ways books do or do not reinforce the attitude."

Their position, as so stated, need not even involve us in any fundamental distinction between "pure" literature and "propaganda" literature, as applied to the "imaginative" field. The effectiveness of the so-called propaganda novels of Mr. John Dos Passos, for example, depends upon the author's *exploitation* of an ideology, just as the effectiveness of any book does. A writer, to have a "powerful" effect, must have found some way of profiting by a pre-established mold of thought in the minds of his readers. He is ringing the bells that lead to salivation. Similarly, the effectiveness of *Uncle Tom's Cabin* did not arise out of the fact that it established an anti-slavery attitude, but out of the fact that it exploited an attitude already alive and flourishing. Its contribution to the strengthening of the attitude resided in the fact that it furnished the public with deeper and fuller imagery for an attitude which heretofore had been sparse in imagery. It profited by the attitude that was already there—but in "repayment" it provided fuller imaginative documentation for this attitude. The sympathy for slaves was now "individuated" in a sympathetic picture of Uncle Tom, so that all slaves became Uncle-Tom slaves. An already flourishing hatred of the auction block was "tapped" by the character-recipe, Simon Legree—and this character in turn made more precise in the popular mind the hatred of the auction block by adding the crack of the whip. There is no difference in procedure here from the procedure of a "pure drama," such as *Macbeth*, which gets its effect by "tapping" our horror of murder, and repays this profit by giving us in exchange, not the vague thing murder, but blood on the hands, and the knock of conscience made into a ribald knocking at the door.

For a distinction between "pure" and "propaganda" literature we must not look to the author's method. We must seek the distinction in the social situation. A book becomes "propaganda" simply by reason of the fact that the ideology upon which it relies for its effectiveness is close to a "burning issue," as with the old "problem novel," which horrified us with pictures of hereditary degeneracy during the decade or so that all social ills were attributed to deterioration of the germ plasm. A writer who exploited some aspect of our ideology having to do with sex perversion, for instance, would be writing "pure literature" in the technical sense so long as people's primary interests were in other fields; but should there be a drive on foot for the propagation or eradication of sexual perverts, this book would become "propagandist." So far as esthetic procedure goes, so far as the literary man profits himself by tapping our attitudes and profits us by giving us a richer and more ramified corpus of imagery for some attitude which otherwise would remain less "documented," there is no fundamental difference in the literary tactics of this sex book, *Uncle Tom's Cabin, 1919,* and the sweet floating imagery by which Shakespeare in *The Tempest* exploits our love of distant music, and in return gives substance to our distant-music imaginings.

Clearly, the author who "weights" his observations in this sense will both contribute to the reinforcing of the serviceable attitude and be rewarded for doing so. If our literate public, for instance, is filled with varying degrees of resentment toward the orthodox capitalist order, a poet unfriendly to this order will both exploit this resentment and reinforce it by the "weighting" of his observations with his particular "gravitational pull" in mind: looking at the unshipped cars in the storage yard of a Detroit manufacturer during the depression, he may see them huddled forlornly and without purpose, whereas if the same yard were beheld in Russia, the poet's eye might see the cars there all aflutter, eager to leap forward in their glad task of gratifying the restive peasantry. One not so greatly touched by this resentment, however, might find such "weighting" excessive, a "rhetorical exaggeration," since his own attitude does not lead him to meet the poet "halfway," so he may observe glumly that a car's a car, and if it's new and shiny in Detroit, it is exactly the same as though it were new and shiny in Russia, or its dinginess in one place is like its dinginess in another—and the observation may help us to understand somewhat why different historic periods have such vastly differing ideas as to what they shall call "mere rhetoric." A work tends to become "mere rhetoric" when it has been strongly weighted by a specific situation and this situation meanwhile has been completely changed so that, the "gravitational pull" being gone, the "weighted" material now seems "gaseous." Hence in particular the "mere rhetoric" of the law courts, which was no mere rhetoric at all at the time it was offered, but a very wise and accurate adjustment to a specific situation. For the things one says when a man is sitting in the dock, alive and breathing, and accused of crimes which, if the charge is proved, will take this particular man, whom one is watching, and put his light out, the things one says under such conditions are so imbued with the particularities of the case that nothing short of the entire scene could restore for us the logic of their "weighting."

So, in the end, all books are "weighted," be they propaganda or pure. A work like Mr. Dos Passos's *1919* might be "weighted" to strengthen serviceable attitudes toward the situation now particularly upon us—the weighting of *The Tempest* might conceivably reside in the fact that its imagery is a corrective to many situations, reinforcing in general our fleeting "adumbrations" of possible gentler existences. The intensity of a book's appeal is always based upon the reader's disposition to "meet the author halfway." A work cannot possibly overwhelm people unless it is a mere spark for "touching off a charge" already accumulated within them. Artists do not load power kegs—they light fuses (though the imagery they assemble may in turn become a powder keg for someone else's fuse, as Mr. A might set Mr. B into a rage by calling him "old Scrooge"). The artist is like the man who cried "Fire!" in a theater. The "brilliancy" of the fellow arose out of the fact that he shouted the word best adapted to "touching off" a stampede under these particular conditions. Thus "pure" literature, as distinguished from "propaganda" literature, would simply be literature "weighted" as regards broader or less burning issues (preferring perhaps those issues which burn with the "hard, gemlike flame"). And as with any other terminology, the appositeness of a writer's images will vary with the change of conditions: the terminology of astrophysics would not generally be found very "pivotal" in a plague.

Agitators and Poets

We dare protest only when Marx-inspired critics attempt to go beyond their prescriptions for the season, offering statements as to the function of imaginative literature in general, which they seek to confine within their wholly malapropos concept of the bourgeois-proletarian dichotomy. What good designate as escape the fruits of some discipline upon which a man may have formed himself for years? If he has got to the present point in his researches and accomplishments after a very rigorous pursuit of his ideas, and thus possesses a range in which he has equipped himself with some especial penetration, what good would there be—should some great plague come upon us—in asking that he learn medicine? If there is a call for action, presumably his body will be worth what any similar body is worth, as a means of carrying the sick or burying corpses—and likewise if a time for action comes in our economic disasters, we may expect to find him lost in the storming of some bastille or other, like the next man. But as regards the purely intellectual realm, let us not expect him to turn from the matters in which he is skilled, to grind out sickly revolutionary exhortations for which his very abilities unfit him. Critics may, it is true, make their Cause look all the worthier by proposing in the name of the Cause that all such earnest workmen be scorned—but if they did not feel that a writer's efforts are turned pointedly enough toward the Cause of emancipation as they conceive it this year, they might with as much justice simply include such a writer among the class whom they would save, restricting the active business of salvation to their own abler hands.

For such protectiveness, the "inapposite" writers should be very grateful. I could imagine nothing more humiliating than the plight of an author who, after giving his best efforts to the conquest of the situation in which he found himself, mastering it finally by an appropriate ordering of vocabulary (after much uncertainty and even breathlessness, as he felt himself lost among imponderabilia and evanescence which seemed too quick for formulation, and really would have been had they not kept returning again and again, their repetitiveness becoming an equivalent for steadiness), and if the author has finally made himself at home in these matters, and has a solid, integrated body of imagery to offer, and puts it down, I can imagine nothing more annoying than for some damned pestilence to arise, or drought, or war, so wholly irrelevant to the main aspects of his triumphs that they become woefully "off the subject." Hence, if sociologically minded critics can whip people into shape, and organize their efforts in such a way that this overwhelming irrelevancy is removed, he may hope that when it is gone, his own preoccupations will again become more relevant. So let him go and sit among agitators, and run them little errands, and bring them trade-lasts, and beg them to hasten the day, assuring them that he is too hopelessly among the downtrodden to be of any great emancipatory benefit as regards the current issue, and confessing how he cannot even properly take delight in his own accomplishments until these agitators have removed the grave problem which, during its fierce hegemony, makes the accomplishments seem as arbitrary as a "full-rigged ship in a bottle," or as violin-playing, or as the loveliness of *The Tempest*.

And out of his gratitude, he may in an humble way partially repay his debt to them even now—for he may assist in preventing what might be called the dangers of "over-agitation." By providing images for issues other than the key issue, he may modestly contribute to the agitators' work by contrast. His own works, somewhat to the side of the burning issue, may prevent people from being agitated and agitated upon the one subject alone until, out of an excess of agitation, they simply let their minds collapse, and take to solving rebuses and puzzles (a devious gratification if ever there was one, as the puzzle-solver puts himself a step behind on taking up the unsolved puzzle, and thus on solving it he can get the feeling of advancement so necessary to "acceptance," though his illusion of progress was obtained by his simply bringing himself up to the place where he had been at the beginning, namely, with a slate wiped clear of puzzles).

Essentially, the work of the "pure" poet and the work of the agitator coincide: each, that is, is contributing to make the mind at home in the fluidities of change. For if the true "agitative" quality of art in general resides in its ability to keep the doors open, to increase our range of receptivity by the building of fragmentary insights into well-documented wholes, the agitators too are involved in the engendering of greater receptivity, though in their case the receptivity is confined to a more limited set of conditions. If pure poetry has caught enough of the evanescent by now to make us at home in Change, the agitators are pledged definitely to one particular Change, carrying the tradition of nineteenth-century evolutionary thinking to the point where it affects the very pocketbook. In this sense, we might hold that the importance of the agitators is not so much in what they say as in the mere fact of their saying it. Perhaps their real service to their Cause is somewhat like the service once done the Faith by the old works of piety, which were prolific in their discovery of cunning and remote and unsuspected sins whereby the man who had thought himself passably good, in an average sort of way, could be proved to bristle with transgressions as a porcupine with quills. It did not much matter what the sins were—the cause or piety was served by the uncovering of *any* sins. So perhaps these agitators perform the best service to their Cause, not by leading us to read one author and shun another, but simply by the fact that their various exhortations and warnings, regardless of whom they apply to, serve to familiarize us with the idea of Change in general, so that their Revolution tends to become something taken for granted, as the problem imperceptibly moves up a peg, no longer being "Shall we have a Revolution?" but "What sort of Revolution shall it be?" In this sense, they would do their Cause as much benefit were all their exhortations and warnings reversed, if only the opposite judgments likewise were offered in the name of Change.

Is There Another Revolution?

There is a way of widening and deepening convictions until they are found to touch upon matters which at first seemed quite unrelated to them—and one may pursue these linkages along courses of their own, seeking to fit into a larger whole the particular concerns which started one on a particular hunt. The "esthetic" would seem to differ from the "practical" not in essence but in degree; the "esthetic" would permit us to go further afield in our search of "linkages." I might illustrate the difference by saying that a dog's discomfiture under fleas is not an "esthetic" matter but a practical one. If the dog but had an interest in theory for its own sake, however, we could take advantage of this purely esthetic curiosity to make him understand how, after the relief of a purifying bath in flea-soap, he gets a fresh population of fleas from his confreres, the esthetic thus helping him to a very practical bit of insight. Meanwhile, he considers it practical to scratch, but we esthetes do not consider this a very practical solution at all.

The esthetic, to be of any significance to the esthete, must ever be founded upon something so practical as an insistent "push away from." Like the practical, it is a search for the "pull toward." It differs from the practical primarily in the range which it would permit itself in the search for the appropriate "pull toward." It finds worthy of deep consideration many possibilities which the practical would dismiss in a flash.

Once a frame of reference is established by general acceptance, this frame becomes "practical." It is practical to confine one's consideration of a problem within the frame of reference generally accepted. When the businessman boasts that he "sticks to hard facts," that he deals only with "realities," he means simply that he will not expand or alter the accepted frame of reference, being totally uninterested, for instance, in Thorstein Veblen's acute ways of exposing the naive metaphysical assumptions upon which business attempts to base itself. The businessman is sticking to hard facts when he evaluates his year's business by the showing on his balance sheet. To envisage the question of profits by any frame of reference beyond this balance sheet is impractical. The socialists who begged him to place this problem in a larger frame were mere "visionaries," a kind of "social esthete," until it finally turns out that the practical frame of reference was pretty much like the practicality of the dog scratching his fleas, while the esthetic, theoretic frame was the one which was really the more practical on the subject of flea-bites.

The balance sheet was, as surveyors would say, the businessman's "bench mark," a bench mark being "one of a number of marks along a survey, affixed to permanent objects, to show where leveling staffs were placed." I have seen old deeds, so imbued with the respect for bench marks, that they guided one so many links north by east so many degrees and minutes to an "oak sapling"; and looking at the yellowed page, one could know without following the old surveyor's lines that there would be no "oak sapling" at that point. There might be a patriarchal tree; there might not even be the vestiges of a stump—but a sapling, no. Or I read of a boundary bordering on "Henry Hart's land," yet all the Harts had long ago died off or filtered into other counties. So, were one to make a second survey, one should change his frame of reference somewhat. If the second survey were of business, and one were a Thorstein Veblen, the equivalent for the "sapling" kind of bench mark might be disclosed in the "fluctuant base-line for the evaluation of collateral."

Practical and Esthetic Frames of Reference

Now, I think the esthetic is a kind of second survey, in the sense that it is always looking along the past bench marks of the practical and noting how many of them are of the "sapling" or "Henry Hart's land" sort. Coming upon these, the esthetic speculates: "At such points there will be something different than is described in the document." In the interests of the practical, of stability, of charting, there is here a wandering into the regions of the impractical, the fluctuant, the uncharted. The esthetic, even if it sees men dying for a Cause, might stop to consider whether a mere rewording of the issue could perhaps transform the entire field of battle into wholly different alignments.

We are now facing the practical and esthetic aspects of revolution. (I say "revolution," though I do not necessarily mean "bloody revolution." There still is a chance that we may transform our unfit institutions by the medium of the ballot. I devoutly hope we do so— as otherwise we lose in democratic safeguards what we gain in the efficiency of dictatorship. I do not share that fine disdain of the people which underlies the Communistic brotherhood. I do not believe that the stablest kinds of social acquisition are gained with the help of a Stalin-herder.) In any event, there are the practical and esthetic aspects of change. The issue has been obscured somewhat by the fact that the formerly esthetic frame now comes forward as the practical one—while the individual businessman, believing that profit is simply a matter of "personal character," and that the situation can be remedied if we have enough men of "real commercial enterprise," emerges as the "visionary," the somnambulist, accomplishing remarkable feats of equilibrium as somnambulists sometimes do, yet walking in his sleep nonetheless. So the propounders of the esthetic frame, which they now see rapidly increasing its candidacy as the practical frame, show some indications that the practical has gone to their heads—for they would deal with nothing now but "reality," and they would scorn the esthetic with fervor. It is by this process that out of the old "esthete" has come the Saul-Paul anti-esthete, as they would now put a stop to the further development of that same fluctuant speculating by which their own esthetic frame was evolved prior to the catching-up of the practical frame. In their proscriptions against further insight, they would even ridicule by implication their own methods of gaining insight.

Meanwhile, the esthetic could not hold for a moment that the fundamentals of any revolution are contained in the mere rearrangement of a few unadjusted laws and commercial practises. Vast social upheavals are the merest symptoms of Change, the surface-manifestations, hardly more than the indication that something is going on. Revolutions must run much deeper than that, if they are not to dry up with the stopping of the spring rains. Who could get elated at the mere thought that Russia might someday have her highways as cluttered with automobiles as America in 1929? Who could thrill to the promise of a new humanity at the realization that if we better distributed our buying power, we might have permanently that tinny prosperity which a large part of our population enjoyed for a few deceptive years? Who could be reassured by the kind of "spiritual rebirth" that comes of taking homeless boys, saying to them, "Come, boys, let's build a railroad," and making "men" of them by enlisting their sturdy efforts in this work? One has seen ministers of the gospel very ably ridiculed for their recent utterances as to how the financial disasters are a "blessing in disguise," since they make so many people destitute, and can thus elevate others by opening in them the founts of Christian charity. Yet what essential difference is there between this ghastly notion of uplift, and the uplift that comes of building a railroad where there is none? Of course we must have a railroad where there is none—but what we in America must seek is the kind of uplift that might come when the railroad is already there.

The possibilities of the "real" revolution are to be bought in another order. We dare salute in the Russian system, not the promise that it may eventually be distributing motor cars as the American system could not continue doing, but the possibility that by this system people might gradually lose interest in motor cars without thereby causing a national disaster. I do not mean that there is anything wrong with motor cars. It is said that when pepper was first brought from the East, people sat down to whole plates of it, and nearly burned out their gizzards before pepper became sufficiently taken for granted for them to use it merely as a seasoning. And likewise with motor cars, which are bad as social platefuls, but very useful as social seasoning. My point is simply that, by the American system, we cannot turn our mechanical commodities from platefuls to mere seasoning in our social life without so ruining "sales" that we cause ghastly disorders to the state. People must continue wanting things terribly, even after they have them. They dare not stop wanting a commodity simply because it is there in sufficient amount to fulfill their industrial needs—they must go on wanting it in excessive amounts, since only a mounting production of it could fulfill their commercial needs. Add now the dilemma that after they have made this hideous adjustment to the productive forces under capitalism, after they have obediently twice-buried themselves by teaching themselves to want more and more of all sorts of tinny things, not as social seasoning but as heaping platefuls, devoting their entire day either to commodity-gourmandizing or to concocting the products for one another's commodity-gourmandizing, add now the unkind fact that the sluicing of profits into too few hands interferes with this obedient surrender against which the "esthetes" had thundered for a century, and you understand why we can place our hopes only in an economic order which can let industrial gourmandizing lapse into industrial seasoning. The esthete may at last take heart, as people may no longer *be called upon to teach themselves to enjoy* the conditions of an economic warfare which, insofar as one man's profits entail another man's loss, differs from thievery only in the sense that when being robbed by a thief, one is not usually expected to take a cooperative part in the enterprise. Or there may be such new promise as might arise were men to say, "There is no further railroad that needs building; hence, we cannot rouse ourselves any longer to ennoblement by calling, 'Come, boys, let's build a railroad'; precisely at this point, historically the beginning of 'degeneration,' we propose to situate the springboard into a different sphere of efforts." In advocating the revolution of expedients, which is the practical revolution arising out of the former esthetic frame, we must keep in mind the new esthetic frame which must begin to take into account the subsequent "pull toward."

Essentially, the new frame must be based, not upon the elation of Antithesis, but upon the fact that *ennoblement* must not arise out of *deprivation*. The entire purpose of the present movement is to bring about a state of affairs eliminating rudimentary deprivation. As a consequence, the kind of exaltedness that comes of buddy-

thinking in the trenches must be minimized, lest people find themselves required to maintain warfare purely in order that they may
buddy-think (as the minister of the gospel advocated destitution as a
way of striking the hard rock and making the waters of charity flow
from it). We must promise to one another the kinds of punishment
that come of walking beneath palms. The new esthetic frame of
rigors must be relegated to a different order—the battle cries which
now make comrades feel good are precisely the aspect of the new
practical frame which becomes, by the esthetic frame still further
along, the scratching of flea-bites. We must embrace the present
Cause cynically, as a mere *devoir* to be performed, lest we open
ourselves to the threat of disintegration through its success. We
must consider it as an attempt to use as seasoning what was once
platefuls, and is now plate-empties.

Critical and Creative as Obverse
and Reverse of One Mintage

Hence, now that the old esthetic frame has gained some practical
validity, and we, from this point of vantage, would set out in search
of new linkages, new bench marks of the "sapling" and "Henry
Hart's land" variety—let us risk, in a vague way, stating the kind of
considerations with which the new esthetic frame might possibly be
concerned. It will concern itself, in some form or other, with three
worlds, which we have called the primary, secondary, and tertiary
worlds—and it will attempt to contrive all kinds of shuttle-concepts
for slipping back and forth easily among them. Its relation to the
primary world (the metaphysical or religious world) will be established mainly as a *yearning*. Its relation to the secondary world (to
directer, more "natural" ways of living, an ampler tapping of the
"primitive") will be established partially by actual attainment and
partially by imaginings. Its relation to the tertiary world (of contingencies, passing problems, "news") will be established by sche-
matization and identification of a much fuller sort than is now
available to us, as we become better learned in what "news" is.
As the sciences gain in rigor, it will perhaps be left to art to venture
the most hazardous "shuttlings" among these primary, secondary,
and tertiary fields. Metaphor, welded to desire, can often give us
glimpses of the primary, at least in the sense that it *gives substance
to our feeling of what it might be like to know the primary*. As for
the secondary world, through the somewhat "recidivistic" trait in
artists (corresponding to the "return" we saw in actors, who restored
the animal totality of "gesture-speech" by adjusting the entire set of

their bodies to the tone of their sentences), we shall be enabled to participate more fully in the ways of this secondary world (a world in which one lets himself be easily aroused to anger, since, by the same token, he may be as easily aroused to good-nature). In part we may incorporate the artist's suggestions into our own lives; in part, we shall leave them on the page, but constantly incorporate them into the *interpretation* of our lives. And art will illuminate the tertiary world by the various devices of comparison, idealization, simplification, summarization, et cetera. It can pull all the sciences together, as neither science nor philosophy nor history can, offering a quick likeness between some process in geology, say, and the way a motor goes, and finding it fruitful through finding it picturesque, through "starting things that it doesn't finish." It can be a kind of squandering of hypotheses, holding them for one flash only, for one phrase or sentence, and then assuming by its next grouping some other hypothesis. It can be a peculiar welding of irresponsibility and discipline, since it is wayward in its use of material, yet this material must always obey an order integral to the opus in which it is contained—and the material, further, can arise only out of erudition (I refer not necessarily to an acquaintance with other texts, though there may be this too—but primarily to a familiarity with the varied assortment of signs which go to make up life itself, and which the artist scans carefully, whether he knows it or not).

In art of this sort, the merging of criticism and poetry will be complete, as people come to feel the same synthetic satisfaction in a formula as in an image, and come to realize that the same "intuitive" step is involved in any progression, be it a raising of the arm, the solving of a problem in mathematics, a growth of narrative, or nice unfoldings of exposition and argumentation. The same modes of insight can be handled by imagery or concepts—and as this fact comes more into prominence, we shall consider the poetic and the critical as obverse and reverse of the same coin. It is agreed that criticism analyzes the processes which poetry exemplifies—it is not sufficiently recognized that poetry throws great light upon the processes which criticism exemplifies. The "background" which the poet or novelist supplies for his events is expanded imperceptibly until it becomes the "essayistic" background of criticism; his story, ever seeking to make itself "typical," covers the same field of understanding as the "case history" of descriptive science. More and more we find writers like Gide and Mann, who offer comment upon their work as an integral part of the work's "message." There is a tendency to seek an interchangeability of the conceptual and the imaginative, as would be natural to a state of thinking whereby vocabulary or terminology is discovered to be a major aspect of "observation," so that we recognize not merely something to be seen and someone seeing it, but also an intermediary process of grouping and linguistic identification which dictates the "essence" of the thing seen. To any poetic "mythology" there is a rigorous, conceptual equivalent. In any work of art there is implicit a set of ethical and esthetic canons, and a methodology. "Understanding," to be complete, attempts to *use* a process, to *describe* the process, and to *orientate* the process with relation to other processes. Hence, insofar as a writer aims to fix a vocabulary, his "critical" and "imaginative" interests merge.

This general welding of the critical and imaginative might terminate a line of thought which was perhaps most clearly inaugurated when people began noting the indistinguishability of poetry and prose, or began considering the boldness—and even at times the rashness—of some scientific or historical doctrines. The establishment of a critical order has to wait upon the unpredictable ways of "insight" just as surely as the writing of a tragedy does. The resonance in the formulae of Newton, as compared with the mere rattle of some contemporary "emotional" drama, will further lead us to be less prompt in dividing the "emotional" from the "unemotional," as we learn instead perhaps to distinguish people not so much by emotionality and lack of it, as by the sort of things they get emotional about and the ways in which they get emotional. Such an alteration would avoid the current blunders that come of calling poems like those of Mr. T. S. Eliot "intellectualistic," despite their intensity of feeling which suggests nothing so much as gnarled anguish, while we grant warmth categorically to some nearly brainless poetess who even fears to read another book lest her own precious personality be nibbled at the edges, and who packs her pages with those body pulsings which one should begin with, to which one should be sensitive before sitting down to write at all, but which he relegates to a minor place in his work purely because enough cannot be done with them. Indeed we might even say that the so-called intellectual writer alone gives the true indications of emotionality, since his emotions are sturdy enough to carry over even into quite abstruse matters, still engrossing him where the brainless lady would have been made quite frigid. There should be different tests for emotionality on a page and in a bed.

"Life Is a Maze"—with Qualifications

The esthetic, then—in science, in art, in philosophy, in criticism—is a process of naming, and of naming in such a way that one seeks to go beyond the points of reference which one finds already available around him. It is a conscious step into the realm of "trial and error," as trial and error applies, not to an animal's mere blind fumblings in an arbitrarily constructed maze, but as it applies to the attempt of an intelligent being who finds himself caught in mazes that have, for all their indifference to him, some underlying logic or order in their construction (at least in the sense that some of their passageways "naturally" give rise to others, or that the whole is constructed by some scheme of mutual adjustments within its parts, and not merely put together for the sake of experimenting upon a hungry and bewildered cat). That is, we have something better to try, in our efforts to extricate ourselves, than a mere slashing about until we happen to hit the latch that releases the trap door. Experimenting, of even the blindest sort, is certainly a large part of the emancipatory process—but we have also the assistance of documents, as though a second cat, never before in such a maze, might pull the latch and get himself out promptly if a prior cat could have left him a message, in perfect Cat, saying, "Pull down this latch to release trap door." And insofar as each maze of history is a new maze, so that the past latches are not quite the ones to work, we are still assisted by our ability to experiment consciously on the basis of *meanings*—that is, the archives as to past experience with mazes have left us with some indications as to the construction of mazes in general, and on the basis of these we may theorize as to what device *ought* to be effective in freeing us, thus making fewer random motions.

Sometimes the novelty of the maze, or the stupidity of prior cats, makes it difficult for us to hit upon any satisfactory device whatsoever. At other times, though we may have found the correct device, we find it difficult to hit upon ways of inducing people to use it. So we become involved in a kind of maze-within-a-maze, as we believe that we have the right device, yet are imprisoned with others, and the device is so heavy that we cannot move it alone, needing the cooperation of others before it can be put to the test, whereas for various reasons they happen to be disinterested in the device, bewildered by the device, or may even think of it with loathing. We learn that before we can get them to try the device, we must examine the mazes of the mind, until we have also laid down a working hypothesis as to the mind's logic, and with the help of this hypothesis (generally assumed rather than explicit) we seek to construct a stimulating device for inducing people to try our emancipatory device.

So it is with the formulation of an economic expedient, and with the problem of making it acceptable to the people (or if not making it acceptable to them, then at least making them accept it). Were the expedient needed, were it adopted, and did it work, I am sure that we should then see our way clear to seek the devices for other emancipations (the need for which arose in part from the fact that the successful operation of the economic device had released us to concern ourselves with broader matters, and in part from the fact that the operating of the economic device had, in itself, given rise to new difficulties as a by-product of its operation).

Then there is the "wayward" factor: how a man will find some detail of interest in the maze, not because it promises to get him out, but because, while seeking a way out, he came upon this detail which he happens to consider remarkable in itself. It may or may not turn out to be the very thing that was needed—but in any case, he has drawn it forth for observation where others had passed it by—in giving it a name, and a place among other names, he has made it an "object." It is now a candidate for further consideration, when other men come to look over the available arcana of resources.

Nor must we always think of devices by this division into the categories of the "stimulating" and the "emancipatory." Since many of our mazes are purely mazes of the mind, the stimulating device and the emancipatory device will be found to have merged into one, the exhortation and the result being identical, the inducement to see in a certain way being also the content of such seeing.

Perhaps our maze, as so qualified, is the maze of the Gestalt, or Configurationist account of meanings, which was formulated as its propounders watched apes get food, and which thus follows empirical facts much more closely than does Marx's optimistic determinism. By this Configurationist theory, a meaning or ideology "suited to" a situation would arise out of the situation only in the sense that the environmental situation presented a problem to be solved. The "solution," however, would be something unpredictably added, a re-adaptation of past meanings to the new situation, requiring a new "combination" so extrinsic to the situation itself that it need never be found at all, and much too tentative to be discussed in terms of "causality," so far as our present vocabulary of causation goes.

By placing in a cage with an ape two separate sticks which could be joined to make a longer one, and by placing food outside the cage beyond the reach of either stick used singly, the investigators observed the rise of a new "meaning" as to the use of sticks. They observed the ape first trying ineffectually to rake in the food with one or the other of the sticks, experimenting so blindly at times that he even tried to reach the food from the opposite side of the cage. They observed him, while playing idly with the sticks, discover in the course of his manipulations that the two could be joined. Shortly after, with something very much like a flash of understanding, the ape ran with his new device to the edge of the cage and raked in the food. Other problems of similar sorts were tried on this ape and other apes. And so little did the nature of the problem determine the solution, that very often some of the apes did not find the requisite meanings or "configurations" at all, did not link their past knowledge in a new way to obtain new results, even though they sometimes had in front of them the examples of apes who had become quite at home in the new meanings and used them regularly.

A "meaning" is a way of grouping relationships. We may call it the "right" meaning if the grouping enables us to get what we have been trying to get—though precisely here, when the result is viewed in terms of more comprehensive configurations, the very impulse behind our discovery of the first meaning may be proved erroneous by the terms of the broader meaning, as would be the case if the food which the ape had sought and captured happened to contain arsenic. In this event, he would require a further set of "meanings" to warn him that it was not the auspicious occasion for him to use his "joining-and-raking-in" configuration at all.

It will thus be seen that there are meanings beyond meanings, or meanings within meanings—and that one might show much cunning in the putting together of one meaning where another meaning was needed, so that he might have been better off in this particular situation had he been stupid enough to find no apposite configuration at all. Perhaps much of the grave economic difficulty in America today arises from the fact that many men were exceptionally cunning within too limited a range of meanings, showing remarkable inventiveness and fieriness in the attaining of their ends as kept within these limits, but too enamored of this "practical" range to concern themselves with any "esthetic" speculation that might have expanded it, and perhaps have disclosed to them that much of the nourishment they raked into their cage with consummate skill was tainted with something very much like arsenic, which can be taken only in very small quantities, and even then not regularly, though it is true that, by the physiological process known ironically enough as "tolerance" or "mithridatism," one can bring himself to the point where his body can stand such amounts of this and similar poisons as would brutally destroy a dozen unaccustomed men.

The Marxian configuration (and such types of economic theorizing as are allied with it) provides a broader configuration, since it carries the question of profit beyond a mere relationship between each employer individually and his workmen, and leads us to see how, out of a group of such isolated orders, each a well-integrated unit in itself, we can get sheer unmitigated disaster as regards the state in its entirety. Hence, as viewed within the scheme of the Marxian configuration, the configuration developed under isolated private enterprise seems very fragmentary. But let the Marxians not persuade either us or themselves that merely because the practical frame of reference shows some sign of catching up with the esthetic frame, we are to suppose that the ultimate configuration of meanings is now discovered, and that henceforth the tentative-esthetic must rot. One can entertain the possibility of still broader configurations, within which Marxism and its similar economic theories must all appear fragmentary in turn. Such broader configurations, for instance, would provide a more "meaningful" account of human impulses in general, not taking contemporary desires and patterns of thought so much for granted as the economists do, placing in the category of *meanings* the aims and ambitions which are still too often regarded as *facts*. It is in the direction of this broader configuration that we must look if we would again erect a purely esthetic frame of revolution one step in advance of the present esthetic-practical merger. By this proposed esthetic frame, the present issue would involve primarily a mere revolution of expedients, perhaps even endangering its own best results at the start, since it tends to rely upon the most reactionary of all devices, the coup d'état and the benevolent dictatorship. These devices may be needed. They may even be secretly upon us already, covertly in the hands of "the enemy." As a consequence, we may find ourselves requiring such dreary old baggage as the counter–coup d'état and the counter-dictatorship. If such is the case, if the new revolution can be put into effect only by a method that endangers its results, we may accept our lot, regretfully, even sullenly—but let us not meet it with acclaim, and the suspect ennoblement of buddy-thinking. Let us say that there is an important economic stride to be taken. This would be exactly like saying that there is an elevator to be gone up in. Some people who go up in an elevator for the first time are quite thrilled by the experience. Others, seeing the glint in their eye, grumble, "Ah, that's not the city at all. That's the pretty part." Let us recall that not even a revolution is a bed of roses. And let us not be surprised to find a Man of Steel in the Kremlin while a man with the erudition, the critical acumen, and the integrity of a Trotsky rots in exile.

Wherein We Reconsider
the Phenomenon of the Twice-Buried

Our notion of the practical-esthetic merger gives us another point of vantage from which to look back upon the literature of "protest." The esthetic frame, which opposed the practical frame for a century, is coming into acceptance, because the practical frame is broken. An absurdity must finally prove itself an absurdity even in its own terms—and if the practical frame was once questioned only *from without* (as viewed from the alien esthetic frame), it is now proved even incapable of fulfilling its own criteria; it is proved impractical precisely by its own scheme of the "good life," since it is unable to uphold the processes of commodity-gourmandizing which it considered the fulcrum of "culture."

The old bourgeois-Bohemian dichotomy of the last century might thus be widened into a general "philistine-intellectual" dichotomy, under which the bourgeois and proletarian alike were attacked by the Artist-Intellectual as tending to fall within the category of the Twice-Buried. Thus the Esthete-Bohemian-Intellectual, who had warned against profit-thinking for a century, was really in the "religious" camp as opposed to Business, no matter how godless he seemed, for he continually offered versions of the "good life" based upon the idea of "spiritual" attainments as opposed to purely material acquisitions and the ideology that went with them. We might even say that the agnostic literature of the romantics carried on the battle against the reign of Business or Profit-Thinking after the churches themselves had abandoned it, as the churches learned to stress the acquiescent aspects of the Faith which would minimize any conflicts between religion and business as a "way of life." Then there gradually arose the "popular art" of the great advertising mediums, magazine fiction defining the good life exactly as it was defined in the advertising columns, and hence paralleling in turn the churchmen's surrender to the authority of Commerce. It was now left for the Individualists, the Last-Standers, the Poets-against-the-World, the aggressive builders of stubborn Ivory Towers, the pure and simple Esthetes, to carry on alone the attack against the accommodation of the Twice Buried.

By this time the breach between the Poet and his Society had become so great as easily to be made greater. Romantics, finding themselves at odds with their fellows on so many points, did not hesitate to put themselves at odds on still further points. One may call this either self-indulgence or spirit, as one chooses. I should prefer simply to designate it as a technical event: odds making for greater odds, just as fortunes make for greater fortunes. There were even "debaucheries" of style, there was the general tendency towards obscurantism, the refusal to be victimized by victims (since the people who had made the accommodation of Twice-Burial, adjusting all their images and desires to the requirements of a Profit economy growing intense under the increases in productive efficiency, were now accepted wholly as "victims," or as a natural phenomenon like bad weather, against which one sheltered himself as well as he could, as one had abandoned the attempts to exorcize the badness from bad weather). The realization had begun to filter in that if so many millions of people were moving in the direction of this Twice-Burial, it must be because they *had to*. They were being carried on the Currents of Necessity.

But merely because they were being carried on the Currents of Necessity was no reason why the Intellectuals should be carried on these Currents of Necessity likewise. "Insight," as De Gourmont noted, was returning to the "catacombs," where it had taken refuge once before without thereby losing its vitality. One sought one's "band." All sorts of colonies arose, not generally in the literal sense of gatherings under one roof (though there were many of these as well), but in the sense that they were united by a common tradition. Literary men, on meeting each other, suggest nothing so much as the mutual tentative smellings of two dogs. There were all kinds of abstruse tests for recognizing members of one's psychic lodge without the need of some definite trick in the handshake.

The underlying principle throughout this entire movement, ranging as it did from explicit anti-commercial satire to the implicitly anti-commercial imagery of the Ivory Tower, remained always the same: the Protest against the phenomenon of the Twice-Buried, a protest which is now being taken up and carried to completion by the Marxians, who have been encouraged to exhort rather than "retire" by the fact that the Practical is now so near to obvious bankruptcy. This collapse was delayed throughout the nineteenth century by the pronounced expansionistic movement of the century, since the progressive inclusion of fresh areas within the circle of capitalistic exploitation put off from year to year the final dilemma of exploitation: the dilemma that when you have taken all, you must give back in order to take more. The very virtues of capitalism for promoting the process of expansion should in themselves lead us to question capitalism as a fitting adaptation for any other historical condition. It could hardly have stimulated expansion so magnificently had not its very genius required expansion. And now that the entire world is pretty well brought within the one economic frame, and the expansionistic movement slows down to a close, the difficulties of continued exploitation become obvious. Hence the esthetic frame of reference now enjoys an advantage in argument which it did not enjoy during the heyday of romantic "protest." The practical frame could then be attacked only by "theorists" and "dreamers," some of them attacking it on economic grounds, others (the romantics generally) attacking it on the grounds of the psychological warpings it required for our accommodation to it. But though the romantics might hate the brutal disintegration which they saw their own Occidental culture forcing upon so-called backward peoples, their protests were ineffectual against the joyous materialist doctrines of "progress" which gave heart to bourgeois and proletarian exploiters alike. This common bourgeois-proletarian hunt, in which the two groups merely haggled over the division of the spoils, now comes to a close—as it would not even now, if we could but find good markets on Mars.

Romantic and Humanistic Protestants

Thus, if we see that there is no fundamental distinction between the Marxian prescriptions and the romantic prescriptions, each arising out of the same esthetic frame of reference as contrasted with the "practical" business frame that took over science and dominated the century, the same point of view leads us to dissolve the contemporary feud between romanticist-naturalist and classicist-humanist. Both camps are found to have been maintaining an esthetic frame of reference broader than the practical frame of reference in which they moved. Both were dealing with the same phenomenon, the tendency of the esthetic frame to languish under the war of attrition waged against it by the powerfully authoritative practical frame (a tendency all the more liable, since, as we have shown before, the esthetic formulations arise out of the same "push away from" as the practical). Both camps were dealing fundamentally with the problem of the Twice-Buried, the tendency of people to accommodate themselves completely to the demands of the contingent, to equip themselves for the battle of living in a society of intense economic strife by adopting such ambitions and desires as would make them most at home in this economic strife.

The ways of symbolizing the dislike of this accommodation varied greatly. Perhaps the most moving version of all, at least when it is read with the pressure of the present difficulties to make us "meet the poet halfway" is that astoundingly firm and inexorable poem of Mr. Edwin Markham, "The Man with the Hoe," in which he pictures the "accommodation" as a sheer blunting of human gentleness and receptivity, a deadening of all one's interests in order that one may incidentally procure the deadening of pain:

> Who made him dead to rapture and despair,
> A thing that grieves not and that never hopes,
> Stolid and stunned, a brother to the ox?
> Who loosened and let down this brutal jaw?
> Whose was the hand that slanted back this brow?
> Whose breath blew out the light within this brain?

And having pictured resignation in so repellent a form, the Poet yet feels that the genius of the organs must still somewhere be crying out, however deeply submerged beneath the contemporary necessities. And so this brutalized thing may someday protest in the interests precisely of gentler ways, yet protesting within the terms of the brutal jaw which has been forced upon it:

> How will it be with kingdoms and with kings—
> With those who shapt him to the thing he is—
> When this dumb Terror shall rise to judge the world,
> After the silence of the centuries?

The line of social satirists, from Flaubert to Sinclair Lewis, saw the same accommodation being made in a much less tragic, but very irritating way, as people became quite at home in the new scheme, and went forth gustily each day to economic strife, thrilled with Californian images of progress. Akin to this satiric movement was the Ivory Tower movement (some of the satirists themselves only came out of their Ivory Tower on occasion to flay the ideological set-up of the Profit-system). In general, as we have suggested, the Ivory Tower movement was more affirmative than that of pure satire, as it went aggressively to work laying out rich schemes of counter-imagery. In this sense, paradoxically enough, we might interpret it as the first clear manifestation of the present tendency toward a definitely stated and positive "ideal." Its "retreat" was given the fullest artistic substantiality. Not contenting itself with the negative criticism of satire, it offered any number of alternate worlds, imagined with fullness. Gradually also there came the discovery of still another phenomenon in this matter of the Twice-Buried, a living being which we might call the synthesis of Markham's symbol with that of the satirists: the "tough," the "plug-ugly," whose brutal jaw was not loosened and let down at all, but cunningly merged the brutality of the desolate peasant seen by Markham with the "joyous" accommodation of Flaubert's Homais or Lewis's Babbitt—the gangster, the racketeer, who is commonly pictured in the papers as "preying" upon business, but is in reality a mere projection of commercial tactics, asking for a private toll, like any businessman, to be interposed at the distributive stage of a product's movement from production to consumption. If he were not integral to the commercial process, he would not be so intertwined with the commercial process.

Thomas Mann was dealing with this same phenomenon of the Twice-Buried when he looked wistfully at bourgeois people whom he considered antithetical to the Bohemian. He watched them with a kind of envious astonishment, since they surrendered so spontaneously that they were not even conscious of making a surrender. He meanwhile, the Bohemian, remained recalcitrant, admiring the ease of their accommodation (which he was psychologist enough to feel as a social necessity) even while accepting a permanent maladjustment as his own lot in life. As the esthete, thoroughly documented in Mediterranean lore (Mann always gives his divided characters an "outlaw" strain of Southern blood), he must make a life problem of precisely the matter to which his naive burghers adapt themselves without thinking. He thus remains "incongruous," a feeling which he symbolized by the invention of grotesque Bohemian characters through whom his own point of view is satirized. He remains an "outsider," going and looking at people, guilty that he is not one of them, yet remaining what he is. The symbolism is confused somewhat by the fact that Mann's own sweetness or humility (as contrasted with the unrepentant disdain of the Flaubertian attitude) led him to give his burghers the "benefit of the doubt" by endowing them with all the "simple virtues" which he found lacking in himself. He tended to picture these people as though they were the preservers of some past gentleness while he was gnarled with newness. The "esthete" of that time did not realize the element of "return" concealed in his so-called deviations and innovations, as the Marxian is not always aware of a similar "return" in his advocacy of collectivism.

The typical esthete was De Gourmont, who thought himself quite wickedly afloat because he had equipped himself with a kind of contemporary learning to which the *homme moyen* was closed. But his "newness," as with the "new" in Baudelaire and Mann, appeared revolutionary largely because it was opposed to the revolutionary changes which had become the "norm." These men were, we might say, objecting in the name of the "organic productive forces," whose ideology was being crushed beneath the demands of the new "social productive forces." This confusion of the issue runs all through the period, as writers again and again refused to acquiesce to a scheme whereby the maladjustments between the Self and the Non-Self would be righted through the surrender of Self, insisting (though less clearly than the Communists) that we must change the Non-Self, must change the social institutions to fit our needs, rather than changing our needs to fit the social institutions—though of course the final adjustment will involve mutual yieldings of both Self and Non-Self. Sometimes this antagonism made for defiance, sometimes for flippancy. In men like Mann, De Gourmont, and Anatole France it led to the development of irony, which may be defined as a recognition of the fact that people surrender only because they *have to*, along with the recognition of the fact that one does not propose to accept such ready forms of integration for himself. As confined to the poet alone, we may define irony as "that type of vacillation which comes of realizing that the traits which one is best equipped to develop are not the traits best making for one's adaptation to his environment."

Once we consider the world of commerce, of Profit-Thinking, as *authoritative*, once we take it as the essential factor affecting everyone and really constituting the modern "royalty," we see how many rival schools become united as allies in the same protestant campaign: social satirists, dwellers in the Ivory Tower, romantics, literary Marxists, classicists, humanists, even royalists and neo-Catholics. Each was contributing to a counter-movement against the dominant order. All were attempting to provide substantial imagery to prevent the non-practical frame of reference from crumbling under the steady drop-by-drop corrosion of the once authoritative, but now itself corroded, practical frame. They all attempt to maintain a corrective, regulatory esthetic frame as opposed to the acquiescent aspect of the practical.

Primarily, the difference between the humanist and romantic groups arises from their different angles of attack upon the same issue. Generally remaining in the universities as custodians of the religious-metaphysical lore which provided the richest traditional imagery for substantiating the distrust of the demands made upon us by strictly contemporary contingencies, the humanists were naturally led by their texts (mostly "pre-evolutionary" texts) to slight the genetic aspect of these matters. They were more inclined to confront the issue in terms of "scriptural" exhortation (quotation from secular and sacred authority) rather than by an analysis of the process involved in the tertiary accommodation itself. They were less interested in asking "how people got that way" than in admonishing them against getting that way. In general, they were more accurate than the romantic in defining the cultural impoverishments of Twice-Burial, and could often find instances of the romanticist's unconscious surrenders.

For the romantic was in the thick of the Twice-Burial process. Each day he felt the clods falling upon him—and this fact of being "within the process" was perhaps a great incentive in leading him to give much more weight to nineteenth-century evolutionary thought (stemming generally from Hegel), so thoroughly imbued as it was with the sense of processes. Frequently involved in very harsh contacts with the tertiary world, often getting his "Mediterranean lore" only in a kind of "stolen moment," he was more able to feel the element of "immersion." But his talk of "protest" and "rebellion" was the symbolization, in one set of terms, for the same anti-commercial ideology which the humanist symbolized in the terminology of "classic repose."

How Now?

We have been at some pains to make a great many old enemies fraternize. We do not expect them forthwith to love one another on the basis of their common aims; but we do believe that, to the technical eye of history, they will all be seen in the end as mere "sectarian differences in the stressing of a common orthodoxy." But what now? The imminent catching-up of the practical frame would seem to put many valiant protesters out of a job—a predicament which sometimes makes the Marxians exult, though I do not see why the enshrining of the old esthetic frame as the new practical frame should not have precisely the same effect upon themselves.

In any case, what does the "esthetic" do next? If it celebrates the marriage of the practical and esthetic frames by "conforming," it risks violating the basic patterns of character out of which it arose. The old dog must learn new tricks. For the basic patterns of character are "protestant," arising as they do out of the esthete's long tradition of refusal to accept the authority of the profit-economy frame. On the other hand, if the esthete remains faithful to these character patterns, he puts himself in the position of attacking the very millennium for which he had pled. So if he sings the joys of merger, he must quiet something very much like the most adventurous portions of his former self. Or if he retains this, he must "move on," as they tell of the first trail-breakers, who would settle at one end of a twenty-mile-long valley, and when someone finally settled at the other end, they would "clear out" because they found the valley too populous. The simile suggests somewhat the dismalness of the move.

This whole dilemma of the Poet who was born into the tradition of protest against the authority of the practical frame, but who now finds his patterns of protest invalidated by the imminent catching-up of the practical frame, is very competently symbolized, I believe, in Malcolm Cowley's poem "Leander," written to the line from Rimbaud, "un noyé pensif parfois descend." This poem comes near the close of Cowley's *Blue Juniata*, a volume which has given us, up to this point, one typical aspect of the "esthetic" protest, the Poet against the World, who has perhaps gone beyond protest to the Ivory-Tower, *sauve-qui-peut* attitude. On mountaintops, beneath coal tipples, in Parisian cafés, in the landscape gardens of defunct noblemen, contemplating dead swans, observing the expert flight of birds across a lonely sky, singing the advantages of an American among the Alps while the exchange was in the Poet's favor, lapsing into pensiveness to recall the ecstasy of the embrace, made nervous by the roar of cities, saying ever good-bye—after such a general picture we find a poem of indignation at the killing of Sacco and Vanzetti, and then the Leander poem, the poem we now propose to discuss, clearly manifesting its romantic clingings by its citation from Rimbaud.

The poem is quite simply an invitation to the swimmer, Leander, to abandon his struggle against the Current (the current of the sea in Leander's case surely symbolizing the Current of History in the case of the Poet). "Between the waves, out of the sight of land, / at nightfall toward an unseen beacon swimming," Leander, in his weariness, is invited to succumb, and there are all kinds of fantastic promises as his reward:

> The waves that lapped his shoulders cried: surrender
> and dead men's bones a thousand fathoms under
> called in their sterner voices: O Leander,
> surrender. . . .

Shoulders—surrender—under—sterner—Leander—surrender: the lure of these assonances is matched by the lure of images, until Leander finally does surrender, as he

> slowly filled his lungs with water, sank
> through immense halls of darkness, infinite
> chambers of dreams. . . .

He thus became simply "a white thing that drifts / southward with the current."

The sea keeps its excessive promises. The corpse undergoes its sea-change. It is carried in its acquiescent course past all kinds of wonders, developing new kinds of beauty as it becomes encrusted with those heretofore untouched existences that go with currents.

These wonders it spontaneously reflects, through the lenses of its dead eyes, "pelagic meadows where the sea-cow grazes," waters boiling with lava, "unicellular gardens of the foam," and even "the wax and wane of moons," as the milkiness of the dead eyes gives back its own equivalent in this frigid sky-milkiness.

Do we not see in this poem the *dual aspect* of the Current, as it would be found in an esthete born, now attempting to renounce his earlier patterns of protest? The invitation to go *with* the Currents of history arises, manifesting its validity in the prodigality of its promises—yet the vestiges of romantic protest linger, as we see in the symbolism of a *drowning*. Since the patterns of protest are ingrained in one's thinking, the magnificent rewards that come of drifting with the Current can be obtained only by *dying*. The symbol of the Current thus contains aspects of both punishment and reward, punishment for the betrayal of one's old pattern, reward for the welcoming of a new pattern. In the symbol of the Current there is thus "catharsis" (i.e., "acceptance"), since it unites both appeal and warning, call and refusal, transgression and retribution.

This is essentially the problem we face. New men may make the adjustment spontaneously, as Mann's burghers made their wrong adjustment spontaneously, and as the quick standardization of an ideology seems to be flourishing in Russia today. But the old "esthete born" cannot simply slough the basic patterns of his thinking, unless he was too trivial to possess basic patterns very basically. He must consciously unite the acquiescent with the protestant, must both salute the catching-up of the practical frame and maintain a more or less critical attitude despite this practical-esthetic merger. Were the world to be made a perfect world by this proposed merger, did each significant "push away from" henceforth possess its adequate "pull toward," I should say that his persistence in the ways of deviation would be worthless indeed. But as we know that any social movement is, in its very nature, a compromise, we may understand why the protestant note, seeking a new esthetic frame beyond the present, will still be thoroughly apropos. The Marxian ways of seeing, by so ably helping us to see somewhat, can prevent us from seeing more. And above all, since there are millions of people to agree with one another, why should we ask that every writer, even down to the last thirty or forty, agree with them all? Even typhoid carriers have helped the state to a better understanding—so it might not be preposterous to expect some value from dissident artists. We must also bear it in mind that the ways of "cooperation" are devious. A man may contribute new and valuable terms to the vocabulary of biology, for instance, precisely through his refusal to conform with the terms already given. Why should the situation differ in the field of literature? Conformity is not in general such a rare gift that we must prize it above all else. And the non-conforming artist will often, by his non-conformity alone, be punished enough, since he cannot enjoy those rich rewards that come of ringing the bells that cause the salivation in most. He cannot enjoy the massive architectural pleasure of arranging the Hoover-titters and the Trotsky-groans in ever-mounting sequences.

The practical frame will still require much widening, broader configurations—and insofar as all the "experimental" is guided by the "mind helping the body think," the dissident artist may realize that his "innovations" may often be but leading us further back toward the "return," may invoke the sound of stifled voices, may disclose the ways in which all of us unawares have "brutal jaws," may attempt to make a still more accurate revealment of basic requirements which the entire machinery of social living (or should we say even mere "environmental living") has led us to neglect—a "going forward" and a "going back" thus becoming strangely indistinguishable, as the *new* understanding of the mind and its relationship to the universe and to other minds can only be the laying open of relationships that have always been, so that the distinctions between forward-lookers, backward-lookers, and lovers of the "pure" present have all their edges gnawed away again, and we "today" . . . "look forward toward" . . . "ideals" which will satisfy the "pushes away from" that come deeply out of the past.

It is perhaps by this kind of "synthesis" that the marvelous upswing of "evolutionary" thought will be brought to a close. It is hardly to be expected that we can retain the all-absorbing infatuation with "change" as exemplified in nineteenth-century thinking (a pattern of thought which has left us with an invaluable mass of evolutionary and revolutionary documentation, and a method for adding as much more of it as we choose). The evolutionary doctrines, as applied specifically to the "descent" of man, really blinded us a bit by the very brilliance of their insight. But as our eyes have become accustomed to the glare, we can distinguish factors which at first were completely blotted out. We realize that there is a point, an important step, in the evolutionary chain which remains as much as ever unaccounted for by naturalistic doctrines. There is the "inspiration" that comes of making an old situation new by clamping a fresh configuration of meanings upon it, locating it in a different scheme of orientation as we discover it among a wholly different galaxy of terms. The nineteenth century did enough in pointing out so fully (substantiating with such elaborate "imagery") the miraculous processes of evolutionary development—it was thoroughly justified in overlooking "miracles" of any other order. But we, to whom evolutionary thought is no longer a very startling thing, and who really cannot do much more with it beyond supplying subsidiary details, or writing red-hot "Evolutions of the Toothbrush," "Metamorphoses of the Word *Aint*," and "Transitions of Transit-Facilities," we, while retaining this remarkable documentation, and the warning in its method, may turn our attention toward the precise spot which evolutionism neglected. Essentially this would amount to an emphasis upon the *quality*, rather than upon the *power*, of our ambitions and attainments.

Closing Orientation

In any event, the process whereby the "esthetes" become generally reborn as Communists should now be clear. We chart the points briefly, thus:

All during the nineteenth century, when the applications of science were inducing a florescence of the "profit-economy" such as the world had never before witnessed, the intellectuals had fortified themselves against this authority of the practical frame by formulating a directly antithetical esthetic frame. Hence, the acute development of individualist protest, which was converted into "colony thinking" as the individualist sought out his band, and wrote for this band alone.

The antithetical aspect of esthetic thought was aggravated by the fact that the profit-economy frame was unanswerable within its own terms so long as capitalism could expand into new areas. The intellectuals could cry out against the accommodations of the Twice-Buried, yet there was really not much else for people to do but twice-bury themselves by accommodating their ambitions and desires to the requirements of the profit-economy frame. The system made them "Victims All," as bourgeois and proletarian alike, farmer and industrialist alike, made the necessary accommodation to it. A bourgeois was a kind of "overpaid proletarian," a proletarian was an "underpaid bourgeois." Both thought in terms of *money* because, in the modern hunt, where one catches his food by purchase, money became exactly what bows and arrows had been in the primitive forest hunt. Against this integral ideological adjustment, with all its ramifications, the intellectuals had braced themselves by antithesis. Sometimes the antithesis was made all the easier for them by the fact that they enjoyed an income, and so could enjoy the paradoxical (and frequently unkind) position of attacking people for acquiescing in the very types of thinking to which they themselves owed their support.

The exhaustion of new areas, however, brings the triumph of capitalism near its close. Its accomplishments, its ideas of the "good life," even as judged by its own criteria of the desirable, are now brought into question. However one may differ with such statements, no one has offered us grounds for anticipating a repetition of such vast capitalistic exaltation as marked the last hundred years, whereas nothing less vast could even manage to keep people employed. Hence the pouring-in of the esthetic through the cracks of the broken practical structure. Whereas, throughout the great upswing of capitalist methods during the nineteenth century, the people's minds were *closed to the esthetic antithesis by necessity*, the advancing break-down of capitalist methods now begins to *open their minds again by necessity*. They must look about them for "new meanings," as the old meanings by which they ordered their lives have brought them into difficulties.

This state of affairs we call the "practical-esthetic merger." The intellectual antithesis to the profit-frame is now matched by fundamental antagonisms within the profit-frame itself. The esthetic thus becomes a candidate for consideration. What then happens to the "esthetes," who had inspirited themselves for a century by defiance, by a refusal to compromise? What happens to this non-conformist pattern so ingrained in their thinking?

The "next move" is affected by the fact that the antithetical attitude of the century, running as it did through the entire esthetic frame, also found its parallel in the sphere of economics. The doctrines of Karl Marx attacked the profit-economy frame, not from the "poetic" side as men like Flaubert had done, but from the "conceptual" side. And since the issue now coming to a head is so overwhelmingly of an economic sort, the esthetes could find in Marxism all that they had already been. Despite the practical-esthetic merger, which threatened to destroy such kind of "inspiration" as had heretofore risen out of a practical-esthetic antithesis, they could retain the same kind of "inspiration" by recourse to another aspect of nineteenth-century antithesis, replacing their old philistine-intellectual (or bourgeois-Bohemian) antithesis by the Marxian bourgeois-proletarian antithesis.

In general, therefore, their sympathies turned toward the Communists, whose political pattern was practically identical with their poetic pattern. Here they could find the equivalent for their past uncompromising "colony thinking," the rigid "with me or against me" attitude which had braced the intellectuals for a century. Their older fanaticism of beauty could now be translated into the terms of the "perfect state." Where there had been thoughts of the Ivory Tower, imagery of ideal existences which they had deemed so desirable as to picture their heroes dying for them, it was a natural transition to think now of the Ivory Tower made general and of themselves as dying for it.

To what degree this is an "acceptance of realities" no one now is in a position to say. We may note the clear presence of an "antagonistic" pattern here which may be functioning as mere "survival," and which has often led the esthete-Communist to *invite persecution* rather than *seek results*. Antithesis, so clearly adapted to a state of affairs wherein people's minds were *necessarily closed*, may not be the best possible accommodation to a state of affairs wherein people's minds are being *necessarily opened again*. For just as antithesis tends to bolster one against other closed minds, so it can tend to close the minds of others.

One might distinguish the "evangelist," who brought new meanings, from the "organizer," who consolidated the convinced. The old esthetic antithesis, with its pronounced "colony thinking," was perfect as a consolidator of the convinced. And likewise Saul, with his Saul-Paul reversal, was well equipped to emphasize an antithesis between the faithful and the unbelievers. He was the ideal man to come upon a little churchly minded group, teaching them to appoint a secretary and treasurer, and sending them "inside" epistles which kept their morale intact. But the wheedler-propagandist Christ minimized the antithetical aspect of his propaganda as far as was humanly possible, even stretching his doctrines to the limit in the interests of "tactics," when he proposed the rendering unto Caesar (and if he was finally destroyed, he was destroyed not by the great alien opposition, but by a rival sect, thus suggesting the socialist-communist relationship). If we carry the analogy somewhat bathetically down to contemporary critical issues, we may say that the "Christ-function," as "bringer of glad tidings," was that of propounding a new configuration of meanings, and making this configuration as appealing as possible. Accordingly, he minimized the antagonistic aspect of his doctrine. The Saul-Paul function (of consolidating the faithful, convincing the convinced) was really not serving the interests of "propaganda" at all. It was not a seeking of recruits—it was an exhorting of the recruited.

The martyrology evolved by the church after it had grown in power has completely obscured the relative proportions of "wheedling" and "antithesis" involved in the later propagation of the Faith. But we do know that the thunderings against the heretics were written almost entirely for the consumption of the faithful, and were thus not propaganda but consolidation. There is a general tendency, since violence is picturesque and outstanding, to lay much emphasis upon the element of violence in revolution, in our accounts of the French Revolution, for instance—but one should consider the enormous amount of wheedling done by the philosophers of the Enlightenment, even in the salons of the nobles. And one might ask himself whether it is here that the true incentives to change are to be found, whereas the violence is a mere by-product, possessing so little appeal as "incentive" that the "emancipator" minimized it until it was upon them. Without the misguidance of Antithesis the propagandist of anti-capitalist doctrine can realize that even in Marx there is ground for emphasizing the *conservative* aspect of the change proposed by the Collectivist, ground for advocating a little more Communism because we have already accepted so much of it. Without Antithesis for inspiration, one might question the profit-economy as unfit for modern conditions, grumbling perhaps that any change is necessary, agreeing that change is a nuisance, that there is nothing alluring about it, and suggesting that, since one shares the general dislike of change, one proposes that we confine ourselves to the fewest changes possible—and that, by this program, *our entire productive, distributive, and consumptive methods can be maintained in their present way of functioning without any important industrial change whatsoever, if we but procure a more Communistic distribution of profits, or buying power.*

But the old esthetic "banding together" in rigidly restricted groups tends to do in disguise exactly what the Marxians might warn against: to overstress the "departmental" aspect of modern thought as against the "collective" aspect, a departmentalization in practice thus being concealed beneath a "universality" of doctrine, and enabling the reborn esthete to reaffirm his old "colony" pattern of the last century precisely when he thinks he is discarding it.

It may be that he has sound logical grounds for maintaining this pattern. Merely because it is a "survival" from the past is no evidence per se that it is not adapted to the present. The issue should be clearly faced, however, and not obscured beneath the exaltation of finding oneself apparently "remade." When the practical Thesis against which the esthetic Antithesis had been formed began to crumble, and people's minds became necessarily opened to "new meanings" just as they had been necessarily closed for a century, the esthetes met this practical-esthetic merger, not by dropping antithesis for something else, but by counter-antithesis. And as the original esthetic antithesis had served for convincing the convinced, might not the same be true of its preservation under this new guise, when the nineteenth-century Saul who had arisen antithetically to the profit-economy frame would now become the twentieth-century Paul by antithesis to his former self?

Can we be so strictly guided in the twentieth century by a pattern of thinking so thoroughly adapted to the nineteenth century? Or must we get our new enthusiasms out of something less clear-cut, something less sharply invigorating, something less "esthetic," than a strictly differentiated bourgeois-proletarian alignment of battle?

The old inspiration, we might say, arose out of a writer-citizen breach. We now turn to a writer-citizen merger. Should we, in doing so, retain as a keystone of our thinking the concept of Antithesis which was so integral to the writer-citizen breach, and was not found in the poet-and-politician, Goethe, who preceded the flowering of the anti-practical esthetic?

Addendum

Perhaps the scene has changed somewhat, even within the few months since these pages were written. At first the movement had seemed to sweep down "like a fierce barbarian invasion from the North." It has since abated; partially as the result of a natural revision, as the "proletarian" prophecies lost their first zest under repetition; partially by reason of the fact that the movement was found, by those who would use it for political ends, to be defeating its main purpose, since it drove so many writers, who had little sympathy with the "system," into an apparent defense of the "system." (That is: there were certain writers and trends which the critics had thought good, which had buttressed and guided them in their dislike of the "New Era" concept of the "good life," but which happened to have flourished during the fierce hegemony of orthodox capitalism. The "proletarian" critics had so framed their statement of the issue that, in defending these writers and trends, a critic was made to look like a defender of the worst forms of "exploitation" and corporate abuse. This unfortunate aspect of the literary scene has since been remedied by the stressing of a distinction between "proletarian" and "revolutionary" literature. The "bourgeois" critics of the "bourgeoisie," instead of being damned as anti-proletarians, are now to be admitted as "revolutionary.")

The charge of "over-eagerness." Friends, on seeing my manuscript, detected too much zeal. They are right. The book is over-eager. But my "vested interests" were endangered. The movement, by and large, seemed an attempt to prove that good writing was a kind of crime against the state. Crude books were extolled in the name of proletarian rescue. By some astounding twists, the "morality of production" was made to look like a kind of self-indulgence, while the most haphazard reporting was given the halo of a savior. Hence, all the books and writers which I most admired were discredited for the qualities which made me most admire them—for their patience, their prodding, their pounding, in short, their "instinct of workmanship." What could one admire if one could not admire this—and how hold up one's head in such disastrous times unless one could greatly and intensely admire something? So my "vested interests" *were* endangered; I admit the fact forthwith. And if I am less over-eager now, it is precisely because this danger has abated somewhat—amusingly destroyed in part by such articles as Mr. Henry Hazlitt's, in which he shows that Marx read Shakespeare with enjoyment (so excessive had the "opposition" become that child-arguments of this sort were imperative).

Difficulty of our task. There is no one strictly "Marxian" doctrine. The critical exegetes of Marxism as applied to literary judgment differ widely from one another. Thus, if one were concerned specifically with "refutation," one should be compelled to consider each critic individually. Mr. Sidney Hook, in *The Symposium*, has written a very able document explaining why this is so. Marxism, he points out, is mainly valuable as a "method." A method is a way of tackling issues; what the user of the method says in a given situation depends largely upon the nature of one's audience. Accordingly, since Marx's writings were addressed to different groups (as widely divergent as staunch Catholics and staunch Communists), they present many inconsistencies if considered purely as a body of doctrine. One must approach these from the "Marxian" point of view, "understanding" a specific statement by taking into account the situation under which it was made, the purpose, etc. Thus I do not flatter myself that a single Marxian critic has been "refuted" in this work. I wished simply to show how pliant the Marxian "method" can be, how readily one can "take it over" and apply it for himself, how spontaneously it can make for "revisionism." I wished to show how the Marxian "method" might be re-applied (with Darwinian-Behavioristic alloys) to relieve some of the "pressure on poets."

Now that the movement has somewhat abated, there are two good results, both of them having major importance. The first was wholly unintentional. It is, namely: How much the Marxian critics have done to restore the dignity of metaphysics by showing its close application to political and economic matters. Friends of mine who had ridiculed metaphysics for years, as a kind of remote parlor game, came out for this doctrine of monistic materialism with a vigor which, in a few weeks, surely canceled off all their scorn of many years. In this respect, in the rehabilitation of metaphysics as the basis of a critic's attitude toward books, the Marxians have done much to destroy an ominous intellectually haphazard kind of approach to matters of art and life which our so-called cultured critics had shared only too much in common with our most superficial sales promoters and hard-headed "go-getters." (Veblen, incidentally, had shown some years before, how much "bad metaphysics" there is lurking in the supposed "hard-headedness" of this group.)

The second valuable result is in the sharpening of our understanding as to the "economic" origin of values (admonishing us once more that "morality" and "wealth," "virtue" and "food," "goodness" and "comfort" are organically intertwined). This doctrine is not exclusive to Marxism. It was thoroughly understood by such utilitarians as Bentham, and by the modern pragmatists. It is "Darwinian" (which is to say, it is the very essence of the nineteenth century)—it is implicit in the attempt to explain the rise of values out of "psychological" or "biological" origins rather than as deriving from transcendental sources, from "divine revelation."

What is next? Our belief that the twentieth century can best be a century of "retrenchment." The nineteenth century has left us with a wealth of revolutionary archives. Surely, in subsequent eras, it will be looked upon as one of the most profuse periods in human thought. It will also, I believe, be called a century of "first drafts." May we make a "classical revision" of its "romantic excesses"? Indeed, is it not absolutely necessary that we do this, if we are not to be destroyed by the sheer force of our inheritance? A brief outline of this revision should necessarily emphasize the conflict between values which have arisen from the body-needs and the proper satisfying of these body-needs. Economic decisions now function as an Occam's Razor for satisfying body-needs in an era of romantic excesses.

And a Parting Glance at Sister Antithesis

"So we need not carry over slavishly from the realm of political agitation into the realm of imaginative, speculative literature the concepts of cooperation that apply to the specific martialing of voters." As a matter of brutal fact, there are even indications that the needs of *practical political agitation* in America are not adequately met by the simplist, Collectivistic ways of thought, as vitiated by the Antithesis concept. The awareness of a "common Cause," with the strong emphasis it has placed upon the demand for ideological homogeneity among those embracing the common Cause, instigates too non-particularistic a way of meeting the problems of propaganda. Thus we see, again and again, agitators going into new regions and haranguing the people there, suffering under one of the worst handicaps imaginable, since they are always talking to *strangers*, and making the matter worse by always calling them *comrades*. It would be illuminating to know what percentage of the men now in our prisons for political offenses were imprisoned for agitation in neighborhoods other than those where they were generally known. (In many cases, like the old "esthetes" of the "exile" variety, they apply to the world in a general way, without particularities.) Underlying the American standardization, there is a tremendous sense of regionalism, of the "home team." Agitation in America must be at least individualistic or particularistic enough in its methods to take these facts properly into account. If one is an engineer, one must plead with his engineer colleagues. If one is a farmer, one must go down the road and talk to the next farmer. This is a peculiarly difficult and repulsive job—in some ways much less appealing than going forth to address the world in general, even though the possibilities of getting one's head cracked are thereby greatly increased.

I am not denying the courage of our political prisoners. There is perhaps no greater distinction in man than the distinction of being punished by society because one has worked for the good of society. It is the distinction upon which great religions have been founded. Whether it is also the distinction upon which political parties are founded, I do not know. I do know that the Communists have talked much of strategy—and I am now considering a problem of strategy. I am saying simply that, if one has a neighborhood and "agitates" there, one must outrage his neighbors to a tremendous extent before they will want to see him imprisoned for his sentences, whereas one can, in a strange locality, easily arouse resentment, and deep resentment, by even so slight an error as calling strangers "comrades." (It would be much better, I believe, if a man put himself forward as one totally alien; if he began by stating that he was not properly acquainted with local conditions; if he offered his advice purely as "doctrine from afar," and asked that his audience consider for itself how much of what he was bringing them from other regions, and even from other shores, might be found to fit their own particular situation.) But "collectivistic" thinking, the encouraging sense of being part of a group which recognizes their "normality" among themselves, gives one boldness and sanction of the wrong sort. One grows too authoritative, too schematic, too *impersonal*. Indeed, if one wants to address his neighbors agitatively in Nebraska, he will promptly think of coming to New York and talking to them on a nationwide hook-up, or perhaps sending them marked copies of a magazine containing an article he had written.

Thus, most of the agitation now being done by this literary group is done for agitators. The rigid collectivistic frame of thinking, which leads the Communists to run in packs, makes them too content with the business of convincing one another over and over again, arranging dances among their confreres, and holding more committee meetings in a week than are needed to run the U.S. Steel Corporation for a year. It is for this reason that literary radicals are sometimes accused of being in a "racket," the "uplift" or "virtue" racket, as they generally sell to a radical market. They are certainly entitled to risk this charge; they are entitled to devote themselves to convincing the convinced, for it is highly important that the convinced be kept convinced. But they should not thereby close their eyes to the full responsibilities of agitation (if agitation is to be their business). Whereas the literary radicals generally have "anchorages" in definite neighborhoods, we find them arranging agitative tours into regions with which they have no contacts whatsoever, while their own home towns, with doorbells leading to parlors, still languish without them.

Or show me the Communist writer on the commuting fringe who, though calling out to high heaven in the name of revolution, will stand in front of the local grocery store and breathe one word of political heterodoxy. His impersonal, collectivist ways of thinking make it seem absolutely natural that he should "agitate" in an impersonal way. Yet if he should breathe the word of political heterodoxy, note that he will breathe it apologetically, wheedlingly, with a "Come, now" attitude. In other words, the first thing he must drop as totally inadequate to his purposes will be the note of *Antithesis*, so ably suited for convincing the convinced, and so thoroughly unsuited to anything else. Far from picturing vast and overwhelming changes, and the great surge of ennoblement that comes of them, he will say as easily as he can, "Why, I begin to believe we might patch things up with the minimum of disaster by some of the changes recommended by the—a—the—a—oh, by the Russians, or by the—a—the—the Communists." He will then show how much Communism there is in the modern state already, and suggest that we need a little more—grumbling perhaps that any change at all is necessary, agreeing that change is a nuisance, that there is nothing alluring about it, and suggesting that, since he shares the general dislike of change, we should confine ourselves to the fewest changes possible. Such minimum changes would seem to lie in the direction of a more Communistically distributed *buying power*. At this point he could appeal to the local grocer, who would certainly agree with him that a better distributed buying power would be a godsend to this here community. Any landlord present would also give eager assent. If there were disagreements, they would be disagreements of a discussable sort, and they would not be such disagreements as added one more political prisoner to our distinguished population of political prisoners.

On the other hand, put in place of this method the method that flows from the Collectivistic, Communistic exaltation, put in the place of this wheedler a prophet fired with the deep convictions of a new Faith, bring him into the town with all his undoubted sincerity, all his pictures of a new world created out of heroic Struggle, all the glorifications of martyrdom, of proletarian rescue, of the Oppressed now at last Emancipated, all his wholesome vigor arising from his sense of "solidarity," his manly awareness of being backed by his Group—and you now have a picture of a man with two choices before him: the local Jug, or prompt departure on a rail. The *impersonal* emphases of their doctrines have closed them completely to a sense of propaganda as propaganda would be carried on if one went back to visit one's parents and stepped out before one's own door to begin talking. The whole enterprise becomes a vague, inspiring orgy, glorious but ineffective. Of course, if you think of "character-building," I will admit that our Communist martyr in this picture has done much to earn our profound admiration. If you think of *strategy*, however, his procedure as inspired by the sanction of total one-ness with his fellows becomes more than worthless. And the Communist would surely be willing to sacrifice his "character-building" in the best interests of his Cause. It is customary to lay much emphasis upon the *violence* involved in the French Revolution—but one may also consider the enormous amount of wheedling done by the philosophers of the Enlightenment, even in the salons of the nobles; and one can suggest that herein lay the true *incentives* to change, while the violence was a mere by-product, totally "soft-pedaled" as a factor until revolution was actually under way. In other words, the so-called agitators were not instigators at all. They merely tried to *guide* the movement that was in progress without them. The same seems to have been true in Russia, where the Revolution began while all the important Bolsheviks were out of the country.

Perhaps "agitators" today could accomplish more if they realized that they are mainly bringers of "new meanings," *evangelists* rather than *organizers*; for an evangelist may even come from afar, perhaps *must* come from afar, so that even our wheedler might best put his suggestions forward as alien doctrines imported. An *organizer*, on the other hand, will work under tremendous difficulties, and perhaps insuperable ones, unless he belongs to the locality. Such difficulties may go far to explain the feuds so frequently arising between

Communist agitators and labor leaders. The Communist does not make it clear enough that he is merely presenting "new meanings." Misled by his overweening group-sense, he thinks so spontaneously of "organization" that he fails to note the tactical distinction between the evangelist and the organizer, the "bringer of glad tidings" and the Saint Paul (whose main work was in convincing the convinced). As a convincer of the convinced, Saul with his Saul-Paul reversal was well equipped to emphasize an antithesis between the "faithful" and the "infidel." But the arch-propagandist, Christ, minimized the "Antithetical" aspect of his propaganda as far as was humanly possible, even stretching his doctrines to the limits in the interests of "tactics" when he proposed the rendering unto Caesar; and it seems to have been one of his few "antithetical" moments that disastrously consolidated the opposition against him. The subsequent martyrology evolved by the church as it grew in power has concealed from us the relative proportions between "wheedling" and "antithesis" throughout the later history of the Faith; but we do know that the thundering against the heretics was written entirely for the consumption of the faithful.

All such considerations would seem to suggest that just as pure Collectivist doctrine, untempered by Individualistic aspects, would be inadequate as a way of meeting the situation in the purely esthetic field, so the Collectivist doctrine as vitiated by the concept of Antithesis is misleading as a guide to procedure in the practical field. If anything must be eliminated from our past patterns of thinking and feeling as the result of the practical-esthetic merger, the element to be eliminated is precisely the notion of *Antithesis* that primed the old esthetic frame in its century-long struggle against the unanswerable authority of the practical frame. So long as capitalism had new areas to plunder, the practical frame within its own terms was triumphant. The only way of coping with it was by a simple *antithesis*, the formulating of an esthetic frame which would be the complete *reversal* of this practical frame—and this means of adjustment, as we have tried to show, ran through the entire esthetic frame of reference erected during the nineteenth century, both in the imaginative sphere and in such purely conceptual doctrines as those of Karl Marx. The exhaustion of new areas brings the triumph of capitalism to a close. Its accomplishments, even when judged by its own criteria of accomplishments, are nearly ended. Hence the pouring-in of the esthetic through the cracks of the broken practical structure. And this practical-esthetic merger should suggest precisely our need of dropping the kind of Antithetical encouragement that distinguished the esthetic thinking of the nineteenth century.

We must now make a distinction between an Antithesis and a

Difference. Such a distinction cannot be made under the notion of a bourgeois-proletarian dichotomy, which too strongly stimulates the notion of conformity to one of two antithetical groups. The old exaltation cannot continue apropos when the situation has been radically changed from the situation under which it arose. Stimulation can no longer appropriately arise out of the simple, invigorating battle-cry of an Antithesis—it must be fed from a subtler source, a Difference. And as simple Antithesis drops from the field of poetry and politics alike, we find that the Saul-Paul reversal would entail the renouncing of too much that must be kept. A Difference will bring new identifications, but these will lie across the old in such a way that much of the old is necessarily retained. "Rebirth" thus becomes Goethean, "growth by accretion," not a matter of mere negation, but the discovery of a broader frame for that which we already have, a discovery too *unpredictable* for us to be guided toward it by the mere automatic guidance of a schematic *opposite*.

The "synthesis" that was expected by Marxian doctrine to *follow* the change must proceed hand in hand *with* the change. The rigid "with me or against me" attitude of the Antithesis must dissolve as the key concept for propaganda under contemporary conditions. The very concept of the "system" should lead rather to the realization that people were "Victims All," that bourgeois and proletarian alike had accommodated their thinking to the imperious demands of a profit-economy, and if some persons fared better than others by the accommodation, the fact remains that the basic ideological adjustments were the same in both groups. Against this integral ideological adjustment the "intellectuals" had braced themselves by Antithesis. And as the Thesis against which their Antithesis was framed threatens to collapse under the practical-esthetic merger, they would now merely undo themselves by turning to a simple counter-antithesis. But let us realize that Paul is for convincing the convinced, as was the nineteenth-century Saul who arose antithetically to the profit-economy frame, and out of which the modern Paul would arise in turn by antithesis to his former Self. Goethe, as both poet and politician, knew no such simple opposites.

3

Aesthetic and Practical Frames of Reference

Burke, Marx, and the Rhetoric of Social Change

Greig E. Henderson

Focusing on *Counter-Statement* and "Auscultation, Creation, and Revision," this chapter traces the dialectic of Burke's early works and examines the pivotal transition from literary criticism (the aesthetic frame) to social and cultural criticism (the practical frame). Like *Permanence and Change*, "Auscultation" is a transitional work par excellence, and it provides a useful angle of vision from which to consider Burke's ongoing dialogue with Marx and the way in which that dialogue develops from *Counter-Statement* to *A Rhetoric of Motives*. I contend that the shift toward praxis in Burke's perspective is not as radical as it appears either to him or to others, and that even *Counter-Statement*—the most overtly aesthetic of his works—moves implicitly in the direction of an aesthetic-practical merger. Burke's strategic innovation is to construe Marx's social theory as predominantly a rhetoric of demystification and a hermeneutics of suspicion. Such a construal ultimately allows Burke to subsume Marxism under the dramatistic categories of his own grammar and rhetoric of motives. Social theory and discourse theory are thereby integrated.[1]

In drawing his famous distinction between positive and negative hermeneutics, between a hermeneutics of restoration and a hermeneutics of suspicion, Paul Ricoeur (1970, 27) points to the essential duplicity of the hermeneutical motive itself: "At one pole, hermeneutics is understood as the manifestation and restoration of a meaning addressed to me in the manner of a message, a proclamation, or as is sometimes said, a kerygma; according to the other, it is understood as a demystification, as a reduction of illusion. . . . Hermeneutics seems . . . to be animated by this double motivation: willingness to suspect, willingness to listen; vow of rigor, vow of obedience."

This double motivation is evident in Marx's writing. On the one hand, dialectical materialism is a positive hermeneutics that advertises itself as a science of history, a science that reduces cultural phenomena in the ideological superstructure to modes of economic production in the material infrastructure. Yet, as Burke points out, even the most unemotional scientific nomenclature is unavoidably suasive. The necessitarian underpinnings of Marx's economic causation theory notwithstanding, the utopianism implicit in his scientific understanding of history furnishes an image for action, and the notion of historical inevitability with its built-in teleology of proletarian victory is rhetorically appealing to the last who shall be first. As a positive hermeneutics, Marxism promises a restoration of plenitude, a life of unalienated labor and leisure, of psychological and social integration. This retrieval of meaning gives to human history a rationally coherent and causally intelligible sense of beginning, middle, and end. It offers nothing less than a totalizing master narrative that travels from genesis to apocalypse and culminates in the triumphant success of the human struggle to wrest a realm of freedom out of a realm of necessity. This master narrative is all the more compelling because it is assumed to be scientifically predestined. Nevertheless, as Burke points out, "whatever may be the claims of Marxism as a 'science,' its terminology is not a neutral 'preparation for action' but 'inducement to action.' In this sense, it is unsleepingly rhetorical," its aim being not only to understand the world but also to change it ([1950a] 1969, 101).

On the other hand, dialectical materialism is a negative hermeneutics that demystifies capitalist and bourgeois discourse by showing how such discourse transforms historically produced socioeconomic conditions into universal essences. Empires striving for world markets, Burke notes, become the ways of universal spirit. "As a critique of capitalist rhetoric, [Marxist analysis] is designed to disclose (unmask) sinister *factional* interests concealed in the bourgeois terms for benign *universal* interests" ([1950a] 1969, 102). We are thus admonished to look for mystification at any point where the social divisiveness caused by property and the division of labor is obscured by unitary terms that conceal factional interests, making them seem natural and universal rather than historical and specific. Capitalist rhetoric gives us "a fog of merger terms where the clarity of division terms is needed" (109). Yet however much Marxism contributes to the critique of ideology and to the demystification of political rhetoric, it remains itself both a rhetoric and an ideology.

From *Counter-Statement* onward, Burke is unremittingly hostile toward Marxism's claim to be a positive hermeneutics grounded in scientific necessity. What changes in Burke's response to Marx is his growing appreciation of the rhetorical genius of Marxism as a negative hermeneutics. And that change begins, albeit tentatively, in the nonaesthetic essays in *Counter-Statement:* "Psychology and Form," "Lexicon Rhetoricae," and "Applications of the Terminology."

Generally speaking, the aesthetic essays in *Counter-Statement* see the aesthetic and the practical as necessarily at odds, art being "naturally antinomian" and serving "to undermine any one rigid scheme of living ([1931] 1968, viii). "Insofar as the conversion of pure science into applied science has made the practical a menace, the aesthetic becomes a means of reclamation. Insofar as mechanization increases the complexity of the social structure . . . the aesthetic must serve as anti-mechanization, the corrective of the practical. . . . The aesthetic [must] ally itself with a Program which might be defined roughly as a modernized version of the earlier bourgeois-Bohemian conflict" (110–11). Whether explicitly or implicitly, the aesthetic "works corrosively upon those expansionistic certainties preparing the way for our social cataclysms. An art may be of value purely through preventing a society from becoming too assertively, too hopelessly, itself" (105). This attitude of counterstatement, however, does not simply translate into an art-for-art's-sake position. Burke's aestheticism is a strategy for encompassing a sociohistorical situation; moreover, it aims to have a corrective or corrosive effect upon that situation and is thus practical; art, for Burke, is anything but useless.

In "The Status of Art," this aestheticism is accompanied by a vigorous attack on causation theories—historicist, economic, and psychoanalytic. According to Burke,

The historical approach may have affected the status of art slightly by questioning art's "permanence." . . . But the "practicality" shibboleth, as introduced by the economic critic, converted this genetic theory of social contexts into a causation theory, with economic forces as prime movers and art as a mere "result." . . . Now, it is not very sound dialectic to assume that, because two things change concomitantly, one can be called exclusively a cause of the other. . . . The theory of economic causation [rests] upon the assumption that there is only one possible aesthetic response to a given situation, and that this situation is solely an economic one. ([1931] 1968, 79–81)

For Burke the dialectical interaction of text and context, this sheer fact of interrelationship, is prior to any of the conceptual categories or rhetorical tropes, such as causality, metonymy, reflection, synecdoche, or analogy, subsequently evolved to explain it. The literary work is not simply a passive reflection of a static objective situation; it is a dynamic and strategic response, something that transforms a subject matter that is itself historically fluid and analyzable as a determinate moment only after the fact. As though for the first time, "the literary work or cultural object . . . brings into being the very situation to which it is a reaction. It articulates its own situation and textualizes it" (Jameson 1981, 82). So although literature necessarily arises out of a particular context, it is not reducible to that context in terms of a one-to-one correspondence between cause and effect. For sociohistorical reality does not cause a particular kind of literary response; it merely sets limitations upon the possibilities of response.

It is possible, for example, that "the work of art 'reflects' society and is historical to the degree that it *refuses* the social, and represents the last refuge of individual subjectivity from the historical forces that threaten to crush it" (Jameson 1971, 34–35). The historicity of any moment in time is just as much the upsurge of the potential as the actual, of the latent as the emergent, and it is captured as much by repression as by expression, by reaction as by revolution, by acceptance as by rejection, by evasion as by confrontation, by nostalgic regression as by utopian projection. A text is always a strategic response to sociohistorical reality, and while it must deal with that reality in some manner, if only through conspicuous neglect, its type of response may be prophesied only after the event. Therefore, as Burke points out, "no categorical distinction can possibly be made between 'effective' and 'ineffective' art. The most fanciful 'unreal,' romance may stimulate by implication the same attitudes towards our environment as a piece of withering satire attempts explicitly" ([1931] 1968, 90). Nostalgia for remembered plenitude, alienation from present reality, or projection toward future plenitude are all capable of functioning as revolutionary stimuli. "People have gone too long with the glib psychoanalytic assumption that an art of 'escape' promotes acquiescence. It may, as easily, assist a reader to clarify his dislike of the environment in which he is placed" (119).

As these quotations suggest, even the supposedly "aesthetic" essays in *Counter-Statement* betray a sophisticated sense of the dialectical relationship between work and background and never lapse into barren formalism. The work of art is always doing something more than simply being itself, and there is no suggestion that the work of art is a self-sufficient object constituting its own hermetically sealed universe of discourse. The nonaesthetic essays take this antiformalism a step further and define form as the psychology, not of the author, but of the audience. In "Psychology and Form," Burke contends that form is the creation of an appetite in the mind of the auditor and the adequate satisfying of that appetite. To focus so explicitly on how an auditor's appetites are created, satisfied, frustrated, and fulfilled is already to be aware that "form is a relationship of manipulation between a text and an audience," that "the definition of text, and textuality, must include the factor of its reception," and that "reception is always firmly planted in the historical world" (Lentricchia 1983, 89). In "Lexicon Rhetoricae" and "Applications of the Terminology," Burke moves even further in the direction of rhetorical and cultural criticism, arguing that categorical expectancies and ideological assumptions are implicit in both the writer's verbal structure and the reader's interpretive strategy, and that these expectancies and assumptions affect both the production and consumption of meaning. Meaning, therefore, is always codetermined, the reader's horizon of expectation attempting to fuse with the writer's. Perfect fusion, of course, is impossible, and an inescapable relativity and indeterminacy are thereby introduced into the notion of interpretation. As Burke reflects, "Any reader surrounds each word and each act in a work of art with a unique set of his own previous experiences (and therefore a unique set of imponderable emotional reactions), communication existing in 'the margin of overlap' between the writer's experience and the reader's" ([1931] 1968, 78).

Overtly rhetorical in their orientation, "Lexicon Rhetoricae" and "Applications of the Terminology" foreground this relationship between writer and reader. "If rhetoric is but 'the use of language in such a way as to produce a desired impression upon the hearer or reader,'" Burke writes, "then 'effective literature' could be nothing else but rhetoric" ([1931] 1968, 120). "A writer is engaged in the producing of effects upon his readers. . . . He will manipulate their ideology, he will exploit his and their patterns of experience" (190). For Burke, psychology, form, ideology, intentionality, and response are interinanimating aspects of rhetoric.

Forms, for Burke, are ways of encompassing experiential and ideological complexities. Although art deals with "the constants of humanity . . . the recurrent emotions, the fundamental attitudes, the typical experiences . . . art is also historical—a particular mode of adjustment to a particular cluster of conditions" ([1931] 1968, 107). "A form is a way of experiencing" (143), and a writer necessarily manipulates readers' ideologies in order to arouse, shape, and control their desires. In Burke's lexicon, the term "ideology" is used descriptively; it is not simply a synonym for "false consciousness."

By an ideology is meant the nodus of beliefs and judgments which the artist can exploit for his effects. It varies from one person to another, and from one age to another—but in so far as its general acceptance and its stability are more stressed than its particular variations from person to person and from age to age, an ideology is a "culture." But there are cultures within cultures, since society can be subdivided into groups with divergent standards and interests. . . . Generally, the ideology of an individual is a slight variant of the ideology distinguishing the class among which he arose. (161–62)

For Burke, then, an ideology is neither static nor monolithic; it "is not a harmonious structure of beliefs or assumptions; some of its beliefs militate against others, and some of its standards militate against our nature. An ideology is an aggregate of beliefs sufficiently at odds with one another to justify opposite kinds of conduct" (163).

In my view, the so-called aestheticism of *Counter-Statement* is largely an optical illusion. Burke always regards form as a functioning structure that rhetorically shapes the responses of an audience and strategically encompasses a personal and historical situation as much as it creatively expresses the self of an author. His aestheticism is not mere Bohemianism or dandyism; it is a counterstatement, and however much it takes its stance *against* the symbols of authority that the practical frame entrenches, the aesthetic frame, too, is meant to have social and hence practical consequences. Implicit in *Counter-Statement* is the idea of perspective by incongruity that animates *Permanence and Change* and *Attitudes toward History* as well as the recognition that "every social formation or historically existing society has in fact consisted of *several* modes of production all at once, including vestiges and survivals of older modes of production, now relegated to structurally dependent positions within the new, as well as anticipatory tendencies which are partially inconsistent with the existing system but have not yet generalized an autonomous space of their own" (Jameson 1981, 95). This is why ideologies are not harmonious structures of beliefs or assumptions and why texts are "crisscrossed and intersected by a variety of impulses from contradictory modes of cultural production all at once" (95).

Texts are not unequivocal expressions of their authors' class consciousness, for even though texts do display evidence of false consciousness, of class bias and ideological programming, this is only part of the story. The individual author, critic, or subject can never become fully conscious of his or her own ideological conditioning; he or she is always positioned within the social totality, and this is the sense of Althusser's insistence on the *permanence* of ideology (1971). For Althusser as for Burke, the decentred subject necessarily lives in ideology. There is for consciousness no untainted free space that escapes ideology's operations, since consciousness is ideology. Even at this early stage of his thinking, Burke's conception of ideology goes well beyond the reductivism of vulgar Marxism and moves toward integrating aesthetic and practical concerns.[2]

Nevertheless, the conflict between the aesthetic and the practical remains unresolved in *Counter-Statement*. There is no escaping the fact that *Counter-Statement* sometimes seems to endorse art-for-art's-sake aestheticism. That this collection of essays should be riddled with ambiguities and tensions is hardly surprising when one considers that it emerges out of the years of the Hoover presidency, a time of economic, social, and political upheaval. *Counter-Statement*, "Auscultation, Creation, and Revision" ("ACR"), *Permanence and Change*, and *Attitudes toward History* all embody and dramatize Burke's intellectual and critical responses to tensions and contradictions in the highly industrialized and economically depressed America of the 1930s.

At first glance, "ACR," the unpublished manuscript that follows *Counter-Statement* and precedes *Permanence and Change*, seems to privilege the aesthetic at the expense of the practical, its aim being, as Burke retrospectively puts it, "to resist the mounting sociological emphasis in criticism, even while dealing with the problems of 'orientation' to which the author had been made uncomfortably sensitive by the brusque contrast between the beginning of Hoover's presidency and its end" ([1931] 1968, 213). But the manuscript has two subtitles—"The Rout of the Esthetes" and "Literature, Marxism, and Beyond." Taken together, they reveal the double-mindedness inherent in Burke's project. "The Rout of the Esthetes" points to the motive of aesthetic retrenchment. Although many of his contemporaries have now converted to the Marxist practical frame, Burke is not prepared to surrender wholesale the aesthetic frame. "Literature, Marxism, and Beyond" points to the motive of dialectical synthesis. Burke is moving toward assimilating the practical frame of reference into a broader perspective and adumbrates ideas he will develop at length in *Permanence and Change* and *Attitudes toward History*. It seems to me that, on the whole, "ACR" is more successful in assimilating the mounting sociological emphasis in criticism than in resisting it. That is, Burke sublates the aesthetic-practical dichotomy by linking forms of social communication with forms of social cooperation. He acknowledges that however much the aesthetic frame valorizes self-expression, even self-expression is anchored in the collective revelation inscribed in the language of the tribe, language itself being a quintessentially social product, "the most collective of all enterprises" ("ACR," 126).

"ACR" begins by "granting the all-importance of the present economic difficulties." Nevertheless, Burke is skeptical about "those critics who, aghast at contemporary disorders, would meet [those disorders] by a 'conversion' mechanism, by the adoption of new standards in direct opposition to those they had formerly held, thus hoping as it were to prepare for the social 'Revolution' by a revolution in their own minds." Such a Saul-Paul reversal, whereby the old individualist aesthete becomes the new collectivist radical, merely replaces an old dichotomy—bourgeois/Bohemian—with a new one—bourgeois/proletarian. What is wrong with this transformation is "the doctrine of 'antithesis'" that undergirds it. There is no fundamental alteration in the born-again critic's basic pattern of thinking. Marx, Burke argues, lays too "much emphasis upon an antithesis between an exploiting, bourgeois class and an exploited, proletarian class" (62), and Marx-inspired critics lay too much emphasis upon an antithesis between bourgeois and proletarian literature. With remarkable poststructuralist prescience, Burke advocates difference rather than antithesis, suggesting that the most effective way to undermine and subvert a hegemonic discourse is from within. Any ideology is inconsistent enough to be turned against itself, and the critic who exploits difference rather than antithesis can aid and abet an ideology's self-deconstruction and thus transvaluate its symbols of authority. Difference is less threatening and less alienating than antithesis; it thus makes for a more effective rhetorical strategy. Burke's characteristic focus on rhetorical strategy will later give rise to the furor surrounding "Revolutionary Symbolism in America," a paper received with hostility by Burke's socialist colleagues, who prefer to regard Marxism as science rather than rhetoric and to practice their rhetoric under the name of no rhetoric.

For Burke, "Marx's so-called scientific theory of history is not scientific at all but involves judgments about the nature of the universe which science cannot make, and ambiguities of definition which make the rigorous Marxian prophecies impossible" ("ACR," 62). Marxism is a rhetoric of social change, not a science, and it downplays the constants of human physiology. The human body, Burke points out, is the initial economic plant.

Burke commences his argument by dismantling the concept of relevance, a concept that buttresses the proletarian denunciation of bourgeois art. To condemn such art as irrelevant is not enough. Like escape and evasion, irrelevance admits of degrees and can be applied categorically only if one mistakenly posits a one-to-one correspondence between aesthetic stimulus and reader response. Depending on the situation, a work can be irrelevant, relevant but inadequate, relevant but evasive, or relevant but wrong. For example, romantic protests against science, materialism, and industrialism are relevant insofar as they identify a problem and dance an antithetical attitude, but inadequate as vehicles for social change. Escape literature is relevant to the extent that gratifying one's fantasies and fulfilling one's wishes have obvious therapeutic value if reality forces one to labor in a soul-destroying environment, but escape literature is evasive if the point is to change the world, not to escape from it. Fascism is relevant to a situation of social, economic, and political chaos, but its solution to the problem, though undeniably efficacious, demands the abandonment of most standards of decency, morality, civilization, and humanity; it is thus wrong for those who value these standards. Desire, Burke observes, can be either a push away from the actual or a pull toward the ideal, and there is no predicting in advance what effect various pictures of, say, the good life will have, whether they take the form of utopian literature, success literature, or cinematic society drama. Consistent with the spirit of *Counter-Statement*, he refuses to "assume that the effects of a given work or school are uniform upon all readers" ("ACR," 94) and thus undermines the concept of relevance. For if uniformity of effect is a chimera, then accepting or rejecting works on the grounds of relevance and social efficacy becomes pointless; no categorical distinction between the relevant and the irrelevant can be made. Taking the same antideterminist stance he takes in *Counter-Statement*, Burke notes that "there is a big difference between saying that a certain attitude *takes a certain factor into account*, and saying that the attitude is *determined* by the factor" (97).

The bourgeois-proletarian dichotomy cannot be converted into a simple-minded distinction between the irrelevant and the relevant. Moreover, even though Marxist advocates of antithesis vociferously condemn bourgeois writing, they still adhere to its canons of logic and reasoning, exemplifying "such classic methods of inductive argument and such traditionally 'environmental,' 'evolutionary' thinking as most strikingly distinguish the contributions of the nineteenth-century bourgeoisie. Surely if the breach between bourgeois and proletarian were thorough enough to justify a proletarian Antithesis, this breach should cut as deeply into our critical methods as into our 'creative' ones" ("ACR," 98). Unlike, say, Dadaists, Marxists are linguistically and conceptually conservative in this regard. The proletarian and bourgeois orientations may be different, but they are not antithetical.

Adumbrating concerns that will inform *Permanence and Change* and *Attitudes toward History*, this focus on difference leads Burke to consider the pivotal role terminology plays in inducing social change. "We are faced," he writes, "with the spectacle of a society including new matter, or failing to include it, or first failing and then succeeding. And if it does enlarge and reshape the cultural frame appropriately, it may then become a new *integer*, possessing a new *order*, and a set of new *meanings*" ("ACR," 100). Vocabulary is all-important because "the authority of the old trend is 'spiritually' broken before the authority of a new trend is established." At transitional moments in cultural history, it is easier

to see or to sense that when we have adopted a vocabulary, the conclusions we shall eventually arrive at are already contained in our terms, that in triumphantly coming upon our conclusions, we are simply thinking things through to the point at which we began, merely making the implicit explicit. For by each vocabulary things are classified in a different way. The man who offers a new terminology will generally bring forward three kinds of suggestions: he will show how, by his vocabulary, a concept formerly considered unified can be divided into two concepts or several; how concepts formerly considered independent of each other can be brought into one; and how the new concepts are sometimes simply on a different plane of discourse than the former ones, "cutting across" them on the bias. By making new patterns, new sortings, new identifications, he is—to all practical purposes—making new things. (101)

When a cultural integer is undergoing disintegration in its attempt to encompass new matter, the notion of difference is superior to that of antithesis in its ability to account for cultural lag. "By the 'cultural lag' is meant simply the fact that some significant changes in our social ways are not paralleled by the simultaneous changing of *all* our social ways, as our attitudes toward a given situation, and our devices for controlling it, will naturally be preserved in our speech and our institutions after the situation has changed. . . . Thinking becomes *different* from what it was, rather than *antithetical* to what it was" ("ACR," 104). Proletarian art, then, is different from bourgeois art rather than antithetical to bourgeois art, and "the two arts may have varying degrees of overlapping and distinctness, in rough correspondence with the varying degrees of overlapping and distinctness of the two environments" (119).

In a similar vein, bourgeois and proletarian ideologies are different rather than antithetical. In arguing that environmental factors determine cultural factors and that the nature of the productive forces determines the nature of the ideology, Marx assumes too readily that environments and ideologies are homogeneous. According to Burke, the complex specialization of modern industrial society entails "an enormous 'heterogeneity' of environments, giving rise to a similar heterogeneity of ideologies" ("ACR," 111). Just as the doctrine of antithesis fails to recognize the ambiguousness of relevance, economic causation theory fails to recognize the ambiguousness of suitability. Burke contends that "any number of ideologies are suited to the present situation" (115). Though their ideological perspectives are radically different, the Fascist, the Luddite, or the international financier have solutions to the problem at hand. Each, as it were, is on top, and "any one of these solutions would be 'economically determined' in that it arose out of the current economic difficulties" (115). Collectivism may be more desirable and realistic than, say, smashing machines, but it is not the one right solution that will necessarily emerge out of the nature of things. "The great emotional appeal behind Marx's purely intellectual formula," Burke points out, "arises . . . out of the optimistic promise implicit in his determinism. By combining an ambiguous concept of the suitable with an unproved causal theory as to how the physical determines the mental, he gives us heart to face the discouraging contemporary complexity. He suggests that the 'right' ideology must inevitably arise out of the new environment" (117). Historical necessity notwithstanding, the proletarian must be persuaded to think antithetical proletarian thoughts and to reclassify his or her consciousness, whereas the bourgeois simply cannot help thinking bourgeois thoughts. Marxists plead for their solution, Burke maintains, "precisely because they have no causal guaranty that it will prevail" (118). "Contraband optimism" is smuggled in "under the misleading label of scientific rigor" (115).

As a vocabulary and rhetoric, Marxism has its insights and uses. However, Burke is interested in establishing a broader perspective and is thus laying the foundations for *Permanence and Change* and *Attitudes toward History.* "The equipment which enables a mind to see things in accordance with [Marxian] interpretation," he writes, "can only arise out of an *equipment for interpretation in general*" ("ACR," 134). There is room for the aesthetic because the goal of agitator and poet is "to make the mind at home in the fluidities of change" (139), the aesthetic differing from the practical not in kind but in degree. The advantage of the aesthetic is that it permits us "to go further afield in our search of 'linkages'" (140). Since "vocabulary or terminology is . . . a major aspect of 'observation,'" the aesthetic can be instrumental in coaching new meanings and new perspectives, for it involves "a process of naming, and of naming in such a way that one seeks to go beyond the points of reference which one finds already available around him" (145–46, 146–47).

To survive the social and economic chaos of the thirties, the aesthetic needs to retain some of its protestant and antinomian character. "If it celebrates the marriage of the practical and esthetic frames by 'conforming,' it risks violating the basic patterns of character out of which it arose. . . . The old 'esthete born' . . . must consciously unite the acquiescent with the protestant, must both salute the catching-up of the practical frame and maintain a more or less critical attitude despite this practical-esthetic merger. . . . The Marxian ways of seeing, by so ably helping us to see somewhat, can prevent us from seeing more" ("ACR," 157 and 159).

"ACR" ends on this ambivalent note. Whereas Burke realizes that some form of an aesthetic-practical merger is inescapable, he is not prepared to endorse the Marxist program unequivocally. Nor is he prepared to retreat to aestheticism per se. In the nineteenth century, the development of an antithetical aesthetic frame helped to consolidate individualist protest against profit-economy and capitalist expansion. But as this expansion exhausted new areas of exploitation, the aesthetic began to pour in "through the cracks of the broken practical structure" ("ACR," 162), for when old meanings are no longer adequate, new meanings seep in. The Marxist doctrine of antithesis attacks the profit-economy not from the poetic side but from the conceptual side, encouraging poets to abandon the old and embrace the new. But in embracing the new, they do not embrace a new way of thinking; their antithetical stance is displaced rather than modified. "When the practical Thesis against which the esthetic Antithesis had been formed began to crumble, and people's minds became necessarily opened to 'new meanings' just as they had been necessarily closed for a century, the esthetes met this practical-esthetic merger, not by dropping antithesis for something else, but by counter-antithesis" (164). The problem is the antithetical frame of mind itself, and poets and critics should think of themselves as evangelists rather than organizers, their function being to bring new meanings rather than to convince the already convinced. "A Difference will bring new identifications, but these will lie across the old in such a way that much of the old is necessarily retained" (172).

What is needed is a more comprehensive perspective based on difference so that we might have growth by accretion, not by mere negation. That perspective, of course, is to be developed in the works that follow. So whereas neither Counter-Statement nor "ACR" develops it fully, they do anticipate such ideas as perspective by incongruity, shifting of allegiance to symbols of authority, and bureaucratization of the imaginative. "ACR" is clearly a work of social and cultural criticism, and it displays a broader interest in history, economics, and politics than anything Burke wrote before. Both Counter-Statement and "ACR" affirm the centrality of the rhetorical motive and demonstrate that at a time of economic, political, and personal crisis, Burke is well on the way to constructing an interpretive and critical system for the analysis of cultural discourse.

Notes

1. See Jay 1989. I am indebted to this excellent article, which also examines the transition in Burke's writings from literary to cultural criticism. Jay uses the Burke-Cowley correspondence and sees *Permanence and Change* as the key transitional moment, especially insofar as it attempts to integrate the Marxist and Freudian orientations. For whatever reasons, he does not consider Burke's unpublished manuscript "Auscultation, Creation, and Revision," but his account of the evolving form of rhetorical criticism that Burke elaborates from the 1930s to the 1950s is cogent and incisive. In this chapter, I build on his insights by foregrounding *Counter-Statement* and "Auscultation." To see how the Freudian closet drama connects with the Marxist problem play and how the two of them function in Burke's overall dramatistic project, one should consult Jay 1989.

2. See Burke (1935a) 1984, 304. In the afterword to this edition, Burke mentions that he had not read *The German Ideology* when he wrote *Counter Statement*. Nevertheless, he defends his nonreductivist usage of the term "ideology" and contends that to regard either ideas (Hegel) or matter (Marx) as the motive force of history is to commit a genetic fallacy. "Regardless of how our aptitude for 'symbolicity' came to be a part of our physiological structure, once it began to develop it manifested a nature of its own." Neither Hegel nor Marx is dialectical enough. Marx turns Hegel upside down but still exemplifies the same patterns of thought, which is why Burke, in *A Grammar of Motives*, can so productively discuss Marxism under the agent term of his pentad.

Part II

Methodological Extensions

4

Kenneth Burke's Concept of Rhetorical Negativity

Richard B. Gregg

In his introduction to the 1965 edition of Kenneth Burke's *Permanence and Change,* Hugh Duncan says of Burke, "He is at once one of the most compact and one of the most 'panoramic' writers of our time" (Burke [1935a] 1965, xiv). Duncan is correct in his observation; in making it, he has identified one of the reasons it sometimes appears difficult to employ Burke's insights and concepts critically. Indeed, Burke's discussion is frequently concrete. In his analyses, he often refers specifically to the data he is examining and marshaling in support of his perspective. At the same time his meanings are always continental in that they carry implications that go well beyond Burke's focus of the moment. Take, for example, the heavy emphasis Burke gives to the study of language and human linguistic behavior. If I were to take literally some of the comments I have heard Burke make in public, I would conclude that his perspective is limited to language behavior. Yet I know from reading Burke's corpus that such limitation does not apply. Human language behavior is possible because of more general and more fundamental symbolic potentialities that we as humans possess. Language is one of the ways we are able systematically to shape meaning symbolically, but it is not the only one, and at its base it shares in the fundamental symbolic substance from which all symbol systems spring. Therefore many comments made by Burke and others regarding language carry implications that go beyond language. As Duncan writes in the very first sentence of his introduction, "In an age of specialists,

Kenneth Burke's writings offend those who are content with a partial view of human motivation. He is offensive to many academicians because he cannot be stuffed into any of the bins whose occupancy brings fame and fortune in the groves of Academe" (xiii).

One further observation of Duncan's is relevant to my concerns as a rhetorical critic: "What Burke offers . . . is a methodology, a *way* of thinking and testing our thinking, about *how* we act as human beings" (Burke [1935a] 1965, xliii). What is valuable about Burke's work is the variety of orientations that issue forth from a fundamental perspective with regard to human behavior rather than any formulary approach to the study of such behavior. To be sure, in Burke's writings, we can find discussion and demonstration of systematic approaches that can be used to guide the work of the critic. In *The Philosophy of Literary Form*, for instance, Burke shows how the idea of "image clusters" in texts can be helpful to the critic who is sensitive to them. Burke's concern here is with the possibility that images bodied forth in the text can be seen to cluster together, to be associated together in terms of a common principle or theme or value. Principles, themes, and values can be key to our understanding of the primary ideological appeal of a particular rhetorical interaction ([1941] 1973, 9–13). In the same essay, Burke turns our attention toward the rhetorical power of the scapegoat, the psychological vessel that is symbolically killed after it is made sacred enough to carry the self-perceived evils of one's being (40–41). And again, Burke points out the significance for the critic of examining beginnings, endings, and middles of texts, and of inspecting points of transition for the rhetorical inducements that often lurk there (70). In his book *Counter-Statement*, Burke presents one of the most helpful descriptions and accounts of the rhetoric of form the rhetorical critic can ever hope to find ([1931] 1957, 124–52).

A number of other works by Burke identify concrete and specific methodological questions and procedures that a rhetorical critic might utilize. We can also examine Burke in countless essays and portions of his work as he demonstrates his own critical principles. Burke offers more directive methodological advice to rhetorical critics than Aristotle and a host of other scholars ever did. But I would return to Duncan's perceptive comment I quoted earlier concerning Burke's contributions to the art of criticism; what Burke gives us is "a *way* of thinking and testing our thinking, about *how* we act as human beings." Without taking anything away from Burke's concrete methodological advice, his most valuable contribution to the rhetorical critic is his insight into the nature of human symbolic behavior and the potential effect of symbolic inducements.

In this spirit I wish to use Burke's insights into the symbolic lure of negativity—that is, the lure of alternity, rejection, exhortative constraint, and denial. I shall examine the rhetoric of negativity in my own way, for ultimately criticism is an individualistic, artistic endeavor, and impossible of replication. I agree with the words of Edwin Black when he writes:

Methods admit of varying degrees of personality. And criticism, on the whole, is near the indeterminate, contingent, personal end of the methodological scale. In consequence of this placement, it is neither possible nor desirable for criticism to be fixed into a system, for critical techniques to be objectified, for critics to be interchangeable for purposes of replication, or for rhetorical criticism to serve as handmaiden of quasi-scientific theory. (1978, xi)

But while going my own way, I shall be guided by the insights of Kenneth Burke with regard to the rhetorical power of the negative. Therefore, let me turn to some of his representative comments about the inducements of negativity.

In his essay "Definition of Man," Burke tells us that from a "dramatistic" perspective, the fundamental stress of the most fundamental negative "should be upon the hortatory negative, 'Thou shalt not.' The negative begins not as a resource of definition or information but as a command—'Don't.'" He goes on to point out the sense in which there is a paradox about "don't"; the negative is not the name of a thing but rather an idea or principle. But then he says, "Whereas an injunction such as 'thou shalt not kill' is understandable enough as a negative idea, it also has about its edges the positive image of killing" (Burke 1966b, 10). At once Burke has introduced us to the complexity of the negative, for negatives take on their particular power from positive others, and often from positive opposites. By the same token, negativity always lingers in the contextual meaning of all positives; when one decides to give something a name, he or she does so from among a number of others that might have been used but were not. Likewise when we choose to direct attention to something to bring it into conscious focus, we do so from a range of other phenomena that might have served as candidates of focus but that were not allowed to do so. They were denied the privileged position, just as any one of them might have denied the candidate selected. At the same time, there can be multiple selections and thus multiple rejections, creating the possibilities for hierarchy both positive and negative, the one implying the other, both employing titular terms. Much of Burke's systematic understanding of the interrelationships of motives can be within the interacting valences of positive and negative forces.

Before exploring and illustrating some of these valences, we need to consider just how fundamental Burke sees the principle of negativity to be. It is so fundamental that it goes to the heart of language acquisition and use and would seem to relate to the origins of language as well. In his *Rhetoric of Religion*, Burke points out that "language, to be used properly, must be 'discounted.' We must remind ourselves that, whatever *Correspondence* there is between a *word* and the *thing* it names, the word is *not* the thing." And further: "The paradox of the negative, then, is simply this: Quite as the *word* 'tree' is verbal and the *thing* 'tree' is non-verbal, so all words for the non-verbal must, by the very nature of the case, discuss the realm of the non-verbal in terms of *what it is not*. Hence, to use words properly, we must spontaneously have a feeling for the *principle of the negative*" (1961, 18).

Wherever words are used to evoke images of things, two concepts that Burke holds to be important are at work: identification and division. For us to perceive meaning from a language symbol or from language symbols, we must understand that the symbols stand for, represent, or evoke some other phenomenon. To this extent the two are identified together. But language symbols are not the same thing as the phenomenon; thus there is a significant difference. So, at the most fundamental level of language use, identification and division occur together, positivity and negativity interact together, the positive gaining an important part of its force from its negative, and the negative from its positive. Burke makes it clear that identification and division are not just central to rhetoric but essential to its life: "Put identification and division ambiguously together, so that you cannot know for certain just where one ends and the other begins, and you have the characteristic invitation to rhetoric" ([1950a] 1969, 25).

The fact that we "discount" language when we use it properly enables us to engage in sophisticated linguistic behavior and intellectual processes. Think, for example, of the metaphor. In *Permanence and Change* Burke indicates not only how important the negative is but, in its way, how fundamental: "Those who have criticized the use of metaphor have for the most part not realized how little removed such description is from the ordinary intellectual method of analysis. They have supposed that in analysis we stick to the fact itself, whereas in using metaphor we substitute for the fact to be described some quite different fact which is only remotely connected with it by a more or less remote analogy" ([1935a] 1965, 95).

We know in a general sense that when using or responding to a metaphoric pattern, we combine two positively known, but not typically connected, orientations to structure a new orientation. But here the positive is heavily tinged with the negative, for we must discount or reject parts of the meaning of the first two orientations to perceive the third accurately. As Burke points out, "All metaphor involves a . . . feeling for the discount. Thus the expression 'to sail the ship of state' is interpreted properly only insofar as we know that statesmen are not sailors and the State is not a ship" (1961, 19).

Various modes of discounting appear prominently throughout Burke's work. Indeed, the discount becomes complicated, sophisticated, even transcendent, as we read Burke's theoretical analyses. When it comes to the principle of the discount, and the relationship of symbolic and linguistic use to patterns of thought, he is assertive regarding the processes involved in synecdoche. As with metaphor, synecdoche involves a two-way discount, or a double negation. At the same time, the interaction of double positive affirmations must occur. Focusing on the nature of synecdoche, Burke writes: "The more I examine both the structure of poetry and the structure of human relations outside of poetry, the more I become convinced that this is the 'basic' figure of speech and that it occurs in many modes besides that of the formal trope. I feel it to be no mere accident of language that we use the same word for sensory, artistic, and political representation" ([1941] 1973, 26).

A synecdoche is a linguistic and mental movement that encourages a symbol that is part of a larger whole to stand for or represent the whole, such that many of the emotional valences evoked by the whole are evoked by the part. Thus, the name of a friend, enemy, or acquaintance we have may call to mind a larger set of attitudes. Verbs like "walk" or "run" or "jump" can stand for a whole set of activities. The image, picture, or name of a lover or spouse or close family member can evoke a complex set of intimacies, behaviors, and conversational mannerisms that are unshared with others but yet constitute a world of their own. In our time the images of celebrities, whether athletes, entertainers, or politicians, have come to stand for visions of reality. For years the label "Communist" stood for a whole ideology, and with a complete and integrated ideology comes the world. Because we cannot be everywhere at once, because we cannot do everything there is to do, because we cannot know all there is to know, our synecdochic abilities can lead us to respond to holistic perceptions that include unverified rumors, matters of imagination, and outright fantasy.

Synecdoche, then, is endemic to our existence. But to work fully, we must know that while the symbolic part must stand for a larger symbolic whole, the discount—the negative—must be at work. Take the noun "Mom." For some, that term might evoke a set of memories that stand for our life through high school. But at the same time, we must know that that one term does not represent all that there was to that life, and that other symbols could evoke yet other sets of memories.

Because the principles of positivity and negativity are necessary to each other, and necessarily intertwined, we should not be surprised to find that our vocabularies are filled—in fact structured—by terms that relate to other terms in a state of opposition. They abound in our communication, in terms for good and bad, better and worse, beautiful and ugly, up and down, in and out, fast and slow, birth and death, white and black, ought and ought not, do and don't, health and illness, leadership and followership, summer and winter, democracy and totalitarianism, and on and on. Of course, between these polar extremes are a plethora of terms indicating gradations of positivity and negativity. The meanings for all of these terms interact—in fact gain inducing power—from their opposites.

That our language system contains terms that are positive and their opposing negatives, coupled with the realization that "opposites" gain strength from a base of common symbolic substance, tells us that the symbolic process of reversal is a principle embedded deeply in our mental activity. Burke emphasizes the point throughout his work. One place where he is emphatic about the matter occurs in *Philosophy of Literary Form:* "Ordinarily, we find three ingredients interwoven in a given utterance: the spell and the counter-spell, the curse; the prayer and the prayer-in-reverse, oath, indictment, invective; the dream, and the dream gone sour, nightmare" ([1941] 1973, 5). Then, in "The Rhetoric of Hitler's Battle," Burke drives the point home in his analysis of Hitler's *Mein Kampf.* In that analysis, in one brief paragraph, Burke brings together the concordant principles of diversity and unity, positivity and negativity, and reversibility and stability.

Every movement that would recruit its followers from among many discordant and divergent bands, must have some spot towards which all roads lead. Each man may get there in his own way, but it must be the one unifying center of reference for all. Hitler considered this matter carefully, and decided that this center must be not merely a centralizing hub of *ideas,* but a mecca geographically located, towards which all eyes could turn at the appointed hours of prayer (or in this case, the appointed hours of prayer-in-reverse, the hours of vituperation). (192)

The ability we have to engage the principle of symbolic reversal manifests itself in a myriad of ways. It means we can manipulate symbols in order to achieve transposition of meaning, substitution, transformation, reduction and production, ambiguity, analytic and dialectical processing, transcendence, and more.

It would also seem that the principle of reversibility would be closely related to, if not the primary undergirding of, the activities of symbolic unmasking. Thus, we are able to examine argumentative claims, specific appeals, lines of expressed thoughts, patterns of examples, or adverbs, adjectives, nouns, or pronouns, to name but a few symbolic phenomena, with an eye toward discounting them in order to discover what underlying meaning might be present. For example, we might look at the television ads employed by the Bush presidential campaign of 1988 featuring Willie Horton and realize, without a great deal of cerebral activity, that the fundamental emotional thrust of those ads was racial. Or, one might look at recent television advertising sponsored by Toyota, note the people in those ads who jump high in the air clicking their heels in celebration of their Toyota vehicle, and decide that such behavior is meant to render positive a negative evaluation made against Toyota that it is extremely lightweight, a factor that can lead to difficulty in winds and tragedy in accidents.

When Burke discusses unmasking, he sometimes refers to the work of Karl Mannheim, who was concerned with uncovering strengths, and particularly weaknesses, of ideologies. Says Burke:

Any such "unmasking" of an ideology's limitations is itself made from a limited point of view. But each such limited perspective can throw light upon the relation between the universal principles of an ideology and the special interests which they are consciously or unconsciously made to serve. Each point of view could thus reveal something about the relation between an ideology (we might call it a systematized verbal act) and its nonverbal conditions (the scene of that act). ([1950a] 1969, 25)

But Burke does not restrict his own practices of unmasking to ideology. He moves throughout his work on a variety of levels running the gamut from ideology to very personal, emotional, and idiosyncratic response. In a way, he is debunking and unmasking throughout his work, redefining and reshaping the thoughts of others, not only so that he may discover hidden meanings and motives, but so that he may use them for his own purposes. He does not steal ideas at all but rather looks beneath the surface of presented meaning to find underlying motives, symbolic connections, and ultimately the principles of human symbolic behavior. To find examples of his work, one only needs to read his analysis of Milton's "Sampson Agonistes" as it appears in A Rhetoric of Motives ([1950a] 1969, 3–6), or his discussions of Edgar Allen Poe or Samuel Taylor Coleridge as they occur throughout his work.

So far we have been looking at the symbolic processes of moving back and forth between contraries, contradictions, or opposites. We can apparently make these moves easily if we feel the need or find reasons to do so. Let us not lose sight of the fact that these symbolic processes occur on a spectrum from rather straightforward symbolic activity to complex and sophisticated activity. There are times when we are conscious of our actions, and other times when we are unconscious of them. Let me try to illustrate a bit of that spectrum.

Earlier, I pointed out that the very act of naming is an act of negativity. While the act of naming is no simple thing, based as it is on all the complexities of perception, on the total spectrum of things, it is rather fundamental. When we perceive a phenomenon and decide to notice it consciously by naming it, we consciously or unconsciously decide to overlook a number of other positive perceptions. When we are presented with phenomena and are told how to label them within some kind of context (e.g., educational, occupational, or social), we are induced to perceive a part of reality only and to ignore many other possibilities. Now if we move from parts to wholes, from single namings to interlocking sets of namings, we move to visions of reality, to worldviews, to ideologies that set forth our moments in time, the problems we face, the solutions we may have, the values we ought to consider, or the goals we ought or must try to achieve. We are talking about a way of life that we have adopted among many possible ways of living. We are dealing with a holistic perspective that precludes other holistic perspectives. Often it is not a matter of knowing what choices we have made, but rather not knowing what choices we might have made because we are blind to them. The positive here is that we perceive something; the negative is that there is much we do not see. We can thus be caught in the trap that Burke refers to as "trained incapacity." It is a term Burke borrows from Thorstein Veblen. It means that "reality" as we know it reeks of negativity. From naming to trained incapacity, we have moved from a fundamental symbolic act to a total symbolic reality that in and of itself may be positive or negative.

Drawing from Veblen, Burke says: "By trained incapacity he meant that state of affairs whereby one's very abilities can function as blindness" ([1935a] 1965, 7). Burke then goes on to illustrate as follows:

Savages could make fires by considering dry wood and friction as appropriate linkages in the process of fire-making. The serviceability of their orientation is less apparent when, because their Christian missionary and doctor wore a rain coat during storms, they linked rain coats with rainy weather, and accordingly begged him to don the rain coat as a medicine against drought. Irrigation would have been a more effective means, yet their attempts to coerce the weather by homeopathic magic were not "escapist" in the restricted sense. They were a faulty selection of means due to a faulty theory of causal relationships. (9)

One does not have to look very far to find instances of trained incapacity; they exist all over the world of academe. Every time students walk into a classroom and become exposed to the point of view of an instructor, they open themselves to the possibility of trained incapacity because all facts and reasons arise from theoretical perspectives, and all theoretical perspectives are partial views of the domain they relate to. To take but one example, consider the theories of physics that have been developed over the years. Each succeeding theory changes perspective, often in a productive way, but at the same time bringing with it an incapacity to comprehend in other ways, thus illustrating, in a very complex area of knowledge, the principle that positivity and negativity work together.

For a reversal, we turn to Burke's discussion of "perspective by incongruity" wherein we examine two phenomena that are not "logically" connected in order to understand one of them in an entirely new way. Often we do this by juxtaposing concepts or sets of language structures that we do not ordinarily think of in the same context. This is not an unconscious or subconscious activity; rather, it is a conscious maneuver, though it can easily involve denial. Take Burke's own example:

The vocabulary of economists, with its abstract and statistical formulations for the description of human conduct, is perhaps the most outstanding instance of incongruity. A man may think of himself as "saving money," but in the economist's categories of description this man may be performing a mere act of "postponed consumption." The economist here says in effect that the savings bank carries in its window a sign reading: "Postpone your consumption, at 3% per annum." ([1935a] 1965, 122–23)

Perspective by incongruity induces us to see the character of a thing in terms of a totally different character that at first often seems of an opposing or contradictory character. In the example above the nature of saving money is understood in the context of spending money. As long as we think of the processes referred to above only in their own single context, in effect we negate or deny the other. But if we engage in a metaphoric move that combines both processes together within the same context, in this case a larger context, we see matters differently, in a sense negating or denying features of the earlier contexts by not allowing them to stand alone and apart.

One can go on and on referring to places throughout Burke's work where the negative is either illustrated or referred to. Indeed, true to his own perspective, critical critiques, advice, and admonitions, the negative lurks everywhere. I hope I have done enough to show how pervasive negativity is, and how sophisticated its existence can be. Before ending this portion of the chapter, I would like to sum up by referring to one of Burke's constructs that leads to an ultimate in negativity: *hierarchy.*

Hierarchy refers to order, to relationship, to a kind of symmetry. Order allows individuals, groups, and societies and cultures to work. It is necessary to avoid anarchy and chaos. The establishment of relationship enables people to interact, to know their position and status in regard to each other, to find individual identity, and to learn to appreciate or hate diversity. Symmetry provides the aesthetic of form, a symbolic lure in its own right. Amid this structure the positive and the negative interact constantly. Let Kenneth Burke describe our situation:

In their societies, they will seek to keep order. If order, then a need to repress the tendencies to disorder. If repression, than responsibility for imposing, accepting, or resisting the repression. If responsibility, then guilt. If guilt, then the need for redemption, which involves sacrifice, which in turn allows for substitution. At this point, the logic of perfection enters. Man can be viewed as perfectly depraved by a formative "first" offense against the foremost authority, an offense in which one man sinned for all. The cycle of life and death intrinsic to the nature of time can now be seen in terms that treat natural death as the result of this "original" sin. And the principle of perfection can be matched on the hopeful side by the idea of a perfect victim. (1961, 314–15)

This is a hierarchical structure as full of negatives as positives. So that we may get along, we identify with others on some basis perceived to be similar. At the same time our differences from others help us identify ourselves. In order to get along together, we deny some of the things we want. In order to achieve self-identification, we deny others and separate ourselves from them. When we transgress the established order we are identified with, we feel guilt. When we feel guilty, we learn to scapegoat, thus projecting and denying characteristics of ourselves. We thus engage in transformation, one kind of negation, and perhaps transcendence, another kind. Throughout social hierarchy projection, transformation and transcendence may occur, so that there may be the symbolic changing of self, the perceived changing of our contexts, and the reversal of societal rankings. Whenever social hierarchy exists, and whatever its structure, it is held together by ultimate terms, or an interrelationship of ultimate terms. Such terms ultimately identify by ignoring, negating, or denying the differences.

Throughout all of his work, we are admonished by Burke as follows: "The more zealously a positive is proclaimed, the more we are admonished to inspect it for evidence of its guidance by a set of thou-shalt-nots" (1966b, 449). To the admonition, we might add an addendum. Wherever, whenever, and, regardless of its minimality, a positive meaning occurs, we might want to include in its potential force the power derived from its negative counterpoint.

Much more could be said theoretically and conceptually about the phenomenon of negativity and about the cooccurrence and inducing interaction of the positive and the negative and their implications. But I shall do no more here so that I might turn to a few examples of negativity at work, attempting to engage them as a rhetorical critic. The examples I pick come from rhetorical situations and rhetorical texts that most of us arc familiar with, that present the interaction I am interested in, in a fairly direct manner, and in a way that had consequences.

For my examples, I pick the public statements of two American presidents of this century: Franklin D. Roosevelt and Ronald W. Reagan. I pick them, not to draw evaluative comparisons or to suggest historical or personal analogies in any way. Rather, their public rhetoric reveals several distinct variations of the function and force of negative rhetorical inducement. I pick presidential statements rather than any others because the rhetorical situations in which presidents issue public statements possess some clearly acknowledged and understood characteristics. Those who occupy the presidency enjoy a position of unique symbolic and pragmatic importance, granting them the inescapable influence of ethos. They are in an immediate positive-negative relationship with publics at large. In general, they are expected to be representative of the American people—both of us and one of us. At the same time they are expected to be other than we are, more than we are, in important dimensions (Cronin 1975, 24). Thus they are at once of us and not of us, commonly identified with but simultaneously apart from us, joined by symbolic purpose but separated by pragmatic potential. Consequently, they can be rhetorical "vessels" of unusual import.

Presidents are guaranteed audiences of various kinds, operating from differing perspectives, generating counterinfluences of various intensity. Multiple commonalities and differences thus exist simultaneously in rhetorical situations. In my analysis to follow, I shall not attempt to account for all the varieties of such phenomena extant in the situations of interest. It must be enough to acknowledge their existence.

When presidents issue public statements, they have the potential to identify and define problems, to announce and explain policy, to urge support for some actions and rejection of others, and to influence the establishing of a public agenda to the exclusion of others. As a result of these endeavors, public climates of opinion are constructed, modified, and deconstructed. Amid all of these phenomena there functions the symbolic inducement of negativity. With an eye on such function, I turn to two examples of presidential rhetoric.

When Franklin Roosevelt assumed the presidency in 1933, the tasks he faced were enormous. The stock market had crashed in a resounding fashion; all across the nation banks failed and closed, farmers could not find markets for their products, unemployment became widespread, and nearly all sectors of the economy were affected. The mood of the American people was sour and despondent. Many Americans lost their jobs, their savings, and their homes, and a growing number found themselves in breadlines. For many, hope seemed gone. The Great Depression constituted a profound and overpowering negative counterpoint to the "American system" of individualism and minimal government interference that Herbert Hoover applauded so positively. Onto this stage of chaos and defeatism came Franklin Roosevelt. Full of confidence, zest for life, even gaiety, Roosevelt seemed to have around him the halo of the positive. Indeed, his rhetoric was laced with the positive. But if we stop here, we miss the fullness of Roosevelt's rhetorical picture. I should like to argue that the role of negative inducement was significant in Roosevelt's rhetorical success and that the positive impact of his rhetoric was tinged at some important places by negativity. It is a case of the positive gaining force from the negative, of the negative being used positively. With a slight extension, we might even say that for many people, the negative operated positively.

The climate of opinion prevailing at the time of Franklin Roosevelt's first inaugural address to the nation assured wide attention to his speech. There was a need for themes of change and optimism, and for many, the president provided those themes. Most quoted and remembered of the words he spoke that March day in 1933 are these: "First of all, let me assert my firm belief that the only thing we have to fear is fear itself—nameless, unreasoning, unjustified terror which paralyzes needed efforts to convert retreat into advance" (Wrage and Baskerville 1962, 157; all subsequent Roosevelt quotations are from this source). Here the "enemy" lacing the contemporary scene with negativity is a psychological state of mind, and in the remainder of Roosevelt's speech he implies that it can be purged by individual and collective acts of will. In fact, rejection of the state of fear occurs in the very statement that identifies it when Roosevelt describes it as "nameless," "unreasoning," and "unjustified." Fear is simultaneously minimized and rejected. In an important sense, Roosevelt put his finger accurately on the emotional pulse throbbing in many sectors of the nation and symbolically presented it for exorcism.

This potent headline from the speech, memorable in historic recollection, stands as a promontory to be surrounded by images of optimism and resolution throughout the remainder of the president's speech. Encirclement begins even before the phrase is uttered as Roosevelt announces that the time has come for truth, honesty, and boldness. Immediately before the "fear" phrase he proclaims, "This great Nation will endure as it has endured, will revive and will prosper." Immediately after the phrase, Roosevelt expressed the directive to the people he would argue for throughout his speech: "In every dark hour of our national life a leadership of frankness and vigor has met with understanding and support of the people themselves which is essential to victory. I am convinced you will again give that support to leadership in these critical days" (157).

With the introduction of the need for leadership, Roosevelt turns to solutions he will adopt in light of specific problems he articulates. Those problems constitute redefinition, as the president casts them in materialistic rather than psychological terms. He refers to shrunken monetary values, individual inability to purchase, the shrinking of income, the loss of family savings and markets for agricultural products. A bit later in his speech, Roosevelt proposes, in general terms, materialistic solutions in keeping with the problems. He suggests the need for the redistribution of resources, increasing the value of agricultural products, moving to prevent home and farm foreclosures, unifying relief efforts, and engaging in various forms of national planning. Such solutions, said the president, will lead to recovery and restoration. They also imply governmental intervention on a scale dramatically different from previous policy.

In isolation, the scale of governmental intervention, control, and management referred to by Roosevelt could be seen as a threat to the people of a nation whose sociopolitical lexicon features "individuality," "freedom of choice," "equal opportunity," and "liberty" as almost sacred terms. Growing involvement of the government in individual lives might seem an unwarranted, if not dangerous, intrusion. However, the felt need to alleviate the economic travail of the time helped to mitigate the negativity of threat and served rather to enhance the positive outcome of leadership and action Roosevelt promised. But in addition to the psychological inducement of hope in the midst of despair, Roosevelt's rhetoric served to alter the dimensions of the national exigency so that threat was reduced and hope encouraged. It is in this function of the rhetoric that the role of negativity plays an interesting role.

Roosevelt begins to alter the dimensions of political ideology as he provides a personified enemy to serve as symbolic scapegoat for national ills. The trouble, he asserts, is caused by the "rulers of exchange of mankind's goods" because of their stubbornness and incompetence. "Practices of the unscrupulous money changers stand indicted in the court of public opinion, rejected by the hearts and minds of men" (158). Operating with "outworn practices, the money changers," Roosevelt charges, "have fled from their high seats in the temple of our civilization. We may now restore that temple to the ancient truths" (158).

By describing the enemy as those who follow the rules of self-seeking, the president pictures a scene in which the promises and possibilities of a free-enterprise democracy had become willfully extended to assume the forms of constrictive oligarchy and monopoly. Positives became stretched until they became negatives. Constructive dimensions of an accepted ideology became confining and destructive. Negative dimensions demanded corrective reshaping.

In discussing the measures needed to provide the corrective, Roosevelt reshaped possible negative attributes of sociopolitical ideology to portray them as positive. The goals of individual striving, achievement, and acquisition must become secondary for the good of all. Rather than operating with unfettered individual ambition and effort, regardless of consequences to others, a new discipline must be practiced so that singular ambition becomes willingly constrained by the ambitions of others.

To make his point, the president announced that international relations must defer to national recovery, explaining that such a view is not narrowly nationalistic but rather an insistence upon recognizing the interdependence of the various "elements in and parts of the United States—a recognition of the old and permanently important manifestations of the American spirit of the pioneer" (159). According to Roosevelt: "If I read the temper of our people correctly, we now realize as we have never realized before our interdependence on each other; that we can not merely take but we must give as well; that if we are to go forward, we must move as a trained and loyal army willing to sacrifice for the good of a common discipline, because without such discipline no progress is made, no leadership becomes effective" (160). Such action, said Roosevelt, may be taken under "the form of government we have inherited from our ancestors. Our Constitution is so simple and practical that it is possible always to meet extraordinary needs by changes in emphasis and arrangement without loss of essential form" (160).

In this example, we see the valences of symbolic negativity to be active on several levels. Rhetorically, the positive qualities of widely accepted ideology become negative through symbolic stretching to the point of extremity, whereas negative qualities become positive through retracting them from extremity to an interpretative frame of moderation. Through this oxymoronic reshaping, Roosevelt has stabilized the uncertainties of change and induced support for the role of leadership he intended to assume and the action he proposed to take. In Roosevelt's first inaugural address, we have a case where negative images and symbols enhanced the approbative force of the positive ones.

President Ronald Reagan provides us with a very different aspect of negativity. It is an aspect that may seem unique to Reagan but that may be more prevalent than we noticed before. I refer to the negative force of denial. In order to pursue the brief line of analysis I shall undertake here, I must explain the particular sense of denial I am concerned with.

Burke rightly points out that any action we undertake, any statement that we utter, any choice that we make, involves the negative. In doing any one thing, we deny a number of others. On many occasions, the denial is innocent and relatively passive. We may, for example, choose one particular object of a particular color from among a host of others out of personal preference rather than active distaste. On other occasions, rejection may be more active, as when in voting for one particular candidate we vote consciously and willfully against another. On other occasions, however, denial may be almost subconscious, as when one's protective psyche induces one to concentrate so hard on certain aspects in the environment that other, less pleasant aspects go unseen. When functioning in this sense, negativity assumes a guise among the phenomena composing the underside of meaning; in the case of much of Ronald Reagan's public rhetoric, it fashions itself as the underside of hope.

The general case for deniability as I refer to it here is outlined by George Steiner:

I believe that the communication of information, of ostensive and verifiable "facts," constitutes only one part, and perhaps a secondary part of human discourse. The potentials of fiction, of counterfactuality, of undecidable futurity profoundly characterize both the origins and nature of speech. They differentiate it ontologically from the many signal systems available to the animal world. They determine the unique, often ambiguous tenor of human consciousness and make the relations of the consciousness to reality tenuous. Through language, so much of which is focused inward to our private selves, we reject the empirical inevitability of the world. Through language, we construct what I call "alternatives of being." (1975, 475)

President Reagan's rhetoric denied empirical reality by focusing steadily and confidently on positive qualities, on affirmations of hope, on examples of achievement, on qualities of advancement rather than retreat and decline. It is instructive to remember that Reagan's immediate predecessor, Jimmy Carter, often spoke in terms of negativity with regard to contemporaneous conditions, urging the American public to refrain from excessive expenditures, to settle for a reduced quality of life, to lower expectations and goals for the future. Reagan did nothing of the sort. His public statements emphasized the possible and the probable. Whereas Carter gave expression to the possible retreat of American stature, Reagan gave voice to the surety of advance. Some political commentators claimed that Reagan was a throwback to earlier times in this country when frontiers remained, resources were plentiful, and opportunities existed in abundance. But an examination of his rhetoric indicates otherwise; he spoke confidently of the future and drew a distinction between his party and his Democrat opponents on these grounds: "Their government sees people only as members of groups. Ours serves all the people of America as individuals. Theirs lives in the past, seeking to apply the old and failed policies to an era that has passed them by. Ours learns from the past and strives to change by boldly charting a new course for the future" (*New York Times*, August 24, 1984). And in his second inaugural he declared: "When I took this oath four years ago, I did so in a time of economical stress. Voices were raised saying we had to look to our past for the greatness and the glory. But we, the present-day Americans, are not given to looking backward. In this blessed land, there is always a better tomorrow" (*Washington Post*, January 22, 1985).

Statements like these are trite in the annals of American political rhetoric, but Reagan's themes stressing a "new beginning" and a "new morning" in America do not seem to rest easily in nostalgia. When Reagan delivers these lines there is an exuberance about them that crackles with an impatience to get on with the future. Reagan's appeal is not simply anachronistic in any simple or significant way. Nor is it accurate to assume that Reagan is calling for a return to an old ideology of conservatism. Reagan's approbative reference to individualism as opposed to group identity should not be seen to carry weighty ideological significance. Throughout the Reagan years, public opinion polls indicated that the general public held more liberal beliefs on individual issues than Reagan did.

A more likely explanation brings the inducements of denial more clearly into view. After the turmoil of protest and confrontation during the years of Lyndon Johnson, the continuing frustration of the Vietnam War and cynicism provoked during the Nixon years by the Watergate episode, and the period of pessimism during the Carter years, Americans wanted to feel good about themselves and their country. Ronald Reagan told them they could. Reagan's campaign advisers were aware of the success the president enjoyed playing positive American themes during his first term and planned his campaign for reelection accordingly. In a memo addressing the matter of campaign strategy written by Richard Darman in June 1984, the following advice appeared: "Paint RR as the personification of all that is right with, or heroized by, America. Leave Mondale in a position where an attack on Reagan is tantamount to an attack of America's idealized image of itself—where a vote against Reagan is, in some subliminal sense, a vote against 'mythic' America" (*Newsweek*, November–December 1984, 38).

Reagan's rhetoric during and after the 1984 campaign reflected Darman's advice. Accepting his party's nomination for the presidency again, he indicated that the nation had successfully rejected the mood of an earlier time and had moved in more positive ways. We can all be proud, he said, that this pessimism is ended; America is coming back and is more confident than ever about the future.

Four years ago we raised a banner of gold colors, no pale pastel. We claimed a dream of an America that would be "a shining city on a hill."

We came together in a "national crusade to make America great again," and to make "a new beginning."

Now it's all coming together. With our beloved nation at peace, we are in the midst of a springtime of hope for America. Greatness lies ahead of us." (*New York Times*, August 24, 1984)

In his second inaugural, Reagan reiterated the theme with renewed vigor: "My fellow citizens, our nation is poised for greatness. We must do what we know is right, and do it with all our might. Let history say of us, these were golden years—when the American Revolution was reborn, when freedom gained new life, and America reached for her best" (*Washington Post*, January 22, 1985). In his 1985 State of the Union address, Reagan declared:

My fellow citizens, this nation is poised for greatness. The time has come to proceed toward a great new challenge—a Second American Revolution of hope and opportunity; a revolution carrying us to new heights of progress by pushing back frontiers of knowledge and space; a revolution of spirit that taps the soul of America, enabling us to summon greater strength than we have ever known, and a revolution that carries beyond our shores the golden promise of human freedom in a world at peace. (*Washington Post*, February 7, 1985)

One can find many other passages from other Reagan speeches across the years that demonstrate this unflappable optimism in America's future, point to its abounding resources and energy, and emphasize the talents of its people.

Themes of heroism were also featured in Reagan's rhetoric. They often took the form of anecdotes, a form of illustration and support that the president was fond of. Anecdotes can serve as arguments or evidence to bolster argumentative claims without appearing to be argumentative. They also serve to personalize in ways that invite easy identification. Reagan made it clear that any one of us might be identified in his anecdotes, for we are the true heroes of the nation. In his first inaugural he said:

Those who say that we're in a time when there are no heroes—they just don't know where to look. You can see heroes every day going in and out of factory gates. Others, a handful in number, produce enough food to feed all of us and then the world beyond.

You meet heroes across a counter—and they're on both sides of that counter. . . .

Now, I have used the words "they" and "their" in speaking of these heroes. I could say "you" and "your" because I'm addressing the heroes of whom I speak—you, the citizens of that blessed land. (*New York Times*, January 21, 1981)

The same speech gave us Martin Treptow, who left his job in a small-town barber shop during World War I to join the Rainbow Division on the Western front, and to die. But before dying, he kept a diary with a personal pledge that Reagan read to good effect.

In a speech on October 27, 1983, dealing with affairs in Lebanon and Grenada, we heard about a young marine, badly wounded, with tubes coming out of his body, who, when visited by Marine Corps Commandant Paul Kelly, scribbled "semper fi" on a pad of paper (*New York Times*, October 28, 1983). Reagan's narrative account of the carrying of the Olympic torch across America at the end of his acceptance speech in 1984 is noteworthy. Featured in the narrative were ninety-nine-year-old Ansel Stubbs, four-year-old Katie Johnson, a robed church choir in Tupelo, Mississippi, a fourteen-year-old boy in a wheelchair in Richardson, Texas, a line of deaf children in West Virginia, crowds singing "America the Beautiful" along the route, and a Vietnamese immigrant and his son in San Francisco cheering a nineteen-year-old black man as he pushed an eighty-eight-year-old white woman in a wheelchair while she carried the torch (*New York Times*, August 24, 1984). Reagan's "Morning Again in America" ads during the 1984 campaign did not show Reagan, but rather ordinary people tilling fields or whitewashing fences. Examples are a bit more elevated in the second inaugural with the praying general at Valley Forge, a pacing Abraham Lincoln in the White House, the defenders of the Alamo, and the singing settler going west, but we understand they symbolize all of us. Having come to expect such anecdotes, one perhaps felt disappointed during Reagan's 1985 State of the Union address as he neared the end without mentioning any ordinary hero. Then suddenly there they were—two of them, not in the speech but actually in the balcony ready to acknowledge applause: Vietnamese Cadet Jean Nguyen about to graduate from West Point, and seventy-nine-year-old Clara Hale from Harlem, who operated a program for the infants of drug addicts.

The effect of Reagan's rhetoric in these and similar instances was to induce a focused concentration on the positive to the denial of the negative. It is a misdirection in that it directs attention away from a growing number of problems that festered during his presidency. The budget deficit grew to alarming proportions. American business and industry lost more of its share of the market to foreign countries. The monetary gap separating the wealthy from the ordinary grew, and the number of people who fell into the poverty class increased. Because of financial pressure, small business and family farms decreased in number, and the nuclear family was declared to be in trouble. The number of AIDS cases multiplied, and there was no noticeable advance on the war against drugs. The list could be easily expanded. But for a time, the majority of Americans felt better about themselves, as the inducements of needing to deny the frustrations of a rapidly changing world gave added power to the simpler positives enumerated by Reagan.

The two examples of the rhetorical function of negativity presented here show the negative operating with considerable force. The intensity of the force will differ from situation to situation, in interaction with all of the elements present in rhetorical situations. Consequently, it does not make sense to attempt to identify and categorize all of their limitless possibilities. Wherever there is symbolic meaning, negativity is present, influencing the outcomes of rhetorical interaction and awaiting the disclosure and explication of the rhetorical critic.

5

Burke's Representative Anecdote as a Critical Method

Arnie Madsen

Most commentators on the 1988 presidential campaign reached similar conclusions about the candidates' discourse: the campaign was devoid of "issue" content, focusing instead on the "personality" of the candidates. Many observers will likely only remember the 1988 campaign through visions of George Bush proudly standing in front of an American flag or Michael Dukakis riding in a tank. Yet deeper examination of selected campaign texts reveals the Republican rhetoric closely tied candidate personality to the selection of policy proposals by a future president. Central to the Republican rhetoric was a vision of the various elements of society working together as a partnership under the able leadership of George Bush. This partnership image serves as a representative anecdote for the 1988 Bush presidential campaign.[1]

This chapter further explicates Kenneth Burke's concept of the representative anecdote. In relation to other dramatistic studies, applications of Burke's representative anecdote are still rare in the critical literature. This omission is significant, as Burke suggests that the identification of an anecdote which sums up the essence of a text is an essential element of dramatistic analysis ([1950a] 1969, 59). Additionally, Burke establishes criteria by which to judge whether an anecdote is representative. If the anecdote fails to meet one or more criteria, the anecdote will not represent the text. If the critic shapes his or her analysis around an unrepresentative anecdote, the analysis will in turn misrepresent the text (59, 323, and 324).

This chapter will initially consider Burke's description of representative anecdotes and applications of the method in the critical literature.[2] The second section uses an anecdotal approach to examine a sample of discourse from the 1988 Bush presidential campaign. The chapter concludes by describing the benefits of an anecdotal approach to rhetorical criticism.

The Representative Anecdote

Defining the Representative Anecdote

Some authors argue that the anecdote refers to an individual linguistic act which is representative of a broader text (Balthrop 1983, 8 and 9; see also Dauber 1984, 42). Other critics equate Burke's use of anecdote to a narrative form embedded within a text (Brummett 1984b, 3–4; Brummett 1984a, 162–63; Chandler 1988, 10). The latter view assumes Burke's description of the representative anecdote as "a form in conformity with which the vocabulary is constructed" ([1950a] 1969, 59). Thus, Rueckert states that a representative anecdote is "the paradigmatic embodiment of the 'pure' or 'ideal' form . . . the archetypal myth, the perfect imitation of the pure essence" (1969b, 381).

David Williams's suggestion, however, is that the representative anecdote may be both act and form (1986, 4). By defining the anecdote in such a manner, Williams widens the circumference of the construct, expanding its utility for both rhetors and critics. As Williams argues, "The representative anecdote is thus both a theoretical construct, a statement of what a motivational complex *is*, and a methodological procedure, or a way of discovering the motivational complex" (4). Viewing the representative anecdote as both act and form allows it to become a precept to guide both critics and rhetors. Critics may use an anecdotal approach to explicate further the motivational framework which underlies a text. In this sense the critic uses the anecdote as a methodological procedure. Rhetors may employ the representative anecdote as they try to produce a representative text to round out a situation. A rhetorical situation may call for a specific response, becoming a normative constraint on the rhetor's strategic choices.

Burke suggests, "If one does not select a *representative* anecdote as an introductory form, in conformity with which to select and shape his terms of analysis, one cannot expect to get representative terms" ([1950a] 1969, 324). Burke's concern is that while there are many anecdotes which may be chosen for an analysis, few of the anecdotes will fully represent the text. If the anecdote is not representative of its accompanying terminology, the critic's analysis will not adequately explicate the text.

The problem of identifying an anecdote which represents a text centers on the difference between Burke's notions of synecdoche and metonymy. Burke defines synecdoche as "part for the whole, whole for the part, container for the contained, sign for the thing signified" ([1950a] 1969, 507). In most cases the term "representation" is synonymous with synecdoche, as the unique characteristics of one construct serve to represent a second construct (503). A representative anecdote thus synecdochically represents its originating text.[3]

Burke contrasts metonymic reduction with synecdochic representation. A metonymic construction of an event would be a misrepresentation or deflection of the essence of the event. Burke argues that in a synecdochically related pair, quantity stands for quality as quality stands for quantity. With metonymy the quality of an experience becomes reduced to quantity, with no corresponding equation connecting quantity back to quality ([1950a] 1969, 509–10). Metonymic reductions would consist of words and phrases not reflecting the essential characteristics of the entire text. Metonymic reductions ignore "the motives and interests that inform the substance of human behavior"; they reduce "all human action to naturalistic correlations, to mere processes"; they "mistake statistical for substantial representation" (Leff 1989, 120).

The issue of what is and is not representative becomes important when critics use the anecdote as method. Nonrepresentative reductions may have some utility in clarifying interrelationships among clusters of terms, but they "cannot represent those relationships and thus cannot serve the corrective function necessary for dramatism to generate critical insights which are grounded in text" (Conrad 1984, 98–99). Thus, Burke argues there is a necessity for textual evidence to support conclusions; the critic "must be able to extract [an] interpretation by explicit quotation from the work itself" ([1941] 1973, 69). This requirement of textual grounding forces the critic to discover the anecdote in the text, not to superimpose an anecdote onto the text.

The alternative to discovering an anecdote within a text is for the critic to employ an anecdote of his or her own making in an attempt to summarize the motivational frame of the text in what the critic perceives to be a representative fashion (David Williams 1986, 24). This process of superimposing a theoretical anecdote onto a text is the prevalent approach in applications of the anecdotal method. Brummett, for example, argues that "the anecdote need not have been explicitly uttered in the discourse under analysis. Instead, the anecdote is a method used by the *critic*. The anecdote is a lens, filter, or template through which the critic studies and reconstructs the discourse. The critic *represents* the essence of discourse by viewing it as if it follows a dramatic plot" (1984a, 163; see also Brummett 1984b, 4). As a result Brummett argues that the anecdote "is a *method* for better understanding the vocabulary of utterances rather than an utterance itself" (1984b, 4), and the critic uses "his or her powers of abstraction" to "represent the discourse" (1984a, 163; see Smith 1987, 253–54; Smith and Golden 1988, 246; or J. P. Williams 1986, 3). Brummett concludes that it is the critic's task to "catalogue . . . representative anecdotes and to link them with the situations" (1984a, 174).

The problem with this approach should be readily apparent; by superimposing an anecdote onto a text, the critic cannot know whether the anecdote represents the text. Any text may have a variety of different anecdotes applied to it. However, given the lack of textual support, superimposed or theoretical anecdotes necessarily undermine the search for the constitutive anecdote which accurately represents the substance of the text's motivational complex (David Williams 1986, 25). By superimposing one anecdote out of the many, the critic ignores the form component of anecdotes. Thus, theoretical anecdotes bypass the idea that an anecdote is both act and form, a structure of discourse and a method for examining discourse. The conclusions drawn from criticisms employing theoretical anecdotes may be metonymic misrepresentations of the symbolic reality of a text rather than synecdochic reflections of that reality. A critic's interpretation of a text through a theoretical anecdote thus risks deflection of the text rather than providing a representative view of the text.

Brummett's 1984 *Southern Speech Communication Journal* article on evangelical rhetoric applies a theoretical anecdote to a body of discourse. In the essay, Brummett argues that a shared anecdote underlies the rhetoric of three diverse examples of evangelical discourse. Brummett finds the basis for the anecdote in the Bible's parables of the house and of the sower. To illustrate the anecdote, Brummett identifies five sets of images which reflect the core principles of the parables. With little effort a critic can apply the same parable anecdote to any text. For example, terms reflecting the five sets of images identified by Brummett are also present in the 1988 "Basic Speech" of George Bush:

Horizontal movement images: Drive, running, behind, going, go, go in, come in, direction, take away, projecting, there, move, moving forward, step, lead, around.

Places, foundations, bases images: Support, strong, strength, strengthen, here, sound, fundamental, basis, area, security, country, nation, free world, world.

Structural or building images, root and plant images: Raise, biological, earth, environment, soil, outdoors, rainy, season, homes, kitchen.

Destructive tides or diseases, physical decay images: Hate, bad, down, squeeze, take, taking, cut, missing, freeze, weaken, hit, combat, army, terrorism, force, weapons, nuclear weapons, chemical and biological weapons, threatened, worst, afraid, fighting, foreign, trouble.

Vertical movement, healings, organic growth images: Up, peace, hope, enhance, raise, heavens, God, bless, perfectly, help, learn, protect, safeguard, good, pride, work, opportunity, expansion, big, much, defense, clean, perfect. (see Bush 1988b, B5)

On the basis of these image sets, one could argue that George Bush has the same motivational base as the three evangelical rhetors described by Brummett. While this conclusion may or may not be correct, Brummett's approach provides no procedure to test the conclusion. The conclusions drawn from application of a theoretical anecdote are incapable of disconfirmation. A cursory reading will find terms which verify the presence of any theoretical anecdote within a text. Use of theoretical anecdotes merely classifies or catalogs a text as belonging to a particular anecdote without identifying an anecdote which actually represents the motivational complex of the text.[4]

Criteria for Representation

The corrective to the problems associated with theoretical anecdotes is to generate criteria by which to examine the representativeness of an anecdote, both as structure and as method.[5] Identifying anecdotes which meet the criteria would better assure representative analysis by a critic. In this regard Burke describes an anecdote as "something sufficiently demarcated in character to make analysis possible, yet sufficiently complex in character to prevent the use of too few terms in one's description" ([1950a] 1969, 324). Similarly, Balthrop indicates several elements which guide a judgment about the representativeness of an anecdote: "The search for the representative anecdote recognizes that it must share the 'essence' of both symbolic action and its derivative, dramatism. That is, the anecdote must exhibit conflicts (agon), synecdoche, and the substance (or 'what is'), and the dialectic and synecdochic reversals contained within the paradox of substance (transformation). It will, as representative of human motivation, have a 'strongly linguistic bias'" (1983, 9). Boiled down, those criteria are basically three: the anecdote must reflect human action and symbol use, and it must simultaneously possess both scope and reduction (Burke [1950a] 1969, 59 and 324; David Williams 1986, 25).[6]

The first criterion is that the anecdote *reflect human action.* As Burke argues, "A representative case of human motivation must have a strongly linguistic bias," as it is "a reduction of the world to the dimensions of words; it is the world in terms of words" ([1950a] 1969, 59 and 96). Anecdotes which reflect motion, determinism, or physical relationships rather than symbolic acts would be inherently metonymic, incapable of adequately representing human actions (Conrad 1984, 98). Burke rejects telegraph lines and train stations as anecdotes for human relations in part because of this physicalist bias ([1950a] 1969, 326–27). Burke's overriding concern is that, since humans are symbol-using animals, we must find terminologies for our discussions which stress symbolism as a motive.[7]

The second criterion for representative anecdotes is that they must *possess adequate scope.* Scope is the principle that the anecdote must faithfully reflect reality. The anecdote chosen must not be "too simplist"; rather, it "must be supple and complex enough to be representative of the subject matter it is designed to calculate. It must have scope" (Burke [1950a] 1969, 60).[8] This function requires that if a particular anecdote is to sum up the entire constellation of a text, the critic must present sufficient evidence to indicate that the anecdote actually does encompass those relationships (Balthrop 1983, 20).[9] Balthrop argues, "A single, specific instance may very well contain the elements of a broader development, but that act is quite different when placed within the larger circumference than when treated in its immediate, circumscribed surrounding. As scenic considerations expand, what had been a representative anecdote in a smaller, more limited scene may lose that representational quality because, as the motivational substance of scene changes, the substantial qualities of the anecdote may not" (12–13).

However, the anecdote must not deflect reality. The third criterion requires the anecdote to be a synecdoche, to *represent the text in its entirety.* A metonymic anecdote, by contrast, would demonstrate some sort of connectedness between the anecdote and text, but it would not reveal the essential nature or substance of the text (Burke [1950a] 1969, 325–26). As Conrad argues, "Although the critic might choose one of many forms in which to express this [representative] principle, the principle itself must be synecdochic. It will not provide a *summary* of the act, a list of its many features. It will instead provide a *summation* of those elements, an expression of the essential dramatic conflict that underlies the act" (1981, 46). The anecdote is a synecdoche, and in that sense "is never simply metonymic, or reductionistic, but rather involves the complexities which obtain in the case of a microcosm which 'stands for' the macrocosm" (David Williams 1986, 3–4). The singular will replace the plural, the part will replace the whole, the consequent will replace the antecedent. Each act within the anecdote will share the essence of the broader scope of acts contained within the text (Balthrop 1975, 3). The elements necessary for inclusion in this synecdochic representation are fundamental principles such as the symbols of dramatic conflict and an underlying agonistic relationship expressed in images of confrontation, trial, and resolution (Conrad 1984, 96; Balthrop 1983, 13–14).[10]

Phases of Dramatistic Analysis

Burke suggests that critics should follow three phases of dramatistic analysis in examinations of rhetorical practice (these are logically distinct and not temporally ordered phases) (Conrad 1984, 95). One of Burke's "rules of thumb" is to examine the dramatic alignment, or what goes with and against what. This is a "statistical" process involving the charting of the text and the relationships contained within it (Burke [1941] 1973, 69 and 18–35). Conrad indicates this phase is "*statistical analysis* of the verbal structures which comprise symbolic acts" (1984, 95). Statistical analysis is "an inductive, constrained search for the dramatic alignment of a work, for the unified and opposing principles that are present in a text" (96).[11]

A second rule of thumb is to examine the "underlying imagery (or groupings of imagery) through which the agonistic trial takes place" (Burke [1941] 1973, 83). This phase includes "a search for a symbol (or symbols) which *represent the essential character* of the acts" (Conrad 1984, 95). In this respect the critic identifies a hierarchy within the text which logically contains the text's principles, relationships between the principles, and any sources of ambiguity in those relationships (102). At the apex of the hierarchy "is a central, synthetic construct which logically contains the matrix of conceptual interrelationships revealed through statistical analysis" (97). The construct at the apex of the hierarchy is a "title of titles," a concept which "sums up" all the particulars contained within the hierarchy (Burke 1961, 25). After identifying the title of titles, other subclasses seem to emanate or radiate from the construct (26). The central construct from which other elements radiate is the representative anecdote. The anecdote, "if it is truly representative," is "some form, which is already *in* the terminology, just as a 'familial' definition is already 'in' the tribal terms" (David Williams 1986, 5).[12]

The third principle is the examination of critical points or watershed moments within the work. This includes examination of beginnings and endings, as well as other critical moments such as the introduction of new qualities, changes in alignment, and so forth (Burke [1941] 1973, 78). This phase of dramatistic criticism is "*pentadic analysis* of the interrelationships among the multiple dimensions of symbolic action. . . . a process through which a critic examines the interrelationships among the constituent elements of symbolic acts" (Conrad 1984, 95 and 99). This phase of analysis is both logically and temporally posterior to the selection of a representative anecdote (99; Burke [1950a] 1969, 59).[13]

The next section of this chapter applies the anecdotal procedure to three speeches delivered by George Bush in the 1988 presidential campaign. The analysis will apply the three phases of dramatistic criticism to the Bush texts, focusing on the representation phase. This section illustrates the utility of the anecdotal approach in examining how one speech serves as anecdote for a set of speeches as well as how a common anecdote can serve as the motivational base for several speeches. This section also illustrates how the rhetorical situation provided normative constraints on Bush's approach to the campaign.

The Representative Anecdote and the 1988 Bush Campaign

This section of the chapter will examine three speeches delivered by George Bush during the 1988 presidential campaign. The first text is the "Announcement Speech," serving to announce the Bush candidacy in Houston, Texas, on October 12, 1987. The second text is the "Acceptance Speech," delivered by Bush to accept the presidential nomination at the Republican National Convention in New Orleans, Louisiana, August 18, 1988. The third text is the "Basic Speech," or stump speech, given during the third week of October 1988, in Illinois. These texts provide samples of discourse from three distinct periods of the 1988 Bush campaign. Analysis of these texts will reveal an underlying anecdote which extends throughout the Bush campaign. This analysis also demonstrates how the acceptance speech functions as anecdote, as representative moment of the campaign.

A brief analysis of the scene serves as the background for analysis of the Bush texts. The vice president delivered his announcement speech during a period of setbacks. George Bush showed poorly against Pat Robertson in the recently concluded Michigan caucuses and had similar discouraging results in an Iowa straw poll (*Facts on File*, October 16, 1987, 757). These problems reinforced the continuing references to the "wimp factor," the damaging perception that Bush lacked the nerve to be his own person (757). For example, President Reagan stated in an interview that Bush was more completely involved in national affairs than any previous vice president. When asked for an example, however, Reagan replied, "I can't answer that in context" (757).

Yet even with the problems facing the campaign, at the time of the announcement speech Bush was the acknowledged front-runner for the Republican nomination. A Roper Poll conducted in September of 1987 showed that Bush was the preferred Republican candidate in the eleven southern states that would hold presidential primaries on Super Tuesday (*Facts on File*, October 16, 1987, 758). At the time of the announcement, Bush had a significant lead over Senator Robert Dole and the rest of the Republic candidates in most national polls (Cook 1987, 2455).

By August of 1988, Bush had emerged from the pack as the Republican nominee for president. Yet Bush remained behind Democratic nominee Michael Dukakis in the opinion polls. At the opening of the Republican National Convention, Dukakis had a lead of 10–14 percentage points over Bush (*Facts on File*, August 12, 1988, 591). Furthermore, Dukakis had the edge with the so-called Reagan Democrats. In most surveys, a solid majority of these registered Democrats who had voted for Ronald Reagan for president preferred Dukakis in 1988 (Barnes 1988, 2081).

Most political commentators suggested that the vice president had to meet at least two goals at the convention to close the gap with Dukakis in the final weeks of the campaign. The first was to demonstrate his leadership ability through the selection of a running mate; the second required an effective address to delegates at the Republican convention. The immediate reaction to the selection of Indiana Senator Dan Quayle as the vice presidential choice was not favorable. Not only was Quayle a relative unknown in national politics, but also there were questions about his background and ability to lead, should a crisis arise (Germond and Witcover 1988, 2208; *Chicago Tribune* editorial, August 19, 1988). As a result of the fallout from the Quayle nomination, the pressure on Bush increased, requiring a strong Bush acceptance speech. The *Philadelphia Inquirer* stated that Bush must both stake out clear differences between himself and President Reagan and articulate sensible solutions to important public policy issues (editorial, August 18, 1988).

Commentary following the speech suggested that Bush managed to exceed all expectations for the address. The *Minneapolis Star and Tribune* editorialized that the most subtle idea in the speech was the careful distancing of Bush from the Reagan administration (August 19, 1988). Bush "emerged from President Reagan's shadow to reveal a forceful but compassionate man with a sense of humor that includes a capacity to poke fun at himself" (*Houston Post*, August 20, 1988). The strength of the address also served to decrease, at least temporarily, the number of questions asked about the choice of Quayle as running mate (*Honolulu Advertiser*, August 19, 1988). Finally, the speech served to demonstrate the differences between the political philosophies of George Bush and Michael Dukakis (*Houston Post*, August 20, 1988).

As Bush campaigned in the last few weeks before the election, the electoral scales were tipping in his favor. By the middle of October a poll by the *Wall Street Journal* and NBC News indicated that Bush had a 17-point advantage over Dukakis (*Facts on File*, October 21, 1988, 769). The media also reported the Democratic candidate was writing off regions of the nation as impossible to win (769; ibid., October 14, 1988, 753). Predictions of an electoral landslide for Bush were starting to appear in media accounts of the campaign (752).

Statistical Analysis

One phase of dramatistic critical procedure is statistical analysis of the texts.[14] Five major themes appear within the three Bush speeches. The first theme is that the United States is leader of the free world. Expression of this theme is manifest in a variety of ways. The United States is the leader of the world, playing a unique role in world politics and working to solve many of the problems of the twentieth century. Similarly, the United States is not in a state of decline; rather, it is a rising nation, a nation that will lead the world into the twenty-first century (references here and below to Bush's speeches are taken from Bush 1987, 1988a, 1988b).

A second unifying theme which crosses the boundaries of the individual texts is the strength of the U.S. economy. The economy was in decline when the Reagan administration took over from the Democrats in 1980. Since then the economy has grown and will continue to improve. The economy was ill but has recovered. There are still some problems with the economy, but a Bush presidency will make progress. The Republicans are the party which rebuilt the economy. The Democrats, if elected, would once again destroy the economy.

The third theme relates to foreign policy. This theme suggests that democracy and peace are on the march because of the U.S. arms buildup. The United States has rebuilt its defenses. Strength and diplomatic negotiations lead to peace, while weakness, concessions, and ambivalence lead to war. Furthermore, the United States must negotiate from a position of strength if peace and democracy are to continue to spread.

A fourth thematic commonality relates to core principles which Bush praises in his discourse. Of primary concern are the individual and the family. The individual and the family are the foundation of society, the "bright center," the "essential unit." Closely related to the individual and family are community and local organizations. The United States is a nation of communities and organizations, a "thousand points of light." Essential to the preservation of the individual, the family, and the community are values centered in ethics and religion. Here Bush advocates prayer in schools, the pledge of allegiance, and the death penalty. He similarly registers his opposition to gun control, abortion, prison furloughs, and tax increases.

A fifth common thread linking the speeches concerns the role of government in society. In general, the nation should minimize government intrusion in society. IRS agents, for example, should not invade the homes of taxpayers. Government should be active in certain areas such as the environment, the economy, education, drug enforcement, and defense. However, beyond those specified areas, government should have no role. Finally, public servants should act to serve the public, not the greed of politicians.

The five themes present an outline of the equations in the Bush speeches. The Bush campaign views certain clusters of terms and policies as positive, and other clusters are harmful to society. Certain policies will serve to promote the interests of a strong United States, the world, the individual, and the family. Other policies will cause the degeneration of the United States, the world, the individual, and the family. The role of the individual, the family, and the community should increase, while government's role should decrease.

Burke's second rule of thumb for dramatistic analysis is the search for a representative anecdote. There are two procedures for identifying an anecdote. One is the process advanced by Balthrop: the search for an act which is representative of an entire set of acts. The acceptance speech of George Bush stands as the representative anecdote for the three texts under examination in this chapter, as an act within a larger body of discourse.

In this sense, the acceptance speech is a text designed to meet the exigencies of the situation.[15] At this point in the campaign Bush was trailing Dukakis in the polls. The address had to serve two functions: it needed both to transform Bush into a viable candidate and to confront the newly defined agonistic relationship with Dukakis.

In the fourth paragraph of the speech, Bush took the opportunity to mention his choice of Dan Quayle as running mate. Beyond that brief reference, Bush chose not to enter the fray over the appropriateness of his vice presidential choice. Furthermore, the closest to a Bush admission that the Republican campaign was behind in the polls is the following remark: "Many of you have asked, 'When will this campaign really begin?' I have come to this hall to tell you, and to tell America: tonight is the night."

Bush instead devoted much of the speech to separating his policy proposals from those of Reagan and Dukakis, as the themes outlined earlier in this section demonstrate. Bush used the following remarks to show the inadequacy of previous governmental actions: "But let's be frank. Things aren't perfect in this country. There are people who haven't tasted the fruits of the [economic] expansion. I've talked to farmers about the bills they can't pay. I've been to the factories that feel the strain of change. I've seen the urban children who play amid the shattered glass and shattered lives. And there are the homeless. And you know, it doesn't do any good to debate endlessly which policy mistake of the '70s is responsible. They're there. We have to help them." Some changes in policy from the Reagan administration will inevitably occur with the election of Bush to the presidency. "Our work is not done; our force is not spent." However, the change will be less drastic than what would occur with the election of the Democratic nominee: "Now, after two great terms, a switch will be made. But when you have to change horses in midstream, doesn't it make sense to switch to the one who's going the same way?" Most press reports agree that Bush in the acceptance address delivered a speech which met the constraints imposed upon him by the situation. He succeeded in outlining a vision of America which was distinct from Ronald Reagan's (thus avoiding the wimp factor) and Michael Dukakis's (thus providing a new impetus for the fall campaign).

The earlier announcement address radiated in toward the Bush campaign, attempting to define the differences between Bush and the other Republican contenders. The Basic Speech radiates out, detailing specific differences between the Bush and Dukakis campaigns. Meanwhile contained within the acceptance address are the five common themes of the speeches, summing up the three texts within itself.[16] The acceptance thus served as the center or hub of the campaign, from which the themes of both the announcement and the Basic Speech could radiate.

Finally, when examined in a temporal sequence, the acceptance address is the first text which can detail the agonistic relationship involved in the 1988 election.[17] While this is not the first Bush speech to refer explicitly to the Democratic opposition, this address is the first legitimate opportunity for Bush to define the campaign as Bush the Republican nominee versus Dukakis the Democrat nominee. Bush thus refers to "my opponent," "he," "our opponents," "three blind mice," "Michael," "they," and "liberal Democrats" within his speech. The introduction of the Dukakis agon also reinforces the idea that the acceptance address possesses adequate scope, as a critical transformation has occurred in the campaign. For example, the announcement speech as anecdote would not account for the transformation in the scene from Republicans versus Democrats to Bush versus Dukakis.

A Form as Representative Anecdote

The second type of anecdote is an underlying form which exists throughout the text(s) under examination. In this sense a single anecdote should lie at the center of the three Bush texts. One phrase initially appears in the announcement speech and subsequently recurs in the acceptance address. In his announcement speech Bush says, "I mean to stand for a new harmony, a greater tolerance, and a renewed recognition that this country is and always has been a partnership." In the acceptance address Bush suggests, "I hope to stand for a new harmony, a greater tolerance." Further explication of the key terms in these phrases will help to shed light on the anecdote advanced here.

Webster's New Collegiate Dictionary provides one definition of "harmony" as "pleasing or congruent arrangement of parts." "Tolerance" is "sympathy or indulgence for beliefs or practices differing from or conflicting with one's own." Finally, a "partnership" is "a relationship . . . usually involving close cooperation between parties having specified and joint rights and responsibilities." This analysis will suggest that the anecdote for the Bush texts is a harmonious and tolerant partnership among the individual, the family, the community, and government.

Described in more detail, the anecdote functions to encompass the interrelationships among the themes outlined in the Bush texts. Each of the spheres in the United States (individual, family, community, and government) has its own separate and distinct rights and responsibilities, as defined by the partnership agreement. If the spheres work together in a harmonious and tolerant fashion, the economy can continue to grow, the United States can continue to be strong in the world, and society can maintain its core values. If one or more of the spheres disrupt the partnership, encroaching on the rights and responsibilities of the other partners, the goals enunciated by Bush will fail to materialize. Thus, if the voting public elects the Republicans in November and Congress enacts the policies advocated by Bush, the partnership will succeed. Only greed, wealth, self-interest, and election of the Democrats will disrupt the partnership.[18]

Pentadic Analysis

The third recursive phase of dramatistic procedure is pentadic analysis of the text. With the Bush texts, the emphasis is on the ratio between agent and scene. Bush portrays himself in the texts as an agent who can maintain and improve the scene, maintain and strengthen the partnership. At the time of Ronald Reagan's election to the presidency in 1980, the Democrats had degraded the scene. Reagan reclaimed the scene, and Bush will be able to lead the nation into the twenty-first century. Here Bush suggests his competence, his experience, his capability of fulfilling the task of being the U.S. president. The alternatives to electing Bush are, first, the Democrats who caused the problems initially and, second, Bush's opponents for the Republican nomination (Bob Dole, Pat Robertson, Al Haig, etc.).

Several statements by Bush reveal this relationship between agent and scene. Bush suggests, "I seek the Presidency for a single purpose, a purpose that has motivated millions of Americans across the years and the ocean voyages. I seek the Presidency to build a better America. It is that simple, and that big." Similarly, Bush claims, "I am here tonight, and I am your candidate, because the most important work of my life is to complete the mission we started in 1980.

How do we complete it? We build on it." Bush indicates his commitment to the strength of the nation when he suggests, "I will not allow this country to be made weak again."

The contrast to the Democrats is obvious throughout the acceptance speech. Here Bush suggests, "The stakes are high this year and the choice is crucial, for the differences between the two candidates are as deep and wide as they have ever been in our long history. Not only two very different men, but two very different ideas of the future will be voted on this Election Day. What it all comes down to is this: my opponent's view of the world sees a long slow decline for our country, an inevitable fall mandated by impersonal historical forces. But America is not in decline. America is a rising nation." Bush states, "Two parties this year ask for your support. Both will speak of growth and peace. But only one has proved it can deliver. Two parties this year ask for your trust, but only one has earned it." The same theme continues when Bush suggests, "The fact is, they talk, we deliver. They promise, we perform." Bush directs a jab toward Dukakis by stating, "Competence makes the trains run on time but doesn't know where they're going. Competence is the creed of the technocrat who makes sure the gears mesh but doesn't for a second understand the magic of the machine." Bush thus suggests that the personal characteristics of the candidates mirror the nature of the country under the guidance of their respective parties. It is only the Republican candidate who can strengthen the partnership agreement. Bush portrays himself as a strong leader, and the Republican party is the party capable of leading a strong nation. Dukakis is incapable of leading the nation, and the Democratic party was responsible for weakening the country in the 1970s. The effect of electing the Democrat is a weakening or dissolution of the partnership.

The relationships between the various elements of the partnership anecdote require the election of Bush to the presidency. Bush concludes, "For seven and a half years I have worked with a President, and I have seen what crosses that big desk. I have seen the unexpected crises that arrive in a cable in a young aide's hand. And I have seen problems that simmer on for decades and suddenly demand resolution. I have seen modest decisions made with anguish, and crucial decisions made with dispatch. And so I know that what it all comes down to, this election . . . is the man at the desk. And who should sit at that desk. My friends, I am that man. . . . I will keep America moving forward, always forward—for a better America, for an endless, enduring dream and a thousand points of light. That is my mission. And I will complete it." Bush portrays himself as the candidate qualified to fulfill the themes outlined in the discourse. The experience and vision of George Bush will allow the mission of the United States to succeed. Only election of the Democratic opposition can stop the progress and destroy the partnership.

Conclusions

Conclusions on the Bush Texts

Several implications follow from this application of the anecdotal approach to Bush's 1988 campaign rhetoric. First, there are noticeable differences between the three texts and the Bush inaugural address delivered in Washington, D.C., on January 20, 1989. While many of the same themes are present in the inaugural, the connections are less explicit. One of the themes is noticeably absent, as the Bush inaugural avoids clear statements of policy. However, the inaugural address does contain explicit references to partnership, as Bush suggests that the executive branch and Congress must work together to solve the nation's problems (Bush 1989, 10). Whether the partnership anecdote continues to represent the discourse as the circumference expands beyond the three Bush texts examined here, however, is beyond the scope of this chapter, as the critic would need to apply the three phases of criticism to the expanded textual circumference.

Second, the use of the anecdotal approach also helps to clarify apparently contradictory themes evident in the Bush campaign rhetoric. At times "compassionate George" spoke of a "kinder and gentler nation" and "a thousand points of light." At other times, "tough George" sought to increase penalties for drug abuse, make abortion illegal, and increase use of the death penalty. The partnership anecdote helps to resolve the tension between these two positions. Bush perceives the emphasis should be on the private and community-based elements of the partnership, the thousand points of light. Providing those elements of the partnership with the necessary responsibilities in society will allow America to become a kinder and gentler nation. Transferring some duties to the private sector would in turn allow the government to focus on the societal problems it is most capable of solving. The Bush rhetoric is not inherently contradictory; rather, it suggests altering the configuration of duties among the various partners.

Third, the partnership anecdote illustrates how the Bush discussion of the personal character of candidates becomes relevant in the 1988 political campaign. The qualities that Bush praises in himself are the qualities he perceives as necessary to preserve the partnership and keep the state on the proper track. Those vital qualities are the ones Bush argues are lacking in the Dukakis persona. Dukakis would instead disrupt the progress of the state by upsetting the balance between elements of the partnership. The partnership anecdote thus functions in a manner analogous to Plato's view of the soul and the state. Plato argues, "Must we not acknowledge . . . that in each of us there are the same principles and habits which there are in the State; and that from the individual they pass into the State?—how else can they come there?" (1937, 435). Applying this principle to contemporary politics, the personal characteristics of a candidate mirror the kind of state they would create.

Fourth, by identifying a representative anecdote and making clear some of the assumptions within a text, the critic can function as a social critic. In this role the critic can judge the motives of the agent delivering the text and call attention to those elements which are appropriate or inappropriate for use under the circumstances of the situation (Brummett 1984b, 5 and 23). For example, while Bush proclaims basic equality for all in his speech acts, the partnership anecdote calls forth images of hierarchical relationships. One example of a partnership agreement is a law firm. When a lawyer becomes a partner, he or she becomes one of the select few at the top of the law firm's hierarchy. Associated with hierarchy are images of the side-effects of hierarchy. At the societal level, the economic hierarchy of the United States has attendant ills likely to result from social stratification such as poverty, unemployment, and environmental degradation. While the explicit language of Bush calls for equality, the underlying imagery of the Bush texts justifies "trickle down" economic policies designed to benefit only the wealthy sectors of society. This reveals the inherent ambiguity of partnership, the aspects of the anecdote allowing Bush to call simultaneously for apparently contradictory policies. A critic could examine the tensions inherent in the Bush speeches in an attempt to provide a corrective to the Bush rhetoric. In this fashion the critic would function as a social critic, examining the normative bases of a rhetor's discourse. As Conrad indicates, reliance on statistical or pentadic analysis alone may lead to a distorted representation of a text. As such, normative judgments made without the assistance of a representative anecdote may be in error.

Finally, other anecdotes likely exist for the Bush texts. The anecdote of "family" is one example implied in many of the speeches. Similarly, as the circumference of the study expands, as the critic examines more of the Bush discourse, the acceptance speech may no longer function as an anecdote for the 1988 Bush campaign. It would be necessary to determine through application of the three phases of criticism whether such alternative anecdotes cohere across the sample, however, to claim they are synecdochic representations of the texts.

Conclusions on the Representative Anecdote

This chapter has served to clarify the requirements of an anecdotal approach to rhetorical analysis. Several conclusions about the anecdotal method are relevant here. First, the representative anecdote is a useful method for analysis of rhetorical texts, but only if it is indeed a *representative* anecdote. It is essential that the critic's textual analysis fulfills all three criteria of representation. Meeting the criteria of representation provides a synecdochal analysis of a text, rather than a metonymic reduction of the text.

Second, any representative anecdote has a fixed circumference. As the critic's view of the act shifts, what may have formerly represented the process may no longer fill that role. An anecdote for a text or a period within a movement may not be an anecdote for a genre of texts or for the entirety of a movement. When the scope of analysis changes, attention to the scope of the anecdote must simultaneously occur.

Third, there are two distinct types of anecdotes, either of which may serve to represent a text. One type of anecdote is an act within a larger body of acts. In this sense the acceptance address serves as anecdote for the Bush campaign. The second type of anecdote is a form appearing throughout a sample or within a broader text. The partnership anecdote is of this type, as partnership is interwoven into all three of the Bush texts.

Fourth, since the representative anecdote is both act and form, the anecdote becomes a precept to guide rhetors as well as critics. A situation may call upon a rhetor to produce representative discourse, exemplified by Bush's reaction to the scene encompassing the acceptance address. The requirement of representation constrains the rhetor, becoming a normative criterion for the situation. The rhetor's ability to identify and respond to the unique situational constraints is a factor which influences the degree of success achieved by a rhetor in a situation.

Fifth, the representative anecdote can serve as a corrective to the critic's own analysis. In this sense the anecdote is an independent check on the results of a critic's cluster analysis. Conrad argues that an anecdote "serves as a touchstone which a critic can use to reevaluate the terministic structure that emerged from his or her statistical analysis" (1984, 97). If the details of the text are inconsistent with the anecdote derived from the hierarchical arrangement of textual principles, the critic has conducted a valuable test of his or her approach to criticism and can subsequently move the analysis to a more representative interpretation (97). Any text contains more than one anecdote, but few anecdotes function as synecdoche for a text.

Finally, the anecdotal approach provides a means for evaluating a body of rhetoric that extends across time. As such, it is a useful critical tool for analyses of rhetorical movements, political campaigns, and rhetorical genres. The use of the representative anecdote for such time-bound studies allows the critic to identify where the various rhetorical periods under examination share (or do not share) a common underlying form (Balthrop 1983; Balthrop 1975; Smith and Golden 1988, 257).

Notes

1. The author wishes to thank Charles M. Kauffman, Leland M. Griffin, David Zarefsky, and V. William Balthrop for their comments on earlier drafts of this chapter.

2. I do not focus on isolated references to the representative anecdote, those works which neither develop the concept nor use it as a methodological approach to criticism. See, for example, Benne 1969, 200–201; Black 1969, 167; Chase 1969, 252–53; Fergusson 1969, 176. Furthermore, this chapter will not examine articles such as Brummett 1981, which uses procedures similar to the representative anecdote. Instead it examines only those works which specifically claim to use the representative anecdote as a method of rhetorical criticism.

3. Balthrop argues that while other anecdotal forms exist, it is "the representative anecdote alone that is summational of the others and provides the title-of-titles that fulfills the noblest synecdoche" (1983, 29). Conversely David Williams argues that admonitory-hortatory and constitutive anecdotes compose "the range of representative anecdotes. That is, if a so-called representative anecdote is neither constitutive nor admonitory-hortatory, what is it? There are no alternatives remaining" (1986, 6–7). Constitutive anecdotes summarize what the substantial nature of being *is*, while admonitory-hortatory anecdotes summarize what the nature of being *would be* if we identify ourselves with available precepts (7–8; see also David Williams 1989, 198–99).

4. I am not suggesting that the critical process is "objective" or results in "a correct" interpretation of a text. Rather, this caution implies that theoretical anecdotes lack the necessary textual support, as a critic can find any anecdote within any text.

5. Several writers on the representative anecdote incorporate the criteria

of representation described in this chapter—for example, Balthrop (1975, 1983, 1986), Conrad (1981, 1984), Dauber (1984), Madsen (1983, 1984, 1986, 1988, 1989), and David Williams (1986, 1989). Most applications of an anecdotal procedure fail to meet one or more of the criteria for representation outlined by Burke. Among those are the studies conducted by Chandler (1988), Marshall (1986), Pondozzi (1986), Scodari (1987), Smith (1987), Smith and Golden (1988), Stuart (1974), Thorpe (1986), and J. P. Williams (1986). In all of these studies either there is no indication that the critic derives the anecdote from within the text, or the critic does not demonstrate that the anecdote meets the criteria of representation outlined in this chapter. This does not deny that an anecdote underlies the texts examined in these studies or that the identified anecdotes do not serve useful critical functions. Rather, this critique suggests that the authors have not necessarily identified representative anecdotes which function as synecdoche for the texts.

6. Dauber suggests seven criteria for representation (1984, 46–57). However, most of her criteria are summaries of the component elements of scope and reduction and are not separate criteria for representation. The three criteria defined in this chapter subsume all Dauber's criteria.

7. Brummett argues that the representative anecdote for a sample of related discourse is *xeroxing*, "the duplication and replacement of humans with evil, inhuman copies that are difficult to detect. . . . This act of duplication is carried out through technological conspiracies" (1984a, 168). In this instance the anecdote is a reflection of a purely mechanical process (motion), the technological duplication of humans, and is not a reflection of human action and symbol use. As Dauber suggests, "Symbolic acts could not be represented by something that is not an expression of conscious will" (1984, 53). As such, xeroxing as anecdote is analogous to the telegraph lines and train stations rejected by Burke as unrepresentative.

8. One of the first applications of the anecdote in studies of rhetorical texts was Griffin 1969. Griffin argued, "The enactment of the Negative may be taken by the student as a 'representative anecdote,' a moment that embodies, implicitly or explicitly, the key terms and equations of the movement. With these terms and equations the study of a movement begins" (463). Balthrop, however, suggests that symbolic restructuring of a movement into an ideology often does not occur until the movement is at a more mature phase than its initial inception. Focusing solely on the movement's beginning fails to acknowledge the potential for scenic transformations within the development of the movement (Balthrop 1975, 4–5).

Yet Balthrop's caution does not restrict the critic to searching for anecdotes only after scenic transformations are complete. Such an approach would restrict the critic to historical studies of movements which have run their course. This would prevent critics from examining movements in their inception phase, or those which have not advanced to a mature state of development. This would foreclose the possibility of analyzing the *different* anecdotes which exist during the various phases of a movement's development. An idealist or admonitory anecdote may represent the inception phase of a movement, as it warns against what society is in danger of becoming. When the movement matures, the critic may discern a constitutive anecdote which reflects the essential nature of what the movement is. As a whole, Griffin 1964, 1969, and 1984 reflect the idea that movements embody different anecdotes at various stages of development.

9. Brummett argues that "the anecdote must be able to incorporate many or most of the terms or particulars of discourse into its plot, dramatis personae, etc." (1984b, 5). If the standard is only that an anecdote should encompass many of the details of a text, there is no guarantee the elements included within the scope of the anecdote are representative of the discourse in its entirety.

10. Scodari argues in her study of the "self-awakening" anecdote embodied in soap operas that some episodes result in damage to this anecdote or render the anecdote inconclusive (1986, 2). If the anecdote becomes damaged or if it is not present in an episode, then the anecdote cannot represent the episode and does not function as a synecdoche for soap operas.

11. Statistical analysis alone can focus so much attention on the details of a text that its character as an overall work becomes lost. Statistical analysis can also lead to the illusion that criticism is empirical and objective (Conrad 1984, 96 and 97). Conrad concludes that statistical analysis by itself cannot ensure that the critic's interpretation of a text is either representative or comprehensive (97).

12. Two risks inhere in this phase. First, a critic may apply a theoretical anecdote to a text. In such a case, the anecdote would be metonymic or a misrepresentation, as it would not be a form *in* the terminology of the text. This problem requires that the critic conduct the representation phase of analysis simultaneously with the other two phases. The second problem is that the anecdote may, by its nature, be unrepresentative. A discussion of criteria for the evaluation of representation appears earlier in this chapter.

13. Conrad suggests that pentadic analysis is potentially deceptive, since disconfirmation of the results from within the system cannot occur (1984, 99). To avoid misrepresentation, the critic must perform pentadic analysis with the other two phases.

14. The critic does not use the three phases of dramatistic criticism in a temporal fashion; rather, the phases are "cognitive processes which occur simultaneously" (Conrad 1984, 95). For ease of reading, however, the three phases are separated in this discussion.

15. In this respect the anecdote meets the first criterion of representation, that the anecdote must reflect human action and symbol use.

16. This demonstrates that the acceptance as anecdote possesses scope, being broad enough to account for the entirety of the discourse.

17. As indicated earlier, an anecdote must account for the agonistic relationships of the situation to embody a synecdochic representation.

18. The partnership anecdote fulfills the three criteria of representation. First, symbolic interaction between agents leads to the creation of a partnership agreement. The agreement is an agency designed by agents to accomplish certain specified purposes; cooperative action by the partners will

maintain the proper functioning of the agreement. Second, contained within the anecdote are the thematic elements and corresponding equations common to the three Bush texts. Third, the anecdote functions as a synecdoche for the texts. It accounts for the agonistic relationships, providing a summation of the discourse without being a mere summary.

6

Kenneth Burke's Conception of Reality

The Process of Transformation and Its Implications for Rhetorical Criticism

Dale A. Bertelsen

Of the many ways in which reality can be conceptualized, two have gained prominence in the study of human communication. One holds that reality is fixed and physical. For instance, the general semanticists' point of view suggests that language refers to a fixed biological reality (Korzybski 1948). A second contrasting conceptualization holds that reality is in flux and is socially determined. As a result, rhetorical epistemologists such as Scott (1967), Farrell (1976), and Orr (1978) argue that reality is socially constructed through communication. Kenneth Burke offers a third alternative in which reality is understood to be influenced by both the physical or biological and the social or symbolic.

This chapter posits that Kenneth Burke views reality as a transformational process composed through a perpetual dialectical relationship between a biological dimension and a social dimension.[1] From this perspective, reality can be thought of as a series of compromises that our conceptualizing selves make between social constraints and inner primitive needs, or as an intralogue between biological and symbolic modes. Correspondingly, Burke's notion of rhetoric establishes a dialectical relationship between an ontological mode (where things can be said to exist) and an epistemological mode (where existence can be understood). This view privileges a somewhat unusual use of the term "rhetoric." In this regard, rhetoric is both figurative and literal, or constitutive and referential. For example, there is the word for mountain and then there is the mountain itself. We use rhetoric denotatively to refer to a mountain, but the word "mountain" can also be used figuratively to mean a symbol of strength.

Stated generally, the process of transformation posits any given moment of reality as a rhetorical compromise between opposing forms. These compromises manifest a view of reality based on an implicit *principle of transformation* that constitutes a theoretical statement about the rhetorical strategies and tactics employed to achieve unity or social cohesion between the biologically unique or otherwise divided (Burke 1974, 329). In *A Grammar of Motives*, Burke tells us that transformations "are not 'illusions,' but citable realities" ([1945] 1969, 57). As such, they constitute the resources for rhetorical inquiry and criticism. Rhetorical criticism, then, becomes a dialectical analysis that examines the structural relationships constituted by the interplay of the ontological and epistemological dimensions of transformations.

A clearer understanding of the process of transformation will help explain how the structural relationships between disparate forms function dialectically to identify reality and serve as the basis for isolating the rhetorical practices employed to create or reconcile human divisiveness. I am intentionally choosing to emphasize divisiveness in this chapter, in contrast to Burke's focus on identification and cohesion. I find featuring divisiveness a productive way to illustrate the redefinition and recontextualization that mark all transformations. This approach complements Burke's work by teasing out the essential notion of redefinition inherent in transformation and the ways in which it occurs. In presenting this viewpoint, a threefold analysis is offered. First, an outline of Burke's view of reality is presented to establish a transformational perspective.[2] Second, four rhetorical functions of the process of transformation are identified (translation, conversion, transcendence, and catharsis). Third, the critical implications of Burke's transformational perspective are proposed.

Transformational Perspective

Transformation—as Burke's conception of reality—is a process established through a perpetual dialectic between biological phenomena and the social context. During a discussion with Satan about the forming of personality in Burke's "Epilogue: Prologue in Heaven," the Lord contends that personality "is itself intermediate, insofar as the human person will be compounded of animality and symbolicity" ([1961] 1970, 310). In like manner, Burke writes that life itself "is suggested by the comparing of eternity to animality indefinitely prolonged" (28). Thus, for Burke, reality remains at all times in process. Humans experience existence through the prism of language, or the social context. At the same time, language constrains the range of explanations available for human perceptions. There is no intrinsic meaning in biological phenomena. It is only through the resources of both the biological and the social that things gain meaning, thus allowing humans to make sense of their world.

Coming to grips with the richness, complexity, and ambiguity of Burke's transformational perspective can be difficult. There is a sense in which we are inclined to ask, "Which came first, the chicken or the egg?" Our tendency to focus on such "firsts" leads to a critical myopia that privileges the chicken or the egg, depending on our focus. But Burke would privilege neither in his scheme, and therein lies the knot that we must unravel if we are to understand his transformational perspective. Burke himself hints at the difficulty while discussing dramatism and scientism as approaches to the study of language and human relations. He contends that dramatism "stresses the 'ontological,'" and scientism "the 'epistemological'—though to say as much is to say that each ends by implicating the other" ([1961] 1970, 39). That is, the inherent reciprocity between being and knowing in a transformational perspective discounts the temporal priority of both biological phenomena and symbolism. Burke's conception of reality encourages us not to sort out the temporal relationship between the chicken and the egg but to acknowledge that "there is a sense in which the *being* and *being-known* are one" (165).

Despite the complexity of Burke's transformational perspective, he rehearses the matter for his readers by regularly showing us, explicitly or implicitly, the process at work. One of the places where he shares this notion is his discussion of the relationship between nonsymbolic motion and symbolic action. This discussion provides an entrance to Burke's conception of reality as a process of transformation.

In *Permanence and Change*, Burke presents a summary of Henri Bergson's perspective of incongruity by observing that "the events of life are continuous, any isolated aspect of reality really merging into all the rest" ([1935a] 1965, 92). Indeed, for Burke "the real course of events is necessarily, at all times, unified" (94). However, in Burke's schema, there is a basic polarity of existence which he characterizes as the distinction between the realm of nonsymbolic motion and the realm of symbolic action (1978a). Nonsymbolic motion is the world of the physiological organism, the world of matter where events are unified and indistinguishable. Burke suggests that "as a practical convenience, we do make distinctions between various parts of reality" ([1935a] 1965, 92). For example, the human organism, the body, because of the centrality of the nervous system, acts as the principle of individuation that divides us from one another (Burke 1966b, 1983a). When extended into the realm of human relations, our uniqueness as biological creatures makes us simultaneously members of the same species and yet divided from one another. At the sociopolitical level, club or party membership determines who and what are "in" and who and what are "out." At the logological level, language includes and excludes. In essence, division is the natural state of human existence.

Our ability to make distinctions between biological phenomena allows us to *act,* and as a result, "We find our way through this everchanging universe by certain blunt schemes of generalization, conceptualization, or verbalization" (Burke [1935a] 1965, 92). In order to interact, even for purely biological reasons, humans resort to symbolic action. In an attempt to move from the inherent biological divisiveness of existence to a context of community, humans develop the capacity to create and use symbols to express feelings, desires, sentiments, and opinions. The realm of symbolic action, then, is the realm of social existence or communal context.

Burke suggests that human biological centrality is unavoidable when discussing the constitution of reality. He proposes that symbolism is a "transformation or rebirth" that expresses the inherent biological divisiveness of the human organism, or a perspective of reality in a context of symbolic action (1974). The transformation of subjective perceptions into objective perceptions, of biological discreteness into communally understood symbols (and implicitly vice versa), "brings us close to the pathetic fallacy in its purity: the tendency to find our own moods in the things outside us. And the equivalent for this, in the intellectual plane, would be the tendency to find our own patterns of thought in the 'texture of events' outside us" ([1935a] 1965, 214).

Symbol systems allow for the expression of biological phenomena, but when those phenomena are expressed, they are individuated according to their own biases. For example, humans differ in gender, race, and sexual preference. In an effort to diminish the social estrangement that often accompanies recognition of those differences, terms such as "women" or "womyn," "black" or "African-American," "Hispanic" or "Latin," and "gay male" or "lesbian" are selected as referents. While these terms may be less prejudicial than others, they still maintain the inherent divisiveness of the human condition. Thus, all of our talk embodies a statement about existence—an ontological statement. The manner in which we conduct our lives is at all times strongly influenced by our nature as biological creatures, including the symbolic context we select to reflect that nature.

Thus far, our discussion might suggest that the biological, if not temporally prior to the symbolic, is certainly logically prior—that being somehow precedes knowing. Even Burke suggests that "always beneath the dance of words there will be the dance of bodies" ([1961] 1970, 288). However, such a suggestion would prematurely conclude our discussion. While the idiosyncratic tendencies of the biological dimension are present in any view of events, I do not mean to suggest that Burke's view of reality is based in relativism or turns on subjectivism or solipsism. Very simply, Burke's conception of reality is inevitably ambiguous. What is knowable for Burke, or identifiable as reality, is the structure of relationships that results from the merger of dialectical polarities. Samuel B. Southwell suggests that for Burke, "the body in negotiation with the culture is the energy of the act that engenders being" (1987, 85). Reality for Burke is what Southwell might describe as the structures of the opening to the world and history that language provides (40). In short, neither the biological nor the social is fundamentally featured in Burke's conception of reality—it is simply both, together. Accordingly, to round out our discussion of Burke's transformational perspective of reality, we need to consider the influence of the social dimension.

Human existence and the range of experiences that accompany that existence do not simply acquire their identity from their nature as biological phenomena. On the contrary, existence and its concomitant experiences "also reflect the character of the way in which we confront them" (Burke [1961] 1970, 169). This character is a product of the resources of the social context in which we find ourselves. In an effort to identify our individual perceptions in a manner that others can understand, we ground those perceptions in language or symbolism. Indeed, no matter how influential the biological dimension might be in shaping reality, the social context plays an equally important role. Burke observes that "however much the individual poet may transform language for his special purposes, the resources with which he begins are 'traditional,' that is: 'social.' And such sociality of meaning is grounded in a sociality of material conduct, or cooperation" ([1935a] 1965, iii). In short, "Man justifies himself in the modes of socialization that go with his society" (lv). Modes of socialization permit the shared understanding of existence. For example, killing animals for food is a common human practice. Those who believe in hunting for food and fur regularly describe their activities as "harvesting." Those who are opposed to such activities cast them as "slaughter" or "murder."

Thus, all of our talk about existence implicitly contains a statement about the way we understand our existence—an epistemological statement.

Without the social context provided by language or symbolism, there would be no means to identify our perceptions as reality. But the social context does not simply provide referents for human perception. On the contrary, just as the way we live and experience the biological realm influences the symbols we select to talk about our existence, so too does the social context provided through the resources of symbolism influence the way we live and experience. Burke chooses an anecdote about an island savage in the South Pacific to make this point. In this account the savage has been hexed—received the symbolic tribal death sentence—and approaches death, despite the intercession of modern medicine. The story clearly illustrates "the point about the way in which the realm of symbolism can affect the sheer motions of a physical body, as manifested by a turn from health to grave illness on the part of a body swayed by symbolism" ([1961] 1970, 17).

The influence of the social context on the biological, of the symbolic on perception, even pervades human thought. That is, thought itself is a result of the structural interplay between sensory perception and the symbolic. We return to Burke's hypothetical discussion between the Lord and Satan in *The Rhetoric of Religion* for clarification. In their talk about thinking, the Lord observes that all languages have properties in common: "principles of order and transformation as will go by the name of grammar and syntax; all languages must have words that put things together and words that take things apart; all tribal idioms will have ways of naming and exhorting. Such elements, common to all languages, coupled with the conditions common to all bodies, will make for a common underlying logic" ([1961] 1970, 297). Indeed, the Lord is even led to say that "all orderly thought will be a function of their symbol systems" (297). But Burke does not privilege the symbolic or knowledge over the biological or being. It is the action composed through the dialectical coupling of language and the body that constitutes thought. From a transformational perspective, being is dependent on knowing insofar as knowing is dependent on being. Both come together in Burke's view, as the action that results from the transformation of sensory perception through symbolism.

Transformation, then, is the process Burke relies on to explain the ineffable movement between subjective perception and social context, from biological to symbolic and vice versa: the redefinition or recontextualization of individuated perception in a socially recognizable form, or the influence of that form on human perception.

Such a conception of reality suggests a foundation for rhetoric that embraces a dialectic between ontological and epistemological dimensions—between the way things are and the way we understand them to be. Consideration of the rhetorical functions inherent in the process of transformation will alert us to the manner in which discrepancies arise between the way experience presents itself and the way we choose to understand it and, by implication, will remind us about the manner in which our understandings can lead to discrepant experiences.

Rhetorical Functions

Because of the constant shifting, or the constant dialectical tension between the biological dimension and the social context, reality itself is a rhetorical product. The way we understand existence and the way we experience that existence are rhetorically constituted. The dialectic intrinsic to the process of transformation always invokes a double-edged meaning of rhetoric as referential and constitutive, literal and figurative, denotative and connotative, ontological and epistemological. In addition, four primary rhetorical functions inhere in the process of transformation: translation, conversion, transcendence, and catharsis. These functions are a direct result of the suspension of dialectical tension between the ontological and epistemic dimensions and necessarily manifest themselves in symbol usage. Consequently, it would be misleading to consider these functions as discrete or sequential—they simply are.

Translation

The symbolic forming of ideation, the substantiation of the dialectical relationship between biological and social dimensions, is the translating of individual perceptions into socially recognizable forms—the individuation and reindividuation of form (Burke [1931] 1968). Human ability to make the move from biological perception to symbolic referent is a result of a feeling for the principle of the negative. Burke writes that "all words for the non-verbal must, by the very nature of the case, discuss the realm of the nonverbal in terms of *what it is not*" ([1961] 1970, 18). That is, no matter what we call a thing, the word for it can never be that thing. Since we are never quite able to find a term or terminology that adequately expresses our perceptions, we engage in a process of revision that adjusts symbols to an approximation of our intent or understanding. For example, we might characterize someone we have a relationship with as an acquaintance, a friend, or a lover, depending on the quality and intensity of the relationship. Thus, our symbolic enactments should be viewed as the identification of an attitude toward the situation in which those enactments occur. Burke suggests that "'implicit' in such revisions there is a set of judgements, or aesthetic norms, which some critic might translate into an explicit set of poetic principles" (1966b, 70). These judgments represent the rhetorical impulse inherent in the constitution of reality.

But translation, as a rhetorical function of the process of transformation, goes beyond merely identifying biological perception in a socially recognizable form. The images chosen to represent biological perception generate their own rhetorical impulse. In order to identify a closer approximation of meaning, each person's symbolic identifications are mediated, shaped, or translated by the available cultural symbols, with each dimension adjusting the other in a constant, simultaneous, rhythmic revision based on the tension between the way we experience things and the way we understand those experiences. In other words, because we are continually translating between perception and symbol, symbol and perception, a transformational perspective of reality is decidedly rhetorical. In Burke's view, "Reality is what things will do to us or for us" ([1935a] 1965, 22).

The influence of the biological orients us to translate our perceptions into a language that will allow others to share our understanding of events. Hence, we express the ineffable in terms of something which it is not. At the same time, the language we employ alters and limits the possible interpretations of events available to us—we understand events in a way that obscures their essence.

Conversion

For Burke, a conversion primarily indicates a view or version of reality. This version of reality positively or negatively orders relationships and will be expressed as a perversion or aversion (Burke 1966b). Indeed, to be converted refers to being oriented or "'turned' in the direction of the excitement" (Burke [1961] 1970, 139). That is, an orientation converts experiences so that those experiences conform to a version of reality, or to a rhetorical perspective. Our orientation "can even induce us to convert the unpleasant into the pleasurable" (Burke [1935a] 1965, 239).

A view of reality is formed by aligning individual perception with culturally understood symbolic referents. In a sense, symbolic enactments are converted by and through adherence to a view of reality. Interaction with others creates a social context that adheres to a hierarchical principle (Burke [1950a] 1969, 141–42). Borrowing as we are from the same cultural storehouse of symbols, there is a degree to which the number of possible interpretations of reality are limited. The choices among possible interpretations are based on a ranking that favors the orientation of the person making the choice. If, for example, we were asked to select a term to identify our characterization of sexual intercourse, we are immediately confronted with a hierarchy of terms ranging from the provincial "screw" or "bang" to the more genteel "making love." Whichever term we choose embodies our momentary attitude toward sexual intercourse. As a result, transformations convert biological perception through a cultural context while maintaining the individuality of that perception. Thus, in establishing social bonds, transformations result in symbolic division. Because transformations have such a recalcitrant nature, symbolic action reveals an attitude (orientation) toward the situation in which the symbols were cast.

We also find a degree of recalcitrance in the symbols we select to identify our perceptions. Burke observes that *"a statement is an attitude rephrased in accordance with the strategy of revision made necessary by the recalcitrance of the materials employed for embodying this attitude"* ([1935a] 1965, 255). In our effort to convey a closer approximation of reality or meaning, the biological dimension is converted by the available cultural symbols. Returning to our example about terms for sexual intercourse, we find that the term or terms we *do* choose to characterize the act permeate our experiencing of the act. The way we choose to understand that act predisposes us to orient ourselves to act in the manner we understand. In fact, Burke identifies a symbol as "the conversion of an experiential pattern into a formula for affecting an audience," and "audience" here would clearly include humans creating their realities ([1931] 1968, 157). Thus, symbolic action satisfies both ontological and epistemological demands and contributes to the rhetorical imperatives of reality. Just as the process of transformation converts experience into symbol, so too does it infuse a symbolic identification of experience with contextual constraints.

Accordingly, the process of transformation converts perception by temporizing or personalizing its essence (Burke [1945] 1969, [1961] 1970, 1974). That is, symbolism temporally embodies the essential motives of the symbol user. For example, politicians regularly engage in activities that appeal to the electorate's frugality. In an election year, candidates discover that budget deficits can be alleviated through more involvement from the private sector or that "improved" accounting procedures can produce a balanced budget, or very simply, they may ask the voters to indulge in faith and "Read my lips! No new taxes." These situational or temporally bound symbolic castings result from the transformation of one essential motive—the desire to respect the edict that voters vote their pocketbooks. Politicians are not necessarily concerned with balanced budgets or budget deficits or even faith. What they are concerned with is reelection; by temporizing, personalizing, or grounding that motive symbolically, taxpayers can be moved to ignore the essential motive by focusing on the temporal ones. But this motive or essence would not be discernible were it not for the dialectical relationship between ontological and epistemological modes that encourages transcendence.

Transcendence

Once we engage in symbol usage, the temporal requirements of symbolism involve us in transcendence. Transcendence is the structural compromise negotiated between opposing forms. That is, we are constantly goaded by the biological dimension and the social context to overcome our biological centrality in a manner that permits others to share our experiences and our understandings of those experiences. However, because language or symbolism articulates our biological, social, or political distinctions in terms that are not adequate to describe them, the process of transformation implicitly maintains the essential paradox of substance between biological and social dimensions. In other words, in an effort to diminish our biological divisiveness, we employ symbols that maintain the quality of that divisiveness while encouraging social identification. Burke suggests that "identification in itself is a kind of transcendence. For instance, since the individual is to some extent distinct from his group, an identifying of him with the group is by the same token a transcending of his distinctness" (1974, 326). The identification or imagistic representation of an idea mediates and distorts the idea by temporally grounding biological phenomena, sheer motion, in the social context. Thus, the process of transformation is transcendent not because it gets beyond the essential paradox of substance but because it filters experience, thereby encouraging action. As Burke says:

If sensation is the realm of motion, idea is the realm of action. And action is possible only insofar as the rational agent transcends the realm of sheer motion—sensory image. He does so, however, by forming adequate ideas of the limitations defining this sensory realm. And insofar as his understanding of the world's necessities approaches perfection, he is correspondingly free: he can "act," rather than being merely "moved," or "affected." (1966b, 430–31)

The personalizing or temporizing of essence necessary to move beyond the estrangement of biological existence to social context forces us to arrange our terms hierarchically. Such arrangement organizes or orders biological phenomena according to the dictates of the prevailing language, symbol system, or sociopolitical system. Suppose, for example, we sought to examine the relationship between those who rule and those who are ruled. We might begin by noting that the master and slave relationship was not an equitable distribution of power, the disproportion resulting from a terminology representing the polar opposites of the possible terms available to describe the relationship. We might surmise that things improve somewhat when we move to feudalism's royalty and peasant, and even more so when we arrive at industrialism's boss and worker. However, symbolism does not alter the basic structural relationship between discrete entities. On the contrary, symbolism places the structural relationship between discrete entities in a temporal arrangement that reflects the existing linguistic, symbolic, or sociopolitical hierarchy. In effect, hierarchy maintains the structure of relationships between the two realms—hierarchy is what gives us transcendence. Thus, a rhetoric that transcends is one that transforms biological phenomena according to the resources of the social context to conform to a closer approximation of reality.

Because the constant dialectic of transformation prohibits the actual transcendence of disparate realms and reaffirms the paradox of substance, Burke notes that a rhetoric formed through the resources of the social context satisfies epistemological expectations and, as a result, conveys belief rather than meaning or reality. He contends that "an indeterminate mixture of motion and action is in effect a poeticized 'psychology,' detailing not what the reader is to 'see' but what 'mental states' he is thus empathically and sympathetically 'imitating' as he reads" (1966b, 208–9).

Humans resort to courtship to overcome this inherent divisiveness. That is, humans rely on their rhetorical skills to transcend biological and social division. And while courtship, the enactment of rhetorical strategies and tactics, "would transcend the social mystery, ending Platonically on a mystic, mythic vision of celestial mystery . . . we would stress rather its nature as a series of formal operations for the dialectical purifying of a rhetorical motive" ([1950a] 1969, 221). If we are bound by our biological or political centrality, yet constantly attempting to transcend that inherent division, then any attempt to articulate reality in a social context is biased by our perception, perspective, or orientation.

In essence, neither the biological nor the social dimension of transformation, when taken alone, affords a transcendent reality. Indeed, "Words being in the realm of the worldly, it follows by the very nature of the case that any words designed to describe a realm by definition transcendent must be inadequate to their real or supposed subject matter" (Burke 1966b, 374). Symbolism, the common means by which we attempt to overcome biological divisiveness, simply masks that divisiveness by recontextualizing the biological in the cloak of the social.

Catharsis

The dialectical movement between the biological realm and the social context engages us in rhetorical compromising between what we experience and how we understand that experience. Our symbols never quite adequately identify the idea we had in mind. Likewise, our initial perceptions are often clouded and distorted as they approach expression. To visualize this notion, one might consider the writer who rushes to the desk to jot down an "insight," only to have the insight dissipate the nearer the desk becomes. In the process of coining the appropriate language to express the insight, the writer has lost sight of the initial thought. Whatever is expressed is a rhetorical compromise negotiated between the biological realm and the social context. While this expression does not precisely account for the writer's initial perception, it does allow the idea to get said. In this way, the rhetorical compromises inherent in the process of transformation are satisfying because they permit the writer to get something said. That is, in our efforts to recontextualize perceptions or biases, we have a sense of perfection—that we have said it as clearly as we can. Thus, we feel satisfied simply by finding the words to express ourselves. However, since we cannot achieve the perfection of transcendence in our symbol using, we encounter unresolved tensions. We are plagued by these tensions only so long as we lack confidence in our symbolic choices.

In addition, it is this cathartic purging that satisfies our need to make our version of events socially palatable. We rely on catharsis to mediate our relationships. In an attempt to resolve human divisiveness, we often engender symbolic enactments designed to induce others to see events the same way we do. Ironically, we often rely on division for cathartic satisfaction. In an attempt to transcend the inherent divisiveness of the human condition, we resort to victimage and scapegoating (Burke 1966b, 1974). Such strategies attempt to purify, cleanse, or make more acceptable a version of reality by creating a symbolic vessel capable of uniting competing versions, groups, or nations. For example, consider the enemy: diabolically evil Japs, ruthless Nazis, treacherous Commies, and bloodthirsty Iraqis. Each depiction served as the primary unifying symbol for the sacrifice of lives and resources. Each depiction mobilized collective action by inducing Americans and their allies to shed their differences for the greater good—the defeat of the enemy. Each depiction cast reality in a manner that allowed others to share an attitude about certain events.

Burke makes it very clear that the nature of language implies attitude ([1961] 1970, 288). What is interesting for us here from a rhetorical standpoint is that the cathartic function of the process of transformation is able to establish an attitude toward events as the reality of those events. Indeed, Burke remarks that "whether in error or not, the attitude will be wholly real while it prevails" ([1961] 1970, 289).

Thus, the transformational process functions rhetorically and permeates human existence. When envisioned as a translation, the process of transformation results in a symbolic identification of reality. This symbolic identification represents a structure of experiences—a conversion, a version of reality. Since this conversion seeks to diminish biological divisiveness, we reorder our transformations according to it. This reordering has a transcendent function that adjusts and is adjusted by situational variations. These situational adjustments have a cathartic effect that allows others to participate sympathetically in our symbolic enactments, thereby sharing meaning and understanding.

Implications

Both the general semanticists' and the rhetorical epistemologists' conceptualizations of reality and rhetoric are incomplete. Reality is not constituted simply through biology or through the social context. Rhetoric is not simply ontological or epistemological. Both tensions work constantly whenever we communicate. Indeed, both are a primary determinant of how we perceive reality and how we understand it. There is an external reality, but equally important, there is a way in which we fix and look at that reality.

Recent Burkeian scholarship focuses on the argument about the degree to which Burkeian explanations of rhetoric are ontological or epistemological (Brock et al. 1985; Brock 1985). This argument becomes spurious when the inevitable tension between the biological and the social are recognized and accepted as the basis of a Burkeian conception of reality. Resolution of this argument promises, then, in true Burkeian fashion, that rhetoric draws its foundation from a dialectical relationship between ontological and epistemological modes (Burke 1985a; Chesebro 1988). Indeed, for Kenneth Burke, insofar as humans can understand existence, that existence is dialectically derived. If we accept this resolution, what does it mean for the practice of rhetorical criticism from a Burkeian perspective? Five critical implications can be identified by maintaining a transformational perspective.

First, a transformational view acknowledges human divisiveness by highlighting an awareness of the ontological and the epistemological dimensions of rhetoric. Many contemporary interpretations of Burke's work focus too much attention on his concept of identification (Bormann 1972, 1973, 1982; Fisher 1984, 1985a, 1985b, 1987). Identification relies on the resources of the social context— the realm of epistemology—for its critical efficacy. As a result, "fantasy" and "story" emerge as the essential rhetorical constructs for reality (Chesebro 1988). Basically, these constructs are cast as social fictions that deny a biological dimension of reality. However, Burke's transformational perspective does not propose a fictional account of the world. On the contrary, the rhetorical functions inherent in the process of transformation provide a base for understanding reality as "demonstrable relationships, and demonstrably affecting relationships" (Burke [1945] 1969, 57–58).

Second, since reality and symbolism are rhetorical by nature, rhetoric becomes a primary means of scholarly inquiry. Burke reminds us that "language in particular and human relations in general can be most directly approached in terms of *action* rather than in terms of *knowledge*" ([1961] 1970, 38). And action is the dialectical interplay between the biological and the social, between the ontic and epistemic. Thus, symbols both are limited in their ability to convey reality and sometimes overdetermine reality. Humans often read more or less meaning into their symbols than is literally there. According to Burke, symbols and symbolic action are "mythic descriptions" of reality; they are belief systems that are factual only insofar as they mediate and maintain the dialectical tension between the ontological and epistemological (1966b, 152). By understanding symbol systems, we do not gain complete understanding, but we do gain a closer approximation of their meanings. We are forever bound to reveal our biological centrality or our sociopolitical biases, regardless of the symbols we select to enact that perspective. For Burke, biological phenomena themselves are not communicable. Instead, reality formed through the process of transformation directs attention—it induces others to share a version of reality. Thus, magic, myth, and science become symbolic mediations that might best be understood as rhetorical modes of inquiry rather than as explanations for existence.

Third, by viewing reality as a transformational process that maintains a dialectic in perpetuity between the biological and the social dimensions, rhetorical criticism becomes a dialectical analysis that studies the structural relations employed to maintain the dialectical tension between ontological and epistemological modes.

It is quite natural and often necessary to resolve dialectical contradictions by moving toward an ultimate term that resolves the dialectical tension through a synthetic unification of antitheses. To do so, however, is for Burke a perversion of the rationality of the process of transformation. To overlook the process itself whereby reality is formed limits the potential to examine or modify that perspective. As Burke notes in *Permanence and Change:* "A man solves a pseudo-problem who takes, not the *motion,* but the two *concepts* of centripetal and centrifugal forces, as the reality, thereupon devoting his energies to a scheme for uniting them into a synthesis" ([1935a] 1965, 93). Burke acknowledges that "nothing is more imperiously there for observation and study than the tactics people employ when they would injure or gratify one another—and one can readily demonstrate the role of substantiation in such tactics" ([1945] 1969, 57).

Fourth, the critic's task is to unmask the divisiveness engendered by the recontextualization or temporizing of biological or sociopolitical biases. From a transformational perspective, the critic locates an area of study by recognizing that the biological dimension of an act is overemphasized or deemphasized. Take, for example, the Exxon Valdez oil spill. Here we have a perfect example of the reality of an act being cast by agents in a fashion that emphasizes the social context at the expense of the biological. The humanism of the oil spill—the inherent biological nature of the act—is ignored or deemphasized in Exxon's discussion of the act. At issue is the destruction of the environment and the death of thousands of fish and animals. But most of Exxon's talk about the act is based in a symbolism that attempts to transcend the biological dimension by focusing on the technological ramifications of the oil spill (economic perils, cleanup costs, and the relative merits of oil transportation in general).

The abortion issue might be envisioned as one that offers an overemphasis of both the biological and the social, depending on one's vantage point. Pro-lifers discount the social implications of denying the right to abortion by focusing almost entirely on the biological dimension and adding a bit of morality as justification. Pro-choicers discount the biological dimension by focusing on social implications under the guise of civil libertarianism. In either case, the critic should make every effort to restore the dialectical tension of the transformational process if we are truly to enhance our understanding of the role of rhetoric in contemporary culture and keep the conversation going.

Fifth, the critic's goal, then, becomes one of identifying the principle of transformation that is enacted to divert attention from the act by recontextualizing the biological dimension. In the case of the Exxon oil spill, that principle of transformation might be identified as the rhetoric of the "bottom line" and can be located through the bureaucratized structural relations necessary to reduce the tension of the act. Rhetorical strategies then, include (1) casting the environment as secondary to the pursuit of wealth—the environment can be jeopardized for the sake of profit, fisheries are assigned a monetary value, and Alaska's economic future is imperiled; (2) denying responsibility for the act on the basis of cost—cleanup will cost millions that will be passed on to the consumer in the form of higher prices; (3) offering a "drunken" sailor as the cathartic scapegoat for purging the denial of the humanism of the act; and, (4) justifying this perspective by aligning it with the communal value of, or need for, energy.

The principle of transformation can also be identified in other symbolic modes. For example, Hollywood films rely heavily on dialectical tension to maintain narrative continuity. Each scene in a film establishes or pursues a dialectic that must be transcended if the narrative is to progress. The critic's task is to identify the principle or principles of transformation being enacted to maintain dialectical tension in the service of narrative continuity. To illustrate, consider Rocky Balboa and Rambo, Sylvester Stallone's icons of American manhood. These characters constantly find themselves embroiled in dialectical tensions with enemies, opponents, family, and friends. In most instances, the principle of transformation that permits the continuance of the narrative in these films alternates between violence and escapism as the rhetorical strategies necessary for survival in the structural relationships between characters.

Conclusion

Burke views the rhetorical motive as a constant in the constitution of reality. The constancy of our making choices represents his notion of the permanence of change required to establish and maintain communal bonds and communal understandings. There is a permanence of change required for social existence, but the central divisiveness of the human organism precludes the symbolic conveyance of meaning. Meaning, and correspondingly understanding, comes to us through the structural relationship created through the dialectic between biological and social dimensions. Symbolic action represents an approximation of sensory perception or a propaganda for permanence or even a permanence of propaganda. Inasmuch as others share that approximation or propaganda or view of reality, we create and share belief that permits us to interact. In a sense, that is all there is when viewing the way humans use symbols. Symbolic action merely "dances" the attitudes of the symbol user (Burke [1941] 1973).

Humans do seek identification in an effort to transcend biological divisiveness, but we should acknowledge that identification is idealistic and beyond the resources of symbolism. Once we acknowledge division as the essential state of human existence, critical analysis might be profitably directed toward understanding the transcendent efforts of symbolic action designed to identify the biological and/or the sociopolitical biases of the symbol user.

As human beings, we are all always critics processing the competing symbols of our own particular reality. Each symbolic identification we make is an act of discrimination that transforms sensory awareness into and according to our individual orientation or belief system. These transformations are essentially acts of criticism that extend from the complexity of the political arena to the simplicity of deciding what to add to our afternoon tea. It is the critical act that keeps political totalitarianism in check and the critical act that allows us to distinguish between sugar and salt. Without the ability to discriminate between competing symbols and symbol systems that attempt to define our perception of reality, we are at the mercy of interpretations dictated by others. As Burkeian critics, when we consider reality as a transformational process with biological and social dimensions, rhetoric becomes an inevitable tension between ontological and epistemological modes. Accordingly, as critics, we should recognize that attempts to deny either mode require us to re-create that tension.

Notes

1. Many current interpretations of Burke feature some understanding of transformation as central to their reading. See, for example, Bertelsen 1985; Chesebro 1988; Heath 1986; Nelson 1989; and David Williams 1989.

2. Drawing on the work of the poststructuralists, Raymie E. McKerrow makes a similar case for a transformational perspective as the ultimate aim of a critical rhetoric (1989). While McKerrow is primarily concerned with identifying critical rhetoric as applied theory and praxis, the similarity between Burke and the poststructuralists should not be overlooked.

Part III

Applied and Societal Extensions

7

Kenneth Burke on Ecology

A Synthesis

Jane Blankenship

> My Great-Gramma Brodie
> Wouldn't let me say "G"
> 'Cause it meant a swear-word.
>
> My Great-Gramma Brodie
> Knew about
> Heck, Holy Smokes, and Darn it.
> She helped me clean them up, too.
>
> My Great-Gramma Brodie
> Taught me a lot
> About Implications.
> (Burke 1968a)

Clearly, the lesson taught to Kenneth Burke by his Great-Gramma Brodie about terms and their implications is illustrated vividly by his treatment of the term "ecology" and its implications. From the 1920s to the 1990s Burke has been talking to us very directly about ecology, ecological balance, nature and counternature, technological progress, the toxic wastes created by all sorts of "medicine men," the "pollution" of war, and the like. The development of his ecological attitude, his "Orientation," and his continuing "search for secular piety" is quite public. Indeed, like his "little hero" in the short story "Herone Liddell," Kenneth Burke's "revelations" are "haunted by ecology" (Burke 1968a, 287) and the implications of that term.

Whether one turns to Burke's lived story at his home in Andover, New Jersey, to his satirical "make believe" story of Helhaven (Burke 1971, 1974), or to the main body of his work, his fundamental concern for matters ecological is readily apparent. The purpose of this chapter is twofold: first, to sketch Kenneth Burke's ecological attitude and its related lexicon; second, to note some connections between that attitude and the larger corpus of his work.[1]

Kenneth Burke's "Ecological Attitude" and Its Related Lexicon

Here we consider Burke's sense of place, his living in "real" and "imagined" communities; his revelations as representative anecdote; and the pivotal terms fundamental to Burke's expression of his ecological attitude.

A Sense of Place: Living in "Real" and "Imagined" Communities

Human story, for Burke, is "located" in natural history (in motion) and in the world of action; that is, it is constructed symbolically through language. Moreover, "even some random spot in the woods is not just that, but has a personal history" (Burke 1981a, 98). Even casual readers of Burke's work quickly understand that his sense of *place* is profound. "Placement" and "location" function centrally in Burke's lifework (Burke [1945] 1969, 3–126, especially 85–91). Burke, the "vagabond scholar," is "rooted" most clearly in Andover, New Jersey. He moved to New Jersey from Pittsburgh with his parents in 1915, well before that state became routed in traffic and polluted by smoke and toxic waste and before it was nicknamed the Garden State. There, "as ever, future-minded," he later bought a house in Andover, having borrowed $300 from his father for a down payment for the mortgage. It was a two-room house, and he "cleared away the horrendous weed-infested litter" that surrounded it (Burke 1981a, 98). Reminiscing about his life in Andover, including his battle with promoters bent on "developing" the land contiguous to his, our self-proclaimed "agro-Bohemian" summons up the new dimensions to "a run-down monarch's saying: 'After me, the deluge'" (98). Listen to Burke writing on the implications of Big Technology in his "adopted" and "adoptive" state:

If more and more pollution is to be our state's future, all such polluters can get themselves the best berths on a sinking ship. And they can die rich in ripe old age, and even honored by their fellow citizens. For the ship that is sinking is the ship of state, and indications are, from all over the nation, that such a state will never go under, wholly. It can just go on sinking and sinking as a place to live in while there's always the likelihood that those with funds enough can invest in better berths not yet so polluted, elsewhere. (98)

Ever reminding us that we are the "instruments of our instruments," driven by notions of "perfection," Burke's Helhaven project, aptly called by William Rueckert "a cruel and painful (for him, as for us) parody and burlesque of Walt Whitman," lets us glimpse what may happen when humans are reduced to instrumentalities of their own making (Rueckert 1978, 71–86; Rueckert 1982, 278–87). In Helhaven, we can "live" completely removed from our "natural condition." In "Towards Helhaven: Three Stages of a Vision," Burke partially sums up his "Anti-Technologistic Humanism" this way:

There still remains the problem of how life on earth can manage to survive the burdens of world-wide pollution that plague the ways of industrial progress. When you consider how much such "effluence" is almost inevitable in such highly developed technologic enterprises as oil refineries, pulp mills, chemical plants—in sum, the profuse production of power by the mining and processing of minerals, the use of agriculture for industrial purposes, and the consumption of either fossil fuels or atomic energy—it becomes hard to imagine how such trends can be adequately neutralized so long as *hypertechnologism* continues to set the pace for mankind's way of life. And the most violent of Communist or Fascist revolutions are far from the depths of radicalism that would have to be reached before the adventurous ideals of exploitation that are associated with modern, industrial, financial, and political ambitions could be transformed into modes of restraint, piety, gratitude, and fear proper to man's awareness of his necessary place in the entire scheme of nature. (Burke 1971, 19)

Observing the "compulsiveness of man's technological genius," our vast capacity for implementing that genius and our propensity to be "happiest when we can plunge on and on," Burke foresees "a self perpetuating cycle quite beyond our ability to adopt any major reforms in our ways of doing things" (Burke 1971, 19). Thus, our "mounting technologic clutter threatens us." Whatever happens in the "real" of Andover, New Jersey, or the "imagined" of Helhaven, we are talking about *our* "place"; the *eco-* in "ecology," after all, comes from the Greek *oikos* (house).

Burke as Representative Anecdote

Some years ago, in chatting with Don Abbott about his youth in Pittsburgh, Burke recalled that he often looked at his world through the mists of "full employment"—of factory smoke and grit, sometimes thinking the diffusion of light through that mist quite beautiful. It was, he recalled, only later that he knew the full dimensions of those earlier mystical moments (Burke 1972b). In high school he came to read Ralph Waldo Emerson's early essay "On Nature" and to inquire, with Emerson and others, on our "uses of nature" and the intimate and fundamental connections between I-Eye-Ay (Burke 1966a, 875–95). He, like his "little hero," came to ponder "Gallantry vs. Ecology":

For the world of gallantry (where science has been carried into industry by the applications of politics and commerce) threatens at every point to disrupt the "ecological balance" of the purely physical world. Man's "dominion" over the "lowlier" species that are put here for his "use" threatens at every point to become manifest in a way whereby he destroys what he needs directly or indirectly for his own survival. (Burke 1968a, 294)

And he came to understand how mighty our "resources of guilt" and to inquire into master polluters of all sorts (e.g., Hitler) and how they claim frequently to act "in the name of" cleansing (Burke [1941] 1973, 191–220). Thus, we "purify" our water, "re-move" our toxic wastes, "save" our energy, and talk about "clean" bombs—all the while demanding our "freedom" to waste, to pollute, and to seek after new ways of "perfecting" ourselves.

William Bowen, in the February 1970 issue of *Fortune*, praises Burke "for having in 1937, been the first critic to predict the coming importance among the sciences, of 'one little fellow named Ecology, and in time we shall pay him more attention'" (Bowen 1979, 198). Although we have already dated Burke's ecological "hankerings" as beginning much earlier, at this point it is worth recalling his 1930 essay "Waste—the Future of Prosperity" (Burke 1930, 10–14; Burke 1957, 322–24). Looking back on that early essay, Burke comments: "I then viewed the cult of excessive technologic 'progress' rather as a mere cultural absurdity than as the grave economic problem it now [1971] shows signs of 'progressively' becoming" (Burke 1972a, 17).

Early Burke drew the connection between kinds of "conservation movements." In the 1955 introduction to the reprinting of *Attitudes*, he speaks of "a truly new situation," "a change in motivational quality":

We refer to the invention of technical devices that would make the rapid obliteration of all human life an easily available possibility. Up to now, human stupidity could go to fantastic lengths of destructiveness, yet always mankind's hopes of recovery could be born anew. . . . But now presumably a truly New Situation is with us, making it all the more imperative that we learn to cherish the mildly charitable ways of the comic discount. For by nothing less than such humanistic allowances can we hope to forestall (if it can be forestalled!) the most idiotic tragedy conceivable: the willful ultimate poisoning of this lovely planet, in conformity with a mistaken heroics of war. (Burke [1937] 1984, v)

In following an anecdote recalling the children's game "King of the Ashpile," in a P.S. dated 1959, Burke comments:

Despite my complaints against "nineteenth-century antithesis-thinking," I often failed to see the full implications of my own stress upon the principle known as the "socialization of losses," which cuts across any flat distinction between "capitalism" and "socialism." And the closely analogous ways in which thermo-nuclear power was developed in U.S.A. and U.S.S.R. suggest that Big Technology *cum* accountancy overrides the current political fictions. (350)

From that view of technologic "progress" to Burke's "search for an attitude" to give humankind "an *overall* purpose" (Burke 1978b, 33), his thinking on ecology has been clearly laid out for us to follow. But it may be most useful for us to recall here that in *Rhetoric, Poetics, and Philosophy*, where he speaks of his search for that "attitude," Burke suggests:

I can offer only one that seems to make wholly rational sense. And to a large extent it has been given to us by the fact that our great prowess with the resources of symbolic action led to the astounding ingenious invention of technology. Now owing to technology's side effect, pollution, mankind clearly has one unquestionable purpose; namely, to seek for ways and means (with correspondingly global attitudes) of undoing the damage being caused by man's failure to control the powers developed by his own genius. . . . With the great flowering of technology, the problem of self-control takes on a possibly fatal new dimension. Man must so control his invented servants that they cease to control him. Until man solves that problem, he has purpose a-plenty. (33)

Whether one talks about ecology as an "orientation" or a "great web" or an "organism metaphor" or as a "less teleological 'ecosystem'" does make indeed a difference (Cronen 1983). Burke has always taught us that "terms have implications"—and it seems worthwhile to note that the lexicon of Burke, himself an ecologist (in practice and in theory), allows us a rich "representative anecdote" for study. A representative anecdote, Burke tells us, is "something sufficiently demarcated in character to make analysis possible, yet sufficiently complex in character to prevent the use of too few terms in one's description" (Burke [1945] 1969, 324).

In this section I list several pivotal terms from Burke's discussions of ecology. For each one, I give illustrative words, phrases, or specific quotations.

ATTITUDE

—As incipient act: An *"attitude* leads to its *enactment"* ([1937] 1984, 413).

CAPACITY

—"A capacity is not something which lies dormant until used—a capacity is a command to act in a certain way" ([1931] 1968, 142).

DETERMINISM

—From a dramatistic perspective: "Along Spinozistic lines, Dramatism would feel safest if one could prove beyond all doubt (as one doubtless never will) that everything in the realm of physics and biology is inexorably determined. Insofar as a state of freedom is possible, Dramatism would seek it in the realm of symbolic action (the dimension that the determinist Spinoza called 'adequate ideas'). And to illustrate my point, I'd offer an anecdote.

"There is a tribe in the far North that gets its livelihood primarily from fish. The tribesmen began ailing. Experts were dispatched—and the source of the trouble was soon spotted. Thanks to industrial progress further south, the local food supply was loaded with mercury. Here was a simple biologically deterministic fact. If these tribesmen continued eating the contaminated fish, they would necessarily become more and more unhealthy.

"Thus, the diagnosis of their situation (a statement of the case based on wholly deterministic principles) was like an 'adequate idea' that freed them from this particular biological bondage. True, many more 'adequate ideas' would be needed before those poor devils could be wholly patched up. As a sorry matter of fact, the best that most of them could probably manage would be for them to go on relief and start buying canned fish, if it still was fish they wanted, and if they could afford it, and if it wasn't also contaminated by industrial progress further down the line" (1972a, 31).

DISSOCIATION

—"We use these damn machines on us. . . . What is going on in me when I'm talking to you? . . . What's going on in my body? And I think for the first time in the world's history, our technological machine has got the resources to check on that. And what we have is a totally new kind of dissociation. I am out there, recorded on a dial! Who am I? Here I am a person, and now that stuff!" (1983a, 13).

—"Attitudinally . . . the two perspectives [the personalistic and the instrumental] are quite at odds. To the extent that Technology succeeds in perfecting instruments of precision designed for the study of the body's behavior as an electro-chemical mechanism, scrupulously discriminating among the physiological processes that match corresponding stages of expression and communication in the realm of 'symbolicity,' to that extent the very documentation of the parallels between those two orders will accentuate our awareness of their difference" ([1937] 1984, 379).

ECOLOGICAL BALANCE
—Used as early as 1937 by Burke; e.g., in (1937) 1984, 150, 154, 167, 173, 300, 355.
—Of the "dubious kind"—"that exports two-dollar wheat and gets in exchange a Dust Bowl" ([1937] 1984, 150).

ECOLOGY
—Technology's "self-criticism" ([1937] 1984, 412).
—The science of ecology "has to do with the kinds of balance that prevail among biological organisms, considered as members of a sub-verbal, extra-verbal, or non-verbal community" ([1935a] 1984, 275).

ENTELECHY
—"[By] 'entelechy' I refer to such use of symbolic resources that potentialities can be said to attain their *perfect fulfillment*" (1972a, 39).
—The "entelechial principle"—"the symbol-guided tracking down of implications, going to the end of the line" ([1937] 1984, 422).
—Entelechy and perfection.
—The "cult of perfection" (1968c, 294).
—Becoming rotten with perfection.

ENTITLEMENT
—See "What Are the Signs of What? Toward a Theory of Entitlement" (Burke 1966b).
—"'Transcendent' entitlement" (1968c, 291).
—"Its unifying function is in effect an addition to the elements it unifies. And in this technical sense it could be called 'cosmic,' or 'supernatural,' or 'religious' (being technically 'religious' in the sense that, like religion, it infuses all things with the essence of the

Word, the Logos, the personality of the 'first' creative fiat)" (1968c, 291).

FREEDOM
  —To waste, to pollute, "not to give a damn" ([1935a] 1984, 331).
  —Freedom as "grounded in the realm of symbolic *action*" (1972a, 32).

GUILT, THE RESOURCES OF
  —See (1937) 1984, 128.

NATURE, COUNTERNATURE, AND SUPERNATURE
  —Counternature as "symbol-guided Technology's realm" ([1937] 1984, 417).
  —As *in* nature: "The various toxic waste dumps are *in* nature; all Counter-Nature (much of it advantageous) is *in* nature. It is 'unnatural' only in the sense that, thanks to the symbol-guided 'labors' of Technology, we have altered the nature of our environment as no other animal's mere 'presence' in the world has been remotely able to do" ([1937] 1984, 426).
  —As "hygenically sterilized": "In the natural biosphere, much such 'dying' leads to kinds of 'decomposition' which form the ground of new growth. . . . [In] the realm of Counter-Nature . . . much that comes into contact with the 'half-life' of some thermonuclear residues will remain 'hygienically sterilized' for, in all likelihood, a long time after any human offspring could possibly still be here" ([1937] 1984, 414).
  —Counternature and "bureaucratization of the imaginative": "Technology can be neither criticized nor controlled nor corrected without recourse to still more Technology. The *opportunities* to produce further and further 'generations' of contrivances are indistinguishable from the *compulsions* to do so. Accordingly, implicit in the concept (or, some philosophers would say, the idea) of bureaucratization thus expanded are the outlines of a Destiny predestined by instruments (often devilishly ingenious) of our own making" ([1937] 1984, 396).

(THE) NEGATIVE
  —As a linguistic invention. Burke maintains, with Bergson, that there are no negatives in nature; nature *is* (1953b; [1961] 1970, 9–21).

PERFECTION
  —Cult of (1968c, 294).
  —Rotten with.

PIETY
  —"The sense of what properly goes with what" ([1935a] 1984, 74).
  —As a schema of orientation.
  —As "a system-builder, a desire to round things out, to fit experiences together into a unified whole" ([1935a] 1984, 74).
  —"Our orientation largely involves matters of expectancy, and affects our choice of means with reference to the future" ([1935a] 1984, 18).

PLACE, SENSE OF
  —Location.
  —Placement.
  —Stance.
  —Context.
  —Environment.
  —Situation.
  —Scene.

PROGRESS
  —The inevitability of.

PURIFICATION, REDEMPTION
  —As needed by Guilt ([1961] 1970, 4–5, 314).

STORY
  —"We assume a time when our primal ancestors became able to go from Sensations to *Words* for sensation. (When they could duplicate the experience of tasting an orange by saying 'the taste of an orange,' that was when story came into the world.)
  "Whereas Nature can do no wrong (whatever it does is 'Nature'), with Story there enters the realm of the true, false, honest, mistaken, the downright lie, the imaginative, the fanciful, the speculative, the visionary).
  "By learning language, the human body, a composite creature, combines the realms of nonsymbolic motion and symbolic action.
  "The body thus provides a principle of individuation that is grounded in the centrality of the nervous system. But this separateness as a physiological organism is 'transcended' by the peculiar collective social nature of human-symbol systems.
  "There's a strictly *logological* counterpart of 'magic.' It *empirically* matches the creative word in the first chapter of Genesis where each decree said '"Let there be"—and there was.' . . . For all *discriminations*, in the purely symbolic realm, the Universes of Discourse, are by definition 'creative' by being creatures of sheer

symbolicity. And such nomenclatures constitute a realm of *discriminations* that human story brought into the world. But in time that will all be gone, thus undoing Emerson's complaint, 'A believer in Unity, a seer of Unity, I yet behold two,' while the realm of nonsymbolic motion continues to discriminate in ways of its own" (Brock et al. 1985, 31–32).

—"The Story of Evolution tells us how, quite as there was a time when the geological and biological processes of Earth went on wholly devoid of Human Story, so the conditions that at present 'comprehend' the human animal will eliminate the creatures whose Stories seek to 'comprehend' them, hence things will again proceed Sans Story" ([1937] 1984, 384).

SUBSTANCE
　—As Paradox ([1945] 1969, 21–34).
　—As a "convertible term" with "motivation" ([1945] 1969, 376).

TECHNOLOGICAL EFFICIENCY
　—"Experts in the 'agribusiness' line can get and are getting profits in their market by demanding methods of 'efficiency' in the use of the soil that earn them maximum immediate monetary yield at the long-run cost of depleting the soil (and at no cost to them, for they will have moved on, to 'bureaucratize' their kind of pliancy by 'efficiently' depleting the soil elsewhere)" ([1937] 1984, 406).

TECHNOLOGICAL PSYCHOSIS
　—Technology as compulsion ([1935a] 1984, 296).
　—A desire to carry "to the end of the line."

TECHNOLOGISM (ALSO CALLED PERSPECTIVE BY INCONGRUITY)
　—The belief that: "The remedy for the problems arising from technology is to be sought in the development of ever more and more technology. . . . On one of the all-night radio programs with which I sometimes while away insomniac hours, I heard an ardent proponent of Technologism (an *anima naturaliter Technologistica*) ridiculing reactionary idealists who kept asking whether it might be possible to clear up the pollution in Lake Erie. They should look forward, not back, he said—and rather than trying to clean up Lake Erie, they should pollute it ten times as much, then find a way to extract from its wastes a new kind of energy" (1972a, 53–54).

TECHNOLOGY
　—As counternature.
　—As symbol guided ([1935a] 1984, 307).

—As "a coefficient of power" ([1941] 1973, 184; 1976, 188); "the resources intrinsic to Technology being what they are, there is a 'natural' invitation for the owner or driver of a powerful contrivance to feel personally powerful" ([1937] 1984, 386).

—As possessing a "kind of built hopefulness" ([1937] 1984, 429).

—As *anti:* -ethical, -magical, -poetic, -religious.

—As humankind's entelechy. Technology "is an ultimate direction indigenous to Bodies That Learn Language, which thereby interactively develop a realm of artificial instruments under such symbolic guidance" ([1935a] 1984, 296).

VICTIM

—"In the Christian system, Jesus is the victim. Here the issue is technology, where everything is positive, free, and supposedly good. We find that the victim is the country itself, the nation. . . . Fifty thousand dump heaps now. Victimage is coming back on us now. It's the most efficiently victimizing system that was ever built!" (1983a, 19).

Burke's Ecological Warning

Humankind's entelechy is symbol-guided technology; that is, technology is an ultimate direction indigenous to Bodies That Learn Language (Burke [1935a] 1984, 296). Technology is a coefficient of power (Burke [1941] 1973, 184; Burke 1976, 188). Indeed, as Burke observes,

Technology is so great a coefficient of power that when it makes a mistake the results can be fantastically disproportionate to the intention. . . . True, technology's ability to magnify our disorders may imply equally great abilities to magnify our powers of improvement, and such is indeed the case. But technology . . . is so highly innovative that we necessarily lag in learning how best for us to live with it, particularly because, in such complicated choices, there are always so many more ways of being wrong than of being right. (188)

Furthermore,

The possibilities of "sabotage" . . . increase proportionately to such a technologic coefficient of power. Ours has become the ideal age of either the highjacker or the guerrilla because such roles are the perfect match for our technologic innovators. Quite as any innovator might hit upon a "breakthrough" that shifts the whole productive-distributive system, so protestors can relate to the fantastically mounting and vulnerable accumulation of technologic resources whereby, if you but cut one wire or punch one hole in a gas tank, inconceivably mighty powers can become weaker than an old nag or one sputtering candle. (188)

Whether one accepts all or only some of Burke's argument at this point, there is a distinctly *antiparliamentary* dimension to much of our new technology which is developed at such a rate of change that we have little time to "talk about" what to *do* with it. Without such talk, means are inclined to become ends. Moreover, even if inclination were present, there may not be time to try the "parliamentary." Talk may simply be(come) too "inefficient," and "human story" may end.

Kenneth Burke's Ecological "Attitude," His Ecological Terminology, and the Larger Corpus of His Work

Pivotal terms can be thought of as an abbreviated concordance (a kind of entitlement). The purpose of composing such a list of landmarks in Burke country is to highlight the relations among them in order to note how they play out in Burke's "ecological attitude." I propose now to arrive at further accountings of these terms and this attitude in Burke's larger corpus. His distinctions between the realms of *motion* and *action*, a primary division that forms the basis for a definition of humankind, still subsumes these lesser discriminations (Burke 1978a, 809–38). In the following discussion I provide a brief description of how these terms coincide with the larger categories that are perhaps more familiar to us.

While there is a wholly unique Human Story, there also exists a story that nature itself is engaged in telling; this story began without us and will continue with or without us. There is a clear indication that the importance of this extrahuman story has escaped the attention of ecologists and others for many years (Cronen 1983, 10–11). For example, Cronen argues that changes in nature must be understood as a function of both humanity's intervention and the forces of nature itself: "As we shall see the period of human occupation in post glacial New England has seen environmental changes of an enormous scale, many of them wholly apart from human influence" (10–11). It is certain that this story remains a mystery to us, regardless of whether we seek its introduction or its conclusion. Our efforts at deciphering this plot are ultimately but mere reflections of our own story.

Ecological matters are inevitably criticisms, the weighing of competing interests. In this arena operate both humanity and nature itself. Between these perspectives lies a judgment favoring some positions and cursing others. These alterations represent a shifting balance of perspectives. As should be clear, Burke contends that the recent past, the period encompassing his own lifetime, has realigned this balance as a dangerous menace for humanity. The acceleration of our technological side effects has taken on a "deadly" dimension.

How could we have reached such a state? Were there no warnings? Surely there were, for the purely physical reincarnation of unintended side effects is itself physical, which we confront in the litter at any street corner in this country. From our technologies there derive manifest effects. The nature of these effects grounds them in nature, or the realm of motion. To these effects we ascribe whatever measure of reality we can discern. Only through adopting language do we attain choice and the possibilities of "no" or, perhaps even more important, "maybe." But nature is so much more single-minded. It *is*. There is a single-minded determination here. And when our industries reduce us to motion, when the biological and physical consequences of our technological compulsions are translated into waste and hazardous by-products, we are, in this sense, little more than victims of our environments. No less prominent among the terms ground in motion are those given over to form. Capacity is pure potential (Burke [1931] 1968, 29–40). It too *is*. There exists no choice at this elemental stage, only capacity for. Within form there is the ultimate determinism, and it exists as a realm of nature, whether human or otherwise.

For the terms "entelechy" and "perfection," we are tempted, momentarily at least, to substitute the single term "determinism." Implicit in all forms are inherent ends whose existence is both mysterious and invisible to human eyes. This invisibility is both literal, in the sense that we cannot see the structure of a DNA molecule, and also figurative, in the sense that we may not comprehend the unintended by-products of our future. At all levels, form consistently operates as appeal unencumbered by anything other than its nature. In this way an acorn is an appeal to oakness.

As creatures engaged, by our very nature, in a process of individuation and by "the creative moment" (Blankenship, Murphy, and Rosenwasser 1974; Blankenship 1989, 128–55), we are finally driven to the recognition of ourselves. This discovery lies at the heart of our most profound moments. At these junctures we stand out and see in our reflections glimmerings of our destiny. Part of these reflections tell us that we are not *un*related to the extrasymbolic or nonsymbolic operations of nature. Grounded in motion, we *are* and, it is hoped, will remain. But we are also grounded in *symbolic* action.

Human Story came into the world when humans could "duplicate the experience of tasting an orange by saying 'the taste of an orange'" (Brock et al. 1985, 31–32). Human Story (as stories in nature) is located in some place, some scene (some environment). The "location" of Human Story resides (1) in the realm of nature (motion) and (2) in the realm of symbolic action. Human Story cannot exist without motion (although motion can exist without Human Story), any more than it could exist without action.

Human Story is brought into the world by the "creative word" (a dim analogue of the creative fiat: "Let there be . . .") (Burke [1961] 1970, 151–85). Human Story brought into the world a realm of *discriminations*. All "*discriminations*, in the purely symbolic realm, the Universes of Discourse, are by definition 'creative' by being creatures of sheer symbolicity" (Brock et al. 1985, 32).

With Human Story enters the negative (a "distinctively linguistic product"). There are "no negatives in nature"—nature merely *is*. With Human Story "there enters the realm of the true, false, honest, mistaken, the downright lie, the imaginative, the fanciful, the speculative, the visionary" (Brock et al. 1985, 32).

Goaded by notions of progress and having developed an awesome counternature (toxic wastes, nuclear weapons, etc.), we victimize our "natural" environment and feel ourselves victimized by our "second-nature" (counternature, technology). We thus suffer a double dissociation.

Having developed powerfully effective resources of guilt (ways of laying waste), we seek redemption by "recovering" the land, "purifying" the water, and "cleaning up" Three Mile Island—maybe. As we perfect both our resources of guilt and our resources of redemption, we occasionally pause to sum up our condition—the human condition—and worry about what that entitlement implies. One implication entails "technological efficiency" and its correlate "technological psychosis," continued dissociation, rationality, and that other "determinism," progress, which Technologism entitles us to.

Progress leads to more progress and, at the end of the line, to PROGRESS—a "fully developed" Andover, a "culture bubble" like unto Helhaven which has completely made the natural "unnatural" and demonstrated, perhaps irrevocably, that we have become instruments of our instruments and thus pushed to the brink of motion. Whether we do reduce ourselves to motion, Burke leaves to us, reminding us of our "place": "There was no story before we came, and when we're gone the universe will go on sans story"—at least sans Human Story (Burke 1983b, 859). But, only if the "imaginative" element in Human Story becomes fully "bureaucratized"—fossilized, perfect—will death occur. For Burke, however, the notion of the "possible" (the maybe) functions as a potentially powerful anti-dote to such perfectionist tendencies.

Burke raises a central question when he asks: "What are the signs of what?" (Burke 1966b, 359–79). I will not attempt a precis of that piece; it is always best to read Burke firsthand. This essay, though, is pivotal to understanding his writings on ecology and, indeed, the larger corpus of his work. By asking this question, Burke engages us in an exercise which requires that we examine "a somewhat para-doxical proposition that experimentally reverses the common-sense view of the relationships between words and things; that is, that words are the signs of things" (369). Burke asks us to invert that view and to argue, at least temporarily, that "things are the signs of words."

Burke starts us off on our inversion by reminding us:

Since language derives its materials from the cooperative acts of men in sociopolitical orders, which are themselves held together by a vast net-work of verbally perfected meanings, might it not follow that man must perceive nature through the fog of symbol-ridden social structures that he has erected atop nature? Material things would thus be like outward mani-festations of the forms which are imposed upon the intuiting of nature by language. (1966b, 378)

If we assume this "might," then, he asks us to continue along with him:

Just as the Word is said by theologians to be a mediatory principle between the world and the supernature, might words be a mediatory principle be-tween ourselves and nature? And just as the theologian might say that we must think of the word as the bond between men and the supernatural, might words (and the social motive implicit in them) be the bond between man and the natural? . . . [M]ight nature be necessarily approached by us through the gift of the spirit of words? (362)

If we take this view, then nature could be conceived as "not just the less-than-verbal thing we take it to be." Could nature not, then, be said to be "infused with the spirit of words?"

Are words the signs of things, or are things the signs of words? For the purpose of making the distinction between the implications of these contrasting perspectives, it may be useful to follow each one to the "end of their lines." First, let us consider the possibilities of the word as the sign of the "natural." We can turn to Burke's satirical Helhaven. Clearly, this essay speculates about where we will be at the end of the "Industrial Age" or the entelechial principle driven solely by rational "determinism." Instead of "merely" the material comforts in this "perfect" future, we find ourselves fugitives on our own planet. Goaded by notions of "progress," we hover above a toxic waste dump. Surely by this point we see that our term "progress" and its correlatives have implications and that we risk carrying these implications to the end of the line. Progress as our entitlement "transcends" nature with unanticipated consequences and is far removed from our original, creative notion of "progress." Nature becomes merely a less-than-verbal thing.

What if, in contrast, things are the signs of words? Here also we could become "rotten with perfection." In the actual essay in *Language as Symbolic Action*, Burke never requires that we "go to the end of the line" with our inversion. (Burke may simply be too much of a "word-man" for that!) Or we may simply misunderstand him on this point. One possible example may be the "noble savages 'return to the land.'" It may be that humans as symbol users are simply precluded from this possibility—that is, because we have the capacity for language, we use that capacity and cannot lay it down like a tool. Words remove us from nature at least partially, although we can return to nature, particularly when we have infused nature with the social content and weightings of words. We are back to Burke's fundamental duality. Action, Burke reiterates, "encompasses the realm of entities that respond to words as such . . . [and] 'motion' encompasses the realm of entities that do not respond to words as words" (1966b, 366). They may not be totally bridgeable, but it is important to note that Burke does talk about an "indeterminate realm."

Unfortunately, there is an intermediate realm, as when sheerly physiological processes (properly to be charted in terms of motion) are affected by [humans'] attitudes, passions, reasonings and the like (properly to be charted in terms of action). Simplest example: The thought of a physiologically wholesome food may produce repugnance in a person whose mores have not established the normality of this food. This margin of overlap is further made possible by the fact that, so far as the empirical realm is concerned at least, though there can be motion without action (cf. the realm of physics, at least as that realm is studied and applied by humans), there can be no action without motion (since every idea, concept, attitude, or even every sheer word, if you will allow man no more consciousness than that, requires its corresponding set of purely physical processes; for though we still may not accurately know what a word is like as regards its sheerly physiological counterpart, we do assume that, within our logic of empirical knowledge at least, its happening even in thought requires certain living functions in a certain neural order, as the physically nonexistent rules of a ballgame cannot be enacted in a game except by eighteen bodies that move, with appropriate physical paraphernalia, by which we mean, at the very least, ball and bat and specified grounds). (366)

Burke seems to ask us to obtain a balanced view here—but not perfectly balanced view in the sense that we find it difficult to hold both views equally, but he does ask us to understand that we word-people are *in* nature, that the world of nature (motion) does not require us, but that the world of humans (action) does require it. Moreover, he urges us to understand that our words (actions, technology) *can* change nature in ways no other natural inhabitants of our globe can. He also requires us to understand that when we change our "place," we change ourselves and that unless we want to undertake a massive relocation, the likes of which we have never before witnessed, we might well long for a *global* understanding such as Burke's "alchemic moment" at a mirror lake in Glacier:

> Here, with the memory of so much undoing
> you stand in the sign of Conservation.
> (On a trail, through woods, there spread
> suddenly one of Nature's clearings, a pond
> and meadow, circled by high trees behind
> much higher peaks downpointing in the
> water. The mystery may be a reflex
> counterpart of all the plunder that had
> been flowing beneath our wheels.
>
> . . . .
> Might we not here, my friends, confront
> the makings of a madness, an
> unacknowledged leap from *This is mine* to
> By God, this is ME! . . . ?
>
> (1968a, 281)

When pondering Kenneth Burke's attempt, lasting fifty or sixty years, to alert us to our "entitlement," one question comes particularly to mind: "How can Burke, knowing all this, remain even a bit optimistic?" Burke provides his own answer. In the spring 1983 issue of *All Area*, a future-minded Burke is talking with his interviewer about his attempts to resist "technology" and to "transcend" the several kinds of "denaturing" we frequently must face.

I'm trying to answer a call across a gulf that can't be crossed. I feel that. Every once in a while, I hit a couple of notes on the piano that just get the damn thing. They get what I wish I could do every time. But not by accident, not by alcohol, but just by doing it that way. I wish I could write a whole thing like that. If you haven't created them spontaneously, you haven't really done them. If you haven't done them with your whole full self. . . . I suddenly get a little notion, all of a sudden, I can be pious again, I can see beyond. There is something! There is something! . . . I don't know. I get a little glimpse of it. I don't know but there it is." (Burke 1983a, 12–13)

Note

1. The author wishes to thank Eric Metcalf for his substantive discussion on this point.

8

Attitudes toward Counternature (with Notes on Nurturing a Poetic Psychosis)

Timothy N. Thompson and Anthony J. Palmeri

> Mark Twain's experience comes to mind, in which, after he had mastered the analytic knowledge needed to pilot the Mississippi River, he discovered the river had lost its beauty. Something *is* always killed. But what is less noticed in the arts—something is always created too. And instead of just dwelling on what is killed it's important also to see what's created and to see the process as a kind of death-birth continuity that is neither good nor bad, but just *is*.
> —Robert M. Pirsig, *Zen and the Art of Motorcycle Maintenance*

In *Zen and the Art of Motorcycle Maintenance*, Robert Pirsig (1974) makes a good case for technology's naturalness. In a search for "quality" the author realizes all that exists has its nature and is a part of the grander Nature; thus even his motorcycle is part of the "buddha-nature." Technology is made from the elements of Nature and runs according to Nature's "laws." However, certain aspects of technology work *against* Nature. The fumes spewed from the cycle's exhaust work against Nature's self-cleansing processes, yet those fumes are acting *with* the process. Technology, like human-kind, is paradoxically both *a part of* and *apart from* Nature.

Throughout the course of industrialization, the social, economic, philosophical, and rhetorical impact of technology has been questioned. The social dynamics of technological development have been of great concern at least since the organizing of Luddites, when Ned Ludd and his coworkers conspired to smash the machines that were replacing human textile workers. Many have commented at length on the social shape of life with machines, from Thoreau's ([1854] 1962) sauntering refusal to keep step with progress to Walter Ong's (1982) maps of the ontological and epistemological changes that accompany technological change. Technology's impact has been assessed through economic questions, from Adam Smith's ([1776] 1985) dissertation on how to turn groups of humans into efficient divisions of labor to an abundance of writings thence which show increased productivity and profits to be gained by employing machines. Philosophically, the impact of technology on human being and knowing has been considered in depth, from earlier works like Samuel Butler's adventures in *Erewhon* ([1872] 1968), where the traveler discovers a land of technology-turned-back, to contemporary interest in the philosophy of science (e.g., Bateson 1972, 1982). All of these perspectives have a rhetorical dimension as they serve a suasive function in adjusting humans to technological conditions. Some works deal specifically with rhetorical and communicative questions, such as the rhetoric of science and current studies of computer and media influences on human communication (e.g., Cathcart and Gumpert 1983; Jamieson 1988; Chesebro 1991). Technology has been studied.

Kenneth Burke has played no minor role in the technology drama. Adjusting to technological "progress" has been a prominent theme in his work, and there are a growing number of variations on that theme (e.g., Blankenship 1990; Brock 1990a; Chesebro 1990; Enholm, Palmeri, and Thompson 1990; Klumpp 1990; Muir 1990). Technology has been addressed from many angles, and yet, just as innovations are turning the new into the old at an accelerating pace, the questions posed by technology (and its spawning ground, science) are forever outpacing the answers in the ongoing march of progress. How is science a self-justifying and extremely persuasive system of thought? What is the nature of the relationship between humans, science, and technology? How do various technologies help or hinder the realization of human "potential" (the vision, entelechy, or telos of human being; or, put another way by Burke, the "principle of thoroughness" which guides perfecting in social order)? What are the economic and social trade-offs in a technologized world? These and other questions will be addressed in this extension of Kenneth Burke's attitudes toward counternature.

Kenneth Burke has been suspicious of technological developments for the greater part of this century. In his first book he wrote: "In contemporary America the distinguishing emergent factor is obviously mechanization, industrialism, as it affects our political institutions, as it alters our way of living, as it makes earlier emphases malapropos or even dangerous" ([1931] 1968, 107). Burke's earlier concerns were tempered with a hope that technology could help achieve humane ends, but by the late 1960s his faith in the machine as an instrument of human happiness waned, a loss of faith evident in the tragic comedy of the Helhaven writings (1971, 1974). The last twenty years of his writings, such as the afterwords in *Permanence and Change* ([1935a] 1984) and *Attitudes toward History* ([1937] 1984), have covered a wide range of terms and attitudes for rejecting and accepting technology. His position has transformed into a kind of comic ambivalence, doubtful yet hopeful: at one moment resigned to the "ever-mounting purely *instrumental* problems intrinsic to the realm of Counter-Nature as 'progressively' developed by the symbol-guided 'creativity' of technological prowess itself" ([1937] 1984, 424–25), but in the next moment hopeful that "Technology has a kind of built-in hopefulness, not just with regard to the resources and corresponding resourcefulness of Technology itself, but even to hoping that a worldwide political system adequate to control its uses and misuses can somehow be contrived" (429–30). While this chapter will not meet the challenge to develop a worldwide political system, it will plant some of Burke's aesthetic seeds with the hope that such political developments may still come to fruition.

This chapter is about countering counternature. This term refers to the by-products and waste created by technological perfecting, which work at odds with the ecosystem's *natural* cleansing abilities, and to technology's impact on the *nature* of the human mind, body, spirit, and social relationships. After reviewing the rise of science and the corresponding "hypertechnologized" way of life it has bred, new paths off of Burke's trail will be presented, pathways meandering through a "comic frame" toward "poetic correctives" of counternature.

Science and Insanity

The human drama is pervaded by the products, by-products, and underlying logic of the "scientific rationalization." Burke maps history through three successive stages: magical, religious, and scientific rationalizations. He appears to use "rationalization" intentionally as a misnaming for orientation, or Weltanschauung. By coupling "science" with "rationalization," Burke begins his "exorcism by misnomer," a planned incongruity which "would suggest that one cast out old devils by *misnaming* them" ([1937] 1984, 133).

The scientific rationalization was preceded by magic, the "rationalization by which man got control over the primitive forces of nature," and then religion, "the rationalization which attempts to control the specifically *human* forces" (Burke [1935a] 1984, 44). Now a third rationalization has gained prominence: "science, the attempt to control for our purposes the forces of technology, or machinery" (44). People within a magical orientation explain things as occurring from mysterious sources. People within a religious orientation explain things as occurring because of the will of a divine or supernatural power. People within a scientific orientation tend to explain things through observable, quantifiable evidence. In later writings Burke notes that all three orientations are active today (307), but he presents the scientific as posing the greatest threat to human existence.

Science has bred technological innovations at an astounding pace, but it has also given birth to various psychoses. Burke equates "psychosis" to overemphasis or, as Dewey used it, a "pronounced character of the mind" ([1935a] 1984, 40). Psychoses develop from thinking and doing things so much in one way that more adaptive ways are ignored. People tend to develop and habituate "ways of seeing" (and being) according to the underlying logic and motivation in their terms for situations. These ways of seeing, whether they are as wide as a Weltanschauung or as brief as a moment's thought, are also, Burke notes, ways of not seeing. Any way of seeing carried to its extreme can become a psychosis.

The "technological psychosis" can be traced to various beginnings, and although "it is customarily traced back to Copernican astronomy, Galilean physics, and the Baconian rationalization of the inductive method, the psychosis cannot be said to have fully blossomed until the time of the Utilitarian philosophers in England, the first country to feel the full shock of systematic technological development" (Burke [1935a] 1984, 44). The utility mindedness of thinkers like Adam Smith, coupled with the accelerated inventiveness of the scientifically efficient exchange of ideas, created radical worldwide change. Developments in mass communication, transportation, energy consumption, and production in general have increased exponentially, resulting in a proliferation of products that are advertised, transported, bought, and sold. Technological innovation has hyperactivated the world's *system of exchanges*—a system that is governed by money.

The system of rapid invention and exchange has led to the moralizing of money. In *Attitudes toward History,* Burke traces part of the roots of the scientific-technological rationale to the invention of credit-debit accounting, which "offered a *quantitative* device for making action rational. The merchant did not have to juggle tenuous notions of vice and virtue when judging his plan of action. He simply consulted his ledgers, and the plan proved 'good' if his balance at the end of the year showed income outweighing costs" ([1937] 1984, 26). Increasing reliance on accountancy was an important "curve in history" because methods of evaluation took a turn from qualitative to a greater emphasis on quantitative, and from interests in religious and moral implications to an increasing interest with secular and economic concerns. The shift to a more pronounced focus on money, weighing costs and benefits in economic terms, became a morality all of its own—the "economic reality"— where right and wrong can be quantified. Money objectifies the subjective realm of value, and because it is efficient and practical, it fits well within the "laws of utility" that guide the scientific rationalization.

Worldwide faith in science, technology, and money has been accompanied by greater faith in quantities. Like Burke, Gregory Bateson saw the turn toward the-numbers-tell-the-truth as key for understanding what he called the epistemological error that continues to structure social evolution:

If you grow up as we do, with a worship of the quantitative aspect and minimal attention to the qualitative aspect, I believe you inevitably land yourself in the dilemmas of our civilization. . . . we are hooked on thinking about quantities, and our whole economic theory is so hooked. Our whole theory of internal satisfactions, our pursuit of happiness and all that, our obsession with property, our measurement of time, and our obsession with money. (1982, 350–54)

Bateson's concern was that quantities had become an overemphasis (a psychosis) in society and in the social sciences and that too great of an emphasis on numbers can drown aesthetic views, as well as place stress on social systems, in the tremendous push toward greater and more efficient numbers.

Quantification is the "objective" basis of the scientific rationalization, and there is little doubt that society is "hooked." Quantities are the basis of political, educational, and corporate decisions, where voter satisfaction, student and faculty productivity, and business progress are made measurable through the accuracy and efficiency of numbers. Moreover, quantities affect the quality of life, as the numbers on scales, watches, and SALE! stickers alter human action.

The quantitative-economic orientation has coevolved with what Burke calls the "cult of new needs" ([1935a] 1984), a tremendous emphasis on the NEW! fostered by fashion, advertising, and the "needs" of consumers. The cult is a social matrix among producers, advertisers, sellers, and buyers, all enmeshed deeply in a courtship maintained by the promise of perfection toward "newer and better ways." Consumers, corporations, and all capitalistic animals are coproducing a drama "sponsored by" the cult of new needs; the pace of which continues to accelerate.

The industrialized world thrives on increasing quantities, striving assiduously toward the production and sale of new goods. But each quantitative gain in production breeds counternature. An increase in the gross national product often indicates an increase in gross natural pollution, and these cycles of production-pollution take their toll on natural and social systems.

Counternature has obvious and subtle effects upon Nature. The obvious includes toxic waste, nuclear waste, medical waste, gas leaks, oil-slicked waters, acid rain, and the cumulative impact of human-made gases on the ozone layer. All are stories found regularly in the daily newspaper, which is itself a contributor, participating in an accelerating deforestation project. Or consider the average car, which puts out its own weight in fumes each year; or the list of leading corporate polluters, who annually put billions of pounds of carcinogens in the air and water. All are obviously working against the self-cleansing processes of Nature, yet the predominant rationalization keeps people striving toward the kind of life that produces counternature.

Less obvious are technology's effects in the social and psychological equations of humankind, or the web of relationships between humans and Nature. Bateson called this connection the eco-mental system, and he described a kind of systemic insanity that results when that relationship is ignored: "You decide that you want to get rid of the by-products of human life and that Lake Erie will be a good place to put them. You forget that the eco-mental system called Lake Erie is part of *your* wider eco-mental system—and that if Lake Erie is driven insane, its insanity is incorporated in the larger system of *your* thought and experience" (1972, 492).

Whether or not one names the system of human thought and experience, "insane" is a matter of personal preference. Some common definitions of the term include "not sane," "crazy," and "extremely foolish," but who is to judge if barrels of nuclear waste at the bottom of a lake fit the definitional criteria? (i.e., one person's insanity is another's economically smart solution to a problem). If, however, insanity has something to do with prolonged exposure to paradoxical injunctions or being in a "bind," then perhaps *humankind is in a bind between economic necessity and ecological sanity.* The compulsions of the produce-pollute model are at odds with the increasing need for a new harmony with Nature.

Recycling programs are on the rise to counteract pollution, but pollution is not the only source of technological guilt. James W. Chesebro noted the guilt of *not knowing much* in an information-saturated society (1990). The information explosion, along with the ubiquity and increasing complexity of technology, leaves most people dwarfed by technology's superiority, ever more guilty of not keeping up with what is "new." Whether it be the glut of "important information" filling mailboxes, newsstands, and file drawers or the loss of confidence to fix the things that make existence "run" (like computerized coffee-makers and fuel injectors), people are increasingly becoming out of touch with the words and things that surround them.

To be out of touch is to be alienated. Technology alienates people as its secrets become shared by fewer and fewer experts. With each new "advance," like computerization and robotics, more people become dependent on technology's healers to maintain the complex gadgetry. "Healers" of all types, not just of gadgets, are depended upon more and more. People are alienated from the legal process, dependent on lawyers and judges to decide the truth of claims; dependent upon doctors to determine what's ailing them; dependent upon psychiatrists and psychologists for tips on how to be sane. Insofar as these functions are taken out of the hands of people, they are alien.

As the scientific rationalization spreads, so do the economic, quantitative, and technological psychoses. Waste, guilt, insanity, and alienation continue to multiply as by-products of progress.

Counternature is proliferating as technology becomes more and more the central agent in the human drama. A metaphor alluded to by Samuel Butler in *Erewhon* captures this theme of technology agent and human agency: Technology is a rapidly reproducing species of conscious being, and humans are the pollinating bees in its reproductive chain. In "The Book of the Machine," the piece of persuasion that led the Erewhonians to destroy all inventions born in the last 271 years, the author makes the case for eradication not so much because of technology's being but fearing what it will become:

I would repeat that I fear none of the existing machines; what I fear is the extraordinary rapidity with which they are becoming something very different to what they are at present. No class of beings have in any time past made so rapid a movement forward. Should not that movement be jealously watched, and checked while we can still check it? And is it not necessary for this end to destroy the more advanced of the machines which are in use at present, though it is admitted that they are in themselves harmless? ([1872] 1968, 264).

The Erewhonians bought the argument and carried their *frame of rejection* to its ultimate—the destruction of all machines. Seeing no similar solution as feasible in the nonfictional here and now, the following will chart critical and poetic correctives from a comic *frame of acceptance.*

To Accept or Reject Counternature? Both, and . . .

How is human action to be named, and how shall it be framed? Whether commenting on science and technology or on a spider spinning its web, we must ask whether it is "good" or "bad," or *both, and* much more? Kenneth Burke has spent a great deal of energy "leaving his options open," using the "both, and" approach as license to explore a fuller range of terms and motivations in the human drama. Such openness is encouraged by a comic frame of acceptance, but one need not accept the comic frame solely in order to remain "open." To reject other ways of seeing, other frames, as less "correct" than the comic would run counter to the ideal openness engendered by a comic frame of acceptance.

For Burke, a *comic* frame does not mean seeing humor in everything but refers to an open and balanced critical stance that is "neither wholly euphemistic, nor wholly debunking—hence it provides the *charitable* attitude towards people that is required for purposes of persuasion and cooperation, but at the same time maintains our shrewdness concerning the simplicities of 'cashing in.' . . . showing us how an act can 'dialectically' contain both transcendental and material ingredients, both imagination and bureaucratic embodiment" ([1937] 1984, 166). The comic frame allows one to remain "loose," free to wander through perspectives, to practice many ways of seeing, to circumscribe the circles of terms available for any given moment. Hence, the human fascination with technology is not only sad, it is funny. Technology is beautiful; it is grotesque, as aesthetically pleasing as the rainbow colors of light dancing on an oil patch.

At the New Harmony Conference, William Rueckert (1990) provided a helpful synthesis of the comic frame: It is a broad frame, an awareness of the comedy, tragedy, and irony of living. It is composed of "liquid attitudes," a flowing openness in one's interpretations. It encourages poets, critics, and those reached to use metaphors as a means of mapping moments, while realizing no metaphor presents a full drama. The comic frame acknowledges the basic principle of ecology, that everything is related to everything else, and that reality is always in process. In short, the comic is a flexible, adaptive frame of *acceptance.*

A frame of acceptance does not mean acquiescence to, says Burke, but "an openness to the factors involved. One may accept a situation in thundering against it. Voltaire accepted. Acceptance is exposure" ([1931] 1968, 108); and again, "the comic frame should enable people *to be observers of themselves while acting.* Its ultimate would not be *passiveness,* but *maximum consciousness*" ([1937] 1984, 171). To accept is to say yes to the drama. Much like the frame embodied in Tao, "The Way," acceptance is an approach of "it is" rather than of "should or should not be." All action and motion are positively yes, and only through human symbolic fabrication can one say no. Acceptance means dealing with the drama of human action as *it is* but allows one the freedom to "thunder against" it.

Here again, Burke does not suggest one must either accept or reject the drama or its reigning authority symbols. Acceptance and rejection are of one and the same dialectic, with "transitional" frames rounding out that dialectic. In *Attitudes toward History* ([1937] 1984), Burke begins by posing William James's choices—to "accept the universe" or to "protest against it"—and notes how "James looks for a way of avoiding both. He will be neither an optimist nor a pessimist, but a 'meliorist'" (3). Burke works from James, through Whitman, to Emerson's doctrine of polarity, which allows him "to confront evil with good cheer" (18); then he lays out his own melioristic chart by recasting the poetic categories within acceptance, rejection, and transitional frames.

Comedy, tragedy, and epic are frames of *acceptance,* or "the more or less organized system of meanings by which a thinking [person] gauges the historical situation and adopts a role in relation to it" ([1937] 1984, 5). Burke places plaint and elegy, satire and burlesque under the frame of *rejection,* which is "but a by-product of 'acceptance.' . . . It is the heretical aspect of an orthodoxy—and as such, it has much in common with the 'frame of acceptance' that it rejects" (21). Grotesque and didactic are *transitional,* where "grotesque focuses on mysticism; the didactic to-day is usually called propaganda" (57). He admits, "None of these poetic categories can be isolated in its chemical purity. They overlap upon one another, involving the qualitative matter of emphasis" (57). All of the poetic forms and frames are useful "to equip us for confronting given historical and personal situations" (57), but it is evident that Burke prefers the comic frame of acceptance as an "attitude of attitudes" that is especially suited for dealing with the problems of progress.

Seen in this light, Burke's preference for satire in the Helhaven project (1971, 1974) does not necessarily reflect a preference for a rejectionist frame, but rather the comic critic's awareness of what a specific situation calls for. Indeed, the satire is built upon comedy and tragedy, as James Klumpp (1990) shows so well. Reviewing a passage from Helhaven, where the privileged of the moon's

"Culture Bubble" look through their telescope down on the damned of a polluted earth, Klumpp notes:

> The image is of those in Helhaven looking back to earth to those still mired in the mines and pollution-clogged technology that has produced the material goods which make up their bubble. . . . Thus, the comic irony brings us into touch with our doublespeak that supports technology. . . .
> [The language of Helhaven] is the language with which we live our lives. It is planning, progress, development; it is the language which we use to place ourselves acceptingly into the warm bubble of technology. The fiction of Helhaven is fiction only in its coherence. The oxymorons of controlled environment; artificially constructed nature; the ironic concept of comfort built on the exploitation of others; these are already a part of our landscape. (12)

The moment on the moon is comic, and comedy may be freely woven through all frames, in any poetic moment. The comic poet/ critic is not trapped within using only the resources of comedy. This ability to employ numerous strategies creatively, not a commitment to comedy exclusively, is a reflection of the "freedom to vary" allowed by the comic frame of acceptance.

A Poetic Rationalization as Preferable Psychosis

Burke (1935a, 1937), Rueckert (1982), Brock (1990a), and Chesebro (1990) have claimed that a move away from the scientific rationalization will require a cultural milieu attuned to a "poetic humanist" orientation. Burke ([1935a] 1984) also points out that all orientations are rationalizations; thus poets, like psychotherapists, cannot rightfully claim "reality" is theirs. Poetry, thought of in its Burkeian extraliterary sense as "equipment for living," must serve as a "corrective" for the current hypertechnologized state. Brock claims "poetic humanism . . . is the challenge of the 21st century" (1990a, 6), and though his examples from feminist and medical self-help movements show poetic humanism to be a growing trend, he is cautious of being overly optimistic, because "entrenched interests are not going to change perspectives easily, so an ideological confrontation more severe than that of the 1960s is inevitably ahead of us. But just as religion transcended magic, and science replaced religion, the weakness of the current orientation will bring a shift toward Poetic Humanism" (8). For Brock, Burke's poetic humanism "stresses language, values, and action" (8). Therefore, rhetoric and communication scholars ought to play a "central role" in implementing this shift, and "the poetic humanist orientation should have a significant impact upon the nature of the future theory and methods within the field" (8).

Speaking of the implications for rhetorical criticism, Chesebro wrote that the critic:

must adopt a decisively skeptical role in which the symbolic constructions created by technology become the target of the rhetorical critic. . . . the desire to construct the "good life," or the fashioning of idealistic and humanistic programs, must be postponed until dramatists have determined how a symbolic perspective can be used to counter technology, assuming—of course—that dramatistic systems are capable of challenging the symbolic power conveyed by technology. (1990, 3)

The poet's battle is uphill. Nevertheless, through symbols the scientific rationalization has spread, and through symbols it may be shunned.

While it is clear that rhetoric and communication scholars must play a central role in the orientation shift, it is not clear that the majority will do so. This is true even for those who carry the label "Burkeian." At the New Harmony conference, Burke was apparently surprised by the lack of contentiousness at most sessions. He does not appear interested in becoming an icon for generations of scholars content to preach to the already converted. Put another way, Burke sees danger in creating and maintaining an entrenched interest while providing opposition to the same.

Burke's aversion to the self-serving intellectual formed part of the basis of his earlier disagreements with Marxists, as pointed out by Lentricchia in his analysis of Burke's 1935 speech to the American Writers' Congress:

Burke's challenge to the Marxist intellectual . . . is to stop making things easy for himself by talking into the mirror of the committed and to enter into dialogue with the uncommitted, the skeptical, even the hostile. His implied, bruising point—it was not misunderstood in 1935—was that the proletarian novel was both a literary and political indulgence: applauded by the already convinced, unread by the working class, quietly alienating to the unconvinced, the proletarian novel took no risk of real dialogue. (1989, 285–86)

Burkeians risk the same fate if they are content only to engage in intellectual gossip with peers—attending conferences and writing great things, where someone is reading or listening, but not those who most need the message.

Poets, critics, and all who work in ways of seeing must step up the efforts in educating, agitating, and legislating toward the Poetic Way.

The way is to exercise the resources and range of symbols, giving wings to "agitating thoughts" so that they might enlist the action of others in these transitional times. Emerson wrote:

The poet also resigns himself to his mood, and that thought which agitated him is expressed, but *alter idem* ["another yet the same"], in a manner totally new. The expression is organic, or the new type which things themselves take when liberated. . . .

The poets are thus liberating gods. The ancient British bards had for the title of their order, "Those who are free throughout the world." They are free, and they make free. ([1842] 1962, 535–37)

The poet liberates through language. The poet stretches imaginations, taking those who will attend through the fullness of moods and moments. The poet plays with many forms and frames and, through "organic expressions," frees people's way of seeing. Kenneth Burke is a poet. The Poetic Way is an overemphasis on expressive freedom, and as such, it is an openness psychosis.

If the poet should develop such a psychosis, it is one that can be lived with; being a slave to shouting "Freedom!" is not such bad servitude. If symptoms develop, do not seek analysis for this psychosis. Instead, let it spread in the hope that others will be afflicted. Let it spread through the mind of science, fogging faith in the gods of utility. Most of all, let it spread through educators, agitators, and legislators.

Poetic Education, Agitation, and Advocacy

Poetic educators make "What does it mean to be the symbol-using animal?" a central question for the academy. Balancing today's largely pragmatic, career-oriented focus of schools, the poet places aesthetics within a liberal tradition in the forefront. In every classroom, it is the poetic educator's goal to address historical and contemporary human action in ways that encourage students to discover constantly the many ranges of terms toward enlightenment. Poets need not scoff at "great books" educational curricula so much as refuse to accept such books as the only way of addressing life. Indeed, the poetic educator exposes students to "great symbols," only some of which may be on the printed page.

The poetic program must go beyond books and classrooms, employing a variety of media to counter the premises and promises of a nonreflective scientism. Poetic/comic educators can use public-access television, radio, and computer-mediated communication to saturate more thoroughly the media-linked marketplace, increasing what advertisers call the "reach" of the message. Some may consider this a contradiction, to be using technologies while pursuing the shift from scientific to poetic. But they are not contradictory means and ends for two reasons. First, the shift should be toward an *emphasis* on the poetic, not the total eradication of technology (which is not possible and probably not desirable at this point in the human-technology "bonding" process). Second, poetic practitioners must use the terms and techniques of the scientific way truly to "reach" people living by technology's terms. As Burke noted, "Any new rationalization must necessarily frame its arguments as far as possible within the scheme of 'proprieties' enjoying prestige in the rationalization which it would displace" ([1935a] 1984, 66). The words and ways of scientific-economic-technological mind-set shall be springboards to poetic insight. Thus, poets can connect with the "bottom line" rewards of Thoreau's sauntering, the "innovation" of Frost's less-traveled road, or the "street-smart, hard-nosed, efficient, time-saving, money-saving practicality" of a Horatio Alger, Jr. hero. By whatever means and messages, poetic/comic educators must "go public."

Agitation is another means of promoting the poetic program, through demonstrations, protests, letter writing, speeches, mainstream and alternative publications, and other routes. Some individuals and organizations are combining agitation with education, as when Greenpeace and Earth First send mass mailings, organize protests, and stand physically in the way of actions damaging to the environment. Without being overly critical of these efforts or minimizing their accomplishments, from the standpoint of the comic frame their methods of agitation leave something to be desired. Specifically, the ultrapolemic, noncompromising style serves to frighten major segments of the public who, when confronted with the image of "environmental extremists," conclude that a more moderate course of action is needed. Then, typically, the moderate course is believed to be that of the corporate world and government officials adept in strategic ambiguity.

A poetic/comic agitator does not debunk but demystifies. The mysteries of human enmeshment with technology must be revealed more than concealed; insightful questions turned up more than technologies torn down. The poet seeks dialogue more than destruction. True, there is a body of literature in rhetoric that suggests conditions in which a confrontational approach works (e.g., Scott 1968; Scott and Smith 1969), but these works address shifts toward student and civil rights. Confrontation serves as a necessary "justificatory" strategy in those movements. A certain dogmatism is necessary and expected so as to reinforce the values of the committed followers. However, the shift to poetics will not benefit from a dogmatic frame and debunking tactics. Those seeking the shift are not typically from an "out" group in society, thus the incorporation of confrontational strategies is not so credible. Poetic demystification of science and technology is more likely to get a hearing than a strong denunciation of the same.

To complete the program, poetic/comic advocates must work toward getting their language in legislation. Burke reminds us of the difficulty in such a task, because of "the grim fact that so many government bureaus, in response to the pressure of private lobbies, function as representatives of the very interests whose excesses they were nominally designed to control" (1971, 19). One problem is that legislation is enacted at local, state, and federal levels in ways that tend to favor "groups" over society as a whole. Another problem is that legislators are themselves trapped in the same hyper-technological consciousness that plagues other segments of society. Consequently, the average legislator automatically sees industrial "growth" as positive, since it correlates with "jobs," "progress," and so on. The task of the poet-advocate is to contrast industrial growth with ecological growth and to word legislation such that it linguistically loosens technology's grip on decision making.

Education, agitation, and legislation, persuasively enhanced by poetic action and a comic frame, are critical paths toward the fruition of a new orientation. This poetic "art of living" gains vitality in attitudes, life through language, and spreads through actions. Amid the scientific-technological-economic babble, it is inspiring and therapeutic to think along poetic and comic lines, but those thoughts must be taken *through language to action* for the Poetic Way to become meaningful for the masses, and perhaps free some souls from a life of quiet desperation.

The Dawn of a Poetic Age

Though the goal in this chapter has not so much been to spark a social movement as it has been to provide the reader a poetic moment, the rhetorical requirements to be met by all working for an orientation shift are similar to those faced by movement leaders. Simons argues that a movement leader must attract an organized group of followers, must gain approval for their "product" by the larger society, and must react to the resistance generated by the larger structure (1970, 3–4). His hope for leaders who "embody a higher wisdom" (10) is consistent with the present poetic program, as are Lee Thayer's ideas on leaders creating "alternities," visions of a world *other* than it is. "It is the leader's stories that *mediate*, for all those who would follow, an alternative way of being, doing, knowing, having, or saying in the world. It is the leader who, in the stories he or she tells, and in his or her unique way of telling them, kindles human and social alternity" (1988, 260). The poetic/comic path needs leadership, though it is not certain at this time that it will look good on a résumé.

In the relatively short span of time since the industrial revolution, the scientific rationalization has developed into a habit that appears impossible to break. With its cluster of associates—technological, economic, and quantitative psychoses, made acute by the "cult of new needs"—the scientific rationalization has bred *pollution* in wasteful modes of production, *alienation* in a highly specialized clutter of gadgetry where few "experts" share the secrets, and the *guilt* of not knowing enough in the constant media bombardment of "fast-food information" (filling but not too nutritious). Pro-technology is an attitude that pays, but it robs people of flexibility, as it reduces choices to actions that are efficient, time saving, money saving, practical, and profitable. It narrows the range of human roles, encouraging people to act as good cost-benefit analysts.

A poetic art of living holds aesthetic and ecological concerns above the instrumental-economic anxieties that goad the industrialized world. The poetic enhances appreciation of Nature and the rapture of living, envisioning humans as something more than profit-taking, privilege-seeking animals. It reveals each life *qualitatively* as a drama aspiring toward transcendence, rather than quantifying life as an ongoing ledger of material holdings, earnings, and assets. The poetic seeks beauty more than utility, in the ecology more than the economy.

Poetic and comic correctives are needed to counter the rapid mutation of counternature before it reaches the "end of the line"—its perfection—where the merger of mind and machine will leave no need for a poem.

Part IV

Philosophical Extensions

9

Instruments of His Own Making

Burke and Media

Robert S. Cathcart

Burke's theory of dramatism has been increasingly subjected to examination by those considering its relevance in a technologized age of information (see Simons 1989; Oravec 1989; David Williams 1989; Klumpp 1989; Chesebro 1990; and Brock 1990a). Chesebro, for example, concludes his paper "Dramatizing Technology" with the question, "Can technology be dramatized, given the theories, concepts, and techniques available within a dramatistic approach?" (1990, 3). I wish to address this question, but in a slightly different form: Can dramatism be technologized, that is, be reconceptualized and revitalized, to a point where it can become the necessary critique in a world dominated by the technological media of communication?

Prior to analyzing the role of dramatism in a technological world, it is necessary to consider Burke's position vis-à-vis this question and to understand why it is that he has not provided us with a clear guide into the postmodern age. It is important that we separate out Burke's own feelings about technology from his dramatistic concept of criticism.

Burke's Skeptical View of Technology

Burke has secured a preeminent position in philosophy and rhetoric and has been a major contributor to literary criticism. But what is the future of Burkean dramatism in a world where literature, specifically poetry, is being supplanted by video and cinematic images and where political rhetoric is conducted by telephone, fax, and TV spots? It is interesting to note that Burke, the critic, has grown increasingly skeptical about his dramatistic system of analysis leading "Towards a Better Life" and more concerned with waging a guerrilla war against technology. With dark skepticism he writes, "The Logological view of this situation is that no political order has yet been envisaged, even on paper, adequate to control the *instrumental* powers of Technology" ([1937] 1984, 424). In *Towards Helhaven: Three Stages of a Vision*, he exclaims, "Frankly, I enroll myself among those who take it for granted that the compulsiveness of man's technological genius, as compulsively implemented by vast compulsions of our vast technologic grid, makes for a self-perpetuating cycle quite beyond our ability to adopt any major reforms in our ways of doing things" (1971, 19).[1] Chesebro also sees this change in Burke and describes Burke's growing skepticism: "For Burke ([1937] 1984), technology now requires that a critic maintain a sustained skepticism. Burke's explicit concern for the development of idealistic and humanistic goals and programs has been displaced by a sustained skepticism, a need to debunk and to deconstruct societal constructions featuring technology" (1990, 2).

We can better understand Burke's doubts and his antipathy toward technology when we examine his views on scientism ("The Technological Psychosis") within his three distinct rationalizations in human history: magic, religion, and science.

Magic was the rationalization by which man got control over the primitive forces of nature. . . . Religion seems to be the rationalization which attempts to control the specifically *human* forces. As civilization became more complex, a highly delicate code of human cooperation was needed. Religious thought became the device in the mental sphere for ordering cooperative habits under complex conditions. We are now concerned with a third great rationalization, science, the attempt to control for our purposes the forces of technology, or machinery. (Burke [1935a] 1984, 44)

At the center of scientism is "the technological psychosis. . . . [it] is the one psychosis which is, perhaps, in its basic patterns, contributing a new principle to the world. It is at the center of our glories and our distress" (44). Although Burke treats these three stages as determined by changing needs in a changing world, he has always been deeply suspicious of the technology aspects of the science stage— not surprising for a man who, while living less than fifty miles from New York City, refused to install electricity until the 1950s and running water until the late 1960s.

In Burke's later years technology replaced fascism as the demon to be confronted by the humanist critic: *"Hyper-technologism* continues to set the pace for mankind's way of life. And the most violent of Communist and Fascist revolutions are far from the depths of radicalism . . . associated with modern, industrial, financial, and political ambitions" (Burke 1971, 19). Chesebro describes this evolution in Burke's attitudes:

In the early 1980s, technology is cast by Burke as one of the two major perspectives dominating society. . . . Hence, from a symbolic viewpoint, Burke's perception of reality has shifted from one of multiple perspectives . . . to his most recent conception of reality, a reality dominated by only two forces in opposition—the individual is pitted against technology. . . . Technology is no longer viewed as an instrument potentially capable of achieving idealistic and humanistic ends . . . as an instrument which could be used for either good or evil. . . . By 1983, technology had become for Burke (Burke [1937] 1984, 379), one of "two perspectives," in which the "instrumental" perspective created by technology is cast in opposition, or "quite at odds," to a "personalistic," democratic, or idealistic perspective. (1990, 2)

In *Attitudes toward History* Burke claims that capitalism creates mercantilists whose interests and profits are pursued at the expense of the nation. "Technology, as driven by the necessities of capitalism [results in a] dubious kind of 'profit' that exports two-dollar wheat and gets in exchange a Dust Bowl" ([1937] 1984, 150). He goes on to explain that capitalism leads to "self interest" and to "alienation"— "that state of affairs wherein man no longer 'owns' his world because, for one reason or another, it seems basically *unreasonable"* (216).

Burke's concerns with technology have heightened with the coming of the "Information Age." He seems to confirm what many fear, that technology is out of control and humans may be unable to stop the destruction of the universe. This has led some to interpret Burke (perhaps too simplistically) to mean that the postmodern or humanist critic must attack or reject technology (Brock 1990a). It is obvious, however, that technology will not disappear, nor will we return to a past when life revolved around a homogenous community of place and where literary criticism was the highest calling of the critic.

Gaining a Perspective on Technology

Technology is not something distinct from the environment or just another tool in our environment. Technology *is* our environment. Humans have been developing technologies since before recorded history, fulfilling what seems to be a natural desire to create instruments that extend the human reach and harness the forces of nature. The technologies of human communication exist as an unbroken line—from cave paintings to print to television to computers—shaping human thought and action. The struggle to define and establish human values has always been framed by the times *and the technologies* that circumscribe human existence.

What has changed is the rapidity of technological development. In less than one hundred years we have moved from an industrial age to an information age. In even less time, the dominant medium of communication has shifted from print to electronic. These explosive changes have led to the creation of mass culture (for the first time) and the relocation of social and political power. We have reached a stage where technologies are no longer simple instruments extending an individual's strength and reach. Technology is now created, financed, and distributed mainly by huge multinational corporations. Some technologies have passed beyond the control of individuals and even elites who could, in the past, for example, use the technology of print to control large groups of semiliterates.[2] Individual uses of technology have been supplemented by social and global uses of technology, which in turn have resulted in the technological uses of humans. We have even reached the point where technologies can use and reproduce themselves without human intervention.

There certainly are frightening aspects to our present orientation to science and technology, but probably no more frightening than certain aspects of the magic or religion stages Burke claims preceded our present scientism stage. It is difficult to imagine how frightening was a world of magic where such a commonplace as a dead bird was an omen of death, or how frightening a world of religion where an inquisition could bring a sudden and violent end to a lifetime of work and devotion.

The problem for the critic at this point is to accept that the long history of technological growth has come to fruition and at the same time to develop a critical stance recognizing the weaknesses within the science/technology rationalization, thus providing the philosophical corrective to advance to the next stage. This transition will not be achieved by those who believe technology, like the church of the Middle Ages, can be brought low through a renaissance of "poetic humanism,"[3] or by those collectivists who believe a "critical school" of media criticism can weaken competitive capitalism and place the control of technology in the hands of "the people."[4] A contemporary dramatistic stance requires the critic to reject the notion that technology alone is the enemy and that *media* technologies are only material tools—only action not motion. The means to this end can be found in the dramatistic philosophy of Kenneth Burke, but only if the new critic can transcend the limits of a literary/print bias that proscribed much of Burke's application of his dramatism.

Burke's Literary Bias

Burke's fear of technology cum scientism and his reluctance to accept the fact that imprintation (writing and printing) are technological media, however, do not negate Burke's philosophy of language and symbolic action (rhetoric) or make it inapplicable as a conceptual basis for analyzing and evaluating our more modern media of communication—cinema, radio, television, and computer. It is necessary to point out where Burke's biases, both intentional and unintentional, have stood in the way of applying his theories to modern mass media and to discuss his concepts of form, function, and identification to indicate why it is appropriate and necessary for the contemporary critic to move beyond the limitations set in *The Philosophy of Literary Form* in search of a dramatistic philosophy of media form.

It is understandable that Burke's writings do not include the technological media of communication as symbolic action. He, like other literary critics, is working from a literary (print technology) perspective on the world. For Burke there is no faith greater than his faith in poetry—that literary form which embodies a complete acceptance of *the magic of written language.*[5] Burke's orientation is toward and from the written word. His métier is literary criticism. The scene for his symbolic study is mutatis mutandis the printed page, a viewpoint that is continually reflected in his work. "It has long been *written* into the nature of the universe; and eventually it must be *written* into the basic patterns of the State" ([1935a] 1984, 62, emphasis added). For Burke, writing and printing (that medium he must use to make his case for language as symbolic action) seem to fall outside his category of technological media. Burke accepts the close tie between tools and language; implements "become a kind of 'second nature,'" and "language is a species of action, symbolic action—and its nature is such that it can be used as a tool" (13–15), but he does not accept the reverse, that some tools (such as media technology) can be both motion and action. Human toolmaking propensities and the resulting network of materials and technology are, for Burke, part of the "property structure." Tools can be only instrumental. Language, too, can be instrumental, but it is primarily symbolic—"the essence of human motivation, the collective means of expression" (15).

Clearly, in *Permanence and Change* ([1935a] 1984), Burke separates implements (tools) from symbol making (action from motion) and connects technology with tools (implements as property). While he makes references to "'Big Technology' ('the new weapons [that] threaten to undo us,')" (20) and "'technological psychosis' [a *pronounced character* of the mind]" (44–47), he never makes clear the connections (or separations) among industrial technology, communicative technology (communicative media), toolmaking/toolusing, and property, nor does he consider their effects on language and symbols. Put another way, Burke does not address specifically how the technological media of communication—an integral part of our using (or misusing) symbols—affect the symbolic process itself. He considers all technological media of communication (with the exception of print language) implements of transmission, that is, channels of information transportation, which have little symbolic import beyond that given to them through the verbal symbols we attach.

Burke ridicules McLuhan's (1964) aphorism "the medium is the message," with the following example:

Primus rushes up breathlessly to his friend Secundus, shouting, "I have a drastic message for you. It's about your worst enemy. He is armed and raging and is—" whereupon Secundus interrupts: "Please! Let's get down to business. Who cares about the contents of a message? My lad, hasn't McLuhan made it clear to you? The *medium* is the message. So quick, tell me the really crucial point. I don't care what the news is. What I want to know is: Did it come by telegraph, telephone, wireless, radio, TV, semaphore signals, or word of mouth?" The moral of my tale is simple. (1966b, 413–14)

The moral of the tale may be simple, but our symbolic processes are more complex. Our everyday experiences indicate that humans do care about and do consider the medium of communication (see Campbell 1983). In times of natural catastrophe, for example, people attach much more symbolic significance to messages (i.e., they are more likely to act on messages) reaching them through the media of radio and television than to those presented face to face by a human messenger. Also, consider the import of the dictum, "Put it in writing."

A medium is not only a channel or channels of communication but also a learned, shared, and arbitrary system of symbols through which human beings interact and communicate. The languages (the visual images) of television and film are a symbol system capable of dramatistic results in their own right and possess all the elements of a linguistic form (see Rogers 1986 and Campbell 1983). Not that the verbal and print content of such media is unimportant, but neither is the medium of communication unimportant or without its symbolic uses. A technological medium is not a neutral instrument to be manipulated and orchestrated at will. Rather, it is a potent system of symbols that transfers data and information and simultaneously alters the way human beings conceive of reality and perceive of themselves and others.[6] Thus, language and medium represent coexisting and reciprocal means of communication (see Gumpert and Cathcart 1990).

Symbolic action, central to Burkean dramatism, has come to mean what it does for Burke largely because of the technological medium of print, which gives form to so much of our symbolic system. When he refers to instruments of our own making that have separated us from our nature, he overlooks the instruments of written language—tools for preservation of the word: an alphabet, type set, paper, books, libraries—and the symbolic action inherent in this medium. Writing and printing require the use of technological implements for their existence. The alphabet, the pen, the typewriter, and the printing press are the instruments of our own making. The alphabet and print technology have done more than all other instruments to separate us from our nature. Though Burke often distinguishes oral presentation (performance) from poetry, writing, and drama, he does not address the role of print and writing, per se, in shaping human discourse and symbolic action.

It is almost impossible for us to conceive what human discourse (symbolic action) would be if there had never been an alphabet or any means of fixing and preserving language signs. There are still a few primitive societies untouched by literacy (and thereby untouched by any philosophy of literary form or any other philosophy of language for that matter), and we know little about their symbol making except in cases where we have been able to render their spoken language into some print semblance that can be studied for its grammar and syntax. Such analyses, of course, immediately remove us from the actual meanings and symbolic practices of these peoples. Even the most primitive people (considered primitive because they do not have *print* technology), however, have used and do use instruments of communication (technology) to transcend time and space—petroglyphs, paintings, weavings, drumbeats, and so forth. These symbolic forms and their instrumentalities also remove primitive peoples from their nature.

Burke, in *Language as Symbolic Action*, explains his preference for separating human linguistic verbalization from human instrumentalities of communication.

In saying that the human powers of symbolicity are interwoven with the capacity for making tools . . . we still haven't answered one objection. . . . In choosing *any definition at all*, one implicitly represents man as the kind of animal that is capable of definition (that is to say, capable of symbolic action). Thus, even if one views the powers of speech and mechanical invention as mutually involving each other, in a technical or formal sense one should make the implications explicit by treating gifts of symbolicity as the "prior" member of the pair. (1966b, 14)

While the power of speech is undoubtedly prior to all human action, the instruments of language, the alphabet, and other media of communication have become part of our symbol making and using (Gumpert and Cathcart 1990). Once these media of communication become operational, it is pointless to speak of what is "prior." Symbolizing does not exist in some pristine state fully formed and developed unrelated to our technologies of communication.

In his "Notes on the Phenomenology of Media," Haynes has pointedly questioned attempts to separate the dominant media of communication from the symbolizing process:

The media through which thoughts are expressed in a culture affect the nature of those thoughts. Because we know how to read and write (and therefore have a literate bias), the point inevitably remains somewhat obscure: if we did not, and if we were unaware of the existence of a process by which ideas could be recorded permanently in symbols on the pages of books, how would we think, what would we think, indeed, what would our lives be about? And what would it be like to speak with others? And what *could* it be like? (1988, 72)

We live in a literate world and our symbol making and symbol using seem "naturally" a part of a print world that has always been that way. As Haynes points out, "Without writing, we could not even, for instance, give meaning to our place in time, for there would be no calenders. Life might be quite pleasant without calenders, but as creatures of a world where time is recorded, we will never know. The point is instructive . . . , it suggests the profundity of the change in the nature of human consciousness brought about by the change in the dominant media of communication" (71).

That there could be a world where print is not the dominant medium seems almost unthinkable—cannot be thought of in other than literary metaphors—if one makes a narrow literary-poetic application of Burkean dramatism. When Burke discusses language and people's symbol making as action, he tends to see the printed word as the only vehicle for symbolization. He is very much in the tradition of Plato. In Plato's view, and in the view of some academics, written (not oral) language is the only appropriate vehicle for the expression of analytic and abstract relationships and for the representation of knowledge gained from the manipulation of abstract symbols (see Havelock 1986 and Scribner and Cole 1981). While Burke himself is well aware of the inroads of modern electronic media as a vehicle for the transmission of information (see his comments on McLuhan), he is less than clear when he describes the role of technological media of communication in the scheme of human symbol making. In the first chapter of *A Rhetoric of Motives*, for example, he discusses the effects of "imagery" in creating "identification."

Taken simply at its face value, imagery invites us to respond in accordance with its nature. Thus, an adolescent eager to "grow up" is trained by our motion pictures to meditate much on the imagery of brutality and murder, as the most noteworthy signs of action in an ideal or imaginary adult world. . . . One can surely expect such imagery to have sinister effects, particularly in view of the fact that the excessive *naturalism* of modern photographic art presents the violence, as nearly as possible, without formal devices that bring out the purely *artistic* or *fictive* nature of such art. There is no difference, in photographic style, between the filming of a murder mystery and the filming of a "documentary." ([1945 and 1950a] 1962, 17–18)

Here, imagery is a mental process provoked by the medium of photography and film and made sinister by the technological form (excessive naturalism) of those media. In contrast, in the same chapter he claims that "the range of images that can be used for concretizing the process of transformation is limited only by the imagination and ingenuity of poets" ([1945 and 1950a] 1962, 12). For Burke, "A poet's identification with imagery of murder or suicide, either one or the other, is, from the 'neutral' point of view, merely a concern with *terms for transformation in general*" (11). Here, imagery is a product of poetic form, but we find no mention of the connection between print technology and poetic form. Certainly Burke is not limiting such "transformation" to oral discourse alone.

Burke is often unclear when he uses the term "medium." In *Language as Symbolic Action* he deals with this issue most directly:

Since practically any artifact can be classified as a medium, and the current widespread use of the term "communication" allows McLuhan to treat any such invention as a medium of *communication*, we might here propose a working distinction, for present purposes. We might speak of *directly* communicative media (such as telephones or television) and *indirectly* communicative media (in the broad sense that cars, refrigerators, foods, clothing, and guns could be called communicative). "Forms" would extend things further (as with the difference between television as a medium of communication and soap opera as a medium of communication). (1966b, 416)

The confusion concerning media channels and media content is evident. While telephones and television provide the electrical and electronic channels of technological media, automobiles, foods, and so on are signs or content and need not have a technological medium interposed between them and the receiver. That is, they are signs to which we attach symbolic meaning beyond their use as tools, and sometimes they can be artifacts to which we can affix verbal messages (license plates, bumper stickers, model names). In that sense, one could say such artifacts are a medium of communication. There is a similar problem with Burke's distinction between television, an electronic medium of communication interposed between a source and a receiver, and soap opera, a dramatic form that realizes its performance in the electronic channels of television and radio but which can also be successfully communicated via print channels (e.g., newspaper and magazine) and iconographic/print channels (e.g., comic strips). Soap opera form, however, cannot be as successfully exploited through poetic/literary (print) channels of communication. In that medium soap opera becomes maudlin and clichéd (flawed) "literature."

In *Permanence and Change* ([1935a] 1984), "language is a communicative medium" (36), and there is "the poetic medium of communication" (66) and "a sound communicative medium" (163), all subsumed by "the communicative medium" (xlix). In *Language as Symbolic Action* (1966b), Burke refers to the "various *media* of symbolism" (52), "an artistic medium," and "the 'static' media (painting and sculpture)" (417). In none of these references does he mean by "medium" a technology interposed between a sender and a receiver, nor is he concerned with channels and information. Rather, Burke views "language" as *the medium*. For Burke, language can be a communicative medium (i.e., it can be factual, descriptive, informative, reportive, etc.), and it can be a poetic medium (i.e., it can be transcendent, universal, motivational, etc.). Language for Burke is a "medium" that can be both instrumental and symbolic. In contrast, communicative media can be "direct" and "indirect," as noted above, but they must always have "content" (language symbols), and it is content that interests Burke rather than the medium that gives form (meaning?) to this content. He bases his discussion of the state of the communicative medium on what he calls the "profession of writing" and describes how writers have adjusted to the "master psychosis" (technology) and allowed poetry to ebb. He does not consider that a true communicative medium, even in an electronic age, can be any other than written.

Burke's position on media is similar to those who maintain that technology is just another form of toolmaking humans have developed and that it does not determine human thought and action. Rather, human needs, desires, and interests determine how tools (technology) are to be used. Paradoxically, Burke must rely on print technology (a tool) to maintain and validate his literary position—a position which in turn is derived from a "linear" thought process that is dependent upon being able to fix and preserve language in print form.

Burke recognizes the thought versus the language/form dilemma in the works of Marshall McLuhan but not in his own work: "McLuhan himself gives a lineal theory of steps into the mechanical age and through it into the electric age. Maybe he'd probingly concede that on this score, his own book (in being printed) is necessarily a somewhat obsolescent way of heralding the anti-Gutenberg future" (Burke 1966b, 418). Though facetious here, Burke nonetheless admits the possibility of the existence of a process of lineality related to the medium of print. There is support for this in his critique of McLuhan:

In *Understanding Media* we find him [McLuhan] concerning himself with the notion that one kind of character is a better fit for television, another kind a better fit for radio. . . . The point is not that a given medium (in the sense of a directly communicative form) does its full work upon us *without* the element of "content." Rather, his study of the difference between painting (or sculpture) and poetry indicates how expert practitioners of a given medium may resort to the kind of contents that the given medium is best equipped to exploit. (416)

Note Burke's references to "expert practitioners" exploiting the capabilities of a medium. He implies any technological medium is a tool available to the *practitioner of language* to utilize to its best. In this view, media are tools for completing the job (of communicating symbols), not a process that creates unique languages and forms which shape the practitioner (cause the practitioner to view the world and develop the message in ways determined by the technology) and shape the message (certain kinds of contents can be developed only by means of certain media).

McLuhan and his colleague Edmund Carpenter, however, indicate that a given medium has its own language and contents that exploit the practitioner. "Media differences . . . mean that it's not simply a question of communicating a single idea in different ways but that a given idea or insight belongs primarily, though not exclusively, to one medium, and can be gained or communicated best through that medium" (Carpenter and McLuhan 1968, 439). And "Each medium, if its bias is properly exploited, reveals and communicates a unique aspect of reality, of truth. Each offers a different perspective, a way of seeing an otherwise hidden dimension of reality. . . . New essentials are brought to the fore, including those made invisible by the 'blinders' of old languages" (445).

One of the difficulties the contemporary critic faces in applying Burke's theory of dramatism to the modern electronic media of communication is Burke's insistence on the separation of images and language. He places "artistic," "static," or "indirect" media in categories quite separate from "direct" communicative media but insists that these, like direct media, must be "read" and interpreted in a narrative or linear way.

Works such as painting and sculpture first confront us in their totality, then we impart a kind of temporal order to them by letting the eye rove over them analytically, thus endowing them with many tiny "histories": as we go from one part to another, feeling the developments and the relationships among the parts. But although no work can come to life as an artistic medium unless we, by our modes of interpretation, sympathetically and "empathically" (or "imaginatively") endow its *positions* and *motions* with the quality of *action*, there is a notable difference between paintings or sculpture on one side and notations for words or music on the other. (1966b, 417)

For Burke, images—pictures, photos—exist only in the realm of motion. When humans interpret these and give them symbolic meaning, they then exert influence as action. In other words, humans respond to all stimuli in the same way, creating a language (i.e., a print language) of symbolic action. It is not the viewer (interpreter) alone, however, who endows visual images (works of art, photography, cinema, and TV) with the quality of action. It is the technological structure and form that engage the viewer in a dialectic which produces a narrative wherein action arises. With traditional pictorial painting and sculpture, it might seem that an accumulation of tiny histories like printed pages produces the narrative form leading to action, but in actuality it is also the technological forms inherent in the medium that allow (require) the viewer to utilize specific interpretive modes.

This point can be better understood when we examine so-called nonrepresentative visual images where artists purposefully manipulate the medium (paint, canvas, film, light, etc.) to ensure that the viewer cannot endow position and motion in a pictorial or linear way. In this case, the viewer must interact with the visual images in ways that the language of that particular form makes possible. The whole of the twentieth-century abstract art movement was committed to making viewers responsive to the art forms of color, texture, space, and so forth as form and not as mere imitation of images that appear on the retina and that have already been categorized in the mind. The same is true of the art of the motion picture where its creator uses cinema technology to pile one image on another or intercut pictures so rapidly that viewers must respond to the form to produce a narrative. It is the form and structure of these visual media that prevent the viewer from standing at an objective distance and reading the message as though it were on a printed page. The technology of a visual medium draws the viewer in and requires the interpreter to use the language of that medium.

Burke points out that different frameworks of interpretation lead to different conclusions about what reality is. He sees symbolic action as grounded in the realm of the nonsymbolic. While motion is necessary to action, action cannot be reduced to motion. The meaning of a sentence, for example, is not reducible "to its sheer physical existence as sound in the air or marks on the page, although material motions of some sort are necessary for the production, transmission, and reception of the sentence" (Burke [1935a] 1984, 36). The same can be said for any technological media of communication. Each, as tools or implements, represents motion, and the media text (a medium's intrinsic forms) is a language that is the basis for the symbolic meanings that humans attach to them—thus, action.

Burke, while not directly subscribing to the concept of media as motion and action, agrees that different frameworks of interpretation alter our interpretations of reality and thus that motives are derived from our communicative forms. Note his position in *Permanence and Change:*

The question of motive brings us to the subject of communication, since motives are distinctly linguistic products. We discern situational patterns by means of the particular vocabulary of the cultural group into which we are born. Our minds, as linguistic products, are composed of concepts (verbally molded) which select certain relationships as meaningful. Other groups may select other relationships as meaningful. These relationships are not *realities*, they are *interpretations* of reality—hence different frameworks of interpretation will lead to different conclusions as to what reality is. ([1935a] 1984, 35)

Dramatism and the New Criticism

It is important for the critic to recognize that Burke's perspective on symbol using, despite his literary/print bias, has shifted over the years from a narrow epistemic view to one that combines the epistemic and ontological into a dialectical mode of confronting a work. Describing Burke's ontological-epistemic shift, Chesebro sees this development as an opportunity to reassess Burke's position and to utilize dramatism as the critical stance in the media age. He points out:

Without overstatement, it is now possible to argue that the electronic media constitute a distinct reality which has displaced experientially understood reality. The most challenging task for the rhetorical critic is to reassert and to employ the distinction between epistemic and ontological, to specify what is real and what has been constructed through human symbol-using, to identify the symbolic-constructions which mislead, and to isolate the range of life-affirming options which can be employed to enhance the quality of life. (1988, 186–87)

If we take dramatism as a critical stance, shorn of Burke's literary/print bias and technological antipathy, and apply it to our postmodern world, we will see that it provides the ground on which the critic can grapple with our technological demons in the same way that Burke dealt with fascist authorities.[7] Dramatism is a recognition that language mediates between the mind and reality, that rhetorical appeal is dependent upon how practitioners excite and satisfy forms that the mind learned by experiencing patterns in nature and art. Even though much of Burke's method of analysis was developed through his study of language and literature, his theory of dramatism can be applied to any area of artistic endeavor and more specifically to the imaging of contemporary communicative media. In his article "Dramatic Form—Tracking Down Implications," Rod explains that Burke's system can be used in relation to nonverbal as well as verbal art forms: "A work is a structure of interrelated terms, and we experience the work *in terms* of these terms. ('Terms' in this sense need not be exclusively verbal, or ever verbal at all. A painting for instance, may be experienced *in terms* of colors and visual forms)" (1982, 24).

Burke initially developed his system through his analysis of literature, grounding many of his ideas of language in verbal text, but at the same time he was deeply concerned with uncovering the underlying conflicts taking place within the rhetor which are acted out symbolically through the rhetor's communication with the external world and evidenced in a variety of communication acts (poems, plays, speeches, symphonies, political tracts, etc.). Burke understood that "all competent art is a means of communication" and would therefore qualify as a fitting subject to be dealt with rhetorically within his framework of analysis. "There is rhetoric like an oration. There is rhetoric like a treatise or a manual on oratory. And there is rhetoric like the analysis of one particular work or figure and/or its use" ([1931] 1957, 73). He acknowledged that the suasive progressive power found in a work of literature or drama was also found in the suasive power of an artwork designed to create an affective change in the viewer. He claimed: "A work of art is a *development* or *transformation* that proceeds *from* something, *through* something, *to* something" (1942, 15).

The critic, by including the grammar and syntax of a communicative medium as part of the language we humans use in the process of symbol making and symbol using (or misusing), can better understand how aesthetic and ethical perspectives are being altered.[8] By decentering the subject and recognizing the structuration of meaning in our present world, one can better apply and appreciate the utility of dramatism as a critical approach. Though Burke is wedded to a verbal-literary view, he has pointed the way to deconstructing the symbolic reality of the image and to the utilization of a semiotic-type analysis to produce a critique that reveals human artistry or devilry.

Despite Burke's trepidations about technology and his restricted view of communicative media, his dramatistic system anticipated (predated) much of the work of the deconstructionists and postmodernists. Burke anticipates the recent ideological turn for many critics (see Wander 1983) by refusing to adopt the positivist's "neutral" stance. According to Fletcher, "He includes himself in the symbolic action of his own arguments. He enters his own discourse as its hero, and dwells there. If the word autobiography did not normally refer to past events, we could say that he has been busy writing his intellectual biography. We could even believe that his life has been what we see in his accumulated body of texts, each of which is a testimony to his presence at the moment of composition" (1982, 162).

Chesebro has recognized the potential that Burke's dramatism offers for a new critique: "The future stance of the dramatistic critic will mimic postmodern philosophy and the techniques of the deconstructive critic. . . . [I]f the transformations revealed in Burke's writings are any indication, technology will blur the distinctions between the dramatistic and deconstructive critics" (1990, 3).

Dramatism and deconstruction come together where critics recognize that technological media of communication are also symbol systems, not only material (property), but languages capable of artistic (poetic) form and motion as well as action (media language can be both instrumental and symbolic). What are the languages of the communicative media, and what forms do they take as symbolic action? These are the questions the dramatism critic must address to come abreast of the current modes of human communication. The language and forms of print technology will no doubt remain with us, just as oral language and its forms persisted long after the invention of print and the alphabetic form. But the print form (literature) and its subsequent logic of reality will no longer dominate. The deconstructionists have already begun the undoing of traditional literary criticism, and the postmodernists are examining new ways of constructing symbolic reality.

It is the recognition of and acceptance of the electronic-cinematic obliteration of proclaimed mass and high culture forms (Kaplan 1987) that most distinguish the postmodern critic from the traditional literary critic. For the postmodern critic the "poetic" has been replaced by the "popular." As Grossberg (1988, 180) explains, "the popular" is precisely the site of the most powerful postmodern forms, not only in textual forms, but in relations between the text and insertion into people's everyday lives. It is the way real people experience popular texts that is important. These texts are inserted into real experience and used to make sense of ordinary lives. He goes on to say: "Postmodern forms are empowering because we do not know what matters, but we do know that *something does*, and that is what is important. This reduces ideology to affect, and becomes a way of negotiating ordinary lives, and an impossible relation to the future" (180).

Postmodernist Baudrillard suggests we no longer live in a Marxist "drama of alienation," but we live in an "ecstacy of communication." He claims we have moved from Freud's universe of the sexual self to the universe of seamless communication that exposes and consumes everything. "Everything is reduced to image, a celebration of the look. Instead of living under the 'sign of alienation,' we now live in a perpetual present that moves away from representation and private interiority" (1983, 128–30). A relentless stream of media information destroys the boundaries of the real and the imaginary and makes nonsense of the signifier and the signified. Baudrillard goes on to state: "Postmodern forms are not merely signs of historic reality but are historic reality itself. Modern iconic communication makes the signifier (the surface) redundant as the image (the sign) becomes the reality" (131).

In her study of MTV, "Pop Stars and Cola Advertising," Rogers examines the nature of video form, revealing its blurring of signified and signifier:

All the above [Bon Jovi's "Bad Medicine," George Michael and Aretha Franklin's "I Knew You Were Waiting," and Phil Collins's "Groovy Kind of Love"] militate against traditional narrative structure. There is no narrative position from where the action unfolds. The artist tells (sings) the scenario, acts it out and watches simultaneously. Editing style mimics Hollywood genres, documentary cliches and home video/movie effects. Both result in the flattening out of the real and image distinction. Within the video text it is unclear what is image and what is the internal "reality." (1989, 50)

With "reality" being constantly blurred by the electronic and cinematic image, the belief there must always be a sign (verbal), a signifier (linguistic symbol), and a spectator to interpret verbal symbols in terms of a historic reality is being called into question. Verbal language signified by its print form gives us a sense of the past, present, and future, with meaning derived from the use of linguistic signifiers. In the postmodern environment, signifieds—images pressed upon us by filmic and electronic media—have forms and meanings quite different from the forms and meanings found in verbal texts.[9]

The notion of "form" has always been one of the most important aspects of Burkean dramatism. Burke has convincingly demonstrated that it is form rather than verbal content that produces action rather than motion. The most important aspect of dramatism, and what makes it most applicable to contemporary mass media, is its focus on form rather than content alone to reveal the processes of symbolic action. When we look to form to reveal symbolic action, we have the key to understanding the languages of the new media.

Burke recognizes, implicitly, that form is not restricted to literary/verbal uses but functions rhetorically in all artistic creations. "We can discuss the basic forms of the human mind under such concepts as crescendo, contrast, comparison, and so forth. But to experience them emotionally, we must have them singularized into an example, an example which will be chosen by the artist from among his emotional and environmental experiences" ([1931] 1957, 49).[10]

Burke's theory of symbolic action matured to conclude that form, idea, and art are inseparable. Through his discussion of form, he recognized the universality of dialectical pairs such as association-dissociation and merger-division. Burkean concepts of form can readily be applied to cinematic and video messages. Producers of electronic and filmic rhetoric must also rely on dialectical pairs, and they must utilize both technical form and emotional form to produce the psychological symbolism that in turn produces an art of eloquence. Where there is eloquence, there is dramatism.

As noted by Gumpert and Cathcart: "Growing up literature in contemporary society means that we must adopt the accouterments of language, written and iconic as well as verbal. A medium is not only a channel or channels of communication, but is also a learned, shared and arbitrary system of symbols. That is, it is one of the languages through which human beings interact and communicate in terms of their common cultural experiences and expectations" (1990, 29).

What is needed now is a Burkean "Philosophy of Media Form" to update his *Philosophy of Literary Form*. It is in the forms of communicative media that we will find the ways to understand how rhetoric functions in the information age. Recognizing that there are forms peculiar to each medium of communication will help us understand how individuals and societies come to make meaning of an exceedingly complex and bewildering mass of mediated information.

In no other media of communication do technical form and emotional form come together with such impact as in electronic and cinematic communication. This amalgam of forms is what makes it so difficult to disentangle the content of modern media from their technical forms. The challenge for the modern critic is to grasp the significance of form as the source of meaning in our modern mass media. As suggested, Burkean dramatism anticipates this need by making form the key to understanding artistry and eloquence (Heath 1984).

Burke explains the notion of form as "the creation of an appetite in the mind of the auditor, and the adequate satisfying of that appetite. . . . A work has form in so far as one part leads [us] to anticipate another part, to be gratified by the sequence ([1931] 1957, 31). And "Form and content cannot be separated. . . . [One] can't possibly make a statement without its falling into some sort of pattern" (1966b, 487). According to Heath, Burke's "theory of symbolic action matured to conclude that form, idea, and art are inseparable" (1986, 80).

Conley, examining the development of Burke's vision of the role of communication in human relations, claims that Burke in *Counter-Statement* lays out a "new aesthetic" based on his conception of "form":

Form is a function not of the subject matter but of the psychology of the audience, of "those curves of emotion which, because they are natural, can bear repetition and loss" [Burke (1931) 1957, 36]. The methods of maintaining interest most natural to the psychology of information . . . are surprise and suspense, whereas, "the method most natural to the psychology of form is eloquence" [Burke (1931) 1957, 37]. So, for Burke, "psychology," "form," and "eloquence" are virtually synonymous, and "eloquence . . . becomes the essence of art" [Burke (1931) 1957, 40]. (1990, 270)

Conley explains further: "The mechanism invented to reproduce the original mood of the artist can be considered to take both an emotional form, in the symbol, and a 'technical form,' the sort [Burke] discussed in 'Psychology and Form' and analyzes in detail later, in the inventory of basic movements of experience that can be exploited by art" (1990, 270).

Not only does dramatism lead the critic to examine the intricate blending of emotional and technical form characteristic of modern media, but its insistence that "text" is more than the formal relationship of words with ideas points the critic in an ontological direction where symbols and stimuli are intertwined. Dramatism seeks out "text," not just in the verbal narrative, but in all the ways object, event, condition, and relationship are interpreted by receivers. In its ontological approach to meanings and motives, Burkean dramatism anticipates the critical work of Fiske (1989) and others who have used semiotics to establish texts and subtexts in the images communicated by modern media. As Jameson describes Burke's approach to text:

Text cannot simply allow reality to persevere in its being outside of itself, inertly, at a distance; it must draw the real into its own texture. . . . Insofar, in other words, as symbolic action—Burke will map it out as "dream," prayer, "or chart"—is a way of doing something to the world, to that degree what we are calling "world" must inhere within it, as the content it has to take up into itself in order to give it form. . . . [T]his simultaneous production and articulation of "reality" by the text is reduplicated by an active, well-nigh instrumental, stance of the text toward the new reality. . . . Such aesthetics of the intrinsic thus reflect the realities of artistic production under the market system itself, and give expression to the free floating portability of artistic texts in search of an impossible public, texts released from the social functionality which once controlled their meanings and uses in pre-capitalistic social formations which have now broken down or been dissolved. (1982, 74–75)

Though Jameson is applying Burkean dramatism to print texts, it is quite clear that the same analysis fits, even more aptly, television and cinematic texts. What is important here is that dramatism moves us away from the notion of a text as a free-floating or universally timeless narrative—an unchanging form. That notion infuses much of the present and past literary criticism but is inadequate to the complexities of the languages and artistry of modern media.

Overlapping Universes

It will not serve us to pass off mediated information as merely knowledge or motion rather than action. Dramatistic analysis integrates the aesthetic, the ethical, and the practical, an appropriate step in the postmodern world, where media forms provide symbol systems that are the bases of symbolic action. By moving dramatism from a strictly verbal/print focus to one more in line with the hyperreality of the postmodernists, it can serve as a critique of mediated communication.

FROM WITHIN OR
FROM OUT OF
THE VAST EXPANSES OF THE
INFINITE WORDLESS UNIVERSE
WE WORDY HUMAN BODIES HAVE CARVED
MANY OVERLAPPING UNIVERSES OF DISCOURSE
WHICH ADD UP TO A
PLURIVERSE OF DISCOURSES
LOCAL DIALECTS OF DIALECTIC

(in Simons and Melia 1989, 263)

Notes

1. "Toward Helhaven" is Burke's projection of a future fictional world where technology and religion are merged and where people have lost control of the symbolic processes that make them human. Though intended to be an ironic view of technology, the work expresses Burke's real fear of a technological future. He ends the essay, "Let there be no turning back of the clock. Or no turning inward. Our Vice-President has rightly cautioned: *No negativism.* We want AFFIRMATION—TOWARDS HELHAVEN. ONWARD, OUTWARD, AND UP!" (1971, 25).

Burke's overwhelming concern for the negative aspects of scientism and technology and his doubts about criticism were noted by Conley in his analysis of Burke's contribution to rhetorical theory: "Recent scholarship has begun to recognize not only how great his contribution to the revival of rhetoric was but also how prophetic Burke really was. But even Burke, in the years just after *A Rhetoric of Motives* was published, seemed to give up the fight" (1990, 277).

2. Crane describes our rapidly evolving new technologies and points to the difficulties of trying to keep abreast: "Technology does not, at least in

this century, stand still. New tools are beginning to address the problems raised by broadcast media—and will doubtless generate their own set of problems in turn. [The latest] hypermedia databases, however, can connect full text, relational databases, motion video, sound, still images, and diagrams together into a single environment. The new technology has the inherent power to provide detailed information for study, to supplement still images and text with motion and sound, and to present complex kinds of information clearly and efficiently" (1990, 32).

3. Brock sees us already making a "shift to a new orientation—Poetic Humanism" (1989, 11). He argues that just as religion transcended magic and science replaced religion, the weaknesses of the current orientation will bring a shift toward Poetic Humanism. Brock claims (17) that Burke has pointed the way toward Poetic Humanism in *Permanence and Change*, where he projects the nature of the new poetic, humanistic orientation: "the view of man as 'poet,' the approach to human motives in terms of action *(with poetic or dramatic terminologies being prized as the paradigms of action, a term that leads happily into the realms of both ethical and poetic piety")* ([1935a] 1984, 168). Burke concludes, "Our thesis is a belief that the ultimate metaphor for discussing the universe and man's relations to it must be the poetic or dramatic metaphor" (263).

4. The "critical school" refers to those media analysts and critics who derive their orientation from the so-called Frankfurt scholars, who argued that the mass media support the established social order by acting as the means of social control and that television in particular is a powerful agent of the dominant ideological apparatus. Early proponents of the "critical" approach were Gramsci (1971), Althusser (1971), and Foucault (1977).

5. In *Permanence and Change* Burke writes, "After all, the devices of poetry are close to the spontaneous genius of man: in framing a corrective philosophy with poetic standards, we should have a point of reference which was in turn 'biologically grounded.'. . . On the other hand, the poetic point of reference is weakened by the fact the poetic medium of communication itself is weakened. The center of authority must be situated in a philosophy, or psychology, of poetry, rather than in a body of poetry. . . . If we are to revise the productive and the distributive patterns of our economy to suit our soundest desires, rather than attempting to revise our desires until they suit the productive and distributive patterns, it would surely be in the region of poetry that the 'concentration point' of human desires should be found" ([1935a] 1984, 66).

Poetry for Burke is not just another literary form but represents a transcendent use of language, leading to the highest form of symbolic action. Reviewing his own evolving concept of symbolic action, he writes autobiographically in the third person: "In keeping with his 'occupational psychosis' as a writer, he thought of such joining in terms of *communication*, which in turn was conceived specifically as ideal *poetic* communication. But whereas he had been mulling over the possibility of a *neutralized* language, a language with no clenched fists, he could not help seeing that Poetry uses to perfection a *weighted* language. Its winged words are weighted words. . . . Later, the author would be able to inquire into the ways whereby a poet can both exemplify group 'weightings' in his use of language and 'transcend' them if the poem follows along a properly ordered series of steps" ([1935a] 1984, liii).

6. Cathcart and Gumpert (1986) examine the ways in which modern media, particularly photography, play a role in the individual's formulation of a self-image. They conclude: "It is our contention that with the invention of photography we embarked on a new era of self awareness in which the notion of self and the process by which we form and develop our self image has been dramatically altered" (100).

7. Chesebro has recognized both the symbolic power of technology and the challenge to the Burkean critic: "Technology is emerging as the foremost symbolic construction. Technology is functioning as an ever-increasing symbolic determinant, affecting all forms of human communication, including our psychological orientation and interpersonal relationships as well as our social, legal, economic and political systems. In the foreseeable future, if Burke's writings are to be our guide, technology and science will be the dramatistic critic's central object of study" (1990, 3).

8. The relationship of media grammars to symbol using is discussed in "A Theory of Mediation": "There is a grammar for each medium based upon the physical-electronic properties which constitute the medium. People acquire grammars, usually informally, of all the media extant in the world at the time they are born. As new media technologies are introduced, persons acquire the new media grammars and become literate in those also" (Gumpert and Cathcart 1990, 29).

9. Jameson deals with the fears of many that postmodernism does away with traditional values and leaves no base for the critic: "To repudiate that ideological tradition, to valorize the decentering of the subject with its optical illusion of centrality, does not, I would argue, have to lead to anarchism or that glorification of the schizophrenic hero and the schizophrenic text which has become one of the latest French fashions and exports; on the contrary, it should signal a transcendence of the older individualism and the appearance of new collective structures and of ways of mapping our own decentered place with respect to them" (1982, 86).

10. Turim examines video as art and concludes: "Video is an art of our future. . . . We have to learn how to play/work with video, how to see the video apparatus not as an entity whose inherent properties determine its limitations but as a tool for diverse art-making projects" (1983, 137).

10

<hr>

The Evolution of Kenneth Burke's Philosophy of Rhetoric

Dialectic between Epistemology and Ontology

Bernard L. Brock

During his over seventy years of scholarly writing, which has included eight major books as well as hundreds of articles on rhetoric, Kenneth Burke's focus has gradually shifted from epistemology toward ontology. Within this philosophical context, Burke expanded the number of key terms he used to describe his system of thought, from just "dramatism" to both "dramatism" and "logology" (Brock et al. 1985, 22). Arguing for the shift, Burke states: "In my early book in 1935, *Permanence and Change*, I used rhetoric and ontological as synonymous terms. Later, I had to modify this equation; I made the shift in my 1968 article 'Dramatism'" (Brock et al. 1985, 22). Later, Burke explains the nature of the shift: "Though my aim is to be secular and empirical, 'dramatism' and 'logology' are analogous respectively to the traditional distinction (in theology and metaphysics) between ontology and epistemology" (Burke 1985a, 89). This change in his system has been discussed in a series of articles culminating in James W. Chesebro's "Epistemology and Ontology as Dialectical Modes in the Writings of Kenneth Burke," when Chesebro argued that since 1968, Burke's philosophy has functioned dialectically with ontological and epistemic dimensions operating simultaneously.[1] In this chapter, I trace the dialectical tension between Burke's epistemology and his ontology to understand his philosophical transformation from 1931 to 1990. Specifically, while Burke's early writing developed an epistemology, it simultaneously *reflected* an ontology, and as Chesebro argued, his later work on ontology draws upon this earlier developed epistemology.

In addition to Burke's admitted shift in his approach to rhetoric, there is confusion among scholars over the nature of Burke's philosophy of rhetoric. For example, Fisher and Brockriede classify Burke as a "linguistic realist" (1984, 38), while Cary Nelson describes him as a poststructuralist (1989, 171). Burke himself has contributed to the confusion by refusing to advance a consistent classification for his theory. For example, when asked if he was a postmodernist, Burke answered, "I hope not" (Burke 1990, 6).

In an effort to clarify, this chapter describes the evolution of Kenneth Burke's philosophy of rhetoric, noting the dialectic between epistemology and ontology in all of his major works on rhetoric. It is specifically argued here that Burke's philosophy has changed from an earlier dualistic emphasis in which human symbol using is distinct from but a response to an external reality, to a more unified system in which the human process of symbol using integrates, shapes, and controls both external and internal realities simultaneously. This philosophical evolution is developed, first, by tracing the tension between epistemology and ontology throughout Burke's major works and, second, by comparing key rhetorical concepts in his earlier and later periods. Because Burke does not directly discuss his rhetorical philosophy, it is admittedly necessary to tease his position out of his works critically. Hence, the question ultimately becomes: What philosophy does Burke's shift from epistemology to ontology *reflect?* As we proceed to address this question in this chapter, epistemology is defined as method or "a second order concern with knowledge about knowledge . . . sometimes called 'theory of knowledge'" (Reese 1980, 151), while ontology is defined as "'knowledge of being' and refers to a division of philosophy having such knowledge as its subject matter" (401).

Evolution of Burke's Philosophy

Kenneth Burke's philosophy of rhetoric is typically embedded in his critical essays. Accordingly, because an explicit philosophy is not intended, Burke's philosophical ideas are frequently interrelated, complex, and sometimes fragmentary. Furthermore, concepts that are eventually developed in great detail in one work may be found in differing degrees of development in his other works. These factors make Burke's philosophy difficult to identify.

In spite of these complexities, insight into the evolution of Kenneth Burke's rhetorical philosophy can be gained by viewing his writing in three stages. In his earliest and formative stage, Burke essentially develops an epistemology as he establishes his general approach to criticism. In this stage the relationship between his epistemology and ontology is clearly evident. In the middle period Burke continues to focus on epistemology as he constructs and applies his specialized critical methods. During this period his ontological system is least evident. In his third stage, Burke's attention shifts explicitly to ontology as he casts dramatism as a philosophical system. These stages, which are not perfectly distinct, are based on the focus of Burke's writing at any given time. Nonetheless, the stages are instructive and a useful way of extracting Burke's philosophy of rhetoric.

Critical Realism

During his earliest period (characterized by his first four books on rhetoric: *Counter-Statement, Permanence and Change, Attitudes toward History,* and *Philosophy of Literary Form*), Burke challenged the dominant scientific thought of the time found in the philosophies of materialism and logical positivism. Assuming the role of the critic, Burke offered a dialectic between material reality and symbol using. Providing a critique of existing critical thoughts, he ultimately established, during this stage, a general critical method. His critical approach and method presumed that human symbol using (an epistemic construct) was distinct from and a response to an external reality (an ontological construct), thereby reflecting a philosophy grounded in a form of *critical realism.* Critical realists hold "that there is an objective physical world" and that "the datum, the immediately intuited evidence of reality, cannot be numerically identical with any part of that reality" (*Encyclopedia of Philosophy,* s.v. "critical realism," 261).

Burke's realism also reflects a form of dualism that "divides the world into two categories or types of thing, or uses two ultimate principles of explanation, or insists that there are two substances or kinds of substance" (ibid., s.v. "monism and pluralism," 364). Dualism aptly describes early Burke because he presents most concepts as paired opposites, such as "mind" and "body" and especially "motion" and "action." Critical realists hold "that the data in perception (that is, what is intuited, what we are directly aware of) are not actually part of external objects but are 'character-complexes . . . taken, in the moment of perception, to be the characters of existing outer objects'" (ibid., s.v. "realism," 81). So critical realists, in contrast with behaviorists, stress "that there [is] an intuited mental content, the character complex of which we [are] directly aware" (82). Burke's early critical method is consistent with accepting "intuited mental content." In *Counter-Statement* Burke formally distinguishes between "natural forms" (external reality) and "art forms" (symbolic constructs). For example, Burke distinguishes the components of music as phenomenal and the meaning of music as symbolic:

There is in reality no such general thing as a crescendo. What does exist is a multiplicity of individual art-works each of which may be arranged as a whole, or in some parts, in a manner which we distinguish as climactic. . . . The accelerated motion of a falling body, the cycle of a storm, the procedure of the sexual act, the ripening of crops—growth here is not merely a linear progression, but a fruition. . . . Thomas Mann's work has many such natural forms converted into art forms. ([1931] 1957, 45)

Thus, Burke concludes, "We think in terms of universals, but we feel particulars" (47). For Burke, our symbolic universals and the particulars "we feel" are separate but related entities.

Furthermore, Burke suggests that a separate reality is central to his program for criticism, because he casts communicative acts as distinct reactions to an external "reality": "But art is also historical—a particular mode of adjustment to a particular cluster of conditions. The cluster of conditions is fluctuant (from age to age, from class to class, from person to person) thus calling for changes of emphasis" ([1931] 1957, 107). Burke, then, stresses the importance of the "particular cluster of conditons" or "situation": "This Program . . . would define the function of the aesthetic as effecting an adjustment to one particular cluster of conditions, at this particular time in history. . . . The artist who wrote a novel called *Vive the Dole* would, most probably, find that his work died with the death of the specific situation for which it was written" (121). He notes that artwork is separate from but dependent upon the situation to which it was a response.

More generally, during this period, symbol using is cast as a counterpart to an external reality. As Burke has succinctly put it, a symbol is "the verbal parallel to a pattern of experience" ([1931] 1957, 152) that "appeals either as the orienting of a situation, or as the adjustment to a situation, or as both" (156). Yet, Burke also holds that symbols have intrinsic properties: "When the poet has converted his pattern of experience into a Symbolic equivalent, the Symbol becomes the guiding principle in itself" (157). Yet, Burke's philosophy of rhetoric is not the thrust of *Counter-Statement*. The relationship between form and norms, epistemological issues, dominate the book (vii). He also points out that "counter" is dialectic in nature because it deals with opposite principles (iii), an approach that is definitely consistent with dualism. During this early period, when his primary concern is epistemological, his critical method reflects a dualistic philosophy—symbol using is interaction between "external reality" and "intuited mental content."

Burke's second book in his early period, *Permanence and Change*, also reflects a dualistic philosophy of critical realism. His opening observation and example are illustrative: "We may begin by noting the fact that all living organisms interpret many of the signs about them. A trout, having snatched at a hook but having had the good luck to escape with a rip in his jaw, may even show by his wiliness thereafter that he can revise his critical appraisals" ([1935a] 1984, 5). Here, Burke's example of a trout critically responding to an external reality accepts the duality of "reality" and "intuited mental content."

Permanence and Change is particularly significant, for Burke explicitly defines "reality" as "what things will do to us or for us" ([1935a] 1984, 22). Burke does not hesitate to talk about reality as it interacts with the use of symbols. Indeed, he makes it clear that linguistic products or symbols and reality are distinct but interacting entities: "Our minds, as linguistic products, are composed of concepts (verbally molded) which select certain relationships as meaningful. These relationships are not *realities*, they are *interpretations* of reality—hence different frameworks of interpretations will lead to different conclusions as to what reality is" (35). In the afterword to the third edition of *Permanence and Change*, Burke acknowledges both the dualistic nature of the book (303) and its focus on the epistemic term "analogy" (324).

Burke's third book, *Attitudes toward History*, continues his dualistic philosophy of critical realism. His opening reference to William James reflects a view in which human symbol using is distinct from and a response to an external reality, "to 'accept the universe' or to 'protest against it'" ([1937] 1961, 3). Burke details this position, one in which policies are viewed as a response to reality: "'Acceptance' and 'rejection' . . . then, start from the problem of evil. In the face of anguish, injustice, disease, and death one adopts policies. One constructs his notion of the universe or history, and shapes attitudes in keeping" (3).

During this period, Burke clearly presents humans with "intuited mental content" as responding to an external reality. This can be seen as Burke attributes a degree of ontological status to symbol using itself, for symbol using is not only a response, but it also shapes humans' perception of reality: "We must name the friendly or unfriendly functions and relationship in such a way that we are able to do something about them. In naming them, we form our characters, since the names embody attitudes; and implicit in the attitudes there are the cues of behavior" ([1937] 1961, 4). Yet, the thrust of *Attitudes toward History* remains epistemic. Burke focuses upon frames of thought and ultimately the transcendence of individual to societal thought: "Our emphasis is not upon individual strategy, but upon the productive and mental patterns developed by aggregates" (111). These "mental patterns" are the "intuited mental content" that interacts with "reality" in Burke's critical realism.

The final book of the early period, *Philosophy of Literary Form*, serves as a transition to the second stage of his philosophy. Burke's development of specific rhetorical methods initiates his move away from dualism toward the more unified philosophy hinted at in his second period and characteristic of his third. In the foreword to the second edition Burke indicates that he was "primarily concerned with theories of method" ([1941] 1973, vii). Yet, in the opening essay the dualism of Burke's ontology is still evident: "Critical and imaginative works are answers to questions posed by the situation in which they arose" (1). In this first stage, Burke's dualism consistently presents symbol using as a response to a situation.

Yet *Philosophy of Literary Form* is a transitional work because Burke's focus pulls away from opposites and moves to the symbols themselves. He writes: "They are not merely answers, they are *strategic* answers, *stylized* answers" ([1941] 1973, 1). In the section "Literature as Equipment for Living," Burke extends his analysis into the sociological, in declaring that "social structures give rise to 'type' situations, subtle subdivisions of the relationships involved in competitive and cooperative acts" (293–94). This shift in focus does not change Burke's basic philosophy, but it does signal the centrality of symbols in his second stage.

Viewing Burke's dualistic philosophy of rhetoric as critical realism is consistent with his discussion of the schools of philosophy in *A Grammar of Motives*. He explains that the philosophy corresponding to featuring of "act" in the pentad is realism ([1945] 1969, 128), and there is little question that Burke features "act." Labeling Burke's first stage critical realism is consistent both with David Cratis Williams, who describes Burke as both realistic and dualistic (1989, 212), and with Fisher and Brockriede, who argue that his philosophy is linguistic realism (1984, 35).

In the 1930s, Burke sought to offer a philosophical alternative to the materialism and logical positivism invoked by science. He cast symbolism as a conceptual equivalent to, but discrete domain from, the "reality" scientists claimed to examine. But as symbolism gained philosophical prominence for Burke, he shifted his philosophical emphasis during the next twenty years, and he developed symbol using as a coherent and independent conceptual system.

Conceptualism

In his second stage (including *A Grammar of Motives*, *A Rhetoric of Motives*, and *A Rhetoric of Religion*), Burke's focus is more explicitly epistemic as he develops special critical methods such as the pentad, identification, and terms for order. Burke is most well known for his work during this period because of the popularity of these critical tools. Philosophically, however, this period is pivotal because Burke gradually shifts from dualism to a more unified conceptual system. Ultimately, Burke's focus on symbols, coupled with the pivotal nature of the period, makes an ontology more difficult to extract from his writings.

In this stage, Burke reads very much like a symbolic interactionist. Herbert Blumer, in his "Society as Symbolic Interaction," could be mistaken for Kenneth Burke.

The term "symbolic interaction" refers, of course, to the peculiar and distinctive character of interaction as it takes place between human beings. The peculiarity consists in the fact that human beings interpret or "define" each other's actions instead of merely reacting to each other's actions. Their "response" is not made directly to the actions of another but instead is based on the meaning which they attach to such actions. Thus, human interaction is mediated by the use of symbols, by interpretation, or by ascertaining the meaning of one another's action. (1967, 139)

Furthermore, symbolic interactionists appear to accept Burke as one of their own. For example, Stone and Farberman's *Social Psychology through Symbolic Interaction* frequently refers to Burke under the categories of theoretical trends, attitude, identification, motivation, and secular conversion.

Yet, symbolic interaction does not adequately capture Burke's philosophical position during this pivotal and central stage. The thrust of Burke's work is to present a critique in which dialectic is more internal to language, even though traces of his earlier dualism remain. Burke has definitely modified his critical realist position, but he has not quite established a unitary system of rhetoric. Conceptualism comes closest to describing Burke's philosophy during this period. Reese's *Dictionary of Philosophy and Religion* defines conceptualism and then relates it to both realism and nominalism: "The position with respect to universals . . . that they exist as entities in the mind but have no extra-mental existence. The position stands between the extremes of Nominalism and Realism" (100).

This middle position of conceptualism captures the ambiguity of Burke's second pivotal stage. His position is similar to that of John

Locke, who believed knowledge "rests (1) on the experience of the external world acquired through the senses, and (2) on that of the inner world of psychical happenings achieved through introspection" (*New Encyclopaedia Britannica*, 15th ed., s.v. "Locke," 232). "Conceptualism" is an appropriate term for Burke's middle period, when he established specific rhetorical tools within the context of a theory—for example, the pentad—and moved systematically from one concept to another (*Encyclopedia of Philosophy*, s.v. "concept," 178). This is precisely what Burke does during this second stage.

Burke introduces *A Grammar of Motives* with the question, "What is involved, when we say what people are doing and why they are doing it?" His answer points away from an external reality toward an internal process, suggesting a distancing from the realism of his first stage: "The book is concerned with the basic forms of thought which, in accordance with the nature of the world as all men necessarily experience it, are exemplified in the attributing of motives" ([1945] 1969, xv). This question leads Burke into a discussion of the pentad, his most popular specialized method.

In the first chapter, "Container and Thing Contained," Burke maintains, yet modifies, his earlier dualistic concern for symbol using as a response to a situation, suggesting that "using 'scene' in the sense of setting, or background, and 'act' in the sense of action, one could say that the scene contains the act" ([1945] 1969, 3). Instead of viewing situation and response as separate-yet-interacting entities, Burke begins to unite the two.

In contrast, Burke continues this dualistic assumption in his discussion of substance, which he defines as "subsistence, reality, real being (as applied to mere appearance), nature, essence" ([1945] 1969, 23). Then in a reference to Locke, Burke undercuts the dualism and moves toward the symbol as a unified concept by indicating that the external substance is within the thing, "a word designating something that a thing *is not*. That is, though used to designate something *within* the thing, *intrinsic* to it, the word etymologically refers to something *outside* the thing, *extrinsic* to it" (23). Burke then makes the point that the external is the world itself. "Rather, we take it that men's linguistic behavior here reflects real paradoxes in the nature of the world itself" (56) and that it is reality: "The transformations which we here study as a Grammar are not 'illusions,' but citable realities. The structural relations involved are observable realities" (57). At this point, Burke moves back and forth between dualism and a more unified rhetorical system.

In *A Rhetoric of Motives* Burke's attention is focused on the concept of symbol as he again moves back and forth between his earlier dualism and a more unified approach. After explaining that "scientific knowledge is thus presented as a terminology that gives an accurate and critically tested description of reality" ([1950a] 1969, 41), Burke's concern for the symbol itself as a concept instead of its correspondence to "reality" can be seen in his definition of rhetoric: "For rhetoric as such is not rooted in any past condition of human society. It is rooted in an essential function of language itself, a function that is wholly realistic, and is continually born anew; the use of language as a symbolic means of inducing cooperation in beings that by nature respond to symbols" (43). Then by utilizing "idea" and "image," Burke is able to make the symbolic an internal conception: "sensory images could be said to embody ideas that transcend the sensory" (88). In *A Rhetoric of Motives*, while at times hinting at dualism, Burke is able to move away from accepting the independent nature of an external reality.

In *The Rhetoric of Religion*, the final book of the second period, Burke appears to be totally absorbed in symbol using, approaching a philosophy in which symbols unify internal and external realities. This unity is expressed in the foreword, in which he writes, "Religion has often been looked upon as a center from which all other forms of human motivation gradually diverged" ([1961] 1970, v). In discussing this "unifying principle," Burke also introduces the term "logology": "Thus it is our 'logological' thesis that, since the theological use of language is thorough, the close study of theology and its forms will provide us with good insight into the nature of language itself as a motive" (vi). In fact, Burke disassociates himself from a dualist realism, suggesting that "overly 'naturalistic' views conceal from us the full scope of language as motive, even in the sheerly empirical sense" (10). Ultimately, by focusing on "symbol-systems," Burke is able to unify external and internal elements: "Logologically, our design involved an approach to all terminology from the standpoint of Order as an empirical problem, compounded of non-verbal materials which the symbol-using animal variously manipulates and to which he is variously related by purposive actions conceived in terms of his symbol-systems" (268). Burke unites external "non-verbal materials" and internal "purposive actions" in his "symbol-systems."

However, in *The Rhetoric of Religion* Burke does not completely abandon his dualism; it is reflected in his fourfold definition of the human being as:

1. The symbol-using animal
2. Inventor of the negative
3. Separated from his natural condition by instruments of his own making

4. And goaded by the spirit of hierarchy. ([1961] 1970, 40)

Humans invent the internal, symbolic negative in contrast to positive, external reality. Then the human ability to be separated from natural conditions acknowledges two distinct entities. At this stage Burke is moving away from dualism—symbol using as a response to an external reality—but there are still traces of this earlier philosophy.

Burke's alternating between dualism and a more unified rhetorical system points toward the middle position of conceptualism for this second pivotal period in his philosophy of rhetoric. Burke does not mention conceptualism in discussing the philosophies related to the pentad, but he does associate the related concept of realism with the featuring of "act," and he indicates that nominalism can be an individualistic emphasis related to all the other philosophies he discusses ([1945] 1969, 128–29). The significance of conceptualism for Burke's central and pivotal period will be seen later, when I argue that Burke's special rhetorical tools created in this middle period can be associated with either his earlier epistemology or his later ontology.

Symbolic Coherence

Burke's third stage, marked by the appearance of his 1968 article "Dramatism" and a variety of other essays, provides an ontological foundation for symbol using, a foundation that specifies the natures of nonsymbolic motion and symbolic action as well as internal and external realities. Burke now is postcritical, as his concern is with human symbol using itself. In *Personal Knowledge*, Michael Polanyi defines a postcritical assumption when he argues that "we must accredit our own judgment as the paramount arbiter of all our intellectual performances" and that we are "competent to pursue intellectual excellence as a token of a hidden reality" (1962, 265). At this stage Burke de-emphasizes dualism, for reality and language are unified within symbol using.

The term "symbolic coherence" characterizes the ontological status Burke has attributed to dramatism as a philosophy. Coherence theory is a unified approach to truth: "To say that a statement (usually called a judgment) is true or false is to say that it coheres or fails to cohere with a system of other statements; that it is a member of a system whose elements are related to each other by ties of logical implication as the elements in a system of pure mathematics are related" (*Encyclopedia of Philosophy*, s.v. "coherence theory of truth," 130). Burke's third stage reflects such a unified theory because he constructs a symbolic system by relating terms to each other. This coherence is best illustrated in his diagram entitled "Cycle of Terms Implicit in the Idea of 'Order'" in *The Rhetoric of Religion* ([1961] 1970, 184). Burke further suggests its coherent nature when he states, "We see the theological way of merging the principle of the natural order with the principle of verbal contract" (186).

Burke's decision to de-emphasize dualism in favor of a coherence approach to symbol using is evident in his arguments that humans learn language "by analogic means" (Brock et al. 1985, 23) and that "by learning language, the human body, a composite creature, combines the realms of nonsymbolic motion and symbolic action" (32). The unification of Burke's theory is vividly reflected in his phrase "bodies that learn language" as a description of the human being. Similarly, Roderick Chisholm posits that there is "a being for whom all truths are evident, but also, that each of us is identical with that being, and therefore with each other" (1966, 113).

Symbol, in logic and science, "is normally used in the sense of an abstract sign" (Reese 1980, 563), and symbolism "refers to the system of symbols employed or to the fact that behaviour is patterned in symbolic fashion in those cases where it is so patterned" (*Encyclopedia of Philosophy*, s.v. "symbolism," 711). The term "symbolic" describes Burke's approach because symbol using is at the center of his concern for "animals that learn language (symbols)." Burke further explains, "Action, as so defined, would involve modes of behavior made possible by the acquiring of a conventional, arbitrary symbol system" (1978a, 809).

A systemic examination of his third stage reveals that Burke moves from his earlier dualism and constructs a unified or coherent symbolic system. This system, however, stops short of monism, which stresses "the oneness or unity of reality in some sense" (*Encyclopedia of Philosophy*, s.v. "monism and pluralism," 363). Burke casts nonsymbolic and symbolic entities as distinct, but unified in the human body. In "(Nonsymbolic) Motion/(Symbolic) Action" Burke describes a coherent rhetorical system that unifies all polarities in "symbolic action":

I have said that the only transcending of the permanent "split" between the two realms (of symbol and nonsymbol) would be as in some ultimate condition like that which orthodox Western religions imagine in promising that the virtuous dead will regain their "purified" bodies in heaven. . . . And the merger with "symbolic action" is embedded in the very constitution of the poetic medium that celebrates her oneness with nature as the ground of all physiologic bodies . . . hence all is as *verbal* as with God's creative word in Genesis. (1978a, 830–31)

This passage indicates that poetic "symbolic action" is capable not only of unifying but also of transcending all divisions in a system of symbolic coherence.

Then, in his introduction to "Dramatism," Burke suggests this more coherent approach is the most direct way of studying human relations: "Dramatism is a method of analysis and a corresponding critique of terminology designed to show that the most direct route to the study of human relations and human motives is via a methodical inquiry into cycles or clusters of terms and their functions" (1968b, 445). Burke focuses on coherence, "cycles or clusters of terms." Having established his approach, he next presents the pentad with its ratios as a way of understanding and elaborating on the full drama or the complete, coherent, symbolic system (446).

As Burke describes dramatism, he makes it clear that human symbol using, a form of action, is not reducible to external physical conditions—is not representational:

1. There can be no action without motion. . . .
2. There can be motion without action.
3. Action is not reducible to terms of motion. (1968b, 447)

This enables Burke to maintain that "'action' is a term for the kind of behavior possible to a typical symbol-using animal (such as man) in contrast to the extra symbolic or non-symbolic operations of nature" (447).

His symbolic coherence, rather than his dualistic system, is discussed further by Burke in "(Nonsymbolic) Motion/(Symbolic) Action." Burke immediately acknowledges the polar terms of "mind-body," "spirit-matter," and "superstructure-substructure" but asserts that none of these matches the "motion-action" pair, which is his primary concern (1978a, 809). He then transcends these distinctions by discussing "symbolicity," which unites them. He does this by merging "Self," the person as an individual, with "Culture" (810): "The Self as a 'person,' member of a community (Culture) characterized by motives in the realm of symbolic action, is not thus differentiated. In this respect the Self becomes a product of the Culture" (813). For Burke, symbol using combines internal and external elements into a unified, coherent system: "The Self, like its corresponding Culture, thus has two sources of reference for its symbolic identity: its nature as a physiological organism, and its nature as a symbol-using animal responsive to the potentialities of symbolicity that have a nature of their own not reducible to a sheerly physiological dimension" (815). In "The Polarity Poetically 'Resolved'" Burke indicates that "symbolic action" transcends and unifies the "two realms (of symbolic and nonsymbolic)" and makes them one "with nature as the ground of all physiologic bodies" (830–31). With the establishment of a coherent system of symbol using, Burke's philosophy of rhetoric has shifted significantly from his earlier dualistic system of symbol using as a response to an external reality.

The centrality and transcendent nature of human symbol using for Burke is similar to Michael Polanyi's fiduciary program in *Personal Knowledge:*

The articulate life of man's mind is his specific contribution to the universe; by the invention of symbolic forms man has given birth and lasting existence to thought. But though our thinking has contrived these artifices, yet they have power to control our own thought. . . . we must accredit our own judgment as the paramount arbiter of all our intellectual performances, and claiming that we are competent to pursue intellectual excellence as a token of a hidden reality. (1962, 264–65)

Polanyi labels his approach and the period postcritical—which is not inconsistent with Cary Nelson's poststructuralism. These terms fit fairly well with the philosophy of symbolic coherence.

Burke does not mention symbolic coherence in his discussion of philosophies in the *Grammar,* making the selection of a label arbitrary. I have used "symbolic coherence" because it best describes Burke's philosophical position in this final stage.

Comparison of Concepts

As Burke's philosophy of rhetoric evolved from a dualistic to a coherent system, one would expect to see an impact on, and a modification of, some of his key rhetorical concepts. So another way to understand Burke's change in philosophy is to compare key concepts—definitions of human being, pentad, substance, and metaphor—between his early dualistic and his later coherent stages.

Definition of the Human Being

At the end of his critical realism period, Burke introduced his four-clause definition of humans in *The Rhetoric of Religion,* as quoted above. It implied a "reality" separate from humans. Then, in *Language as Symbolic Action* during his middle period, Burke revises his definition, making it more symbolic and less clearly dualistic.

Man is
the symbol-using (symbol-making, symbol-misusing) animal
inventor of the negative (or moralized by the negative)
separated from his natural condition by instruments of his own
    making
goaded by the spirit of hierarchy (or moved by the sense of order)
and rotten with perfection. (1966b, 16)

The addition of "symbol-making," "symbol-misusing," "moralized by the negative," and "moved by the sense of order" directs attention toward the internal process of symbol using, and "rotten with perfection" makes the definition more completely symbolic. These changes definitely reduce the dualistic nature of the definition.

Making yet another shift, Burke offers a different definition that is more consistent with his final symbolic coherence stage. In "bodies that learn language" (Brock et al. 1985, 28) and in his essay "(Nonsymbolic) Motion/(Symbolic) Action," Burke emphasizes a coexistence and interrelationship between the realms of the symbolic and the physical. He notes, "In their bodies (as physiological organisms in the realm of motion) there developed the ability to learn the kind of tribal idiom that is here meant by 'symbolic action'" (1978a, 811). In this definition Burke merges nonsymbolic "bodies" with "language" into a unified concept of "symbolic action." This new definition no longer highlights the dualism of an external reality as a counterpart to symbol using, and it makes symbol using a unified, coherent process. In this merger bodies as "symbol-systems" transcend the physical. Burke states: "The body thus provides a principle of individuation that is grounded in the centrality of the nervous system. But this separateness as a physiological organism is 'transcended' by the peculiar collective social nature of human symbol-systems" (Brock et al. 1985, 32).

Subsequently, in discussing this "transcendence" and applying it to a Wordsworth poem, Burke elevates it further to the word of God, "hence all is as *verbal* as with God's creative word in Genesis." Burke concludes, "In his nature as the typically symbol-using animal, man would make an *Unus Mundas* by making everything symbolic" (1978a, 831). Burke merges the symbolic and nonsymbolic as coexisting and related spheres of action and motion. This merger is a coherent system, since humans have made "everything symbolic."

However, typical of Burke's not wanting to be limited to a single philosophy, in *The Legacy of Kenneth Burke* he combines his two definitions of humans in a poem,

BEING BODIES THAT LEARN LANGUAGE
THEREBY BECOMING WORDLINGS
HUMANS ARE THE
SYMBOL-MAKING, SYMBOL-USING, SYMBOL-MISUSING ANIMAL
INVENTOR OF THE NEGATIVE
SEPARATED FROM OUR NATURAL CONDITION
BY INSTRUMENTS OF OUR OWN MAKING
GOADED BY THE SPIRIT OF HIERARCHY
ACQUIRING FOREKNOWLEDGE OF DEATH
AND ROTTEN WITH PERFECTION
(in Simons and Melia 1989, 263)

This merger of his dualistic and unified definitions of humans continues Burke's efforts to frustrate classification of his work. However, the shift in philosophy from dualism to coherence between the two stages is still evident.

The Pentad

Burke's philosophic evolution is also reflected in his treatment of the pentad. In *A Grammar of Motives* Burke introduces the pentad—act, agent, scene, purpose, and agency—to attribute motives in response to "the nature of the world" as all people "experience it" ([1945] 1969, xv). The "world" and "experience" reflect the dualism of Burke's early writing. Furthermore, he makes it clear that any one of the five terms can be dominant, and "we may even treat all five in terms of one, by 'reducing' them all to the one or (what amounts to the same thing) 'deducing' them all from the one as their common terminal ancestor" (127). Burke then discusses the philosophies consistent with the featuring of each of the five terms (128). This approach is consistent with a dualism of human symbol using, since motives are a derived response to an external reality in which any of the five terms can be dominant.

As Burke's concern for ontology emerged, however, a change in the use of the pentad occurred. In "Dramatism" Burke makes "act" the central term in the pentad: "'Act' is thus a terministic center from which many related considerations can be shown to 'radiate,' as though it were a 'god-term' from which a whole universe of terms is derived" (1968b, 445). He next discusses the remaining terms as they relate to "act." Burke then introduces a sixth term, "attitude," making it a hexad, as he suggests that the ratios of the other terms reflect an *attitude* that is "an ambiguous term for *incipient* action" (446). It is now clear that the pentad has become an internal, coherent system for understanding symbol using that unites internal and external realities as "attitudes" with the "act" or *action* as the way humans relate to the external, nonsymbolic world.

Substance

The most significant change in Burke's philosophy is found in the concept of substance. As Burke moved away from symbol using as a representational system toward an internal, coherent approach, the concept of substance is no longer as closely tied to an external reality. In *A Grammar of Motives* substance is presented as "a scenic word" that is "literally, a person's or a thing's sub-stance . . . that stands beneath or supports the person or thing" ([1945] 1969, 22). Burke then explains its metaphysical meaning: "subsistence, reality, real being (as applied to mere appearance), nature, essence" (23). At this point Burke takes the dualistic position that the symbolic manipulations in the pentad represent an external reality: "The transformations which we here study as a Grammar are not 'illusions,' but citable realities. The structural relations involved are observable realities" (57).

But later in "Dramatism," when Burke constructs a coherent system, the "act" becomes the terministic center of the pentadic ratios that reflect an "attitude." In "Dramatism" there is *no* discussion of substance. Where earlier "scene" and "reality" were the ground for the pentad, now "attitude" appears to be the internal ground with "act" as the link to the external; "the pattern is incipiently a hexad when viewed in connection with the different but complementary analysis of *attitude* (as an ambiguous term for *incipient action*)" (1968b, 446). By substituting attitude for substance, Burke again has moved from a dualistic to a more unified or coherent symbolic system.

Metaphor

Metaphor is the final concept to be compared between Burke's earlier and later writing. In his first epistemological stage metaphor is central to his philosophy, while in his later ontological stage it becomes secondary. In *Permanence and Change* Burke establishes "'orientation' (or general view of reality)," which becomes "perspective," as the subject of the book. Then Burke discusses "Perspective as Metaphor" ([1935a] 1984, 89). This view of metaphor is dualistic because symbols in a general sense represent "reality." Later, in his 1954 prologue to *Permanence and Change*, Burke states, "Another way of characterizing *P & C* would be to say that it lays primary stress upon the many differences of *perspective* that go with a world of much occupational diversity" (lvi). Burke goes on to say, "Our treatment of perspective in terms of 'metaphor' concerns what the social scientists now often discuss in terms of 'models'" (lvii). Burke's models or methods are his major concepts—definition of man, identification, pentad, and terms for order—and the centrality of metaphor to these concepts has already been explained in another essay (Brock 1985, 95–99). Burke's early use of metaphor is thus dualistic in nature.

However, in Burke's final ontological stage, as he moves from dualism to symbolic coherence, metaphor is no longer a central term. In "Dramatism," Burke asks the question, Is dramatism merely metaphorical? His answer is no, for the human being "is defined literally as an animal characterized by his special aptitude for 'symbolic action,' which is itself a literal term. And from there on, drama is employed, not as a metaphor but as a fixed form that helps us discover what the implications of the terms 'act' and 'person' *really are*" (1968b, 448). In rejecting dramatism as metaphoric, Burke did not say dramatism is "reality"—a term that he does not hesitate to use in his critical realism period. Instead, he says it is "literal." This strategic labeling places symbol using as an integrative, coherent system within humans where "bodies learn language." In the process the symbolic characteristics of language, rather than the nonsymbolic and physiological aspects of the body, have become controlling.

In *Philosophy of Literary Form* Burke explains Paul Weiss's transcendent strategy of biologizing physics: "[He] would move by transformations from the realm of physics to the realm of biology . . . by treating both physical and biological processes in terms of a biological metaphor: the metaphor of eating, of digestion, of assimilation" ([1941] 1973, 392). Burke adds that a third realm, ethics, could ethicize physics and biology instead of physicizing biology and ethics. In a similar manner Burke in his third stage symbolizes both physics and biology in contrast to having symbol using function as a metaphor. This is quite consistent with Berger and Luckmann's *Social Construction of Reality* (1967). One could say that, for Kenneth Burke, "dramatism" is human construction of a coherent symbolic reality. As the concern of Burke's writing shifts from epistemology to ontology, metaphor, instead of being central to a dualistic system, becomes integrated into a coherent, symbolic system.

Burke has maintained that two rhetorical systems exist, which he labels "logology" and "dramatism." In this analysis, these two rhetorical systems are cast as products of three stages. The special tools presented during his middle period are central to both systems; however, as demonstrated earlier, they take a different form when used in each system. "Logology," developed during Burke's first and second stages, embodies his concern for epistemology and reflects the dualism of his realistic and conceptual periods. "Dramatism," embodying the ontology of Burke's third stage and including his special methods, reflects the rhetorical unity of symbolic coherence.

The idea that Burke really has two rhetorical systems helps account for the confusion in labeling Burke's philosophy. Fisher and Brockriede, who focus on his first and second stages, argue that Burke's philosophy is linguistic realism. In contrast, Cary Nelson, in "Writing as the Accomplice of Language: Kenneth Burke and Poststructuralism," focuses on Burke's second and third stages and argues for a different interpretation:

I would rather say explicitly that I want to offer a counter-Burke to the humanistic Burke of Marie Nichols, Bernard Brock, Leland Griffin, Lloyd Bitzer, and, more recently, Wayne Booth and Denis Donoghue. . . .

Put somewhat baldly, the issue is whether one sees the symbol-using animal in Burke as an independent agent or as a figure occupying the role of agency within a verbal drama that is in a sense already written for us. (1989, 158)

Nelson, relying heavily on "(Nonsymbolic) Motion/(Symbolic) Action," reads Burke as a poststructuralist: "Dramatism is equally an arbitrary terminological filling out of a linguistic structure already given to him by culture" (166). These contradictory interpretations of Burke are due primarily to focusing on different rhetorical systems. David Williams takes a similar position as he labels early Burke "dualist realism" (1989, 212), yet throughout the article he compares Burke's later writing to Derrida. Chesebro has made it clear that both epistemological and ontological perspectives are necessary for a complete understanding of Burke's rhetoric (1988, 178—79). The evolution of Burke's philosophy of rhetoric forces writers to identify which rhetorical system they are discussing.

Conclusion

One can never know *why* Kenneth Burke's philosophy evolved as it has, but one can speculate based upon his primary concern at each stage of the process. In the first stage, Burke assumed the role of a critic responding to literature and the events of his day. He questioned the positivism of his day but accepted an external reality and symbols as separate entities. As a critic, he discovered the significance of symbols and their use in explaining, understanding, and reformulating these externals, so his philosophy represented the dualism of these two realms. By the second stage, Burke focused more directly on symbol using itself as he constructed tools for analyzing this process and posited that it was central to being human. So his conceptualism reflects his attempt to use language to transcend these polar concepts. In the third period, Burke views symbol using as central not only to being human but to all experience as well, unifying nonsymbolic motion and symbolic action into a coherent rhetorical system. Essentially, the evolution of Burke's philosophy of rhetoric is the increased centrality of symbol using. After Burke discovered that symbols were the key to understanding experience, he created the tools that then became "real" and unified all other elements into a coherent system of symbols.

Another aspect of the evolution of his philosophy of rhetoric is that Burke, within the framework of his time, has been in the forefront of a movement toward a more symbolic approach to reality. In the 1930s in *Permanence and Change* Burke wrote about the dominant scientific rationalization and indicated that its goal was "to control for our purposes the forces of technology, or machinery." He further stated, "The doctrine of use, as the prime mover of judgments, formally established the *secular* as the point of reference by which to consider questions of valuation" ([1935a] 1984, 44–45). Not only did people at the time accept the existence of an external reality, but they made it controlling. Yet, Burke, in advance of the time, recognized the weaknesses of this rationalization and forecast its breakdown and acceptance of a more symbolic orientation: poetic humanism (61–66).[2]

In the late 1950s and culminating in the 1960s, Burke, again in advance of his time, described an ontology uniting internal and external elements symbolically within "bodies that learn language." His "dramatism" is consistent with Berger and Luckmann's landmark work *The Social Construction of Reality: A Treatise in the Sociology of Knowledge* (1967). For Burke, individual reality is a coherent system of symbols.

As scholars rely on Burke's logology and dramatism in their

efforts to expand our knowledge of human symbol using, it is essential for them to understand his epistemological and ontological rhetorical systems. This understanding will be especially important and useful as critics consider extensions of the Burkeian system.

Notes

1. Burke's shift from epistemology to ontology and its implications are discussed in Brock et al. 1985; Burke 1985a; Brock 1985; Chesebro 1988.
2. For an analysis of Burke's stages in society, see Brock 1990a.

References

Althusser, Louis. 1971. *Lenin and Philosophy and Other Essays.* Translated by Ben Brewster. New York: Monthly Review Press.

Balthrop, V. William. 1975. The Representative Anecdote: An Approach to Movement Study. Paper read at the annual meeting of the Speech Communication Association, Houston.

———. 1983. The Representative Anecdote as an Approach to Movement Study. Paper read at the annual meeting of the Speech Communication Association, Washington, D.C.

———. 1986. Ian Paisley's "Call to the Protestants of Ulster": A Representative Anecdote for Ulster Loyalism. Paper read at the annual meeting of the Speech Communication Association, Chicago.

Barnes, James A. 1988. The Comeback Trail. *National Journal* 13 (August): 2080–84.

Bateson, Gregory. 1972. *Steps to an Ecology of Mind.* San Francisco: Chandler Publishing.

———. 1982. Paradigmatic Conservatism. In *Rigor and Imagination: Essays from the Legacy of Gregory Bateson,* edited by C. Wilder and J. H. Weakland, 347–56. New York: Praeger Publishers.

Baudrillard, Jean. 1983. The Ecstacy of Communication. In *The Anti-Aesthetic: Essays on Postmodern Culture,* edited by Hal Foster, 126–34. Port Townsend, Wash.: Bay Press.

Benne, Kenneth D. 1969. Toward a Grammar of Educational Motives. In *Critical Responses to Kenneth Burke, 1924–1966,* edited by William H. Rueckert, 199–207. Minneapolis: University of Minnesota Press.

Berger, Peter, and Thomas Luckmann. 1967. *The Social Construction of Reality: A Treatise in the Sociology of Knowledge.* Garden City, N.Y.: Doubleday, Anchor Books.

Berman, Art. 1988. *From the New Criticism to Deconstruction: The Reception of Structuralism and Post-Structuralism.* Urbana: University of Illinois Press.

Bertelsen, Dale A. 1985. Kenneth Burke's Use of the Term "Transformation" in Four Major Works: A Clarification of His Rhetorical Theory. Master's thesis, Pennsylvania State University, University Park, Pa.

———. 1990. Synopsis of the 1990 National Kenneth Burke Society Conference. *Kenneth Burke Society Newsletter* 6 (April): 1–6.

Black, Edwin. 1965. *Rhetorical Criticism: A Study in Method.* New York: Macmillan.

———. 1978. *Rhetorical Criticism: A Study in Method.* Reprint. Madison: University of Wisconsin Press.

Black, Max. 1969. A Review of *A Grammar of Motives.* In *Critical Responses to Kenneth Burke, 1924–1966,* edited by William H. Rueckert, 166–69. Minneapolis: University of Minnesota Press.

Blankenship, Jane. 1989. "Magic" and "Mystery" in the Works of Kenneth Burke. In *The Legacy of Kenneth Burke,* edited by Herbert W. Simons and Trevor Melia, 246–76. Madison: University of Wisconsin Press.

———. 1990. Kenneth Burke on Ecology. *Kenneth Burke Society Newsletter* 6 (April): 13–19.

Blankenship, Jane, Edward Murphy, and Marie Rosenwasser. 1974. Pivotal Terms in the Early Works of Kenneth Burke. *Philosophy and Rhetoric* 7 (Winter): 1–24.

Blumer, Herbert. 1967. Society as Symbolic Interaction. In *Symbolic Interaction: A Reader in Social Psychology,* edited by Jerome G. Manis and Bernard N. Meltzer, 139–48. Boston: Allyn and Bacon.

Bormann, Ernest G. 1972. Fantasy and Rhetorical Vision: The Rhetorical Criticism of Social Reality. *Quarterly Journal of Speech* 58: 396–407.

———. 1973. The Eagleton Affair: A Fantasy Theme Analysis. *Quarterly Journal of Speech* 59: 143–59.

———. 1982. A Fantasy Theme Analysis of the Television Coverage of the Hostage Release and the Reagan Inaugural. *Quarterly Journal of Speech* 68: 133–45.

Bowen, William. 1970. Our Awareness of the Great Web. *Fortune,* February, 198.

Brock, Bernard L. 1985. Epistemology and Ontology in Kenneth Burke's Dramatism. *Communication Quarterly* 33: 94–104.

———. 1990a. Kenneth Burke and the Twenty-first Century. *Kenneth Burke Society Newsletter* 6 (April): 4–9.

———. 1990b. Rhetorical Criticism. A Burkeian Approach Revisited. In *Methods of Rhetorical Criticism: A Twentieth-Century Perspective,* 3d ed., edited by Bernard L. Brock, Robert L. Scott, and James W. Chesebro, 183–95. Detroit: Wayne State University Press.

Brock, Bernard L., Parke G. Burgess, Kenneth Burke, and Herbert W. Simons. 1985. Dramatism as Ontology or Epistemology: A Symposium. *Communication Quarterly* 33: 17–33.

Brummett, Barry. 1981. Gastronomic Reference, Synecdoche, and Political Images. *Quarterly Journal of Speech* 67: 138–45.

————. 1984a. Burke's Representative Anecdote as a Method in Media Criticism. *Critical Studies in Mass Communication* 1: 161–76.

————. 1984b. The Representative Anecdote as a Burkean Method, Applied to Evangelical Rhetoric. *Southern Speech Communication Journal* 50: 1–23.

Burke, Kenneth. 1924. *The White Oxen and Other Stories.* New York: Albert and Charles Boni.

————. 1925. Psychology and Form. *Dial* 79: 34–46.

————. 1930. Waste—the Future of Prosperity. *New Republic* 73: 228–31.

————. 1931. *Counter-Statement.* New York: Harcourt, Brace.

————. [1931] 1953. *Counter-Statement.* Rev. 2d ed. Los Altos, Calif.: Hermes Publications.

————. [1931] 1957. *Counter-Statement.* Chicago: University of Chicago Press.

————. [1931] 1968. *Counter-Statement.* Berkeley and Los Angeles: University of California Press.

————. 1932. *Towards a Better Life: Being a Series of Epistles, or Declamations.* New York: Harcourt, Brace.

————. [1932] 1966. *Towards a Better Life: Being a Series of Epistles, or Declamations.* Reprint. Berkeley and Los Angeles: University of California Press.

————. [1932] 1982. *Towards a Better Life: Being a Series of Epistles, or Declamations.* Reprint. Berkeley and Los Angeles: University of California Press.

————. 1935a. *Permanence and Change: An Anatomy of Purpose.* New York: New Republic.

————. [1935a] 1954. *Permanence and Change: An Anatomy of Purpose.* Reprint, rev. 2d ed. Los Altos, Calif.: Hermes Publications.

————. [1935a] 1965. *Permanence and Change: An Anatomy of Purpose.* Reprint. Indianapolis: Bobbs-Merrill.

————. [1935a] 1984. *Permanence and Change: An Anatomy of Purpose.* Reprint, rev. 3d ed. Berkeley: University of California Press.

————. 1935b. Revolutionary Symbolism in America. In *American Writers' Congress,* edited by Henry Hart, 87–95. New York: International Publishers.

————. 1937. *Attitudes toward History.* 2 vols. New York: New Republic.

————. [1937] 1959. *Attitudes toward History.* Reprint, rev. 2d ed. Los Altos, Calif.: Hermes Publications.

————. [1937] 1961. *Attitudes toward History.* Reprint. Boston: Beacon Press.

————. [1937] 1984. *Attitudes toward History.* Reprint, rev. Berkeley: University of California Press.

————. 1941. *The Philosophy of Literary Form: Studies in Symbolic Action.* Baton Rouge: Louisiana State University Press.

————. [1941] 1957. *The Philosophy of Literary Form: Studies in Symbolic Action.* Reprint, rev. 2d ed. New York: Vintage Books.

————. [1941] 1973. *The Philosophy of Literary Form: Studies in Symbolic Action.* Reprint, rev. 3d ed. Berkeley: University of California Press.

———. 1942. The Study of Symbolic Action. *Chimera* 1 (Spring): 7–16.

———. 1945. *A Grammar of Motives.* New York: Prentice-Hall.

———. [1945] 1955. *A Grammar of Motives.* Reprint. New York: George Braziller.

———. [1945] 1969. *A Grammar of Motives.* Reprint. Berkeley: University of California Press.

———. [1945 and 1950a] 1962. *A Grammar of Motives and A Rhetoric of Motives.* Reprint as 1 vol. Cleveland: World Publishing, Meridian Books.

———. 1950a. *A Rhetoric of Motives.* New York: Prentice-Hall.

———. [1950a] 1955. *A Rhetoric of Motives.* Reprint. New York: George Braziller.

———. [1950a] 1969. *A Rhetoric of Motives.* Reprint. Berkeley: University of California Press.

———. 1950b. Vegetal Radicalism of Theodore Roethke. *Sewanee Review* 58: 68–108.

———. 1952a. A Dramatistic View of the Origins of Language, Part I. *Quarterly Journal of Speech* 38 (October): 251–64.

———. 1952b. A Dramatistic View of the Origins of Language, Part II. *Quarterly Journal of Speech* 38 (December): 446–60.

———. 1952c. Form and Persecution in the *Oresteia. Sewanee Review* 60: 377–96.

———. 1953a. A Dramatistic View of the Origins of Language, Part III. *Quarterly Journal of Speech* 38 (February): 79–92.

———. 1953b. Postscripts on the Negative. *Quarterly Journal of Speech* 38 (April): 209–16.

———. 1954. Fact, Inference, and Proof in the Analysis of Literary Symbolism. In *Symbols and Values: An Initial Study, Thirteenth Symposium of the Conference on Science, Philosophy, and Religion,* edited by Lyman Bryson et al., 283–306. New York: Harper and Brothers.

———. 1955. *Book of Moments, Poems, 1915–1954.* Los Altos, Calif.: Hermes Publications.

———. 1957. Progress: Promise and Problems. *Nation,* April, 322–24.

———. 1961. *The Rhetoric of Religion: Studies in Logology.* Boston: Beacon Press.

———. [1961] 1970. *The Rhetoric of Religion: Studies in Logology.* Reprint. Berkeley: University of California Press.

———. 1963. The Thinking of the Body: Comments on the Imagery of Catharsis in Literature. *Psychoanalytic Review* 50 (Fall): 25–68.

———. 1966a. I, Eye, Ay—Emerson's Early Essay on "Nature": Thoughts on the Machinery of Transcendence. *Sewanee Review* 74: 875–95.

———. 1966b. *Language as Symbolic Action: Essays on Life, Literature, and Method.* Berkeley and Los Angeles: University of California Press.

———. 1966c. *Towards a Better Life: Being a Series of Epistles, or Declamations.* Berkeley and Los Angeles: University of California Press.

———. 1967. Dramatism. In *Communication: Conceptions and Perspectives,* edited by Lee Thayer, 327–60. Washington, D.C.: Spartan Books.

———. 1968a. *Collected Poems, 1915–1967.* Berkeley and Los Angeles: University of California Press.

———. 1968b. Dramatism. In *The International Encyclopedia of the Social Sciences*, edited by D. L. Sills, 445–52. New York: Macmillan/Free Press.

———. 1968c. *The Complete White Oxen: Collected Short Fiction*. Berkeley and Los Angeles: University of California Press.

———. 1970. On Stress, Its Seeking. In *Why Men Take Chances*, edited by Samuel Z. Kausner. New York: Anchor Books.

———. 1971. Toward Helhaven: Three Stages of a Vision. *Sewanee Review* 79: 11–25.

———. 1972a. *Dramatism and Development*. Barre, Mass.: Clark University Press.

———. 1972b. Interview by Don P. Abbott. Tape recording, in Middleton, Conn.

———. 1974. Why Satire, with a Plan for Writing One. *Michigan Quarterly Review* 13: 307–37.

———. 1976. Towards Looking Back. *Journal of General Education* 28: 167–89.

———. 1978a. (Nonsymbolic) Motion/(Symbolic) Action. *Critical Inquiry* 4: 809–38.

———. 1978b. Rhetoric, Poetics, and Philosophy. In *Rhetoric, Philosophy, and Literature: An Exploration*, edited by Don M. Burks, 15–33. West Lafayette, Ind.: Purdue University Press.

———. 1981a. My Adopted, and I Hope Adoptive, State. *New Jersey Monthly*, November, 67–68, 98.

———. 1981b. Variations on "Providence." *Notre Dame English Journal* 13 (Summer): 155–83.

———. 1982. The Interactive Bind. In *Rigor and Imagination: Essays from the Legacy of Gregory Bateson*, edited by C. Wilder and J. H. Weakland, 331–40. New York: Praeger Publishers.

———. 1983a. Counter-Gridlock: An Interview with Kenneth Burke. *All Area No. 2*, pp. 4–33.

———. 1983b. Dramatism and Logology. *London Times Literary Supplement*, August 12, p. 859.

———. 1985a. Dramatism and Logology. *Communication Quarterly* 33 (Spring): 89–93.

———. 1985b. In Haste. *Pre/Text* 6 (Fall/Winter): 329–77.

———. 1990. Interview by James W. Chesebro and Dale A. Bertelsen. Tape recording, Kenneth Burke Society convention, May 7, New Harmony, Ind.

Bush, George. 1987. Excerpts of Remarks for Vice President George Bush Announcement Speech, Houston, Texas, Monday, October 12, 1987. George Bush for President Press Release, October 17, 1987.

———. 1988a. Acceptance Speech. *Vital Speeches of the Day*, October 15, pp. 2–5.

———. 1988b. The Basic Speech: "When I Talk about a Kinder and Gentler Nation, I Mean It." *New York Times*, October 24, B5.

———. 1989. Transcript of Bush's Inaugural Address. *New York Times*, January 21, p. 10.

Butler, Samuel. [1872] 1968. *Erewhon*. New York: Magnum Books.

Campbell, J. 1983. *Grammatical Man: Information, Entropy, Language, and Life*. New York: Simon and Schuster.

Carpenter, E., and Marshall McLuhan. 1968. *Explorations in Communication*. Boston: Beacon Press.

Cathcart, Robert, and Gary Gumpert. 1983. Mediated Interpersonal Communication: Towards a New Typology. *Quarterly Journal of Speech* 69: 267–77.

———. 1986. I Am a Camera: The Mediated Self. *Communication Quarterly* 34 (Spring): 89–102.

Chandler, Robert C. 1988. Representative Anecdotes in Organizational Communication: Corporate Annual Reports as a Case Study. *Journal of Communication Studies* 6: 10–14.

Chase, Richard. 1969. Rhetoric of Rhetoric. In *Critical Responses to Kenneth Burke, 1924–1966*, edited by William H. Rueckert, 251–54. Minneapolis: University of Minnesota Press.

Chesebro, James W. 1967. Kenneth Burke's "Dramatism" Applied to the Analysis of Rhetorical Strategies. Master's thesis, Illinois State University, Normal, Department of Communication.

———. 1972. The Radical Revolutionary in America: Analysis of a Rhetorical Movement, 1960–1972. Ph.D. diss., University of Minnesota, Minneapolis, Department of Speech Communication.

———. 1988. Epistemology and Ontology as Dialectical Modes in the Writings of Kenneth Burke. *Communication Quarterly* 36 (Summer): 175–91.

———. 1990. Dramatizing Technology: Extrapolating a Future from the Writings of Kenneth Burke. *Kenneth Burke Society Newsletter* 6 (April): 1–3.

———. 1991. Communication Technologies as Cognitive Systems. Paper read at the annual meeting of the Speech Communication Association, Atlanta.

———. 1992. Extensions of the Burkeian System. *Quarterly Journal of Speech* 78 (August): 356–68.

———. In press. Kenneth Burke and Jacques Derrida. In *Kenneth Burke and Contemporary Western Thought*, edited by Bernard L. Brock.

Chisholm, Roderick. 1966. *Theory of Knowledge*. Englewood Cliffs, N.J.: Prentice-Hall.

Conley, Thomas M. 1990. *Rhetoric in the European Tradition*. New York: Longman.

Conrad, Charles. 1981. Agon and Rhetorical Form: The Essence of "Old Feminist" Rhetoric. *Central States Speech Journal* 32: 45–53.

———. 1984. Phases, Pentads, and Dramatistic Critical Process. *Central States Speech Journal* 35: 84–93.

Cook, Rhodes. 1987. As Bush Wades In On His Own Strength, Image a Puzzle. *Congressional Quarterly Weekly Report* 10 (October): 2455–58.

Cowley, Malcolm. 1985. Being Old Old. *New York Times Magazines*, May 26, sec. 6, p. 58.

Crane, G. 1990. Challenging the Individual: The Traditions of Hypermedia Databases. *Academic Computing* 4 (January): 22–23, 31–38.

Cronen, William C. 1983. *Changes in the Land*. New York: Hill and Wang.

Cronin, Thomas E. 1975. *The State of the Presidency.* Boston: Little, Brown.

Crusius, Tim. 1981. Kenneth Burke on His "Morbid Selph": *The Collected Poems* as Comedy. *CEA Critic* 43 (May): 18–32.

———. 1988. Kenneth Burke's *Auscultation:* A "De-struction" of Marxist Dialectic and Rhetoric. *Rhetorica* 6 (Autumn): 355–79.

Dauber, Corinne. 1984. The "Call to Halt the Nuclear Arms Race" as Representative Anecdote: A Burkean Analysis. Master's thesis, University of North Carolina, Chapel Hill.

Emerson, Ralph W. [1842] 1962. The Poet. In *Major Writers of America,* edited by Perry Miller, 530–39. New York: Harcourt, Brace and World.

Enholm, Donald K., Anthony J. Palmeri, and Timothy N. Thompson. 1990. A Debate on the Dialectics of Rotten Perfection. Panel at the annual meeting of the Central States Communication Association, Detroit.

Farrell, T. B. 1976. Knowledge, Consensus, and Rhetorical Theory. *Quarterly Journal of Speech* 62: 1–14.

Fergusson, Francis. 1969. Kenneth Burke's *Grammar of Motives.* In *Critical Responses to Kenneth Burke, 1924–1966,* edited by William H. Rueckert, 173–81. Minneapolis: University of Minnesota Press.

Fisher, Walter R. 1984. Narration as a Human Communication Paradigm: The Case of Public Moral Argument. *Communication Monographs* 51: 1–22.

———. 1985a. The Narrative Paradigm: An Elaboration. *Communication Monographs* 52: 347–67.

———. 1985b. The Narrative Paradigm: In the Beginning. *Journal of Communication* 35: 74–89.

———. 1987. *Human Communication as Narration: Toward a Philosophy of Reason, Value, and Action.* Columbia: University of South Carolina Press.

Fisher, Walter, and Wayne Brockriede. 1984. Kenneth Burke's Realism. *Central States Speech Journal* 35: 35–42.

Fiske, J. 1989. *Television Culture.* London: Routledge.

Fletcher, A. 1982. Volume and Body in Burke's Criticism; or, Stalled in the Right Place. In *Representing Kenneth Burke,* edited by H. White and M. Brose. Baltimore: Johns Hopkins University Press.

Foucault, Michel. 1977. *The Archaeology of Knowledge.* London: Tavistock.

Frank, Armin Paul. 1969. *Kenneth Burke.* New York: Twayne.

Germond, Jack W., and Jules Witcover. 1988. Nine Weeks to Go, and the Race Is Up for Grabs. *National Journal* 3 (September): 2208.

Gramsci, A. 1971. *Selections from the Prison Notebooks.* London: Lawrence and Wishart.

Griffin, Leland M. 1964. The Rhetorical Structure of the "New Left" Movement, Part I. *Quarterly Journal of Speech* 50: 113–35.

———. 1969. A Dramatistic Theory of the Rhetoric of Movement. In *Critical Responses to Kenneth Burke, 1924–1966,* edited by William H. Rueckert, 456–78. Minneapolis: University of Minnesota Press.

———. 1984. When Dreams Collide: Rhetorical Trajectories in the Assassination of President Kennedy. *Quarterly Journal of Speech* 70: 111–31.

Grossberg, Lawrence. 1988. Putting Pop Back into Postmodernism. In *Uni-*

versal Abandon: The Politics of Postmodernism, edited by A. Ross. Edinburgh: University of Edinburgh Press.

Gumpert, Gary, and Robert Cathcart. 1990. A Theory of Mediation. In *Mediation, Information, and Culture: Information and Behavior,* edited by Brent Ruben and L. Lievrouw, vol. 3. New Brunswick, N.J.: Transaction Publishers.

Havelock, E. A. 1986. *The Muse Learns to Write: Reflections on Orality and Literacy from Antiquity to the Present.* New Haven, Conn.: Yale University Press.

Haynes, W. Lance. 1988. Of That Which We Cannot Write: Some Notes on the Phenomenology of Media. *Quarterly Journal of Speech* 74: 71–97.

Heath, R. L. 1984. Kenneth Burke's Break with Formalism. *Quarterly Journal of Speech* 70: 132–43.

———. 1986. *Realism and Relativism: A Perspective on Kenneth Burke.* Macon, Ga.: Mercer University Press.

Henderson, Greig E. 1988. *Kenneth Burke: Literature and Language as Symbolic Action.* Athens: University of Georgia Press.

Hyman, Stanley Edgar. 1955. *The Armed Vision: A Study in the Methods of Modern Literary Criticism.* Rev. ed. New York: Vintage Books.

Hyman, Stanley Edgar, with the assistance of Barbara Karmiller, eds. 1964a. *Perspectives by Incongruity.* Bloomington: Indiana University Press.

———. 1964b. *Terms for Order.* Bloomington: Indiana University Press.

Jameson, Fredric. 1971. *Marxism and Form.* Princeton, N.J.: Princeton University Press.

———. 1981. *The Political Unconscious: Narrative as a Socially Symbolic Act.* Ithaca, N.Y.: Cornell University Press.

———. 1982. The Symbolic Inference; or, Kenneth Burke and Ideological Analysis. In *Representing Kenneth Burke,* edited by H. White and M. Brose. Baltimore: Johns Hopkins University Press.

———. 1983. Postmodernism and Consumer Society. In *The Anti-Aesthetic: Essays on Postmodern Culture,* edited by Hal Foster, 111–25. Port Townsend, Wash.: Bay Press.

Jamieson, Kathleen Hall. 1988. *Eloquence in an Electronic Age: The Transformation of Political Speechmaking.* New York: Oxford University Press.

Jay, Paul, ed. 1988. *The Selected Correspondence of Kenneth Burke and Malcolm Cowley, 1916–1981.* New York: Viking.

———. 1989. Kenneth Burke and the Motives of Rhetoric. *American Literary History* 1 (Winter): 535–53.

Kaplan, E. A. 1987. *Rocking around the Clock.* New York: Methuen.

Klumpp, James F. 1990. Vision of Critique: Kenneth Burke and Civic Discourse in the Twenty-first Century. *Kenneth Burke Society Newsletter* 6 (April): 9–13.

Korzybski, A. 1948. *Science and Sanity.* 3d ed. Lakeville, Conn.: International Non-Aristotelian Library Publishing.

Kostelanetz, Richard. 1981. About Kenneth Burke: A Mind That Cannot Stop Exploding. *New York Times Book Review,* May 15, pp. 11 and 24–27.

Leff, Michael. 1989. Burke's Ciceronianism. In *The Legacy of Kenneth*

Burke, edited by Herbert W. Simons and Trevor Melia, 115–27. Madison: University of Wisconsin Press.

Lentricchia, Frank. 1983. *Criticism and Social Change.* Chicago: University of Chicago Press.

———. 1989. Analysis of Burke's Speech. In *The Legacy of Kenneth Burke,* edited by Herbert W. Simons and Trevor Melia, 281–96. Madison: University of Wisconsin Press.

McKerrow, Raymie E. 1989. Critical Rhetoric: Theory and Praxis. *Communication Monographs* 56: 91–111.

McLuhan, Marshall. 1964. *Understanding Media: The Extensions of Man.* New York: McGraw-Hill.

Madsen, Arnie. 1983. The Constitution as Representative Anecdote: A Burkean Analysis of the Arguments Presented in *United States v. Nixon.* Master's thesis, Wake Forest University, Wake Forest, N.C.

———. 1984. The Structure of Constitutional Argument: *United States v. Nixon.* Paper read at the annual meeting of the Southern Speech Communication Association, Baton Rouge, La.

———. 1986. The Constitution as Representative Anecdote in *United States v. Nixon.* Paper read at the annual meeting of the Speech Communication Association, Chicago.

———. 1988. "You Shall Have No Other Gods before Me" or "Honor Your Father and Your Mother": The Representative Anecdote and the Religious Right. Paper read at the annual meeting of the Western Speech Communication Association, San Diego, Calif.

———. 1989. Presidential Election '88: Vanity Fair. Paper read at the annual meeting of the Central States Communication Association, Kansas City, Mo.

Marshall, Scott W. 1986. The Representative Anecdote and Myth: An Approach to Rhetorical Criticism of Television Programming. Paper read at the annual meeting of the Speech Communication Association, Chicago.

Muir, Star A. 1990. Form and Technique in Helhaven: Counter-Nature's "Invitation to Participate" and the Ethics of Ecology. Paper presented at the convention of the Kenneth Burke Society, May 5, New Harmony, Ind.

Nelson, Cary. 1989. Writing as the Accomplice of Language: Kenneth Burke and Poststructuralism. In *The Legacy of Kenneth Burke,* edited by Herbert W. Simons and Trevor Melia, 156–73. Madison: University of Wisconsin Press.

Ong, Walter J. 1982. *Orality and Literacy.* New York: Methuen.

Oravec, Christine. 1989. Kenneth Burke's Concept of Association and the Complexity of Identity. In *The Legacy of Kenneth Burke,* edited by Herbert W. Simons and Trevor Melia, 174–95. Madison: University of Wisconsin Press.

Orr, C. Jack. 1978. How Shall We Say: "Reality Is Socially Constructed through Communication"? *Central States Speech Journal* 29: 263–74.

Pirsig, Robert M. 1974. *Zen and the Art of Motorcycle Maintenance: An Inquiry into Values.* New York: Bantam Books.

Plato. 1937. The Republic. In *The Dialogues of Plato*, translated by B. Jowett, vol. 1. New York: Random House.

Polanyi, Michael. 1962. *Personal Knowledge: Towards a Post-Critical Philosophy.* Chicago: University of Chicago Press.

Pondozzi, Jeannine. 1986. "When It's Good, It's Very, Very Good": Equipment for Living in *Cagney and Lacey.* Paper read at the annual meeting of the Speech Communication Association, Chicago.

Reese, W. L. 1980. *Dictionary of Philosophy and Religion.* Atlantic Highlands, N.J.: Humanities Press.

Ricoeur, Paul. 1970. *Freud and Philosophy.* Translated by D. Savage. New Haven, Conn.: Yale University Press.

Rod, D. K. 1982. Kenneth Burke's Concept of Entitlement. *Communication Monographs* 49: 20–32.

Rogers, F. 1989. *George Michael and Madonna: Post Modern Stars.* San Diego, Calif.: San Diego State University.

Rosenfield, Lawrence W. 1989. Round Table Discussion: *Selected Correspondence of Kenneth Burke and Malcolm Cowley, 1915–1981.* Paper read at annual meeting of the Speech Communication Association of Puerto Rico, December, San Juan.

Rueckert, William H. 1963. *Kenneth Burke and the Drama of Human Relations.* Minneapolis: University of Minnesota Press.

———, ed. 1969a. *Critical Responses to Kenneth Burke, 1924–1966.* Minneapolis: University of Minnesota Press.

———. 1969b. Tragedy as a Representative Anecdote. In *Critical Responses to Kenneth Burke, 1924–1966*, edited by William H. Rueckert, 380–96. Minneapolis: University of Minnesota Press.

———. 1978. Literary Criticism and Ecology: An Experiment in Ecocriticism. *Iowa Review,* 71–86.

———. 1982. *Kenneth Burke and the Drama of Human Relations.* 2d ed. Berkeley: University of California Press.

———. 1988. Kenneth Burke's Encounters with Walt Whitman. *WWQR* 6 (Fall): 61–90.

———. 1989. Rereading Kenneth Burke: Doctrine without Dogma, Action with Passion. In *The Legacy of Kenneth Burke*, edited by Herbert W. Simons and Trevor Melia, 128–55. Madison: University of Wisconsin Press.

———. 1990. Criticism as a Way of Life. Paper presented at the convention of the Kenneth Burke Society, May 5, New Harmony, Ind.

Scodari, Christine. 1986. Fractured Anecdotes and Damaged Equipment: Coping with the Soap Opera. Paper read at the annual meeting of the Speech Communication Association, Chicago.

———. 1987. Contemporary Film and the Representative Anecdote of "Unmasking": Coping Strategies for a Narcissistic Society. *Central States Speech Journal* 38: 111–21.

Scott, Robert L. 1967. On Viewing Rhetoric as Epistemic. *Central States Speech Journal* 18: 9–17.

———. 1968. Justifying Violence: The Rhetoric of Black Power. *Central States Speech Journal* 19: 96–104.

————. 1974. Editor's Note. *Quarterly Journal of Speech* 60: 234.

Scott, Robert L., and Donald K. Smith. 1969. The Rhetoric of Confrontation. *Quarterly Journal of Speech* 55: 1–8.

Scribner, S., and M. Cole. 1981. *The Psychology of Literacy.* Cambridge: MIT Press.

Simons, Herbert W. 1970. Requirements, Problems, and Strategies: A Theory of Persuasion for Social Movements. *Quarterly Journal of Speech* 56: 1–11.

————. 1989. Introduction. In *The Legacy of Kenneth Burke*, edited by Herbert W. Simons and Trevor Melia, 3–27. Madison: University of Wisconsin Press.

Simons, Herbert W., and Trevor Melia, eds. 1989. *The Legacy of Kenneth Burke.* Madison: University of Wisconsin Press.

Smith, Adam. [1776] 1985. In *Economic Evolution*, 2d ed., by Elbert V. Bowden. Cincinnati: South-Western Publishing.

Smith, Larry David. 1987. The Nominating Convention as Purveyor of Political Medicine: An Anecdotal Analysis of the Democrats and Republicans of 1984. *Central States Speech Journal* 38: 252–61.

Smith, Larry David, and James L. Golden. 1988. Electronic Storytelling in Electoral Politics: An Anecdotal Analysis of Television Advertising in the Helms-Hunt Senate Race. *Southern Speech Communication Journal* 53: 244–58.

Southwell, S. B. 1987. *Kenneth Burke and Martin Heidegger: With a Note against Deconstruction.* Gainesville: University of Florida Press.

Steiner, George. 1975. *After Babel.* London: Oxford University Press.

Stone, Gregory P., and Harvey A. Farberman. 1970. *Social Psychology through Symbolic Interaction.* Waltham, Mass.: Ginn-Blaisdell.

Stuart, Charlotte L. 1974. The Constitution as "Summational Anecdote." *Central States Speech Journal* 25: 111–18.

Thayer, Lee. 1988. Leadership/Communication: A Critical Review and a Modest Proposal. In *Handbook of Organizational Communication*, edited by G. M. Goldhaber and G. A. Barnett, 231–61. Norwood, N.J.: Ablex Publishing.

Thirty Years Later: Memories of the First American Writers' Congress. 1966. *American Scholar* 35: 495–516.

Thonssen, Lester, and A. Craig Baird. 1948. *Speech Criticism: The Development of Standards for Rhetorical Appraisal.* New York: Ronald Press.

Thonssen, Lester, A. Craig Baird, and Waldo W. Braden. 1970. *Speech Criticism.* New York: Ronald Press.

Thoreau, Henry D. [1854] 1962. Where I Lived and What I Lived For. In *Major Writers of America*, edited by Perry Miller, 635–40. New York: Harcourt, Brace and World.

Thorpe, Judie Mosier. 1986. An Examination of Lee Iacocca's Spokesman Ads for Chrysler: A Paradigm for the Representative Anecdote. Paper read at the annual meeting of the Speech Communication Association, Chicago.

Turim, M. 1983. Video Art: Theory for a Future. In *Regarding Television*, edited by E. A. Kaplan, 130–37. Los Angeles: University Publications of America.

Wander, P. 1983. The Ideological Turn in Modern Criticism. *Central States Speech Journal* 34: 1–18.

White, Hayden, and Margaret Brose, eds. 1982. *Representing Kenneth Burke.* Baltimore: Johns Hopkins University Press.

Williams, David Cratis. 1986. "Drama" and "Nuclear War" as Representative Anecdotes of Burke's Theories of Ontology and Epistemology. Paper read at the annual meeting of the Speech Communication Association, Chicago.

———. 1989. Under the Sign of (An)Nihilation: Burke in the Age of Nuclear Destruction and Critical Deconstruction. In *The Legacy of Kenneth Burke,* edited by Herbert W. Simons and Trevor Melia, 196–223. Madison: University of Wisconsin Press.

Williams, J. P. 1986. *Man or Superman?* Application of the Representative Anecdote to Sequential Art. Paper read at the annual meeting of the Speech Communication Association, Chicago.

Wrage, Ernest J., and Barnet Baskerville, eds. 1962. *Contemporary Forum: Contemporary Speeches on Twentieth Century Issues.* New York: Harper and Brothers.

Yagoda, Ben. 1980. Kenneth Burke: The Greatest Living Critic since Coleridge? *Horizon,* June, 66–69.

Contributors

Dale A. Bertelsen (Ph.D., Pennsylvania State University) is assistant professor in the Department of Communication Studies at Bloomsburg University in Bloomsburg, Pennsylvania. In addition to his work on Kenneth Burke, his published research explores the methods and perspectives of rhetorical criticism that have appeared in journals such as *Communication Education*. He has served as editor of the *Kenneth Burke Society Newsletter* and as the editor of publications of the National Kenneth Burke Society.

Jane Blankenship (Ph.D., University of Illinois) is professor in the Department of Communication at the University of Massachusetts in Amherst. She is author of *Public Speaking: A Rhetorical Perspective* (1966; 2d ed., 1972), and her articles and monographs have appeared in major speech communication journals, including the *Quarterly Journal of Speech* and *Communication Education*. Since 1962 she has published extensively on Burke's conceptions and has applied his critical principles. In 1984 she was a member of the steering committee that established the Kenneth Burke Society.

Bernard L. Brock (Ph.D., Northwestern University) is professor in the Department of Speech Communication at Wayne State University in Detroit. He has consistently employed the writings of Kenneth Burke as a foundation for his publications since 1965. His essay "Rhetorical Criticism: A Burkeian Approach," which has appeared in the several editions of his edited book *Methods of Rhetorical Criticism: A Twentieth-Century Perspective* (1972, 1980, 1990), is one of the most frequently read introductions to Kenneth Burke for students of communication.

Robert S. Cathcart (Ph.D., Northwestern University), now retired, was professor in the Department of Communication Arts and Sciences at Queens College of the City University of New York. His works have appeared in speech communication journals such as the *Quarterly Journal of Speech* and *Critical Studies in Mass Communication*. He has authored and edited several books, including three editions of *Inter/Media: Interpersonal Communication in a Media World* (1979, 1982, 1986).

James W. Chesebro (Ph.D., University of Minnesota) is chair and professor in the Department of Communication at Indiana State University, Terre Haute. He has published *Computer-Mediated Communication: Human Relationships in a Computerized World* (1989). His articles have appeared in speech communications journals such as the *Quarterly Journal of Speech, Communication Monographs, Communication Education,* and *Critical Studies in Mass Communication.* He was a member of the steering committee that established the Kenneth Burke Society in 1984 and is the chief convention planner for the 1993 National Kenneth Burke Society Convention.

Richard B. Gregg (Ph.D., University of Pittsburgh) is professor in the Department of Speech Communication at Pennsylvania State University in University Park. He began his considerations of Burke's writings in 1969. He has published *Symbolic Inducement and Knowing: A Study in the Foundations of Rhetoric* (1984), in which he asserts, "It would be difficult in our time to locate any scholar of rhetoric who has more thoroughly explored and employed the symbolic perspective than Kenneth Burke."

Greig E. Henderson is associate professor in the Department of English at the University of Toronto. He has published articles on Burke as well as the volume *Kenneth Burke: Literature and Language as Symbolic Action* (1988).

Arnie Madsen (Ph.D., Northwestern University) is assistant professor in the Department of Communication at the University of Pittsburgh. He has presented ten convention papers on the application of Burke's theories to rhetoric and argumentation.

Anthony J. Palmeri (Ph.D., Wayne State University) is assistant professor in the Department of Communication at the University of Wisconsin in Oshkosh. His publications have appeared in *Speaker and Gavel*, the *Gallatin Review*, and the state journals of the Michigan and Wisconsin communication associations.

William H. Rueckert, now retired, was professor in the Department of English at the State University of New York in Geneseo. He is one of the leading intellectual biographers of Kenneth Burke. He has published *Kenneth Burke and the Drama of Human Relations* (1963; 2d ed., 1982). In 1984 he was a member of the steering committee that established the Kenneth Burke Society. In 1990 he was elected the first president of the National Kenneth Burke Society.

Timothy N. Thompson (Ph.D., Bowling Green State University) is assistant professor in the Department of Speech Communication at Edinboro University in Edinboro, Pennsylvania. His publications have appeared in journals such as the *Journal of Creative Behavior* and the *Michigan Association of Speech Communication Journal*. He has worked as a newspaper columnist and cartoonist and has published poetry dedicated to Kenneth Burke's life and work.

Index

About the Series

STUDIES IN RHETORIC AND COMMUNICATION
General Editors:
E. Culpepper Clark, Raymie E. McKerrow, and David Zarefsky

The University of Alabama Press has established this series to publish major new works in the general area of rhetoric and communication, including books treating the symbolic manifestations of political discourse, argument as social knowledge, the impact of machine technology on patterns of communication behavior, and other topics related to the nature of impact of symbolic communication. We actively solicit studies involving historical, critical, or theoretical analyses of human discourse.